SELENIUM WEBDRIVER

Rajeev Gupta

New Delhi

Pearson

ISBN 978-93-325-2629-7

First Impression

Published by Pearson India Education Services Pvt. Ltd, CIN: U72200TN2005PTC057128.

Head Office: 15th Floor, Tower-B, World Trade Tower, Plot No. 1, Block-C, Sector 16, Noida 201 301, Uttar Pradesh, India.
Registered Office: 7th Floor, SDB2, ODC 7, 8 & 9, Survey No. 01 ELCOT IT/ ITES-SEZ, Sholinganallur,
Chennai – 600 119, Tamilnadu, India.
Phone: 044-66540100
Website: in.pearson.com, Email: companysecretary.india@pearson.com

Printed in India by Repro India Limited

Contents

Preface

Selenium WebDriver is among the most widely used tool for automating browser based applications. Selenium was originally developed by Jason Huggins in 2004. This software was further developed by programmers and testers at ThoughtWorks and Google. It is open source software which can be downloaded free of cost from Selenium.

The first version of Selenium was Selenium IDE (Integrated Development Environment). Selenium IDE provides a record/playback tool for authoring tests. It also provides a test domain-specific language (Selenese) to write tests in a number of popular languages say Java, C#, Groovy, Perl, PHP, Python and Ruby. A major leap to Selenium came from the development of WebDriver API. WebDriver was created by Simon Stewart. WebDriver API overcame most of the challenges that Selenium 1.0 had for test automation say file upload/download issues, pop-up and alert boxes issues, etc. The new version of Selenium with WebDriver API is called Selenium WebDriver. The latest version of Selenium WebDriver that is available for download at the time of writing this book is Selenium WebDriver 2.4.

This book discusses in detail the concepts of Selenium WebDriver and its APIs. The objective of this book is to help novice users to learn to code in Selenium WebDriver environment and help advanced users to master the skills on Selenium WebDriver. The book is replete with practical life problems faced in Selenium WebDriver environment and their possible solutions to enable the readers quickly master the skills of Selenium WebDriver. The book is designed in a way that readers can learn and employ the best Selenium automation techniques in their work areas on their own. The book assumes that the reader has little or no knowledge of programming environment. A separate section on Java is devoted to help the readers learn Java language. A section on 'Getting Started' gives an introduction of Selenium WebDriver and helps the reader to install Selenium and write their first lines of Selenium WebDriver code. Another section on 'Basic Selenium' helps readers learn how to automate a browser based application. Next the book describes how to work with various data files, databases and email clients. I understand that my readers are serious programmers who aspire to be Selenium experts. To fulfill this need, a separate section on advanced Selenium concepts has been designed. Implementing automation within agile teams is gaining popularity day by day. A separate chapter on 'Agile Methodology' describing agile team dynamics and its working mechanism has been written for this book. This chapter will help readers understand agile environment and how to carry out test automation within agile environment. Developing an efficient test automation framework is most important part of test automation. With no proper framework, test automation project can result in huge losses. A dedicated chapter on Selenium automation framework is designed to help readers learn how to design, develop and use the first object oriented automation framework called 'Agile Automation Framework'.

About the Author

Rajeev Gupta is currently working with Tata Consultancy Services as Automation Consultant. He is an expert in Test Automation and QTP/UFT/Selenium–Solution. He is also an author of most widely read automation book *Test Automation and QTP*. He has expertise in Test Auto-mation using various technologies such as Java, JavaScript, VB, VBScript, C#, Macros, etc. He has extensive experience in setting up automation projects for Web applications, Java applications, POS application, SAP application, Power Builder application and Mobile web application.

Rajeev Gupta is the one of the few automation experts who has worked to develop enterprise level automation frameworks that best meets the customer requirements and help achieve high ROI. He is the designer and developer of widely used 'Agile Automation Framework', first object-oriented automation framework that helps to effectively carry out test automation within agile environment.

He is also a corporate trainer for agile test automation, QTP, UFT and Selenium WebDriver courses. He has been instrumental in setting up and guiding many core automation projects for many MNC companies.

Acknowledgements

I would like to express my gratitude to all who saw me through this book, provided support, talked things over, read, wrote, offered comments and assisted in the complete process of making the book.

I would also like to thank my colleagues and friends for the inspiration, knowledge and learning opportunities provided by them.

A special thanks to Steven French for providing valuable insights on the book. The discussions I had with him have gone a long mile in making this book one stop shop for Selenium users. It was a pleasure working with him.

I would also like to thank Omar Mohammed for providing his valuable knowledge on presentation skills. Working with him was always a good learning experience.

Finally, I want to thank my parents and rest of the family, who supported and encouraged me in spite of all the time it took me away from them.

Synopsis

Selenium WebDriver is among the most widely used tools for automating browser-based applications. Selenium was originally developed by Jason Huggins in 2004. This software was further developed by programmers and testers at ThoughtWorks and Google. It is an open source software which can be downloaded free of charge from Selenium.

The first version of Selenium was Selenium IDE (Integrated Development Environment). Selenium IDE provides a record/playback tool for authoring tests. It also provides a test domain-specific language (Selenese) to write tests in a number of popular languages like Java, C#, Groovy, Perl, PHP, Python and Ruby. A major leap to Selenium came from the development of WebDriver API. WebDriver was created by Simon Stewart. WebDriver API overcame most of the challenges that Selenium 1.0 had for test automation like file upload, download issues, pop-up and alert boxes issues, etc. The new version of Selenium with WebDriver API is called Selenium WebDriver. The latest version of Selenium WebDriver that is available for download at the time of writing this book is Selenium WebDriver 2.31.2.

This book discusses in detail the concepts of Selenium WebDriver and its APIs. The objective of this book is to help beginners learn to code in Selenium WebDriver environment and help advanced users to master the skills on Selenium WebDriver. The book is replete with real-life problems faced in the Selenium WebDriver environment and their possible solutions to enable the readers to quickly master the skills. It is designed in a way that readers can learn and employ the best Selenium automation techniques in their work areas on their own. The book assumes that the reader has little or no knowledge of the programming environment. A separate section is devoted to help the readers learn Java language. A section on 'Getting Started' helps the reader install Selenium and write their first lines of Selenium WebDriver code. Another section on 'Basic Selenium' helps readers learn how to automate a browser-based application. The book also describes how to work with various data files, databases and e-mail clients. For those of my readers who aspire to become experts in Selenium, a separate section on advanced Selenium concepts has been designed. Developing an efficient test automation framework is the most important part of test automation. With no proper framework, a test automation project can result in huge losses. A section on 'Selenium Automation Framework' is designed to help readers learn how to design, develop and use 'Page Object Model Framework'.

About This Book

This book has been divided into six sections – Java Introduction, Getting Started, Basic Selenium, Advanced Selenium, Agile Methodology and Selenium Automation Frameworks. Section on Java helps readers to build their basic skills on Java language required for developing tests in Selenium environment. Getting Started section helps novice users to understand and get started with Selenium. This section also guides readers on how to setup the Selenium WebDriver automation environment and write and execute their first line of selenium code. 'Basic Selenium' section is designed to help readers learn and master the skills of designing the most stable location identifiers. This section focusses to help readers learn how to code for various browser elements say edit box, radio buttons, list box, web tables, frames, pop-up boxes, etc. This section also explains how to work with cookies, how to implement verification points, how to data-drive and parameterize tests, how to implement synchronization between running Selenium code and application under tests response time, how to handle test errors and how to develop user friendly test result reports. This section also describes how to create and execute a test suite and how to debug a test script code in Eclipse. In test automation, interactions with various data files, databases and email clients are very obvious. The next section on 'Advanced Selenium' is designed to help readers learn how to code to retrieve and write data to various files and databases say MS Word, MS Excel, Notepad, Oracle, etc. 'Advanced Selenium' section also covers advanced user interactions, executing selenium tests in parallel, learning how to develop and use annotations, writing test code for HTML5 and mobile browser applications, advanced test reporting, and learning how to execute tests using Selenium Grid. The next section on 'Agile Methodology' is designed to help readers understand agile software development concept and the role of automation engineers in there. Lastly, we learn how to design, develop and use 'Agile Automation Framework'.

This book consists of 28 chapters.

Chapter 1 – Introduction to Java, helps you to learn Java language sufficient enough to get you going with developing Selenium Webdriver tests. This chapter covers various data types of Java, variables, operators, conditional statements, looping statements, method overloading and method overriding, enum interfaces, abstract classes and exception handling.

Chapter 2 – Introduction to Selenium, will walk you through Selenium describing its history and tool suite. This chapter describes various Selenium APIs and packages within Selenium Tool Suite and when to use them.

Chapter 3 – Installation, gives a step by step detail on installing Selenium. Separate installation steps are provided for readers who want to install Selenium WebDriver for learning and for readers who want to install Selenium WebDriver automation project for a client or a company. This chapter provides details steps for Firefox setup, Firefox add-ons setup, Eclipse setup, Selenium setup, Eclipse configuration, Basic framework setup, and writing first WebDriver test.

Chapter 4 – Environment Variables, explains how to define the test automation as well as application under test environment variables for a Selenium project. This chapter explains various types of environment variables and how to describe and use them in Selenium tests. This section describes multiple ways of defining environment variables. Depending upon the nature of the project, one of the mechanisms is to be chosen.

Chapter 5 – Locating Elements, introduces you to element identifier mechanisms supported by Selenium WebDriver for locating static and dynamic elements in a web page. Selenium WebDriver provides multiple location strategies to locate elements such as DOM, Xpath and CSS. This chapter will also help you to get started with Selenium WebDriver locator API.

Chapter 6 – Locating Elements using CSSSelectors, first briefly explains the concept of CSS and then describes how to locate an element using its CSS path. This chapter describes to you how to develop a CSS path which is effective in locating the element in every test run. It focusses on helping you to learn to develop a very stable CSS path expression which is least impacted by changes to page or other page elements. This chapter also describes various CSS mechanism which can be used to locate static and dynamic elements such as element attributes such as locating elements using CSS selectors, css absolute path, css relative path, element attributes (*id, class, etc.*), partial element attributes match, Pseudo class selectors, jQuery selectors etc. It also helps you to learn how to use locate an element using multiple attributes such as locating an element using its *id, class* and *name* attribute. Lastly, this chapter also helps you learn how to capture element attributes and text values from a web page during test run.

Chapter 7 – Locating Elements using XPath, first briefly explains the concept of CSS and then describes how to locate an element using its xpath. This chapter describes to you how to develop an effective and stable xpath expression which is least impacted by changes to page or other page elements. This chapter also describes various xpath mechanism which can be used to locate static and dynamic elements such as locating elements using absolute xpath, relative xpath, element attributes (*id, class, etc.*), partial element attributes match, xpath axis etc. . It also helps you to learn how to use locate an element using multiple attributes such as locating an element using its *id, class* and *name* attribute. Lastly, this chapter also helps you learn how to capture element attributes and text values from a web page during test run.

Chapter 8 – UI Map, explains you how to create and use a separate locator class to store identification attributes of all elements. This class is like an element repository class and helps to create a one-point maintenance framework for all elements used in the project.

Chapter 9 – Working with Browser, helps you learn how to execute tests against various browsers – Firefox, Chrome and Internet Explorer. This chapter explains WebDriver methods – *get, getCurrentURL, getTitle, findElement, getPageSource, navigate, getWindowHandles, getWindowHandle, switchTo, close, quit, mange, etc.* This chapter also describes how to maximized and minimize a browser window.

Chapter 10 – Working with Browser Elements, introduces you to various elements that can be present on a web page and how to write code to locate them using Webdriver code. This chapter helps you to learn how to write test code to work with various page elements such as text box, button, link, image, checkbox, radio button, radio button group, dropdown box, and list box, web tables, pop-up windows and frames.

Chapter 11 – Working with Web Tables, introduces you to web tables and describes how to locate them. This chapter also helps you to learn how to locate static and dynamic elements within web tables (child elements of web table). This chapter provides a ready to use WebTable API to work with web tables and web table elements. This API also supports capturing web table attributes; web table element attributes and web table cell text during test run.

Chapter 12 – Working with Popup Windows, first introduces you to various types of pop-up windows. Then it explains the various ways to locate pop-up windows and simulate user action on them. This chapter also describes to you how to work with JavaScript alert and prompt box windows.

Chapter 13 – Working with Frames, describes to you the various types of frames and various WebDriver methods to locate them. This chapter explains how to work with frames and elements present within frames.

Chapter 14 – Working with Cookies, discusses what is cookie and its usage purpose in web applications. It describes how to view cookie information of a web page in Firefox browser. This chapter explains in detail the various WebDriver methods to retrieve as well as modify cookie data.

Chapter 15 – Synchronization, first describes to you the importance of synchronizing the Selenium code execution speed with application response time. Then it discusses in detail that various ways to synchronize test code run with application response time.

Chapter 16 – Checkpoints, first describes the importance of verification points in test code. Then it explains in detail how to write code for various types of checkpoints such as attribute checkpoint, text checkpoint, image checkpoint, bitmap checkpoint, table checkpoint, database checkpoint, XML checkpoint, and file checkpoint. This chapter also explains to you how to check elements presence, verify elements status and capture messages displayed on the page.

Chapter 17 – Data Driven Testing, discusses in detail the importance of data driving tests and how to data drive tests. This chapter explains both JUnit and TestNG framework for data driving tests. Next it describes how to data drive tests using flat file and MS Excel file. This chapter also explains you the best way of data driving tests.

Chapter 18 – Test Results, describes to you the importance of generating a easily human readable test report. This chapter describes to you how to generate customized test reports and test reports with application screenshots. It also explains how to capture video of complete test run.

Chapter 19 – Advanced User Interactions, demonstrates to you how to write WebDriver code to simulate complex mouse and keyboard operations. Next, it describes how to read and write to clipboard. Lastly, this chapter discusses how to execute JavaScript code within a browser page.

Chapter 20 – Extending Selenium, discusses how to extend Selenium WebDriver API and add features for building a scalable test automation framework. This chapter provides ready to use APIs (Selenium Extensions) for working with jQuery widgets, disabled text boxes, highlighting elements during test run, capturing screenshots during test run and comparing two images.

Chapter 21 – Testing HTML5 Web Applications, discusses in detail how to write code to test HTML 5 video player, canvas element and web storage.

Chapter 22 – Working with Flat Files, demonstrates how to read, write and append data to notepad and CSV file. This chapter also describes the best way to define test data in flat files. This chapter also provides a ready to use API for reading test data from flat files.

Chapter 23 – Working with MS Excel, introduces to you how MS Excel to define test data. It describes two methods of working with MS Excel file contents – MS Excel as worksheet and MS Excel as database. This chapter describes how to write code to read/write data to MS Excel file, format cell and cell text attributes and as well to define cell formula. It also discusses how to access MS Excel as database and read/write data to it. Lastly, it provides a ready to use API for working with MS Excel file.

Chapter 24 – Working with Database, discusses in detail how to work with Oracle, IBM DB2 and MS Access database.

Chapter 25 – Working with XML, first introduces an XML file to you. Next it discusses how to create, edit and read an XML file using XML DOM. This chapter also discusses how to read a XML file using XPath query.

Chapter 26 – Selenium Server, discusses in detail how to setup and configure Selenium Server (Selenium Grid) on server and client machine. This chapter describes how to create a test suite and execute it against multiple client machines using Selenium Server. It also describes how to execute multiple tests in parallel.

Chapter 27 – Agile Methodology, introduces to you the concept of software development using agile methodology. This chapter describes in detail the team dynamics, working mechanism, programming mechanism, build deployment mechanism and project management mechanism as used in agile projects. It discusses most popular agile software development methods and practices such as Scrum, Scrum of Scrums, Kanban, Feature Driven Development (FDD), Extreme Programming (XP), Test Driven Development (TDD), Continuous Integration (CI) and DevOps. This chapter describes in detail the role, scope and importance of test automation in agile teams.

Chapter 28 – Agile Automation Framework, describes in detail how to design and develop a enterprise level test automation framework for Selenium WebDriver project.

Who This Book Is For

If you are quality assurance/testing professional, automation architect, automation engineer, software developer engineer in test or software developer looking to create automation test scripts, this is the perfect guide for you! This book attempts to provide easily consumable information on all major aspects of developing Selenium tests. This book has been designed to suffice learning needs of both novice users as well as expert users. By the end of this book you will have acquired expert level knowledge in developing Selenium WebDriver automated tests.

This book also meets the needs of aspiring candidates who want to make sure they are ready for their next interview. It is also a great resource for interviewers as well.

Questions and Feedback Related to This Book

I encourage feedback and any thought from readers whether like or dislike for the enhancements of the book. Readers feedback is important for the development of the book in a more efficient way. For any feedback or query readers can contact the author through https://www.facebook.com/seleniumbook and @rajeevzone (Twitter).

1
CHAPTER

Introduction to Java

Java is an object-oriented programming language (OOP) developed by Sun Microsystems. Modelled after C++, the Java language was designed to be small, simple and portable across platforms and operating systems both at the source and the binary level. Java is a platform-independent language, i.e., Java programs can be executed on any machine.

Java is an OOP language which enables programmers to create flexible, modular and reusable codes. The important features of OOP language which help programmers achieve this are encapsulation, polymorphism and inheritance.

- **Encapsulation:** It is a mechanism that binds together codes and data and manipulates to keep the code safe from outside interference and misuse. Java implements encapsulation by defining the accessibility conditions of variables, methods and classes (private, protected, default public and public). Java's basic unit of encapsulation is *class*. A class specifies the data and the code that will operate on the data. Class specification is used to construct *objects* which are instances of a class.
- **Polymorphism:** It is an OOP feature that enables an object to determine which method to implement or invoke upon receiving a method call. One of the ways Java implements this is through *method overloading* and *method overriding*.
- **Inheritance:** It is an OOP feature which enables building new classes from the existing ones. With inheritance, subclasses get access to all the attributes of its super class. This allows one object to acquire properties of another. One way of implementing this in Java is by defining *abstract* classes.

1.1 | CLASSES

One of the fundamental ways in which Java handles complexity is *abstraction*. A *class* models an abstraction by defining the properties and behaviours for *objects* representing the abstraction. Class acts as a blueprint for creating objects.

1.1.1 | Writing First Java Class Program

The following steps describe how to create a new java class and write a code to it.

1. Open Eclipse and create a new project, say 'SeleniumAutomation'.
2. Right click on the default package 'src' and select *New* → *Class*. 'New Java Class' window pops is opened.

3. Specify class name say 'MyFirstClass' and click on 'Finish' button. Specified class is created as shown in Figure 1.1.

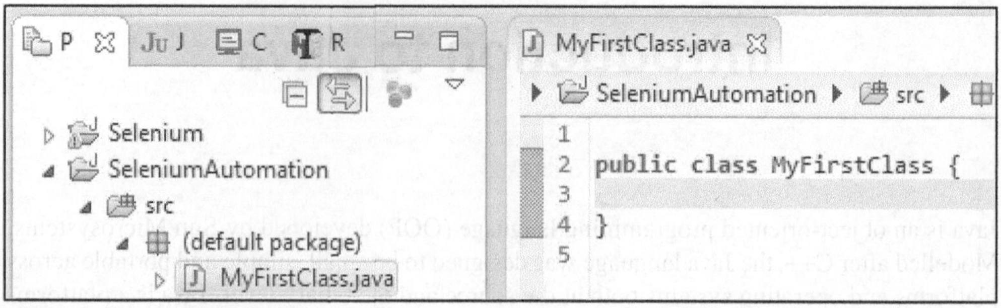

FIGURE 1.1 | Creating a new class

4. Write code for the class. Figure 1.2 shows a simple class code with 'main' method to display 'Hello World!!!' on console window of Eclipse.

```

public class MyFirstClass {
    public static void main(String[] args){
       System.out.println("Hello World!!!");
    }
}

```

FIGURE 1.2 | Writing first Java class program

5. To execute this code from Eclipse, right click on the Eclipse editor window and select *Run As → Java Application*.

1.2 | DATA TYPES

Each variable declaration in Java must define the data type of the variable. The data type defines what values a variable can store. The variable type can be as follows:

- One of the eight basic primitive data types
- An array
- The name of class

The eight primitive data types hold values for integers, floating-point numbers, characters and Boolean values. They are called primitive because they are built into the system and are not actual objects. This makes them more efficient to use. Table 1.1 shows the primitive data types.

TABLE 1.1 | Primitive data types

Data type	Width (bits)	Minimum value/Maximum value
`boolean`	NA	true, false
`byte`	8	$-2^7, 2^7 - 1$
`short`	16	$-2^{15}, 2^{15} - 1$
`char`	16	0 × 0, 0 × ffff
`int`	32	$-2^{31}, 2^{31} - 1$
`long`	64	$-2^{63}, 2^{63} - 1$
`float`	32	±1.40129846432481707e − 45f, ±3.40282347663852886e + 38f
`double`	64	±4.94065645841246544e − 324, ±1.79769313486231570e + 308

1.3 | LITERALS

A literal denotes a constant value, i.e., the value that a literal holds. A literal can represent boolean, numerical, character, string or a null value (Table 1.2).

TABLE 1.2 | Literals

Literal	Literal Type	Example
Integer	Decimal	8, 10L, −90
	Octal	010, 012L, −0132
	Hexadecimal	0 × 8, 0 × aL, −05 × a
Floating	Double	0.41, 4100e^{-2}, .41e^{2}
	Float	0.41F, .4100e^{-2}F, .41e^{2}F
Boolean		true, false
Character		' ', '1', 'A', 'a'
	Escape Sequences	\b, \t, \n, \f, \', \", \\
String		"This is String."

Note: The default data type on an integer literal is always `int` but it can also be specified as `long` by suffixing *L* or *l*.

1.4 | VARIABLE DECLARATION

A variable stores a value of specific type. Variable declaration is used to specify the type and name of the variable. The following code shows how to declare and initiate variables.

```
int i;          //Declaring integer variable
i=1;            //Initializing integer variable
int j=2;        //Declaring and initializing integer variable
long k=2L;      //Declaring and initializing integer variable
```

```
boolean status=false; //Declaring and initializing boolean variable

//Declaring and initializing float variable
float f1 = i/3;                  //Output::0.0
float f2 = (float) (i/3.0);      //Output::0.33333334

//Type casting (converting the variable from one data type to
  another)
int f3 = (int) (i/3.0);          //Output::0

String str = "This is String."; //Declaring and initializing
                                  String variable
```

1.5 | EXPRESSIONS AND OPERATORS

Expressions are statements in Java that return a value. Operators are special symbols that perform an operation, for example, add and subtract.

1.5.1 | Arithmetic Operators

Table 1.3 lists Java arithmetic operators.

TABLE 1.3 | Arithmetic operators

Operator	Description	Example
+	Addition	5 + 2 = 7
–	Subtraction	5 – 2 = 3
*	Multiplication	5 * 2 = 10
/	Division	5/2 = 2
%	Modulus	5%2 = 1

1.5.2 | Comparison Operators

All Java comparators return a boolean value. Table 1.4 shows comparison operators.

TABLE 1.4 | Comparison operators

Operator	Description	Example
==	Equal	5==2 = false
!=	Not Equal	5!=2 = true
<	Less Than	5<2 = false
>	Greater Than	5>2 = true
<=	Less Than Equal To	5<=2 = false
>=	Greater Than Equal To	5>=2 = true

1.5.3 | Logical Operators

Logical operators are used to implement logical AND, OR, XOR and NOT condition. Table 1.5 shows logical operators.

TABLE 1.5 | Logical operators

<table>
<tr><th>Operator</th><th>Description</th><th>Example</th></tr>
<tr><td>&&</td><td>AND</td><td>(5<2)&&(2>10)</td></tr>
<tr><td>||</td><td>OR</td><td>(5<2)||(2>10)</td></tr>
<tr><td>^</td><td>XOR</td><td>(5<2)^(2>10)</td></tr>
<tr><td>!</td><td>NOT</td><td>!(5<2)</td></tr>
</table>

1.5.4 | Bitwise Operators

Bitwise operators perform operations on individual bits in integers. Table 1.6 shows bitwise operators.

TABLE 1.6 | Bitwise operators

<table>
<tr><th>Operator</th><th>Description</th><th>Example</th></tr>
<tr><td>&</td><td>Bitwise AND</td><td></td></tr>
<tr><td>|</td><td>Bitwise OR</td><td></td></tr>
<tr><td>^</td><td>Bitwise XOR</td><td></td></tr>
<tr><td><<</td><td>Left shift</td><td></td></tr>
<tr><td>>></td><td>Right shift</td><td></td></tr>
<tr><td>>>></td><td>Zero fill right shift</td><td></td></tr>
<tr><td>–</td><td>Bitwise complement</td><td></td></tr>
<tr><td><<=</td><td>Left shift assignment</td><td></td></tr>
<tr><td>>>=</td><td>Right shift assignment</td><td></td></tr>
<tr><td>x&=y</td><td>AND assignment</td><td>Equivalent to x=x&y</td></tr>
<tr><td>x|=y</td><td>OR assignment</td><td>Equivalent to x=x|y</td></tr>
<tr><td>x^=y</td><td>NOT assignment</td><td>Equivalent to x=x^y</td></tr>
</table>

1.6 | ARRAYS

An array is a data structure that stores a collection of values of the same data type. Values stored in an array are accessible through array index.

```
//declaring an array of integers
int arr1[];
//creating an integer array with values
int[] arr0 = {2,3,4,5,6};
```

```
//creating an integer array which can hold 100 integers
int arr2[] = new int[100];
//creating a multi-dimensional array using variables
int arraySize=100;
int arr3[] = new int[arraySize];
//creating an String array which can hold 100 integers
String arr4[] = new String[100];
//assigning values to array
arr3[0] = 1;
arr3[1] = 1;
arr4[0]="This";
arr4[1]="This is String array";
//accessing array values
for (int i=0;i<arr3.length;i++){
    System.out.println("arr3[" + I + "]=" + arr3[i]);
}
//Or,
for (int element:arr3){
    System.out.println(element + ",");
}

//copying array
int[] arr5 = arr3;
String[] arr6 = arr4;
```

1.6.1 | Multi-dimensional Arrays

Multi-dimensional arrays are arrays of an array. They use more than one index to store and access values.

```
//declaring a multi-dimensional array
int[][] arr0;
//creating a multi-dimensional array
int[][] arr1 = {
                {1,2,3,},
                {4,5,6},
                {7,8,9}
              };
//creating a muti-dimensional array of size 2*3
int[][] arr2 = new int[2][3];

//creating a multi-dimensional array using variables
int arrayXSize = 3;
int arrayYSize = 3;
int[][] arr3 = new int[arrayXSize][arrayYSize];
```

```
//assigning values to multi-dimensional arrays
arr3[0][0]= 1;
arr3[0][2]= 3;

//accessing values from multidimensional arrays
for (int i=0;i<arr2.length;i++){
    for(int j=0;j<arr2[i].length;j++){
        System.out.println("arr1[" +i + "][" + j + "]=" +
          arr1[i][j]);
    }
}

//copying multi-dimensional arrays
int[][] arr4 = arr3;
```

1.7 | CONTROL FLOW

Java, like any other programming language, supports both conditional and loop statements to control code flow.

1.7.1 | Conditional Statements

In Java, we have four conditional statements:

1. **`if(condition=true){}`:** Executes a set of code when the specified condition is *true*.
2. **`if(condition=true){}else{}`:** Executes first block of code when the specified condition is *true* else executes the second block of code.
3. **`if(condition1=true){}elseif(condition2=true){}else{}`:** Executes the first block of code for which the condition is *true*. If no condition is found *true* and else block exists, then this block of code is executed. If no condition is found *true* and else block does not exists, then none of the `if` block code is executed.
4. **`switch(choice)...case`:** Executes a set of code for which the *choice* condition is *true*. `switch...case` is used when the number of available alternatives and options are many and at a time only one holds true. Though the same can be implemented using `if` condition too, but that makes the code cumbersome and less readable.

`if...` Statement

Consider scenario where code logic to be implemented is as follows:

- If the specified number is < 5, then print "number < 5",
- `Elseif` the specified number is > = 5 and < 10, then print "number is between 5 and 10",
- `Elseif` the specified number is > = 10 and < 20, then print "number is between 10 and 20",
- Else, print "number is > = 20".

```
public class SwitchTest {
        public static void main(String[] args){
                int i=5;
                if (i<5){
                        System.out.println("number<5");
                }else if (i>=5 && i<10){
                        System.out.println("number is between
                         5 and 10");
                }else if (i>=10 && i<20){
                        System.out.println("number is between
                         10 and 20");
                }else {
                        System.out.println("number is >=20");
                }
        }
}
```

switch... Statement

Consider a scenario where the code logic to be implemented is as follows:

- If grade = 5, then print "Excellent",
- If grade = 4, then print "Very Good",
- If grade = 3, then print "Good",
- Else, print "Poor".

```
public class SwitchTest {
        public static void main(String[] args){
                Scanner in = new Scanner(System.in);
                System.out.print("Select an option (1,2,3,4,5)...");
                int choice = in.nextInt();
                switch(choice){
                        case 5:
                                System.out.print("Excellent");
                                break;
                        case 4:
                                System.out.print("Very Good");
                                break;
                        case 3:
                                System.out.print("Good");
                                break;
                        default:
                                System.out.print("Poor");
                                break;
                }
        }
}
```

1.7.2 | Looping Statements

Java supports four looping statements.

1. `for`...statement
2. `for`...each statement
3. `while`...statement
4. `do`...`while` statement

`for(;;)`... Statement

`for(;;)`...statement executes a block of code specified number of times.
For example, the code below prints numbers from 1 to 9.

```
public class TestForLoop {
        public static void main(String[] args){
                for (int i=1;i<10;i++){
                        System.out.println(i);
                }
        }
}
```

`for`... Statement

`for`...statement executes a block of code for each item in a collection or each element in an array.
For example, the code below prints all numbers in an array.

```
int[] arr={1,2,3,4,5};
for (int element:arr){
        System.out.println(element);
}
```

`while`... Statement

`while`...statement executes a block of code while or until the condition is true.
For example, code below executes the loop till array value <4.

```
int[] arr={1,2,3,4,5};
int i=0;
while (arr[i]<4){
        System.out.println(arr[i]);
        i=i+1;
}
```

do...while Statement

do...while statement executes a block of code until the condition becomes false.

```
int[] arr={1,2,3,4,5};
int i=0;
do{
        System.out.println(arr[i]);
        i=i+1;
}while (arr[i]<4);
```

Note: while loop is executed only if the condition is true. So while loop can execute zero or more times. Whereas do...while loop is executed first time without validating the condition, i.e., it will always execute for the first time. At the end of first loop execution condition is checked. So, do...while loop always executes 1 or more times.

1.7.3 | Transfer Statements

Java provides six language constructs to transfer control or exit loops in a program.

1. break
2. continue
3. return
4. try...catch...finally
5. throw
6. assert

break... Statement

break...statement terminates a loop.

For example, the following code shows how to terminate a while and for loop.

```
//exit while loop if i==3
int[] arr={1,2,3,4,5};
int i=0;
do{
        System.out.println(arr[i] + ",");
        if (i==3) break;
        i=i+1;
}while (arr[i]<5);

//exit for loop if i==3
for (int i=1;i<10;i++){
        if (i==3) break;
        System.out.print(i + ",");
}
//Output::1,2,
```

continue... Statement

`continue`...statement exits the current iteration and starts execution the next iteration. For example, the following code prints all numbers except number 3.

```
//exit current loop and execute next iteration if i==3
for (int i=1;i<10;i++){
        if (i==3) continue;
        System.out.print(i + ",");
}
//Output::1,2,4,5,6,7,8,9,
```

return... Statement

`return`...statement stops code execution of a method and transfers control back to the calling code.

```
public class TestReturn {
        public static void main(String[] args){
                printNum(1);
                printNum(2);
                printNum(3);

        }

        public static void printNum(int i){
                System.out.print("\n entering loop");
                if (i==2) return;
                System.out.print("," + i + ",");
                System.out.print("exiting loop");
        }
}
//Output::
entering loop,1,exiting loop
entering loop
entering loop,3,exiting loop
```

try...catch...finally... Statement

`try...catch...finally`...statement is used for handling exceptions. (Further discussed in section 'Exception Handling'.)

throws... Statement

`throws`...statement is used for handling exceptions. (Further discussed in section 'Exception Handling'.)

assert... Statement

`assert` statements are used to validate the assumptions made about the program. Assertions are expected to be *true* when `assert` statements are executed. In case it is *false*, the Java Virtual Machine (JVM) throws a special error of `AssertionError` class. Assertion errors are not handled but allowed to propagate to the top level.

Note: Assertion facility can be enabled or disabled at runtime. If disabled, *assert* statements are not executed during run-time.

1.8 | CLASS

A class is the template from which objects are created. A class declaration typically contains a set of attributes (*instance variables*) and functions (*methods*).

```
public class ArithmeticClass {
        private Boolean status;
        protected int x,y;
        public long sum;

        ...
}
```

1.9 | METHODS

In Java, functions and procedures are called *methods*. Methods can include zero or more input parameters and zero or one return parameter. The following code shows some method declarations. Arithmetic class has two methods `printSum` and `getSum`. Method `printSum` has two input parameters both of integer type and no return parameter. While method `getSum` has two integer type input parameters and one integer type return parameter.

```
public class ArithmeticClass {
        //method to print sum
        public void printSum(int x, int y){
                System.out.println("Sum=" + (x+y));
        }
        //method to get sum
        public int getSum(int x, int y){
                return (x+y);
        }
}
```

1.9.1 | Method Overloading

In Java, method overloading occurs when two or more methods in the same class have the same name but different parameters. Two method can be considered overloaded if any of the below conditions are true:

- Number of parameters is different for the methods.
- The parameter types (input or return) are different.

Class `ArithmeticClass` below has two methods with same name `getSum`. These two methods are overloaded as the number of input parameters is different of both.

```
public class ArithmeticClass {
        //method to get sum as int
        public int getSum(int x, int y){
                return (x+y);
        }
        //method to get sum as int
        public int getSum(int x, int y, int z){
                return (x+y+z);
        }
}
```

1.9.2 | Method Overriding

Overriding a method involves defining a method in a subclass that has the same signature (input and return parameter) as a method in a superclass. Then, when that method is called, the method in the subclass is found and executed instead of the one in the superclass. The following code overrides method `print`. Code below shows classes `SuperClass` and `SubClass`. `SubClass` overrides `print` method of its super class. `MainClass` shows different ways of calling the overridden method of subclass as well as the original method of super class.

```
public class SuperClass {
        int i=1;
        public void print(){
                System.out.println("i=" + i);
        }
}
public class SubClass extends SuperClass {
        int i=2;
        public void print(){
                System.out.println("i=" + i);
        }
}
public class MainClass {
        public static void main(String[] args){
                SubClass subClass1 = new SubClass();
                subClass1.print();//Output::i=2
                SuperClass superClass1 = new SubClass();
                superClass1.print();//Output::i=2
                SuperClass superClass2 = new SuperClass();
                superClass2.print();//Output::i=1
        }
}
```

1.9.3 | Variable and Method Scope

Java has reserved keywords to define the scope of variables methods and classes. `private` keyword is used to declare variables and methods that are to be accessible only within the class. `protected` keyword is used to declare variables and methods that are to be accessible only within the class or any class that extends to this class. `public` keyword is used to declare variables and methods that are to be accessible within the class and as well as outside class.

1.10 | CONSTRUCTORS

Constructor declarations are similar to method declarations. However, constructors name must be the same as class name and it cannot return a value. The main objective of constructors is to set the initial state of an object, when the object is created by using the new operator. The following code shows how to declare constructors with and without input parameters.

```
public class ConstructorClass {
        //Contructor
        ConstructorClass(){
                System.out.println("constructor");
        }
        //Constructor with parameters
        ConstructorClass(String param){
                System.out.println("constructor:" + param);
        }
        //method
        public void method(){
                System.out.println("method");
        }
}

public class MainClass {
        public static void main(String[] args){
                ConstructorClass cc1 = new ConstructorClass();
                //Output::constructor
                cc1.method();
                //Output::method
                ConstructorClass cc2 = new ConstructorClass
                  ("Parameter");
                //Output::constructor:Parameter
                cc2.method();
                //Output::method
        }
}
```

1.11 | ENUM

Enum is a Java keyword used to represent fixed number of well-known values. For example, number of days in a week, number of planets in the solar system, etc.

EXAMPLE 1.1 Simple enums of weekdays.

```
public class EnumClass {
        public enum Day {
            SUN, MON, TUES, WED, THU, FRI, SAT;
        }
        public static void main(String[] args){
                System.out.print(Day.WED.toString() + ":" +
                  Day.WED.ordinal());
                //Output::WED:3
        }
}
```

EXAMPLE 1.2 Simple enums of weekdays with weekday number.

```
public class EnumClass {
        public enum Day {
            SUN(1), MON(2), TUES(3), WED(4), THU(5), FRI(6), SAT(7);

            private int daySeq;

              private Day(int daySeq){
                    this.daySeq = daySeq;
              }

              public int getDaySeq(){
                    return this.daySeq;
              }
        }
        public static void main(String[] args){
              System.out.print(Day.WED.toString() + ":" +
                Day.WED.getDaySeq());
              //Output::WED:4
        }
}
```

EXAMPLE 1.3 An enum defining weekday full name and weekday number.

```
public class EnumClass {

        public enum DayDetails{
                SUN("SUNDAY",1),
                MON("MONDAY",2),
                TUE("TUESDAY",3),
                WED("WEDNESDAY",4),
```

```
        THU("THURSDAY",5),
        FRI("FRIDAY",6),
        SAT("SATURDAY",7);

        private String dayFullname;
        private int daySeq;

        private DayDetails(String dayFullname, int daySeq){
            this.dayFullname = dayFullname;
            this.daySeq = daySeq;
        }

        public String getDayFullname(){
            return this.dayFullname;
        }

        public int getDaySeq(){
            return this.daySeq;
        }
    }

    public static void main(String[] args){
        System.out.print(DayDetails.WED.getDayFullname()
          + ":" + DayDetails.WED.getDaySeq());
        //Output::WEDNESDAY:4
    }
}
```

1.12 | INHERITANCE

Inheritance is a mechanism which allows classes to *inherit* the attributes of an existing class. It is used in situations where the subclass (which inherits attributes) is a subset of the superclass (whose attributes) are inherited. For example, suppose there are three classes—employee, developer and tester. In this case, both developers and testers are employees. Here, employee class can define generic attributes of employees. Specific attributes of developers can be defined in developer class, while specific attributes of testers can be defined in tester class. Both developer and tester class can inherit employee class to inherit generic employee attributes. Here developer and tester are subclasses while employee is a super class. A class can inherit other class attributes using the keyword ‘extends’.

1.12.1 | Employee.Java

The following code shows the inherit attributes of another class.

```
public class Employee {
    private long id;
    private String name;
    private Date joiningDate;

    public Employee (long id, String name, Date joiningDate)
```

```
    {
        this.id = id;
        this.name = name;
        this.joiningDate = joiningDate;
    }

    public long getId() {
        return id;
    }

    public String getName() {
        return name;
    }
    public Date getJoiningDate() {
        return joiningDate;
    }

}
```

1.12.2 | Developer.Java

```
public class Developer extends Employee{
    private double baseSalary;

    public Developer (Employee e){
       super(e.getId(), e.getName(), e.getJoiningDate());
       this.baseSalary=1000.00;
    }

    public Developer (Employee e, double salary){
       super(e.getId(), e.getName(), e.getJoiningDate());
       this.baseSalary=salary;
    }

    public double getBaseSalary(){
       return this.baseSalary;
    }

}
```

Similar to class Developer.java, a separate class Tester.java can be defined for defining tester attributes.

Class below 'Company.java' shows how to use the above defined classes for adding and viewing employee details.

1.12.3 | Company.Java

```
public class Company {
    private ArrayList<Employee> employees = new
      ArrayList
        <Employee>();
```

```
    .....
    public void hire (Employee e, double startSalary)
    {
        Employee e = new Employee(e,startSalary);
        this.addEmployee(e);
    }
}
```

1.13 | INTERFACES

An interface is a group of related methods with empty bodies. In other words, it is a collection of *abstract* methods. An interface is not a class. A class implements an interface to inherit the abstract methods of the interface.

The following code shows an interface *Cars*, that has methods `make()` and `price()`.

```
interface Cars {
        void make();
        void price();
}
```

The following code shows class *Nissan* which implements *Cars* interface and defines its abstract methods `make()` and `price()`.

```
public class Nissan implements Cars {
        @Override
        public void make() {
                System.out.println("Nissan");
        }
        @Override
        public void price() {
                System.out.println("$30000");
        }
        public static void main(String[] args) {
                Nissan nissan = new Nissan();
                nissan.make();//Output::Nissan
                nissan.price();//Output::$30000
        }
}
```

1.14 | EXCEPTION HANDLING

Exceptions in Java are objects. All exceptions are derived from the java.lang.Throwable class. Exceptions can be handled in Java using `try-catch-finally` construct. Exceptions thrown by the *try* block of code is caught (handled) by the *catch* block.

The following code shows an example of *try-catch-finally* construct.

```
public double division(int a, int b){
       double result;
       result = 1/0;

       try{
              result= a/b;
       } catch(ArithmeticException e){
              System.out.println("Value of b is 0");
       } finally{
              System.out.println("Execution Complete.");
       }
       return result;
}
```

Whenever an exception is thrown by try block of code, it looks for *catch* construct which handles that exception. If no *catch* construct is found which handles the exception, then the exception is handled by default exception handler. `Catch` construct is not executed if no exception is thrown or if the respective *catch* construct does not handle the specific exception. For example, in the code above, the *catch* construct only catches *ArithmeticException.* Any other exception, say *FileNotFound* will not be handled by this catch construct. *Finally* code block is executed, no matter an exception is thrown or not. An example for use of *finally* construct can be to write a code that closes DB connections. This will ensure that DB connection is closed, no matter an error happens or not during data retrieval from DB.

1.15 | ANNOTATION

Annotation is a form of metadata that provides data about a program that is not part of the program itself. Annotations have no direct effect on the operation of the code which is annotated. Annotation has a number of uses and few of them are as follows:

- Annotation can be used by the compiler to detect errors or suppress warnings.
- Annotations can be examined at runtime.
- Software tools can be written that process annotation information to generate code, XML files, etc.

An important use of annotation in test automation is to define the test type (functional, regression) and test functional area (customer accounts, funds transfer, etc., for a banking application). Once these information are defined as annotation in tests, tools can be written to selectively execute specific type of test. Also, tools can provide info about the test coverage in each functional area.

1.15.1 | Built-in Annotations

Java provides some built in annotations. Few of them are listed below:

- **@Override:** Verifies that the specific method is an override. It causes a compile error, if the method is not found in one of the parent classes or implemented interfaces.

- **@Deprecated:** Marks the specific method as obsolete. It causes a compile time error, if the specific method is used.
- **@SuppressWarnings:** Instructs the compiler to suppress the compile time warnings which matches the annotation parameters.

Section 'Interfaces' above shows use of *@Override* annotation.

Annotations can also be used to annotate annotations. Listed as follows are few annotations that define the behaviour of an annotation:

- **@Retention:** Specifies how the annotation is stored—whether in code only or compiles into the class or available at runtime through reflection.
- **@Documented:** Marks another annotation for inclusion in the documentation.
- **@Target:** Marks another annotation to restrict the kind of java elements the annotation may be applied to.
- **@Inherited:** Marks another annotation to be inherited to subclass of annotated class.

1.15.2 | Custom Annotations

Java provides the flexibility to define custom annotations as per need. An annotation is defined with at-sign (@) preceding the interface keyword. The following steps show how to create and use custom annotations.

- Open Eclipse
- Select the package where annotation needs to be created.
- Right click and select *New → Annotation* as shown in Figure 1.3.

FIGURE 1.3 | Creating a new annotation file

- Specify annotation name say `RegressionTest`.
  The following code shows annotation code with no annotations and parameters.

```
public @interface RegressionTest {
}
```

Above annotation can be directly used in code as:

```
@RegressionTest
public void testAccountCreation(){
        ...
}
```

- Annotate the annotation as required.
  The following code shows how to create an annotation which defines the test type being automated (functional or regression). This annotation also defines the retention policy and the applicability of the *TestDetails* annotation.

```
import java.lang.annotation.ElementType;
import java.lang.annotation.Retention;
import java.lang.annotation.RetentionPolicy;
import java.lang.annotation.Target;

//Make this annotation accessible at runtime via reflection.
@Retention(RetentionPolicy.RUNTIME)
//This annotation can only be applied to class methods.
@Target(ElementType.METHOD)

public @interface TestDetails {

}
```

- Define the parameters of annotation, if any.
  The following code below shows how to define two parameters for test information—test developed by and test modified by.

```
public @interface TestDetails {
        String developedBy() default "Unknown";
        String[] lastModifiedBy();
}
```

- Use the annotation while developing code wherever required.
  The following code uses the annotation *TestDetails* for test 'testPurchaseOrder'.

```
@TestDetails(testType=Enums.TestType.GUI,
        developedBy="Steve",
        lastModifiedBy={"Ann", "Dan", "Fran"})
public void testPurchaseOrder(){
        ... ...
}
```

EXAMPLE 1.4 Write a custom annotation that defines the following test details:

- **TestType:** GUI or API or UNIT test.
- **TestBucket:** Functional or regression test.
- **TestFunctionalArea:** Account or PurchaseOrder or navigation or security or other.
- **TestStatus:** In development or complete or repair.
- **DevelopedBy:** Person who developed the test.
- **LastModifiedBy:** Persons who modified the test.

First of all, we can create a class that defines enums for fixed values of `TestType`, `TestBucket`, `TestFunctionalArea` and `TestStatus`. The following code shows the code that defines these enums.

```
TestHeader.java
public class TestHeader {
        public enum TestType {GUI,API,UNIT};
        public enum TestBucket {FUNCTIONAL, REGRESSION};
        public enum FunctionalArea {ACCOUNT, PURCHASEORDER,
          NAVIGATION, SECURITY,OTHER};
        public enum TestStatus {INDEVELOPMENT,COMPLETE,REPAIR};
}
```

Next let us create an annotation *TestDetails* that defines the automated test information.

```
TestDetails.java
@Retention(RetentionPolicy.RUNTIME)
@Target(ElementType.METHOD)

public @interface TestDetails {
        TestHeader.TestTypetestType() default
          TestHeader.TestType.UNIT;
        TestHeader.TestBuckettestBucket() default
          TestHeader.TestBucket.FUNCTIONAL;
        TestHeader.FunctionalAreafunctionalArea() default
          TestHeader.FunctionalArea.OTHER;
        TestHeader.TestStatustestStatus() default
          TestHeader.TestStatus.INDEVELOPMENT;

        String developedBy() default "Unknown";
        String[] lastModifiedBy();
}
```

Next let us see how we can use this method in our code.

```
@TestDetails(testType=TestHeader.TestType.GUI,
        testBucket=TestHeader.TestBucket.REGRESSION,
        functionalArea=TestHeader.FunctionalArea.PURCHASEORDER,
        testStatus=TestHeader.TestStatus.COMPLETE,
        developedBy="Steve",
        lastModifiedBy={"Ann", "Dan", "Frank"})

public void testPurchaseOrder(){
        ... ...
}
```

2 CHAPTER

Introduction to Selenium

Selenium is an open source test automation tool package for automating web applications. It is a group of tools providing the flexibility to create record/playback as well as descriptive programmed tests. It provides the ability to write tests in a number of popular programming languages including Java, C#, Perl, PHP, Python and Ruby. Selenium tests can be run against most modern web browsers such as Firefox, Chrome and Internet Explorer. Selenium can be deployed on Windows, Linux and Macintosh platforms.

2.1 | HISTORY

Selenium was first developed by Jason Huggins in year 2004 at ThoughWorks. Selenium was developed as JavaScript library that could drive interactions with the web page. The Javascript library had the flexibility to run the same selenium tests against multiple browsers. This library eventually became *Selenium Core*. Selenium Core eventually drives all functionality of *Selenium Remote Control* (RC) and *Selenium IDE*. Selenium RC instantly gained popularity because of its ability to simulate user actions on a browser through a programming language of choice.

Though Selenium was a tremendous tool, it had its own drawbacks. Since browsers apply security limitations to Javascript, selenium being a Javascript-based automation tool, it was impossible for selenium to simulate various user interactions with browsers. As browsers added new features, these restrictions become more evident leaving automation using selenium more complicated.

In 2006, Simon Stewart, an engineer at Google started to work on a project called *WebDriver*. Google had long been a heavy user of selenium but its testers had to work around the limitations of the product. Simon's WebDriver projects aimed at developing a test automation tool that directly talks to the browser using 'native' methods of the browser and the operating system. This was an effective way to avoid the restrictions that selenium faced being a sandboxed Javascript environment.

In 2008, a need was felt to merge selenium and WebDriver as a single tool. Selenium had massive community and commercial support and WebDriver was the tool of the future. The merging of these two tools had advantages of offering common set of features to all users and also bringing the brightest minds in test automation under one roof.

2.2 | SELENIUM TOOL SUITE

Selenium is composed of multiple software tools each designed with a specific purpose. Table 2.1 lists out the various software tools available at the time of writing of this book.

TABLE 2.1 I Selenium tool suite

Filename	Summary
Selenium-ide-2.3.0.xpi	Selenium IDE
IEDriverServer_x64_2.35.3.zip	InternetExplorerDriver standalone server for 64-bit IE
IEDriverServer_Win32_2.35.3.zip	InternetExplorerDriver standalone server for 32-bit IE
selenium-dotnet-strongnamed-2.35.0.zip	Strong-named .NET assemblies for Selenium, including the RC and WebDriver APIs. Not recommended for most users.
selenium-server-2.35.0.zip	All variants of the Selenium Server: standalone, jar with dependencies and sources
selenium-java-2.35.0.zip	The Java bindings for Selenium 2, including the WebDriver API and the Selenium RC clients. Download this if plan is to just use the client-side pieces of Selenium
selenium-server-standalone-2.35.0.jar	Use this if requirement is to use the Selenium RC or Remote WebDriver or use Grid 2 without needing any additional dependencies Featured
selenium-dotnet-2.35.0.zip	.NET bindings for Selenium, including the RC and WebDriver APIs
android-server-2.32.0.apk	Android Driver server apk
android-server-2.21.0.apk	android-server-2.21.apk
chromedriver downloads.txt	Visit http://chromedriver.googlecode.com/ for the binary needed by the ChromeDriver

Note: Above tools can be downloaded from http://code.google.com/p/selenium/downloads/list.

2.2.1 | Selenium IDE

Selenium IDE (Integrated Development Environment) is a record/playback tool for building tests. It exists as Firefox plugin. This tool records user interactions with browser and plays them back during execution. Selenium IDE is used when there is a requirement to create small and simple test scripts or use and throw test scripts to aid in testing. Selenium IDE tests can be exported as Remote Control or WebDriver tests.

Selenium IDE can be downloaded from http://docs.seleniumhq.org/download/. Selenium IDE is discussed further. Selenium IDE is not the right tool for any serious automation. It is advisable to use Selenium WebDriver to build a robust and reliable test automation project.

2.2.2 | Selenium Client

Selenium client is a language-specific client driver to develop selenium automated tests. Selenium client needs to be installed on all the machines which are to be used for developing selenium tests. Separate driver exists for each programming language chosen. Table 2.2 shows some of the common language bindings that exist at the time of writing this book.

TABLE 2.2 | Selenium client language bindings

Language	Client version
Java	2.35.0
C#	2.35.0
Ruby	2.35.0
Python	2.35.0
Javascript (Node)	2.35.0

Note: Appropriate language bindings can be downloaded from http://docs.seleniumhq.org/download/

We will also learn how to write WebDriver code using Java.

2.2.3 | Selenium Server

Selenium server tool is used to execute selenium tests (Selenium RC or Remote Selenium WebDriver) against multiple machines. It is used to run large test suites against multiple environments (machines). It also allows running tests in parallel, i.e., two or more tests can run on the same machine at the same time. Selenium server reduces the test execution time considerably by scheduling selenium test execution against multiple machines in parallel. Selenium Server can be downloaded from the sites mentioned in Table 2.1.

Note: The test execution may be unpredictable if tests chosen to run parallel are not selected wisely. For example, two tests that sets cookies (say add to cart) if runs in parallel against the same browser, then they will override the browser cookies of each other leading to unpredictable behaviour during test execution.

Internet Explorer Driver Server

Internet Explorer Driver Server is required for using the latest supported features of WebDriver InternetExplorerDriver. This can be downloaded from the sites mentioned in Table 2.1.

Note: In order for the IE driver to work as expected, path of this file should be set on $PATH (or windows environment variable %PATH& for windows).

Supported Browsers and Platforms

Selenium WebDriver supports wide range of browsers and operating system (OS) platforms.

The list of browsers supported by Selenium WebDriver 2.35 is as follows:

- Google Chrome 12.0.712.0+
- Internet Explorer 7, 8, 9 (Both 32- and 64-bit versions)
- Firefox 4, 5, 6, 7, 8, 9, 10...23
- Safari 2, 3
- Opera 8, 9

The list of OS supported by Selenium WebDriver is as follows::

- Windows
- OS X
- Linux
- Solaris

Supported Mobile Automation Frameworks

Selenium provides mobile drivers for two major mobile platforms: Android and iOS (iPhone and iPad), the list of tools that support mobile automation is mentioned below:

- **Android WebDriver:** Android WebDriver allows running automated end-to-end tests on Android browser
- **Appium (iOS and Android):** Appium is an open source test automation framework for automating iOS and Android apps. It uses WebDriver JSON wire protocol for driving tests
- **iOS Requirements:** Mac OSX 10.7+ XCode 4.5+ w/ Command Line Tools
- **Android Requirements:** Mac OSX 10.7+ or Windows 7+ or Linux Android SDK ≥ 16 (SDK < 16 in Selendroid mode)

Supported Testing Frameworks

Testing frameworks are very useful for building a robust and reliable regression suite. The list of testing frameworks supported by WebDriver is as follows:

- JUnit
- TestNG
- Bromine
- NUnit
- RSpec(Ruby)
- Test::Unit(Ruby)
- Unittest(Python)
- Robot Framework Selenium Library
- ISFW
- Hermes

We will also learn how to develop selenium tests using JUnit/TestNG frameworks.

2.2.4 | Selenium WebDriver

Selenium WebDriver or Selenium 2.0 is the result of integration of WebDriver and Selenium. Selenium WebDriver was developed to provide a simple and more concise programming interface in addition to addressing some limitations in Selenium-RC. WebDriver better supports dynamic pages. Selenium WebDriver makes direct calls to the browser using each browser's native support for simulating user actions on browser.

Depending on the nature of automation project, Selenium Server may or may not be required for Selenium Automation Project. If automation project is small and simple and requires executing all tests against single machine and browser, then WebDriver API alone will be able to achieve this. However, if regression suite size is big and requires executing test against multiple remote machines and multiple browsers, then Selenium Server also is to be used. Some of the situations which calls for using Selenium Server along with Selenium WebDriver are mentioned below:

- Requirement is to use Selenium-Grid to distribute test execution over multiple machines.
- Requirement is to execute tests against specific remote machine configurations and browser instances.
- Selenium automation is being carried out using HtmlUnitDriver (non-Java binding).

Setup

Selenium WebDriver supports various programming languages for automating tests. The following section briefly describes Selenium WebDriver project installation steps.

Java

The easiest way to set Selenium WebDriver Java project is to use Maven. Maven automatically creates the project and downloads the Java bindings (Selenium WebDriver java client library) and all its dependencies using a maven pom.xml (project configuration) file. Once the project is created, it can then be imported in Eclipse IDE or IntelliJ IDEA.

Alternatively, Selenium WebDriver jar files can be downloaded from the site http://selenium.googlecode.com/files/selenium-java-2.35.0.zip. Once downloaded, the file needs to be unzipped. The unzipped jar files than needs to be added as external jar files. Steps to add Selenium-Java jar files to the project are as follows.

- Open eclipse and select the project.
- Right click and select *Properties*. *Properties*...window opens up.
- Select options *Java Build Path*.
- Select tab *Library*
- Click on button *Add External JARs*... and add the unzipped Selenium-Java jar files.
- Click on *Ok* button.

Eclipse also provides an option of attaching Javadoc and source files of the jar file to the jar file. In order to attach Javadoc to the jar file, the below mentioned steps are to be followed:

- Download the JavaDoc and save it or note the JavaDoc URL (http://selenium.googlecode.com/git/docs/api/java/index.html)
- Open eclipse and select the project.
- Right click and select *Properties*. *Properties*...window opens up.

- Select options *Java Build Path.*
- Select tab *Library.*
- Double click the jar file so that the tree opens up as shown in Figure 2.1.

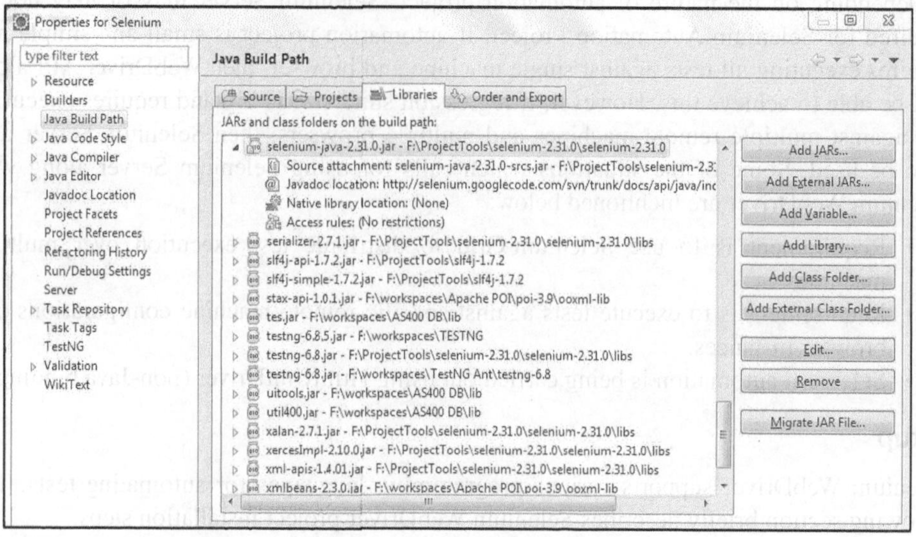

FIGURE 2.1 | Associating Javadoc and source code files to a jar file

- Select *Javadoc Location* and click *Edit* button. *Source Attachment Configuration* window opens up.
- If JavaDoc URL is known, then select option *JavaDoc URL* and provide the URL from the first step.
- Else if JavaDoc files are saved in hard drive, then select option *Javadoc in archive* and then add the file path.

In order to attach source files (source Java code) to the jar file, follow the following steps:

- Download the source code and save it on the hard drive.
- Follow steps 1–6 from above.
- Select *Source Attachment* and click *Edit* button. *Source Attachment Configuration* window opens up.
- Specify the path of the source file and click *OK* button.

How to setup a Selenium WebDriver Java automation project is discussed in Chapter 3.

C#

Selenium 2.2.0 onwards, the C# bindings are being distributed as set of signed dlls (dynamic link libraries) along with dependency dlls. These dlls can be downloaded from link as mentioned in Table 2.1. To setup the Selenium WebDriver automation project, unzip these files and add a reference of the unzipped files in Visual Studio (or IDE of choice).

Note: If OS is Win 7 or above, the zipped files need to be unblocked before unzipping. To unblock the zipped filed: Right click on the zip file " click Properties" click Unblock" click OK.

Python

Selenium Webdriver Python project can be setup by adding the selenium files to the Python environment. To add selenium to the Python environment, the following command is to be executed from a command line.

```
pip install selenium
```

Pip requires pip to be installed. Pip also has a dependency on setuptools.

Notes:

1. For details on pip, refer link http://pypi.python.org/pypi/pip
2. For details on setup tools, refer link http://pypi.python.org/pypi/setuptools

Ruby

Selenium Webdriver Ruby project can be setup by adding the selenium files to the Python environment. To add selenium to the Python environment, the following command is to be executed from a command line.

```
gem install selenium-webdriver
```

Perl

Perl bindings are provided by a third party. Refer link https://metacpan.org/module/Selenium::Remote::Driver for creating a Selenium WebDriver Perl project.

PHP

PHP bindings are provided by a third party. Refer links https://github.com/chibimagic/WebDriver-PHP/, http://code.google.com/p/php-webdriver-bindings/ and https://github.com/facebook/php-webdriver for details on how to setup a Selenium WebDriver PHP project.

2.2.5 | Selenium WebDriver's Driver

WebDriver is the key interface that drives user actions against browsers. There are several implementations of this interface in Selenium WebDriver. Described as follows are the various driver interfaces that can be used to simulate user actions against various browsers.

HtmlUnitDriver

HtmlUnitDriver is a Java-based implementation of a WebBrowser without a GUI. This is the fastest and most lightweight implementation on webDriver. For any language binding except Java, the Selenium Server is required to use this driver.

Usage

- **Java:** `WebDriver driver = new HtmlUnitDriver();`
- **C#:** `IWebDriver driver = new RemoteWebDriver(new Uri(" http://127.0.0.1:4444/wd/hub"), DesiredCapabilities.HtmlUnit());`

Table 2.3 lists the pros and cons of this driver.

TABLE 2.3 | Pros and cons of HtmlUnitDriver

Pros	Cons
Fastest implementation of WebDriver	Emulates browsers' Javascript behavior
Pure java implementation, so platform-independent	
Supports Javascript	

In today's world, most of the websites rely on Javascript. Since, each browser has its own quirks and differences in their implementation of DOM and how Javascript interacts with it, HtmlUnit Javascript capabilities may cause problems that manifests themselves. This is also because, though HtmlUnit has an impressively complete implementation of DOM and has good support for using Javascript, it has its own quirks. Because of these problems, Javascript is disabled by default in HtmlUnit driver.

Firefox Driver

FirefoxDriver simulates user actions against Firefox browser using a Firefox plugin. The Firefox profile is stripped down from what is installed on the machine to only include the Selenium WebDriver plugin (WebDriver.xpi). Firefox driver supports Windows, Mac and Linux platforms. Latest version of FirefoxDriver supports Firefox 27, at the time of writing this book.

Usage

- **Java:** `WebDriver driver = new FirefoxDriver();`
- **C#:** `IWebDriver driver = new FirefoxDriver();`

Table 2.4 lists the pros and cons of this driver.

TABLE 2.4 | Pros and cons of Firefox driver

Pros	Cons
Runs in real browser and supports Javascript.	Slower than HtmlUnit driver
Faster than InternetExplorer driver	

Modifying Firefox Profile

FirefoxDriver provides the flexibility to launch Firefox with modified settings such as using specific plugins. There are two ways of modifying Firefox profile before test execution initiation: one through command line and other by explicitly writing code for it (Table 2.5).

Command "firefox–ProfileManager" is to be used to modify the Firefox profile while executing a test from command line.

Alternatively, desired Firefox profile can also be set using code as shown as follows:

```
FirefoxProfile profile = new FirefoxProfile();
//accept untrusted certificates
profile.setAcceptUntrustedCertificates(true);
//enable firefox native events
profile.setEnableNativeEvents(true);
//load new Firefox profile
WebDriver driver = new FirefoxDriver(profile)
```

Following code shows how to execute tests against Firefox with firebug plugin loaded.

```
//Download the firebug xpi file from Mozilla
File file = new File("firebug-1.8.1.xpi");
FirefoxProfile profile = new FirefoxProfile();
profile.addExtension(file);
profile.setPreference("extensions.firebug.currentVersion",
"1.8.1");
WebDriver driver = new FirefoxDriver(profile);
```

Note: By default, Firefox native events are disabled in Selenium WebDriver 2.35.

TABLE 2.5 | Firefox profile configurations

Property	Description
webdriver.accept.untrusted.certs	Accept untrusted certificate
webdriver.assume.untrusted.issuer	Untrusted certificate issuer
webdriver.development	Never use in production Indicates that we're in development mode
webdriver.enable.native.events	Enable/disable browser native events
webdriver.firefox.bin	The location of the binary used to control firefox
webdriver.firefox.port	Port number Firefox driver to use to connect to local host.
webdriver.firefox.profile	The name of the profile to use when starting firefox. This defaults to webdriver creating an anonymous profile
webdriver.firefox.useExisting	Never use in production Use a running instance of firefox if one is present
webdriver.log.file	Log file to dump javascript console logging to
webdriver.firefox.logfile	Log file to dump firefox stdout/stderr to
webdriver.reap_profile	Should be "true" if temporary files and profiles should not be deleted

2.2.6 | InternetExplorer Driver

InternetExplorer driver simulates user actions against Microsoft Internet Explorer browser. Selenium WebDriver 2.35 supports IE 6, 7 and 8 on XP and IE 9 on Win 7.The driver supports running both 32-bit and 64-bit versions of the browser. This driver is controlled by a .dll (dynamic link library). This driver can be downloaded from the site as mentioned in Table 2.1.

Setup

`InternetExplorerDriver` is a standalone server which implements WebDriver's wire protocol. This standalone server is to be downloaded from the site as mentioned in Table 2.1. The downloaded file is to be unzipped at some location in the hard drive. Next, environment PATH variable needs to be configured to point to these unzipped files. In order to configure *Environment Variables* path in Win 7 environment, follow the following steps:

- Open *Windows Explorer* (or press key + E [windows+E]).
- Navigate to *Control Panel\All Control Panel Items\System. Control Panel Home* screen opens up.
- Click on *Advance System Settings* link. *System Properties* pop-window opens.
- Click on tab *Advanced.*
- Click button *Environment Variables.Environment Variables* pop-window opens.
- Look for variable named *Path in User Variables* section.
- If the *Path* variable exists, then click on button *Edit.*
- Else, click on button *New.*
- Specify *Variable name* as *Path,* if not already defined.
- Concatenate the location of the driver to the *Variable value.*
- Click button *OK.*

Usage

- **Java:** `WebDriver driver = new InternetExplorerDriver();`
- **C#:** `IWebDriver driver = new InternetExplorerDriver();`

Table 2.6 lists the pros and cons of this driver.

TABLE 2.6 | Pros and cons of InternetExplorer driver

Pros	Cons
Runs against real IE browser	Slow as compared to HtmlUnit driver
Supports Javascript with all quirks which end users see	XPath is not natively supported in many versions. Sizzle is automatically injected but its significantly slow.
	CSS selectors in IE 8 and 9 are native, but those browsers don't fully support CSS3

2.2.7 | Chrome Driver

Chrome driver simulates user actions against Chrome browser. ChromeDriver supports Mac, Linux and Windows OS.

Setup

ChromeDriver can be downloaded from the site http://code.google.com/p/chromedriver/downloads/list

The downloaded file is to be unzipped at some location in the hard drive. Next, environment PATH variable needs to be configured to point to these unzipped files. In order to configure *Environment Variables* path in Win 7 environment, follow the setup steps as mentioned for aforementioned InternetExplorerDriver.

Usage

- **Java:** `WebDriver driver = new ChromeDriver();`
- **C#:** `IWebDriver driver = new ChromeDriver();`

Table 2.7 lists the pros and cons of this driver.

TABLE 2.7 | Pros and cons of Chrome driver

Pros	Cons
Runs against real Chrome browser Supports Javascript	Slow as compared to HtmlUnit driver XPath is not natively supported in many versions. Sizzle is automatically injected but it is significantly slow. CSS selectors in IE 8 and 9 are native, but those browsers don't fully support CSS3.

Note: Since Chrome is a Webkit-based browser it may allow to verify whether a web app works in Safari. JavaScript execution may differ as Chrome uses its own V8 JavaScript engine rather than Safari's Nitro engine.

3 CHAPTER

Installation

In this chapter, we will discuss how to setup a test automation project. Initially, we will discuss how to quickly install Selenium WebDriver project for beginners. Finally, we will learn to how to setup a Selenium Automation project for enterprise level applications.

3.1 | GETTING STARTED

This automation project will use Eclipse as IDE (Integrated Development Environment), Java as programming language, Firefox as browser and Firefox plugin Firebug for developing element identifiers which will help beginners to understand how to quickly install the Selenium WebDriver project.

3.1.1 | Downloads

Table 3.1 describes applications that need to be downloaded before starting the installation.

TABLE 3.1 | Essential downloads for getting started with selenium Java automation

Downloadable App	Objective	Site
Firefox 23	Browser against which tests would run	http://www.mozilla.org/en-US/
Firebug plugin for Firefox	• For analysing element attributes • For developing element identifiers	https://addons.mozilla.org/en-us/firefox/addon/firebug/ (this needs to be downloaded once Firefox is installed)
Java Platform JDK	For developing Java programs	http://www.oracle.com/technetwork/java/javase/downloads/index.html
Eclipse IDE for Java EE Developers	IDE for developing tests	http://www.eclipse.org/downloads/
JUnit	Testing framework	https://github.com/junit-team/junit/wiki/Download-and-Install

(*continued*)

TABLE 3.1 | *(continued)*

Downloadable App	Objective	Site
TestNG	Testing framework	http://testing.org/doc/download.html
Selenium-Java	Java-based Selenium WebDriver Test automation framework	http://selenium.googlecode.com/files/selenium-java-2.35.0.zip

3.1.2 | Setup

The installation steps are described in detail as follows:

Installing Firefox

- Download and install Firefox latest version.
- Install Firefox plugin Firebug
  - Open Firefox
  - Navigate to the URL https://addons.mozilla.org/en-us/firefox/addon/firebug. Page as shown in Figure 3.1 opens.
  - Click on the button *Add to Firefox*.

Alternatively, the Firefox add-ons can also be installed from within Firefox.

- Open Firefox
- Navigate *Tools* → *Add-ons*. *Get Add-ons* page opens as shown in Figure 3.2.

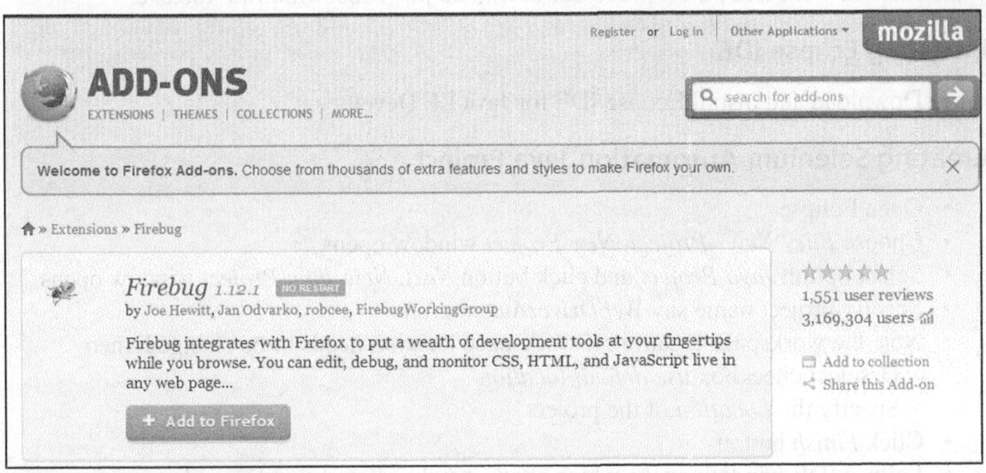

FIGURE 3.1 | Installing Firefox add-ons

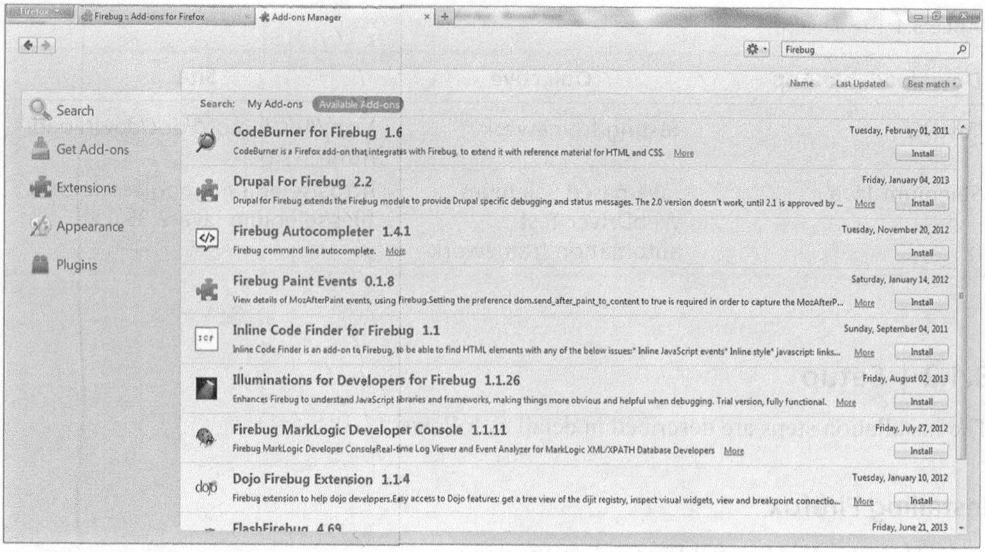

FIGURE 3.2 | Firefox add-ons page

- Search for "Firebug". Firefox search results in a list of add-ons which matches the search criteria as shown in Figure 3.2.
- Click the *Install* button to install the specific add-on.

Installing Java Platform (JDK)

- Download and install latest version of Java Platform (JDK)

Note: Choose the right version of JDK depending upon the operating system and processor bit. For example, for Win 7 OS and 64-bit processor download jdk-7u25-windows-x64.exe, while for Win 7 OS and 32-bit processor download jdk-7u25-windows-x86.exe.

Installing Eclipse IDE

- Download and install Eclipse IDE for Java EE Developers.

Creating Selenium Automation Java Project

- Open Eclipse
- Choose *File* "*New*" *Project*. *New Project* window opens
- Select option *Java Project* and click button *Next*. *New Java Project* window opens
- Specify project name say *WebDriverAutomation*
- Note the workspace location. If workspace location needs to be changed, then
  - Deselect checkbox *use default location*
  - Specify the *Location* of the project
- Click *Finish* button
- Eclipse IDE window opens which shows newly created WebDriverAutomation project with default package *src* as shown in Figure 3.3.

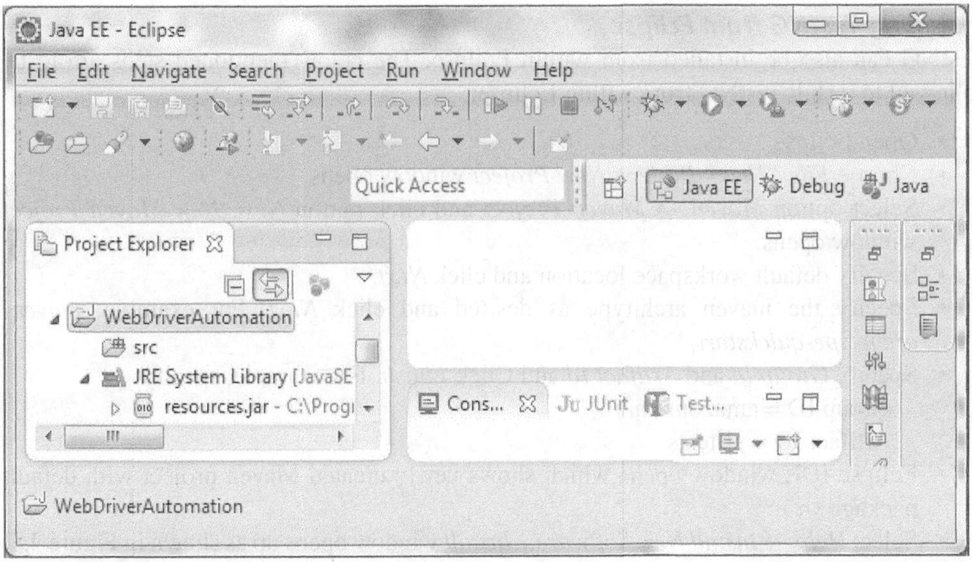

FIGURE 3.3 | Eclipse IDE

Creating Selenium Automation Java Maven Project from Eclipse

Instead of creating a Java project, we can also create a Maven project for Selenium WebDriver automation. Steps below show how to create a Maven project for Selenium WebDriver automation.

Installing JUnit

- Download the JUnit JAR file (junit.jar)
- Open Eclipse
  - Right click on the automation project (WebDriverAutomation) and select *Properties. Properties for WebDriverAutomation* window opens up
  - Select option *Java Build Path.*
  - Select tab *Libraries*
  - Click button *Add External JARs…* and add the junit.jar file
  - Click *OK* button

Note: Eclipse installation by default includes JUnit package. If the installed jUnit package is not latest then follow the above steps to install latest version of JUnit.

Installing TestNG

- Download TestNG JAR file for Eclipse (http://beust.com/eclipse).
- Install the jar file by following steps 1–5 of "Installing JUnit" section to install TestNG jar file.

Installing TestNG from Eclipse

TestNG can also be installed from within Eclipse. The below mentioned steps are to be followed to install TestNG from within Eclipse:

- Open Eclipse.
- Choose *File "New" Project. New Project* window opens.
- Select option *Maven → Maven Project* and click button *Next. New Maven Project* window opens.
- Specify default workspace location and click *Next.*
- Specify the maven architype as desired and click *Next.* For example, *maven-archetype-quickstart.*
- Specify *Group Id* and *Artifact Id* and Click *Finish.* For example, specify:
  Group ID = amazonretail
  Artifact ID = ui-tests
- Eclipse IDE window opens which shows newly created Maven project with default package *src.*
- Select *Help → Install New Software…Install* window opens up as shown in Figure 3.4.
- Specify URL http://beust.com/eclipse. Eclipse will automatically pull up and show TestNG option as shown in Figure 3.4.

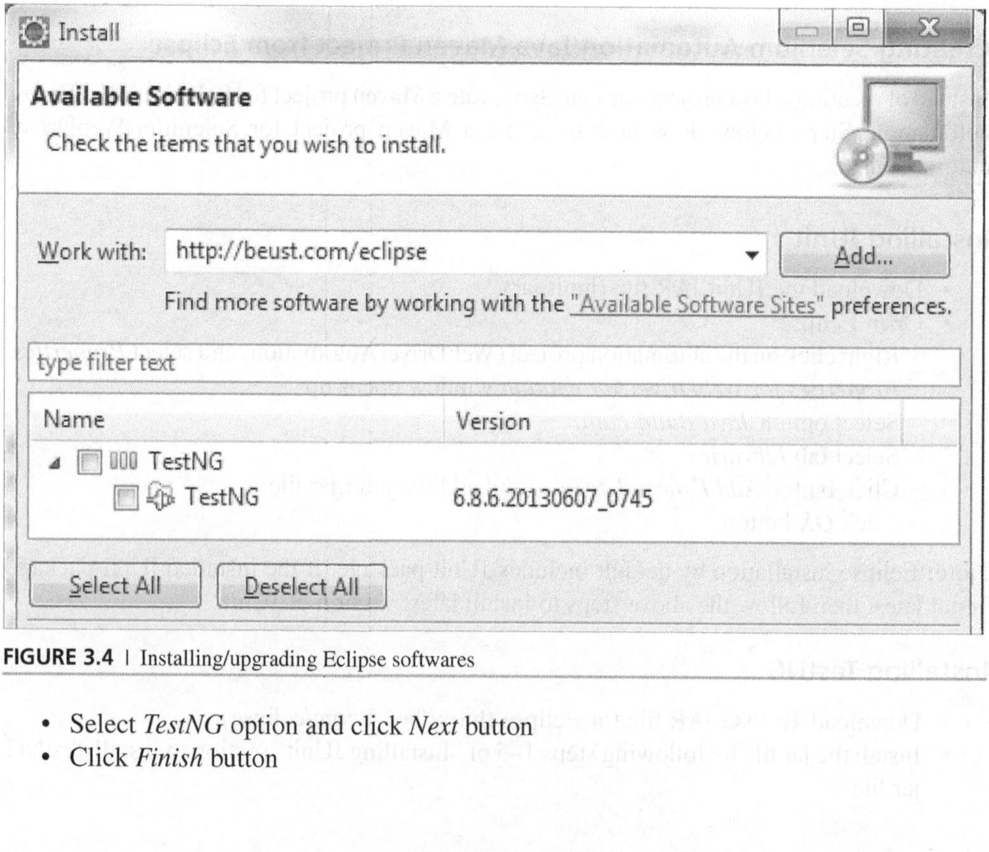

FIGURE 3.4 | Installing/upgrading Eclipse softwares

- Select *TestNG* option and click *Next* button
- Click *Finish* button

Note: Both JUnit and TestNG are testing frameworks. It is advisable to use only one of the frameworks while implementing an actual automation project. For learning purposes, both can be installed for the same project.

Installing Selenium WebDriver

- Download Selenium-Java.zip file.
- Unzip the file to extract JARs.
- Install the Selenium-Java.jar and all Library jars file by following steps 1–5 of "Installing JUnit" section to install Selenium WebDriver Java jar files.
- Install source code and Javadoc, if required, by following the steps of installation as mentioned in Chapter 2.

3.1.3 | Developing First Test

- On Eclipse IDE, select the default package *src* of project *WebDriverAutomation*
- Right click and select *New → Other*. *Select a Wizard* window opens
- Select option *JUnit Test Case* or *TestNG* class and click *Next* button
  - For creating a JUnit test class, select option *JUnit Test Case.*
  - For creating a TestNG test class, select option *TestNG class.*
- Specify the name of the class, say *JUnitTest* and click *Finish* button.
- Eclipse IDE window opens with the newly created class as shown in Figure 3.5.

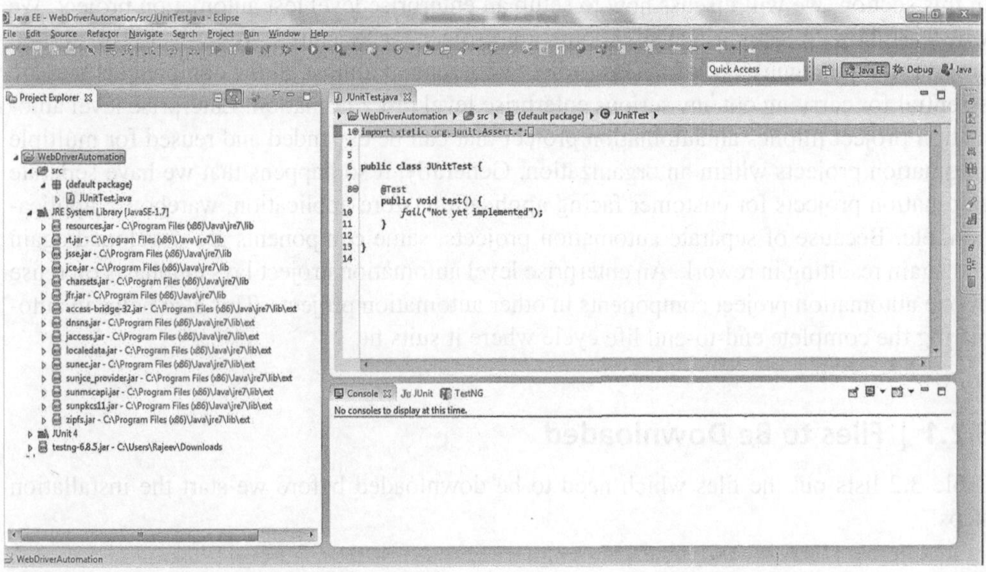

FIGURE 3.5 | Creating a JUnit test class

- Write the following code.

  Below is the WebDriver test code to open Google Search page and search for text 'Selenium WebDriver'.

```
@Test
public void test() {
        FirefoxDriver driver = new FirefoxDriver();
        //open google search site
        driver.get("http://www.google.com");
        //search for text "Selenium WebDriver"
        driver.findElement(By.name("q")).sendKeys("Selenium
          Webdriver");
        driver.findElement(By.name("btnG")).click();
}
```

- Execute the above code.
  - For JUnit test, select the @Test method and do a right mouse click. Select *Run As"JUnit Test.*
  - For TestNG test, select the @Test method and do a right mouse click. Select *Run As"TestNG Test*

3.2 | INSTALLING SELENIUM WEBDRIVER JAVA MAVEN AUTOMATION PROJECT

In this section, we will discuss how to setup an enterprise level test automation project. We will learn how to setup a maven automation project for Selenium WebDriver. The chosen programming language is Java. This project will contain almost all the components that are essential for carrying out any serious enterprise level test automation. Enterprise level automation project implies an automation project that can be expanded and reused for multiple automation projects within an organization. Generally, it so happens that we have separate automation projects for customer facing application, store application, warehouse application, etc. Because of separate automation projects, same components are developed again and again resulting in rework. An enterprise level automation project lays emphasis on reuse of one automation project components in other automation projects. This also helps in automating the complete end-to-end life cycle where it suits fit.

3.2.1 | Files to Be Downloaded

Table 3.2 lists out the files which need to be downloaded before we start the installation steps.

TABLE 3.2 | Generic downloads for setting up Selenium Java Maven Automation Project

Application	Objective	Site
Firefox 23	Test browser	http://www.mozilla.org/en-US/
Plugins		
• Firebug	To edit, debug and monitor CSS, HTML and JavaScript live in any web page	http://getfirebug.com/
• Omnibug	To test analytics	https://addons.mozilla.org/En-us/firefox/addon/omnibug/?src=ss
• Firepath	To edit, inspect and generate XPath expressions, CSS3 selectors and jQuery selectors	http://code.google.com/p/firepath/
• XPather	To generate XPath	https://addons.mozilla.org/en-US/firefox/addon/XPather/
• CSS Viewer	To analyse CSS attributes of an element	https://addons.mozilla.org/en-US/firefox/addon/css-viewer/?src=api
• Web Developer	Tools to effectively test a web application	http://chrispederick.com/work/web-developer/
• Regular Expression Tester	To design/evaluate regular expressions	https://addons.mozilla.org/en-us/firefox/addon/rext/
• RestClient	To test restful web services	http://restclient.net/ https://addons.mozilla.org/en-US/firefox/addon/soa-client/?src=api
• SOAClient	To test web services (WSDL, SOAP, UDDI)	https://addons.mozilla.org/en-us/firefox/addon/soa-client/?src=search
JDK	For developing Java programs	http://www.oracle.com/technetwork/java/javase/downloads/index.html
Eclipse IDE for Java EE Developers	IDE for developing tests	http://www.eclipse.org/downloads/
Maven integration for Eclipse	Maven integration for Eclipse	
TestNG integration for Eclipse	TestNG integration for Eclipse	http://beust.com/eclipse
eGit	To checkin code to Git repository (Install this if code repository is Git and not SVN)	
Apache Maven	To setup maven project (apache-maven-3.1.0-bin.zip)	http://maven.apache.org/download.cgi
Selenium-Java	Java-based Selenium WebDriver Test Automation framework	http://selenium.googlecode.com/files/selenium-java-2.35.0.zip
JUnit	Testing framework	https://github.com/junit-team/junit/wiki/Download-and-Install

TestNG	Testing framework	http://testng.org/doc/download.html
SLF4J	Java API for test result logging	http://www.slf4j.org/download.html
ODBC	Java API to connect to Oracle database	http://www.oracle.com/technetwork/database/enterprise-edition/jdbc-112010-090769.html
JTOpen	Java API to connect to IBM DB2 (AS400) database	http://sourceforge.net/projects/jt400/
ApachePOI	Java API for creating/modifying Microsoft Documents such as Word, Excel, etc.	http://poi.apache.org/download.html
PDFBox	Java API to work with PDF documents	http://pdfbox.apache.org/downloads.html
CommonIO	Java API to assist with developing IO functionality	http://commons.apache.org/proper/commons-io/download_io.cgi
JavaMail	Java API to programmatically read/send e-mail and perform other e-mailing options	http://www.oracle.com/technetwork/java/javamail/index-138643.html
COM4J	Java library that allows Java applications to seamlessly interoperate with Microsoft Component Object Model.	https://java.net/projects/com4j/downloads

Note: The links provided above is the default download page link for all versions of applications and JAR files. The above links may contain applications/JAR files for various supported OS and browsers. Depending on the system where the automation project needs to be setup, appropriate applications/JAR files are to be downloaded. In this chapter, we will learn how to setup an automation project on Win 7 64-bit system.

Installing Firefox

- Download and install Firefox 23
- Install Firefox plugins

Installing Java Platform (JDK)

- Download and install latest version of Java Platform (JDK)
  Note: Choose the right version of JDK depending upon the operating system and processor bit. For example, for Win 7 OS and 64-bit processor download jdk-7u25-windows-x64.exe, while for Win 7 OS and 32-bit processor download jdk-7u25-windows-x86.exe.
- Set Java environment variable
  - Set the JAVA_HOME environment variable to point to the base directory location where Java is installed on the machine

Follow the steps to set Java environment path variable in Win 7 OS:

- Open windows explorer and navigate to *Control Panel\All Control Panel Items\System. Control Panel Home* screen opens.
- Click on the link *Advanced system settings. System Properties* window opens.
- Click on the button *Environment Variables*. Environment Variables window opens.
- Under *user variables ...* section (or *system variables...* section), click on the *New..* button. *New User Variable* window opens.
- Specify variable name as JAVA_HOME and variable value as JDK installation path say *C:\Program Files\Java\jdk1.7.0_25*.
- Click *OK* button to set the Java environment variable.

Table 3.3 shows the Java environment variable settings for various OS.

TABLE 3.3 | Environment variable settings for Java

OS	Output
Windows	Set the environment variable JAVA_HOME to C:\Program Files\Java\jdk1.7.0_25;
Linux	export JAVA_HOME=/usr/local/java-current
Mac	export JAVA_HOME=/Library/Java/Home

- Append Java compiler location to System Path
  Follow the steps to set Java compiler location in Win 7 OS:
  - Follow steps 1–3 of above section to open environment variables window
  - Under *user variables...* section (or *system variables...* section), verify if *PATH* variable exists or not.If it doesn't exists, then click on the *New..*button. Else select the variable and click *Edit* button. *User Variable* window opens
  - Specify variable name as PATH and append variable value as bin path of JDK installation, say *;%JAVA_HOME%\bin;*
  - Click *OK* button to set the environment variable

Table 3.4 shows the Java environment variable settings for various OS.

TABLE 3.4 | Environment variable settings for Java

OS	Output
Windows	Append the string %JAVA_HOME%\bin; to the end of the system variablePath.
Linux	export PATH=$PATH:$JAVA_HOME/bin/
Mac	not required

Note: If the environment variable already exists, then just edit the environment variable and add the variable value. (Ensure existing values are not overwritten).

Note: To verify if Java environment has been properly configured, open command prompt and type *java –version*. The response should look as shown in Figure 3.6.

```
c:\>java -version
java version "1.7.0_25"
Java(TM) SE Runtime Environment (build 1.7.0_25-b17)
Java HotSpot(TM) 64-Bit Server VM (build 23.25-b01, mixed mode)
```

FIGURE 3.6 | Setting environment variable for Java

Installing Eclipse IDE

Download and install Eclipse IDE for Java EE Developers

Install Maven Integration for Eclipse

- Open Eclipse
- Navigate *Help → Eclipse Marketplace...Eclipse Marketplace* window opens as shown in Figure 3.7
- Search for *Maven*. The search list will generate as shown in Figure 3.7
- Select the appropriate integration and click *Install* button

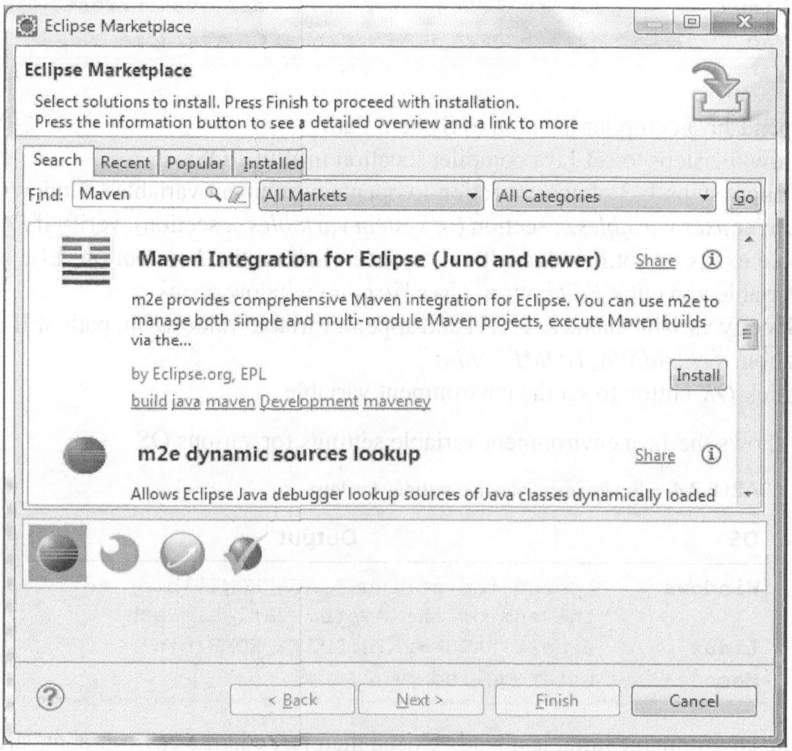

FIGURE 3.7 | Installing Eclipse integrations from Eclipse

Install TestNG Integration for Eclipse

Follow steps 1–4 of section "Install Maven integration for Eclipse" to install TestNG integration for Eclipse.

Install eGit Integration for Eclipse

Follow steps 1–4 of section "Install Maven integration for Eclipse" with search term 'eGit' to install eGit integration for Eclipse.

Installing Apache Maven

Apache Maven is a software project management and a build automation tool for Java projects. It is based on the concept of a project object model (POM). Maven can manage a project's build, reporting and documentation from a central piece of information. Maven dynamically downloads Java libraries and maven plug-ins from one or more repositories such as the Maven 2 Central Repository and stores them in a local cache.

Maven follows a common directory layout for any java project. If we prefer to deviate from this structure, then the settings are to be overridden via the project descriptor.

TABLE 3.5 | Maven directory structure

Maven Directory	Objective
src/main/java	Application/Library sources
src/main/resources	Application/Library resources
src/main/filters	Resource filter files
src/main/assembly	Assembly descriptors
src/main/config	Configuration files
src/main/scripts	Application/Library scripts
src/main/webapp	Web application sources
src/test/java	Test sources
src/test/resources	Test resources
src/test/filters	Test resource filter files
src/site	Site
LICENSE.txt	Project's license
NOTICE.txt	Notices and attributions required by libraries that the project depends on
README.txt	Project's readme

Following steps describe how to install maven.

- Download Apache Maven.
- Unzip maven file to location, say *c:\automation-tools*
- Set environment variable for maven.
  - Follow steps 1–3 of section "Set Java environment variable" to open *Environment Variable* window
  - Under *user variables...* section (or *system variables...* section), click on the *New..* button. *New User Variable* window opens.

- Specify variable name as M2_HOME and variable value as *C:\automation-tools\apache-maven-3.1.0.*
- *Click OK* button.
- Under *user variables...* section (or *system variables...* section),select variable *PATH* and click *Edit* button.
- Append value*; %M2_HOME%\bin;* to the PATH variable value.
- Click *OK* button set maven path.

Note: To verify if maven environment has been properly configured, open command prompt and type *mvn -version*. The response should look as shown in Figure 3.8.

FIGURE 3.8 | Setting environment variable for maven

Installing Selenium WebDriver Java Maven Project

- Create a new workspace folder, say C:\automation-workspace\amazon-retail (c:\automation-workspace\<app-name>)
- Create a new project folder, say *ui-tests* as "C:\automation-workspace\amazon-retail *\ui-tests*".
- Create a new file pom.xml inside project folder 'ui-tests'.
- Write the following contents to pom.xml file

```
<?xml version="1.0" encoding="UTF-8"?>
<project xmlns="http://maven.apache.org/POM/4.0.0"
        xmlns:xsi="http://www.w3.org/2001/XMLSchema-instance"
        xsi:schemaLocation="http://maven.apache.org/POM/4.0.0
          http://maven.apache.org/xsd/maven-4.0.0.xsd">
    <modelVersion>4.0.0</modelVersion>
    <groupId>amazonretail</groupId>
    <artifactId>ui-tests</artifactId>
    <version>99.0</version>
    <dependencies>
        <dependency>
                <groupId>org.seleniumhq.selenium</groupId>
                <artifactId>selenium-java</artifactId>
                <version>2.35.0</version>
        </dependency>
    </dependencies>
</project>
```

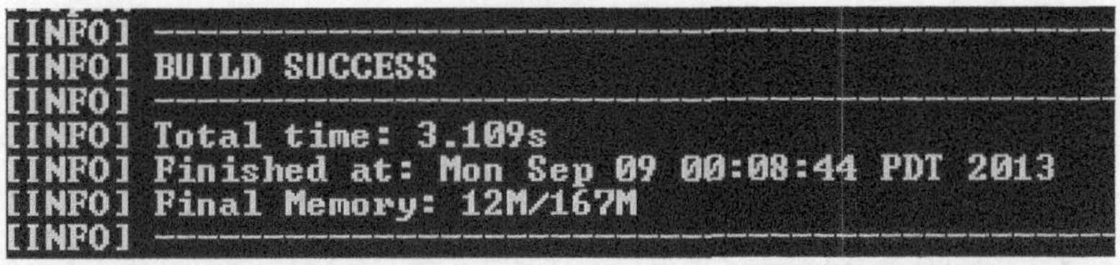
```
[INFO] ------------------------------------------------------------
[INFO] BUILD SUCCESS
[INFO] ------------------------------------------------------------
[INFO] Total time: 3.109s
[INFO] Finished at: Mon Sep 09 00:08:44 PDT 2013
[INFO] Final Memory: 12M/167M
[INFO] ------------------------------------------------------------
```

FIGURE 3.9 | Installing maven project

Note: Replace text strings 'amazon-retail' (or amazonretail) with the name of the choice (companyname-projectname)

- Open command prompt
- Navigate to the project folder, say *C:\automation-workspace*\amazon-retail\ui-tests
- Type "mvn clean install"

Note: Ensure internet connectivity is working as this command downloads all required files for creating a maven project

- Once installation is successful, information as shown in Figure 3.9 will be written to command prompt
- Navigate to the directory "C:\automation-workspace\amazon-retail *\ui-tests*".
- Create folders "C:\automation-workspace\amazon-retail *\ui-tests\src\main\java"*.
- Create folders "C:\automation-workspace\amazon-retail *\ui-tests\src\test\java"*.
- Create folders "C:\automation-workspace\amazon-retail *\ui-tests\src\test\resources"*.

Note: For installing Selenium-Server, specify selenium server dependency in the pom.xml file instead of selenium-java dependency.

```
<dependency>
        <groupId>org.seleniumhq.selenium</groupId>
        <artifactId>selenium-server</artifactId>
        <version>2.35.0</version>
</dependency>
```

3.2.2 | Importing Maven Project in Eclipse

- Open Eclipse
- Navigate *File* → *Import*. *Import* window opens
- Select *Maven* → *Existing Maven Projects* as shown in Figure 3.10
- Click *Next* button. *Import Maven Projects* window opens.
- Click *Browse* button and add the 'WebDriverAutomation' project.
- Click *Finish* button. The maven project will be visible on *Project Explorer* window of Eclipse IDE as shown in Figure 3.11.

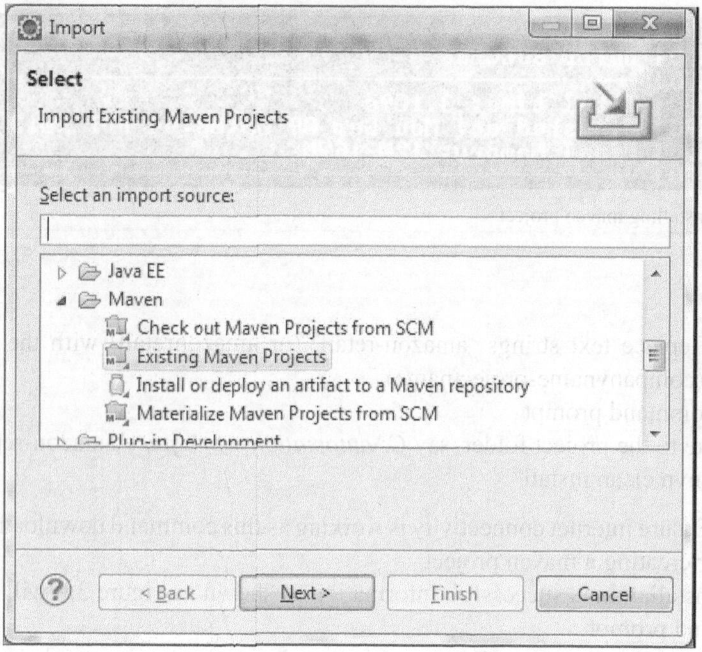

FIGURE 3.10 | Importing maven project

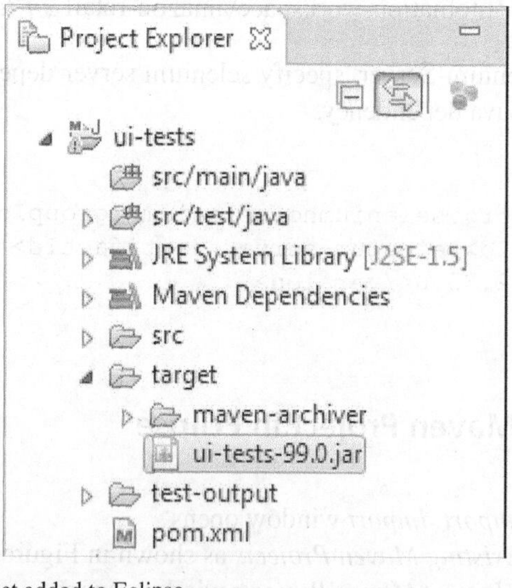

FIGURE 3.11 | Maven project added to Eclipse

Note: Note the ui-tests-99.0.jar file created as shown in Figure 3.11. Any other maven automation project can access the resources of this project by creating a maven dependency of this JAR file.

3.2.3 | Creating Automation Project Framework Components

Next step would be to create the framework (framework components) of the automation project. Listed in Table 3.6 is the list of framework components that needs to be created to implement agile automation framework or page object model framework. Refer chapter 'Agile Automation Framework' for more details on automation frameworks benefits and implementation.

Framework components can be implemented in Eclipse by creating a package for each framework component. Each package can then contain various classes to implement the intended objective of the framework components. The following steps are to be used to create a package:

1. Right click on the source folder (src/test/java) and select *New"Package. New Java Package* window opens.
2. Specify name of the package, say *com.amazonretail.envvariables*. (com.<appname>.envvariables)
3. Click *Finish* button. New package with the specified name will be created as shown in Figure 3.12.

TABLE 3.6 | Agile automation framework components

Framework component	Objective
configuration	Defines automation project environment data and application under test settings.
envvariables	Defines application under test environment data such as application URL, login credentials, etc.
pages	Contains code to automate page functionality.
pagecomponents	Contains code to automate functionality that is common to more than one page such as an advertisement on multiple saying "Free shipping on items greater than $100".
businesscomponents	Contains code that automates a reusable business functionality such as account creation, order placement, etc.
testdata	Defines test data
library	Contains non-UI code that can be reused within the project.
uimap	Defines element identification attributes. This component may or may not be used depending on whether the element attributes are being defined separately or within the page and page components.

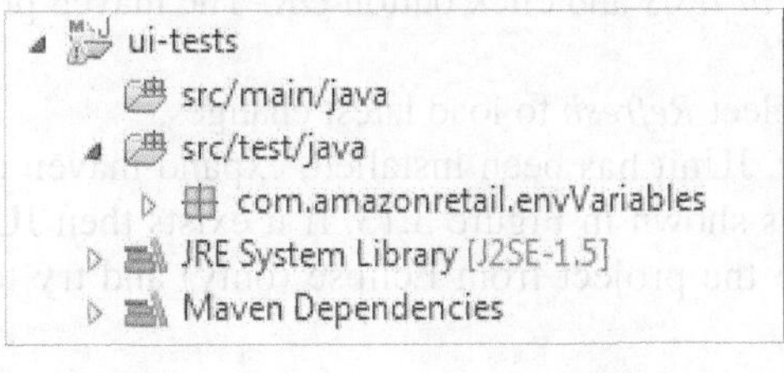

FIGURE 3.12 | Creating new package

Note: The naming convention is standard naming convention being used in Java. Packages can also be created with simple names as 'envVariables'.

4. Repeat steps 1–3 of above to create all the packages.
   Note: Maven embraces the idea of convention over configuration and hence comes with lots of defaults. Changing these defaults involves lots of rework. For Selenium automation, all automation frameworks should be created under hierarchy folder *src/test/java*. Also, the standard naming convention of packages, as mentioned above, is to be followed.

Installing JUnit for Maven Project

JUnit is a testing framework. This needs to be installed only if we plan to implement JUnit and not TestNG as automation projects testing framework. JUnit framework comes bundled with Eclipse. However, it may not always have the latest maven version of JUnit. In order to install latest version of JUnit, follow the steps:

1. Edit the pom file and add the below dependency.

```
<dependency>
    <groupId>junit</groupId>
    <artifactId>junit</artifactId>
    <version>4.11</version>
    <scope>test</scope>
</dependency>
```

   Note: `<version>` tag value needs to be modified to match the latest version.

   The latest maven dependency can be referred from the site http://mvnrepository.com/artifact/junit/junit
2. Save pom.xml file and close it.
3. Open command prompt and navigate to the directory "C:\automation-workspace\amazon-retail *\ui-tests*".
4. Execute command "mvn clean install".
5. On Eclipse *Project Explorer* window, select the project "ui-tests".
6. Right click and select *Maven "Update Project... Update maven Project* window opens.
7. Select the project *ui-tests* and click button *OK.* The maven project in Eclipse will be updated.
8. Right click and select *Refresh* to load latest changes.
9. In order to verify, JUnit has been installed, expand maven dependencies and look for *junit* jar file as shown in Figure 3.13. If it exists then JUnit has been installed. If not then delete the project from Eclipse (only) and try to re-import the maven project.

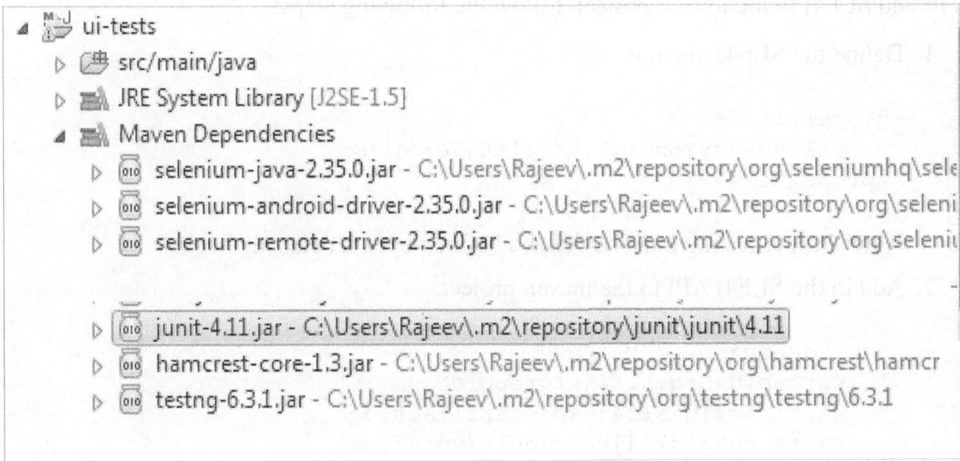

FIGURE 3.13 | Configuring JUnit for maven

Note: In order to configure JUnit or any other framework (JAR file) for a maven project, its dependency needs to be defined in the pom.xml file. Once the dependency is defined, command 'mvn clean install' needs to be executed as shown above. It is good to define all dependencies first in the pom.xml file before doing a clean install of maven. From now onwards, we will just discuss the dependency xml string for various JAR files.

Installing TestNG for Maven Project

TestNG is a testing framework. This needs to be installed only if we plan to implement TestNG and not JUnit as automation projects testing framework. To get started with TestNG, include the following dependency in the projects pom.xml file.

```
<dependency>
        <groupId>org.testng</groupId>
        <artifactId>testng</artifactId>
        <version>6.8.5</version>
        <scope>test</scope>
</dependency>
```

The latest maven dependency can be referred from the site: http://mvnrepository.com/artifact/org.testng/testng

For configuring TestNG for maven project, follow steps 2–9 of section "Configuring JUnit for Maven Project" above.

Installing SLF4J for Maven Project

SLF4J API is used as logging façade when working with JUnit framework. There is no need to install this API if working with TestNG testing framework as TestNG has inbuilt support for logging.

To add SLF4j to the maven project, follow the following steps:

1. Define the SLF4J version.

```
<properties>
    <slf4jVersion>1.7.5</slf4jVersion>
</properties>
```

Note: Properties tag must be defined before dependencies tag begins.

2. Add in the SLF4j API to the maven project.

```
<dependency>
    <groupId>org.slf4j</groupId>
    <artifactId>slf4j-api</artifactId>
    <version>${slf4jVersion}</version>
</dependency>
```

The latest maven dependency can be referred from the site: http://mvnrepository.com/artifact/org.slf4j/slf4j-api

3. The next step is to choose a binding library. Details of binding libraries can be found at site http://www.slf4j.org/manual.html#binding. Here, we will use slf4j-simple.jar as biding library.

```
<dependency>
    <groupId>org.slf4j</groupId>
    <artifactId>slf4j-simple</artifactId>
    <version>${slf4jVersion}</version>
</dependency>
```

For configuring SLF4J for maven project, follow steps 2–9 of section “Configuring JUnit for Maven Project” above.

Installing Java ODBC for Maven Project

- **Get ODBC driver:** Download appropriate Java ODBC driver as per OS and processor bit configuration from the site mentioned in Table 3.2. Assume ojdbc6.jar has been downloaded at location c:\automation-tools\java-odbc\ojdbc6.jar

  Note: Note the release version of ojdbc jar from the downloaded site or refer ReadMe.txt file of the download to find the version. Assume version here is 11.1.0.7.0.
- **Install ODBC driver:** To install your Oracle jdbc driver, type the following command on command prompt:

```
mvninstall:install-file -Dfile=c:\automation-tools\java-odbc\
ojdbc6.jar -DgroupId=com.oracle -DartifactId=ojdbc6 -Dversion=
11.1.0.7.0 -Dpackaging=jar
```

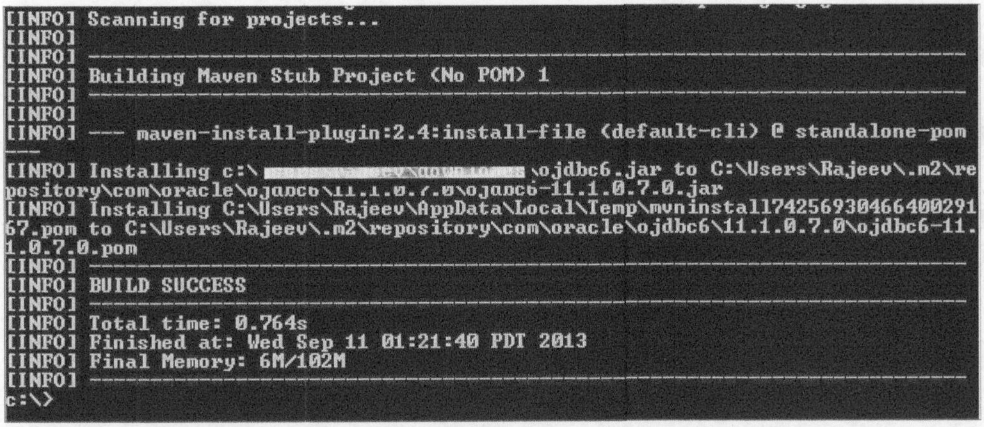

FIGURE 3.14 | Installing Java ODBC for maven project

Figure 3.14 shows the output in command prompt.

- **Define the dependency in pom.xml file:** Update maven project and then include the following dependency to the pom.xml file.

```
<dependency>
    <groupId>com.oracle</groupId>
    <artifactId>ojdbc6</artifactId>
    <version>11.1.0.7.0</version>
  </dependency>
```

For configuring Java ODBC for maven project, follow steps 2–9 of section "Configuring JUnit for Maven Project" above.

Installing JT Open for Maven Project

JT400 is Java API library to connect to AsS400 systems using java code. This API is used to connect to IBM DB2 database. To get started with JT400, include the following dependency in the projects pom.xml file.

```
<dependency>
        <groupId>net.sf.jt400</groupId>
        <artifactId>jt400-full</artifactId>
        <version>6.0</version>
</dependency>
```

The latest maven dependency can be referred from the site: http://mvnrepository.com/artifact/net.sf.jt400/jt400-full

For configuring JT400 for maven project, follow steps 2–9 of section "Configuring JUnit for Maven Project" above.

Installing Apache POI for Maven Project

Apache POI is Java API developed by Apache to work with Microsoft files such as Word, Excel, PowerPoint, etc., using Java code. To get started with ApachePOI, include the following dependency in the projects pom.xml file.

```
<dependency>
        <groupId>org.apache.poi</groupId>
        <artifactId>poi</artifactId>
        <version>3.9</version>
</dependency>
```

The latest maven dependency can be referred from the site: http://mvnrepository.com/artifact/org.apache.poi/poi

For configuring ApachePOI for maven project, follow steps 2–9 of section "Configuring JUnit for Maven Project" above.

Installing Apache PDFBox for Maven Project

Apache PDFBox library is an open source Java tool for working with PDF files. It allows creation of PDF documents, manipulation of existing documents and content extraction from documents. To get started with Apache PDFBox, include the following dependency in the projects pom.xml file.

```
<dependency>
        <groupId>org.apache.pdfbox</groupId>
        <artifactId>pdfbox</artifactId>
        <version>1.8.2</version>
</dependency>
```

The latest maven dependency can be referred from the site: http://mvnrepository.com/artifact/pdfbox/pdfbox

Optional Dependencies

Some features of PDFBox depend on external libraries. These features can be enabled by including the required libraries as dependencies. One of the most notable features is the one meant for PDF encryption. PDFBox uses libraries from *Legion of the Bouncy Castle* for encryption. These libraries can be included in the maven project using the following dependencies.

```
<dependency>
        <groupId>org.bouncycastle</groupId>
        <artifactId>bcprov-jdk15</artifactId>
```

```
        <version>1.44</version>
    </dependency>
    <dependency>
        <groupId>org.bouncycastle</groupId>
        <artifactId>bcmail-jdk15</artifactId>
        <version>1.44</version>
    </dependency>
```

Note: Optional dependencies are not included in the pom.xml file discussed later in this chapter.

For configuring Apache PDFBox for maven project, follow steps 2–9 of section "Configuring JUnit for Maven Project" above.

Installing Apache Commons IO for Maven Project

Apache Commons IO is Java library to assist with developing IO functionality. It contains utility classes for common tasks, input classes for input stream and reader implementation, output classes for output stream and writer implementation, filter classes for filter implementation, comparator classes for file comparison and file monitor classes for monitoring file system events. To get started with Apache Commons IO, include the following dependency in the projects pom.xml file.

```
<dependency>
        <groupId>org.apache.commons</groupId>
        <artifactId>commons-io</artifactId>
        <version>1.3.2</version>
</dependency>
```

The latest maven dependency can be referred from the site: http://mvnrepository.com/artifact/org.apache.commons/commons-io

For configuring Apache Apache Commons IO for maven project, follow steps 2–9 of section "Configuring JUnit for Maven Project" above.

Installing Apache Commons E-mail for Maven Project

Apache Commons E-mail is an open source Java API for reading and sending e-mails. It is built on top of the Java Mail API. JavaMail is an open source. API is platform-independent and protocol-independent framework to build mail and messaging applications. To get started with Apache Commons E-mail, include the following dependency in the projects pom.xml file.

```
<dependency>
        <groupId>org.apache.commons</groupId>
        <artifactId>commons-email</artifactId>
        <version>1.3.1</version>
</dependency>
```

The latest maven dependency can be referred from the site: http://mvnrepository.com/artifact/org.apache.commons/commons-email

For configuring Apache Apache Commons Email for maven project, follow steps 2–9 of section "Configuring JUnit for Maven Project" above.

Installing COM4J for Maven Project

COM4J is a Java library that allows Java applications to seamlessly interoperate with Microsoft Component Object Model. It is a tool that imports a COM type library and generates the Java definitions for that library. The objective of COM4J project is to provide a better integration of Java and COM. To get started with COM4J, include the following dependency in the projects pom.xml file.

```
<dependency>
        <groupId>org.jvnet.com4j</groupId>
        <artifactId>com4j</artifactId>
        <version>20110320</version>
</dependency>
```

The latest maven dependency can be referred from the site: http://mvnrepository.com/artifact/org.jvnet.com4j/com4j

For configuring Apache Apache Commons Email for maven project, follow steps 2–9 of section "Configuring JUnit for Maven Project" above.

POM.xml File for JUnit Framework

The consolidated pom.xml file for JUnit testing framework is as follows:

```
<?xml version="1.0" encoding="UTF-8"?>
<project xmlns="http://maven.apache.org/POM/4.0.0"
        xmlns:xsi="http://www.w3.org/2001/XMLSchema-instance"
              xsi:schemaLocation="http://maven.apache.org/POM/4.0.0
               http://maven.apache.org/xsd/maven-4.0.0.xsd">
      <modelVersion>4.0.0</modelVersion>
      <groupId>amazonretail</groupId>
      <artifactId>ui-tests</artifactId>
      <version>1.0</version>
      <properties>
            <slf4jVersion>1.7.5</slf4jVersion>
        </properties>
        <build>
            <directory>target</directory>
            <outputDirectory>target/classes</outputDirectory>
            <finalName>${project.artifactId}-${project.
             version}</finalName>
            <testOutputDirectory>target/test-classes</
             testOutputDirectory>
```

```
        <sourceDirectory>src/main/java</sourceDirectory>
        <testSourceDirectory>src/test/java</
          testSourceDirectory>
          <resources>
                  <resource>
                  <directory>src/main/resources</directory>
                  </resource>
            </resources>
            <testResources>
                  <testResource>
                  <directory>src/test/resources</directory>
                  </testResource>
            </testResources>
            <plugins>
                  <plugin>
                        <groupId>org.apache.maven.plugins</
                          groupId>
                  <artifactId>maven-compiler-plugin</
                    artifactId>
                        <version>3.1</version>
                  <configuration>
                              <source>1.7</source>
                              <target>1.7</target>
                  </configuration>
                  </plugin>
                  <plugin>
                        <groupId>org.apache.maven.plugins</
                          groupId>
                        <artifactId>maven-surefire-plugin</
                          artifactId>
                        <version>2.5</version>
                        <configuration>
                              <parallel>methods</parallel>
                              <threadCount>4</threadCount>
                              <perCoreThreadCount>true</
                                perCoreThreadCount>
                        </configuration>
                  </plugin>
            </plugins>
    </build>
   <dependencies>
    <dependency>
            <groupId>org.seleniumhq.selenium</groupId>
            <artifactId>selenium-java</artifactId>
            <version>2.35.0</version>
    </dependency>
```

```
        <dependency>
                <groupId>junit</groupId>
                <artifactId>junit</artifactId>
                <version>4.8.1</version>
                <scope>test</scope>
                </dependency>
        <dependency>
                    <groupId>org.slf4j</groupId>
                    <artifactId>slf4j-api</artifactId>
                    <version>${slf4jVersion}</version>
            </dependency>
            <dependency>
                    <groupId>org.slf4j</groupId>
                    <artifactId>slf4j-simple</artifactId>
                    <version>${slf4jVersion}</version>
                    </dependency>
            <dependency>
                    <groupId>com.oracle</groupId>
                    <artifactId>ojdbc6</artifactId>
                    <version>11.1.0.7.0</version>
            </dependency>
            <dependency>
                    <groupId>net.sf.jt400</groupId>
                    <artifactId>jt400-full</artifactId>
                    <version>6.0</version>
            </dependency>
            <dependency>
                    <groupId>org.apache.poi</groupId>
                    <artifactId>poi</artifactId>
                    <version>3.9</version>
                    </dependency>
          <dependency>
                    <groupId>org.apache.pdfbox</groupId>
                    <artifactId>pdfbox</artifactId>
                    <version>1.8.2</version>
                    </dependency>
           <dependency>
                    <groupId>org.apache.commons</groupId>
                    <artifactId>commons-io</artifactId>
                    <version>1.3.2</version>
                    </dependency>
           <dependency>
                    <groupId>org.apache.commons</groupId>
                    <artifactId>commons-email</artifactId>
                    <version>1.3.1</version>
                    </dependency>
           <dependency>
```

```
                <groupId>org.jvnet.com4j</groupId>
                <artifactId>com4j</artifactId>
                <version>20110320</version>
            </dependency>
        </dependencies>

</project>
```

POM.xml File for TestNG Framework

The consolidated pom.xml file for TestNG testing framework is as follows:

```
<?xml version="1.0" encoding="UTF-8"?>
<project xmlns="http://maven.apache.org/POM/4.0.0"
         xmlns:xsi="http://www.w3.org/2001/XMLSchema-instance"
           xsi:schemaLocation="http://maven.apache.org/POM/4.0.0
           http://maven.apache.org/xsd/maven-4.0.0.xsd">
     <modelVersion>4.0.0</modelVersion>
     <groupId>amazonretail</groupId>
     <artifactId>ui-tests</artifactId>
     <version>1.0</version>
     <properties>
             <slf4jVersion>1.7.5</slf4jVersion>
        </properties>
        <build>
             <directory>target</directory>
             <outputDirectory>target/classes</outputDirectory>
             <finalName>${project.artifactId}-${project.
               version}</finalName>
             <testOutputDirectory>target/test-classes</
               testOutputDirectory>
             <sourceDirectory>src/main/java</sourceDirectory>
             <testSourceDirectory>src/test/java</
               testSourceDirectory>
             <resources>
                     <resource>
                     <directory>src/main/resources</
                       directory>
                     </resource>
             </resources>
             <testResources>
                     <testResource>
                     <directory>src/test/resources</directory>
                     </testResource>
             </testResources>

             <plugins>
```

```
            <plugin>
                  <groupId>org.apache.maven.plugins</
                   groupId>
            <artifactId>maven-compiler-plugin</
             artifactId>
                  <version>3.1</version>
            <configuration>
                     <source>1.7</source>
                     <target>1.7</target>
            </configuration>
            </plugin>
            <plugin>
                  <groupId>org.apache.maven.plugins</
                   groupId>
                  <artifactId>maven-surefire-plugin</
                   artifactId>
                  <version>2.5</version>
                  <configuration>
                     <parallel>methods</parallel>
                     <threadCount>4</threadCount>
                     <perCoreThreadCount>true</
                       perCoreThreadCount>
                     <suiteXmlFiles>
                              <suiteXmlFile>src/
                                test/resources/
                                testng.xml</
                              suiteXmlFile>
                  </suiteXmlFiles>
                  </configuration>
            </plugin>
      </plugins>
</build>
 <dependencies>
     <dependency>
            <groupId>org.seleniumhq.selenium</groupId>
            <artifactId>selenium-java</artifactId>
            <version>2.35.0</version>
     </dependency>
            <dependency>
                  <groupId>org.testng</groupId>
                  <artifactId>testng</artifactId>
                  <version>6.8.5</version>
                  <scope>test</scope>
            </dependency>
            <dependency>
                  <groupId>org.slf4j</groupId>
                  <artifactId>slf4j-api</artifactId>
```

```
                <version>${slf4jVersion}</version>
          </dependency>
          <dependency>
                <groupId>org.slf4j</groupId>
                <artifactId>slf4j-simple</artifactId>
                <version>${slf4jVersion}</version>
                </dependency>
          <dependency>
                <groupId>com.oracle</groupId>
                <artifactId>ojdbc6</artifactId>
                <version>11.1.0.7.0</version>
          </dependency>
          <dependency>
                <groupId>net.sf.jt400</groupId>
                <artifactId>jt400-full</artifactId>
                <version>6.0</version>
          </dependency>
          <dependency>
                <groupId>org.apache.poi</groupId>
                <artifactId>poi</artifactId>
                <version>3.9</version>
                </dependency>
      <dependency>
                <groupId>org.apache.pdfbox</groupId>
                <artifactId>pdfbox</artifactId>
                <version>1.8.2</version>
         </dependency>
         <dependency>
                <groupId>org.apache.commons</groupId>
                <artifactId>commons-io</artifactId>
                <version>1.3.2</version>
         </dependency>
     <dependency>
                <groupId>org.apache.commons</groupId>
                <artifactId>commons-email</
                artifactId>
                <version>1.3.1</version>
                </dependency>
     <dependency>
                <groupId>org.jvnet.com4j</groupId>
                <artifactId>com4j</artifactId>
                <version>20110320</version>

         </dependency>
    </dependencies>

</project>
```

Writing First Test Using JUnit

Executing Maven Tests

Command below shows how to execute a WebDriver test 'mytest' from command prompt.

```
mvn -Dtest=TestCircle#mytest test
```

We can also use regular expressions to execute a set of tests from command line. For example, if we want to execute all tests whose name begins with 'test', then command will be as shown below.

```
mvn -Dtest=TestCircle#test* test
```

As of surefire 2.12.1, we can also execute selective multiple tests from command prompt. Command below shows how to execute two WebDriver tests (methods) 'testOne' and 'testTwo' from command prompt.

```
mvn -Dtest=TestCircle#testOne+testTwo test
```

INTERVIEW QUESTIONS

1. Which plug-in you will use to find?
   a) XPath of a button element
   b) CSS path of a image element
2. Which Java API will you use to edit?
   a) MS Word file
   b) PDF file
3. Which Java API will you use to?
   a) Create files and folders on Win 7 OS.
   b) Retrieve folder details such as creation time of a folder on Win 7 OS.
4. Explain the steps to setup a maven project for Selenium WebDriver.
5. Assume all the regression tests in Webdriver automation project start with text 'regression'. Write the command to execute all regression tests from command prompt.

4 CHAPTER

Environment Variables

An environment variable in test automation is a variable whose scope is visible throughout the automation project. These variables are to be accessible through all the components of the automation framework. They are generally used to define application login details, application URLs, database connection strings, etc. Environment variables can also be used to store run-time data. For example, data returned by a SQL query or pass/fail status of the test script. These variables can be declared to be modifiable (static) or non-modifiable (static final). Environment objects can also be used to store values of multiple environment variables.

4.1 | TYPES OF ENVIRONMENT VARIABLES

There are a variety of reasons for using environment variables in test automation. These include:

- Using environment variables to store configuration data
- Using environment variables to store test environment data
- Using environment variables to store run-time data

4.1.1 | Configuration Environment Variables

These variables store information related to application configuration settings or automation project configuration settings for a test run.

AUT configuration settings may include variables that define the way an application behaves under test. Generally, every application has property values that turns on or off specific application features. A simple example would be 'customer chat services' on any web application portal. These services are enabled during day time and generally turned off during the night. These switches (enabling/disabling chat service) are to be defined as *application configuration/environment variables*. These variables can be used to set the AUT to a specific state before initiating the test run. Another use of these variables would be to load and execute specific pre-defined set of test scripts that tests the application in a given state.

Automation project configuration settings include variables that define the default settings of the automation project for a test run. Generally, values of these variables do not change overtime. It is important to define these variables because it makes the automation project easily packagable and portable. That is, the complete automation project can be packaged and moved to a different location as and when required without much effort. These variables can also be used to set up the test run environment before the actual test suite execution happens. These include settings such as default browser settings on which AUT is to be tested, absolute/relative path of automation framework components, etc. These variables are called *automation project configuration variables.*

4.1.2 | Test Environment Variables

These variables define information that needs to be used globally across various components of the test automation framework. For example, browser type and version on which AUT needs to be tested, application login credentials, database connection string, default synchronization wait time, etc. Different parts of the framework say utility scripts, test scripts, page class scripts may need to use the same information to perform different actions on UI. These variables essentially define the test execution settings and hence are called *test environment variables.*

4.1.3 | Run-time Environment Variables

These variables define information gathered during test execution that needs to be shared across different sections of code or framework components. For example, results returned by SQL query may be required as input data for various sections of code. Since the information stored in these variables is generated at run-time, these variables are called *run-time environment variables.*

Note: There are no global variables in java. We can declare public static field in some class or private static field with public static assessors.

4.2 | ENVIRONMENT VARIABLE FILES

There are various ways of defining environment variables. They can either be defined in a properties file, XML file or a class file.

- Properties file
- Class file
- XML file

4.2.1 | Properties Environment Variable File

.properties is a file extension. It is mainly used in Java to store configurable parameters. This file can then be referenced in various class files to access the environment variables.

Creating a Properties File

The steps to create a property file using Eclipse IDE are mentioned below:

- Open *Package Explorer* window in Eclipse.
- Select the specific package for which a property file needs to be created as shown in Figure 4.1. For example: *com.webdriver.envvariables.*

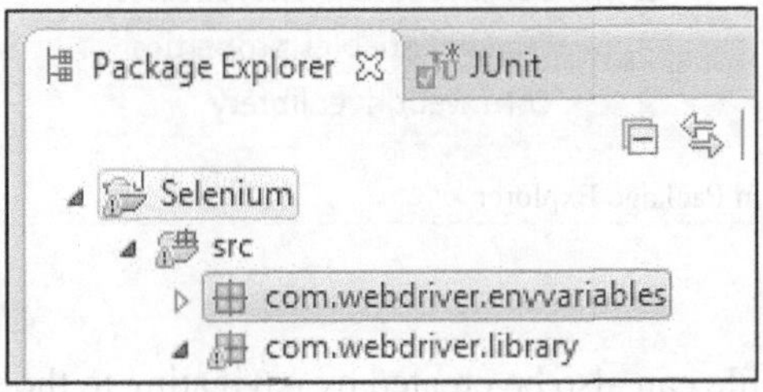

FIGURE 4.1 | Package Explorer

- Right click on the package and select *New → File*. *New File* window opens.
- Select the specific folder under which the file needs to be created as shown in Figure 4.2.

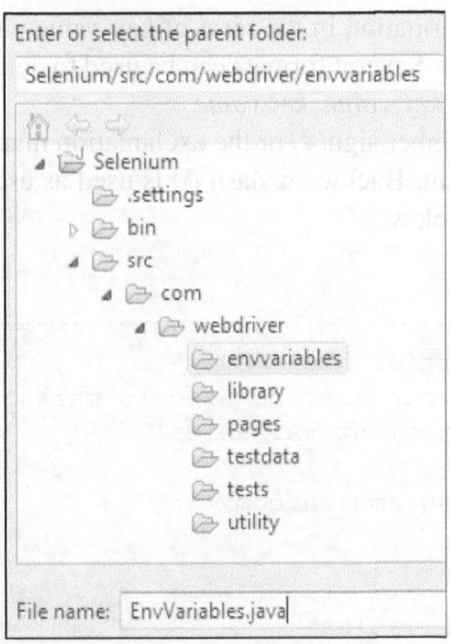

FIGURE 4.2 | Creating a new file from Eclipse

- Specify the file name. For example, *EnvVariables.properties.*
- Click on the *Finish* button.
- The *Project Explorer* window will show the new file now as shown in Figure 4.3.

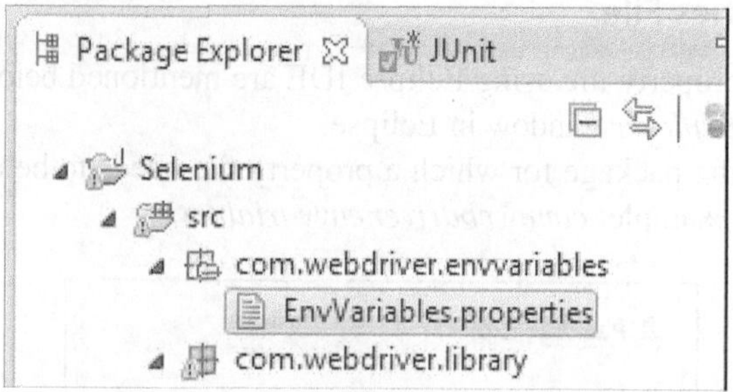

FIGURE 4.3 | Viewing files in Package Explorer

Note: Alternatively, the file can also be created by navigating to the specific windows folder and creating a file with the same name. To see the changes in Eclipse, on *Project Explorer* window, do a *Right Click → Refresh.*

Defining Environment Variables in a Property File

The property file stores information in the form of key-value pairs. Each line in a property file stores one key-value pair. Several formats can be used to define the key-value pairs. Few of them include: *key=value, key:value, key value*

.properties file use the number sign*(#)* or the exclamation mark *(!)* to specify that the current line of text is a comment. Backward slash *(\)* is used as escape character. An example of properties file is shown below.

```
# This is a .properties file
! Exclamation mark can also be used to mark text as comments
# Application environment variables
appName = Amazon
app.url = http://www.amazon.com
app.username=user1
app.password=password

# DB environment variables
# Separating key-value pairs using colon
db.name:QAOracle11g
db.user:admin
# Separating key-value pairs using white space
db.password password
# Backslash tells the application to continue reading the value
  onto the next
# line
```

```
db.connectionstring=DataSource=(DESCRIPTION=(ADDRESS\
  LIST=(ADDRESS=… (CONNECT_DATA=(SERVER=DEDICATED)(SERVICE\
  NAME=MyOracleSID)));
# Adding spaces to the key
db2\ password = key value is "db2 password"
```

Reading Environment Variables from a Property File

Let us assume the above property file is created inside *com/webdriver/envvariables* package. Also the code to read the property file is created inside library package *com.webdriver.library*. Figure 4.4 shows hierarchy organization of various packages/files inside the *Selenium* project.

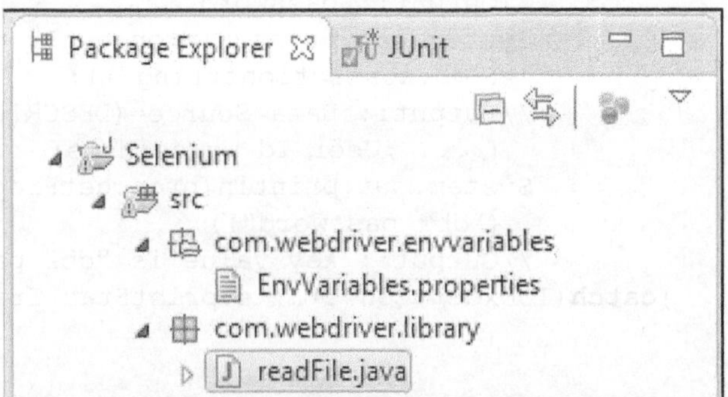

FIGURE 4.4 | Hierarchy organization of various packages/files

Java code shown below can be used to read property values from a property file. `ReadFile.java` is the class file with method `propertyReader`. This method reads property values from the property file.

```
import java.io.File;
import java.io.IOException;
import java.io.InputStream;
import java.util.Properties;

import org.junit.Test;
import org.slf4j.Logger;
import org.slf4j.LoggerFactory;

public class ReadFile {
        @Test
        public void propertyReader() {
                String filePath = "/com/webdriver/envvariables/
                  EnvVariables.properties";
                InputStream file = getClass().getResource
                  AsStream(filePath);
```

```
        Properties prop = new Properties();
        try{
            prop.load(file);
            System.out.println(prop.get
              Property("appName"));
            //Output:: Amazon
            System.out.println(prop.get
              Property("app.url"));
            //Output:: http://www.amazon.com
            System.out.println(prop.getProperty
              ("db.user"));
            //Output:: admin
            System.out.println(prop.getProperty
              ("db.password"));
            //Output:: password
            System.out.println(prop.getProperty
              ("db.connectionstring"));
            //Output:: Data Source=(DESCRIPTION=
              ( ... ;User Id=myUsername;
            System.out.println(prop.getProperty
              ("db2 password"));
            //Output:: key value is "db2 password"
        }catch(IOException e) { e.printStackTrace();}
    }
}
```

Property values can be changed during run-time by using the setProperty method of properties object. The code below modifies the value of the appName property to Selenium.

```
prop.setProperty("appName", "Selenium");
```

Note: Please note dot '.' is treated as a normal string in a property file. We can either specify the key as appUrl or app.url. The complete text is considered as a string.

4.2.2 | Class Environment Variable File

Environment variables can also be defined inside a class file. The environment variables can be defined inside the class file as enumeration objects.

Creating a Class File

Follow the steps below to create a Class file in Eclipse:

- Open *Package Explorer* window in Eclipse.
- Select the specific package for which a property file needs to be created. For example: *com.webdriver.envvariables.*

- Right click on the package and select *New → JUnit Test Case. New JUnit Test Case* window opens.
- Specify the file name. For example, *EnvVariables.java.*
- Click on the *Finish* button.
- The *Project Explorer* window now will display a new file as shown in Figure 4.5.

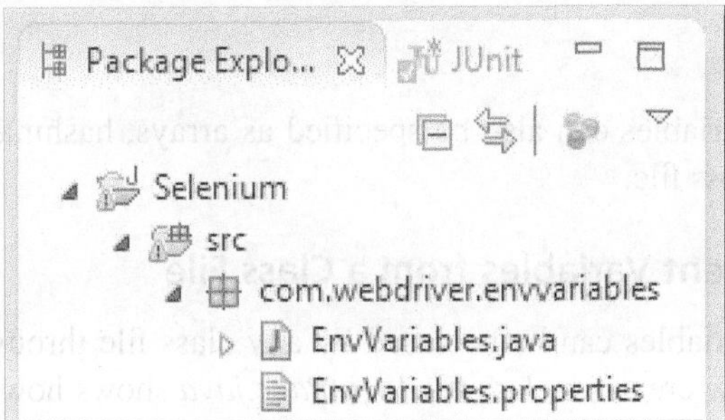

FIGURE 4.5 | Creating a class environment file

Defining Environment Variables in a Class File

Environment variables can be defined inside *Class* file (JUnit Test Case) as enumeration collection objects. Code below shows how to define environment variables as enumeration objects.

```
public class EnvVariables {
        public enum appVars{
                APPURL("http://www.amazon.com"),
                APPUSERNAME("user1"),
                APPPASSWORD("password");

                private String appVariables;

                appVars(String appVariables) {
                this.appVariables = appVariables;
            }

            public String getValue() {
                return this.appVariables;
            }
        }

        public enum dbVars{
            DBNAME("QAOracle11g"),
            DBUSERNAME("admin"),
            DBPASSWORD("password");

                private String dbVariables;
```

```
            dbVars(String dbVariables) {
            this.dbVariables = dbVariables;
        }

        public String getValue() {
            return this.dbVariables;
        }
    }
}
```

Note: Environment variables can also be specified as arrays, hashmap tables or as simple variables inside the class file.

Reading Environment Variables from a Class File

These environment variables can be accessed by any class file throughout the automation project. Example below creates a class file *loginPage.java* shows how to access these environment variables using code. Class file (JUnit Test Case) is created inside package *com.webdriver.library* as shown in Figure 4.6.

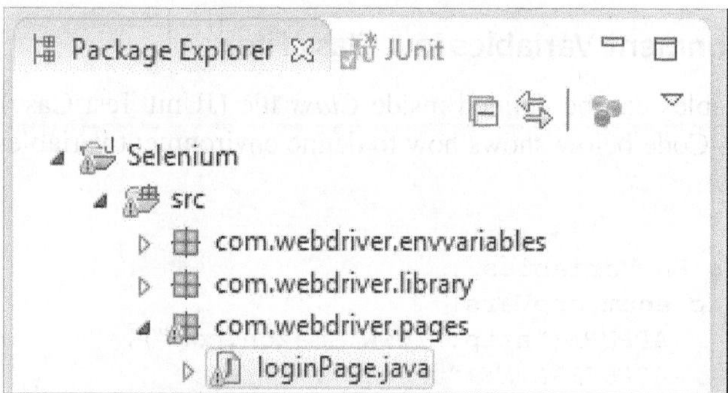

FIGURE 4.6 | Reading environment variables from a class file

```
import org.junit.Test;
import org.openqa.selenium.WebDriver;
import org.openqa.selenium.firefox.FirefoxDriver;

import com.webdriver.envvariables.EnvVariables.appVars;

public class loginPage {
    //login to amazon.com
    public void login(){
        //create an instance of webdriver object
        WebDriver driver = new FirefoxDriver();
        //launch firefox and open url amazon.com
        driver.get(appVars.APPURL.getValue());
    }
}
```

4.2.3 | XML Environment Variable File

Environment variables can also be defined in a XML file. The environment variables exist as tag value pairs in a XML file.

Creating a XML File

A XML file can be created from Eclipse in the same way property file has been created in the section "Creating a properties file". While specifying the file name, file extension is to be specified as *xml*. For example, figure shows *EnvironmentVariables.xml* file created inside package *com.webdriver.envvariables*.

Defining Environment Variables in a XML File

Environment variables are specified as tags and variable values as tag values in a XML file. Code below shows *EnvironmentVariables.xml* file with AUT and DB environment variables definition.

```
<envvariables>
        <appvariables>
                <url>http://www.amazon.com</url>
                <username>UserName</username>
                <password>Password</password>
        </appvariables>
        <dbvariables>
                <dbname>QAOracle11g</dbname>
                <dbuser>admin</dbuser>
                <dbpassword>password</dbpassword>
        </dbvariables>
</envvariables>
```

Reading Environment Variables from a XML File

Let us assume the above XML file is created inside package *com/webdriver/envvariables*. And the code to read the XML file is created inside library package *com.webdriver.library*. Figure 4.7 shows hierarchy organization of various packages/files for the *Selenium* project.

Example below shows how to read a XML file. `ReadFile.java` is the class file with method `xmlReader`. This method reads tag values from the XML file by specifying the tag name.

```
import java.io.File;
import org.w3c.dom.Document;
import org.w3c.dom.Element;
import org.w3c.dom.Node;
import org.w3c.dom.NodeList;

import javax.xml.parsers.DocumentBuilderFactory;
import javax.xml.parsers.DocumentBuilder;
```

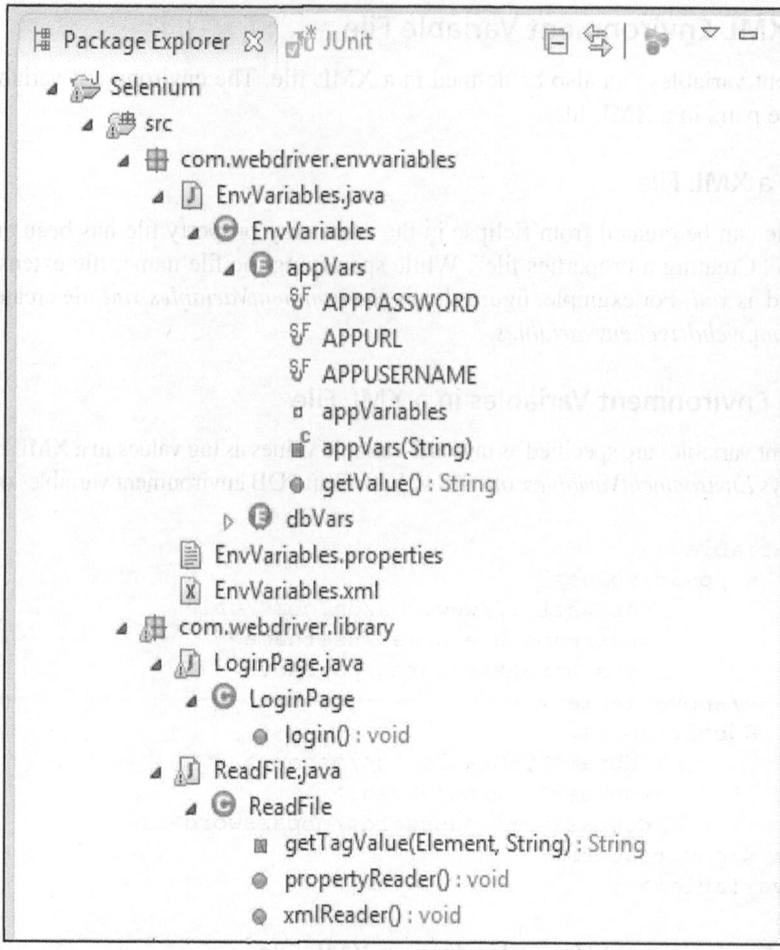

FIGURE 4.7 | Hierarchy organization of various packages/files

```
import java.io.IOException;
import java.util.Properties;

import org.junit.Test;
import org.slf4j.Logger;
import org.slf4j.LoggerFactory;

public class readFile {
        @Test
        public void xmlReader() {
                Logger logger = LoggerFactory.
                  getLogger(getClass());
                String filePath = "/com/webdriver/envvariables/
                  EnvVariables.xml";
                try{
```

```
            InputStream file = getClass().getResource
              AsStream(filePath);
            DocumentBuilderFactorydocBuilderFactory =
              DocumentBuilderFactory.newInstance();
        DocumentBuilderdocBuilder = docBuilderFactory.
          newDocumentBuilder();
        Document doc = docBuilder.parse (file);

        //normalize text representation
        doc.getDocumentElement ().normalize ();
        logger.info("Root element of the doc is" +
            doc.getDocumentElement().getNodeName());
        NodeList nl= doc.getElementsByTagName("appvariables");
        Node node = nl.item(0);
        Element element = (Element) node;
        logger.info(this.getTagValue(element, "url"));
        logger.info(this.getTagValue(element, "username"));
        }catch (Exception e) {
            e.printStackTrace();
        }
    }
private String getTagValue(Element element, String
  tagName){
        NodeList nodes =
            element.getElementsByTagName(tagName).
              item(0).getChildNodes();
        Node node = (Node) nodes.item(0);
      return (node.getNodeValue());
    }
}
```

Using hashtable to store sql query results

INTERVIEW QUESTIONS

1. What are environment variables?
2. Which types of variables can be defined as environment variables in test automation?
3. How to access a .properties file defined in another package?
4. How to define the dependencies in pom.xml file?
5. How to find canonical and absolute path of a file?
6. Which Java APIs will you use for reading?
   a) Flat file
   b) MS Excel file
   c) XML file
   d) JSON file

5
CHAPTER
Locating Elements

All text boxes, buttons, lists and other GUI objects of a page are referred as *elements* of the web page. The property that helps identify an element in a web page is termed as *attribute* of the element. The value associated with the attribute is called *attribute value*. For example, in a login page, the 'login' button element can be identified using the attribute 'name' of the button element. Suppose the attribute value of the 'name' property is 'login'. During script execution, WebDriver searches for an element in the UI whose *name* attribute value is 'login'. The interface that allows accessing and manipulating the elements of a web page is called *method* of the element. For example, *login* button element has *click* method to simulate mouse-click on the button.

Elements organization in an HTML document is described by document object model (DOM). HTML DOM provides an interface to interact with the elements. It provides methods to modify/retrieve *attributes* and *attribute values* of all elements.

5.1 | HTML DOM

HTML DOM is a platform and language-independent programming interface for accessing and manipulating elements in HTML documents. HTML DOM is a tree structure. All nodes of the tree can be accessed as per the hierarchical order of the tree. The nodes in the node tree have a hierarchical relationship to each other.

- The top node is called the root node.
- Every node, except the root, has exactly one parent node.
- A leaf is a node with no children.
- Siblings are nodes with same children.

Consider the HTML source code mentioned below. Figure 5.1 shows the web page rendering for the HTML code mentioned below.

```
<!DOCTYPE html>
    <head>
        <title>HTML Document</title>
    </head>
    <body>
        <h1>HTML Page</h1>
        <p>Page Content</p>
        <input id="googleSearch">
```

```
        <a name="googleLink" href="http://www.google.com">
          Google Search</a>
     </body>
  </html>
```

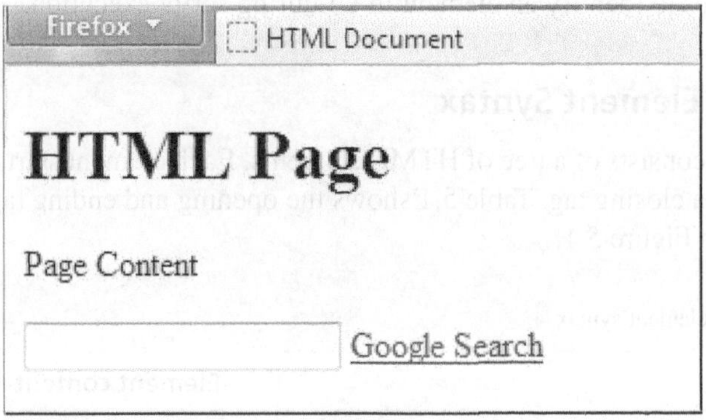

FIGURE 5.1 | HTML page

For the above mentioned HTML code:

- <html> has no parent node, therefore, it is the root node
- <html> node has two child nodes <head> and <body>
- <head> node has one child node <title>
- <body> node has four child nodes <h1>, <p>, <input> and <a>
- <h1>, <p>, <input> and <a> are sibling nodes as they have the same parent node <body>
- <html> is the parent node of <head> and <body>

Tree structure for the above HTML code is shown in Figure 5.2.

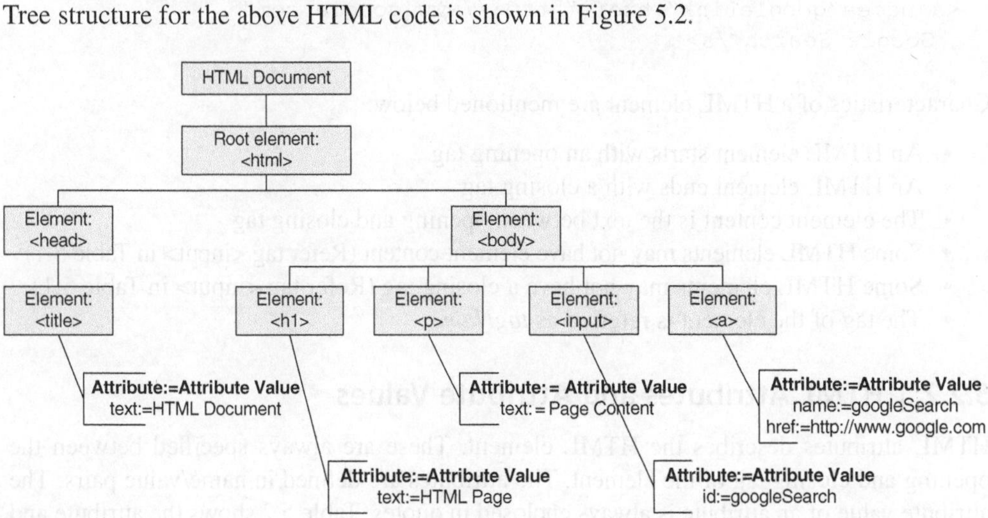

FIGURE 5.2 | DOM tree structure

5.2 | HTML ELEMENT

All text boxes, buttons, lists and other GUI objects of a page are referred as *elements* of the web page. The properties that define an element are termed as *attributes* of the element. The value associated with the attribute is called *attribute value*. Selenium uses these *attributes* and *attribute values* to identify an element in UI during script execution.

5.2.1 | HTML Element Syntax

HTML document consists of a tree of HTML elements. Each element starts with an opening tag and ends with a closing tag. Table 5.1 shows the opening and ending tags of some of the elements shown in Figure 5.1.

TABLE 5.1 | HTML element syntax

Start tag	Element content	End tag
`<h1>`	HTML page	`</h1>`
`<p>`	Page content	`</p>`
`<input id="googleSearch">`		
`<a name="googleLink" href="http://www.google.com">`	Google search	`</a>`

The description between opening and ending tag defines the properties of the HTML element. For example, consider the 'Google Search' link element shown in Figure 5.1. The html code of this element is:

```
<a name="googleLink" href="http://www.google.com">
  Google Search</a>
```

Characteristics of a HTML element are mentioned below:

- An HTML element starts with an opening tag
- An HTML element ends with a closing tag
- The element content is the text between opening and closing tag
- Some HTML elements may not have element content (Refer tag <input> in Table 5.1)
- Some HTML elements may not have a closing tag (Refer tag <input> in Table 5.1)
- The tag of the element is referred as *tagName*

5.2.2 | HTML Attributes and Attribute Values

HTML attributes describes the HTML element. These are always specified between the opening and closing tag of the element. The attributes are defined in name/value pairs. The attribute value of an attribute is always enclosed in quotes. Table 5.2 shows the attribute and attribute values of 'Google Search' link element.

TABLE 5. 2 | HTML element attributes

Attribute	Attribute value
tagName	a
name	googleLink
href	http://www.google.com

Table 5.3 explains some of the generic HTML attributes.

TABLE 5.3 | Some common attributes

Attribute	Description
class	Defines the class name of an element
id	Defines a unique id for an element
tagName	Defines the type of the element
style	Defines an inline CSS style for an element
title	Defines extra information about an element (displayed as a tool tip)
name	Defines the name of the element

Notes:

- All the elements within the HTML document must have a unique value for the attribute '*id*'.
- 'name' attribute defines the name of the element whose tagname is <input>. This attribute is used to reference elements in a Javascript. It is also used to reference form data after submitting a form.

Consider the new account creation page of amazon.com site. We will use this page as example throughout this chapter. Figure 5.3 shows some of the elements of this page.

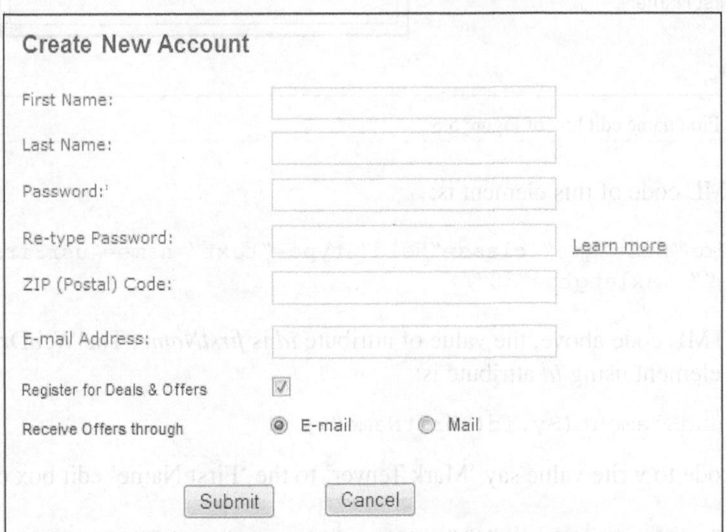

FIGURE 5.3 | Create new account page of amazon.com site

5.3 | WEBDRIVER METHODS FOR IDENTIFYING ELEMENTS

Selenium Webdriver provides a set of methods to uniquely identify an element in a HTML document during run-time. The UI element (say text box, button, checkbox, etc.) is referred as element or web element in WebDriver. WebDriver uses attributes of the web element say *tagName*, *class*, *id*, etc., to locate them during run-time. The various WebDriver methods which can be used to identify an element in GUI are as follows:

- id
- className
- tagName
- name
- linkText
- partialLinkText
- cssLocator
- XPath

5.3.1 | id

The *id* method uses the 'id' attribute to identify an HTML element. All the elements within the HTML document must have a unique 'id' value.

EXAMPLE 5.1 Consider the 'First Name' edit box of Figure 5.3.

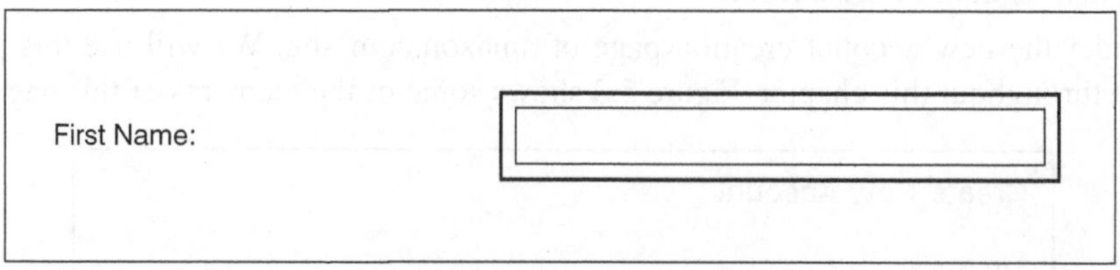

FIGURE 5.4 | First name edit box of Figure 5.3

Assume HTML code of this element is:

```
<input id="firstName" class="field" type="text" name="usrFirstName"
  value="" maxlength="30"/>
```

For the HTML code above, the value of attribute *id* is *firstName*. The WebDriver code to identify this element using *id* attribute is:

```
driver.findElement(By.id("firstName"))
```

WebDriver code to write value say 'Mark Tenver' to the 'First Name' edit box can be:

```
driver.findElement(By.id("firstName")).sendKeys("Mark Tenver")
```

Note: The *id* attribute is the most reliable identification attribute of an element. This is because this property is unique for an element in the entire HTML document.

5.3.2 | className

The *className* method uses the 'class' attribute to identify an element in UI.

Example 5.2 Let us take the example of 'First Name' edit box again. HTML code of this element is:

```
<input id="firstName" class="field" type="text" name="usrFirstName"
  value="" maxlength="30"/>
```

For the html code above, *class* attribute value is *field*. The WebDriver code to identify this element using *class* attribute can be:

```
driver.findElement(By.className("field"))
```

WebDriver code to write value say 'Mark Tenver' to the 'First Name' edit box can be:

```
driver.findElement(By.className("field")).sendKeys("Mark Tenver")
```

Notes:

1. Attribute 'value' denotes the string entered by the user in the text box.
2. Attribute 'maxlength' denotes the length of the acceptable text length limit for the editbox.
3. Two or more elements can have the 'className' attribute value same. Therefore, it is not always a reliable attribute to identify an element. For example, suppose the HTML code for 'Last Name' edit box is:

```
<input id="lastName" class="field" type="text" name="usrLastName"
  value="" maxlength="30"/>
```

As evident from the code, both edit boxes – 'First Name' and 'Last Name'– have the same attribute value *field* for attribute *class*. So, if the code above is used, then during run-time WebDriver will return the first matched element which in this case would be 'First Name' element. This may cause the script to fail in scenarios where we want to work on the 'Last Name' edit box element.

5.3.3 | tagName

The *tagName* method uses the 'tagName' (node name) attribute to identify an element in GUI.

EXAMPLE 5.3 *tagName* of the 'First Name' element is *input* as shown in the HTML code below.

```
<input id="firstName" class="field" type="text" name="usrFirstName"
  value="" maxlength="30"/>
```

WebDriver code to identify this element during run-time can be:

```
driver.findElement(By.tagName("input"))
```

EXAMPLE 5.4 Suppose the HTML code for text 'Create New Account' shown in Figure 5.3 is as follows:

```
<h1>Create New Account</h1>
```

Then, *tagName* of the above element is `<h1>`.

WebDriver code to identify this element during run-time can be:

```
driver.findElement(By.tagName("h1"))
```

EXAMPLE 5.5 Let us consider one more example of link element 'Learn More' as shown in Figure 5.5.

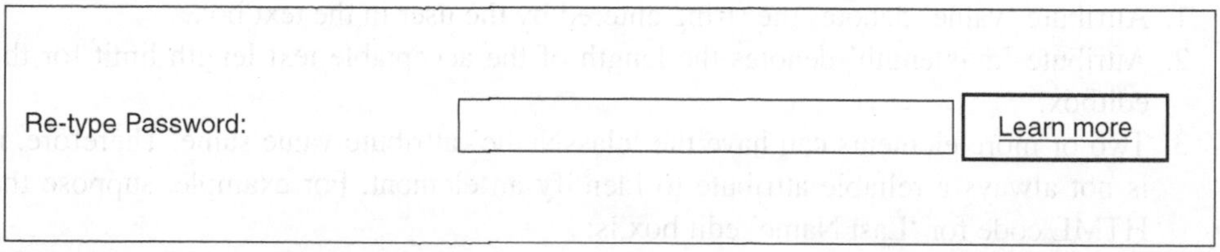

FIGURE 5.5 | Link element 'Learn More'

The HTML code of this element is:

```
<a href="http://www.google.com"> Learn more </a>
```

The *tagName* of this element is *'a'*. Node name *'a'* is used for link elements. Suppose there are 10 links in a page which needs to be tested. In this case, in order to identify all these links during run-time, WebDriver code shown below can be used:

```
List<WebElement> links = driver.findElements(By.tagName("a"))
```

The above code captures all the elements in HTML document whose *tagName* attribute value is *'a'*.

5.3.4 | name

The *name* method uses the 'name' attribute of the element to identify it in UI.

EXAMPLE 5.6 Let us assume the HTML code of the 'First Name' edit box is as follows:

```
<input id="firstName" class="field" type="text" name="usrFirstName"
  value="" maxlength="30"/>
```

For the html code above, *name* attribute value is *usrFirstName*. The WebDriver code to identify this element can be

```
driver.findElement(By.name("usrFirstName"))
```

WebDriver code to write value say 'Mark Tenver' to the 'First Name' edit box can be:

```
driver.findElement(By.name("usrFirstName")).sendKeys("Mark Tenver")
```

Note: When a form is submitted, values of only those elements are passed which have a *name* attribute.

5.3.5 | linkText

The *linkText* method identifies an element by the visible text associated with the hyperlink element. HTML tag <a> is used to define a link element.

EXAMPLE 5.7 Let us assume the HTML code of the hyperlink 'Learn More' is as follows:

```
<a href="http://www.google.com">Learn more</a>
```

WebDriver code to click on this link element will be:

```
driver.findElement(By.linkText("Learn more")).Click
```

Note: *href* is very important attribute of a link element. It indicates the page (URL) to which the page will navigate to on clicking on this element.

5.3.6 | partialLinkText

The *partialLinkText* method identifies an element by the visible text associated with the hyperlink. The difference between *linkText* and *partialLinkText* method is that the former looks for an exact match while the latter accepts a partial match. For example, let us consider the 'Learn More' link mentioned in the above example. The 'Learn More' link can be identified during run-time using any of the below codes:

```
driver.findElement(By.partialLinkText("Learn")).Click
```

Or,

```
driver.findElement(By.partialLinkText("more")).Click
```

Or,

```
driver.findElement(By.partialLinkText("rn mo")).Click
```

partialLinkText method is generally used in stituations where the link visible text value is dynamic in nature, i.e., its value changes with each execution.

EXAMPLE 5.8 Consider the order confirmation page of amazon.com.

Suppose, the *text* attribute value of order number link is – Order Number is: <Order Number>, where <Order Number> is a 10 digit number. Let us assume the visible *text* attribute value is – Order Number is: 2543213654.

The above string consists of static value 'Order Number is:' and dynamically changing value '2543213654'.

The *linkText* method will fail to recognize this element during run-time because of the presence of dynamic value. In such situations, *partialLinkText* method is used to recognize an element based on its static value. The dynamically changing string is ignored for element identification. The WebDriver code to recognize this element can be:

```
driver.findElement(By.partialLinkText("Order Number is:")).Click
```

5.3.7 | cssSelector

Cascading style sheets (CSS) is a style sheet language used to define the presentation semantics (look and feel) of HTML elements.

Prior to CSS, nearly all of the presentational attributes of HTML documents were defined within the HTML document. All font colours, background styles, element alignments, borders and sizes had to be explicitly described, often repeatedly, within the HTML. CSS allows to move much of these information to another file called the *style sheet*. This results in considerably simpler HTML as well easy and centralized maintenance. Style sheets can be inserted in HTML documents in three ways – external style sheet, internal style sheet and inline style. An external style sheet file (say file.css) can be associated with an HTML document using the following syntax:

```
<link href="path/to/file.css" rel="stylesheet">
```

CSS defines a list of rules and a number of English keywords to specify the name of various style properties. The style properties (or patterns) used to select the elements for styling are called *Selectors*. Table 5.4 shows few of the CSS Selectors.

TABLE 5.4 | CSS selectors

Selector	Example	Description
#id	#firstName	Selects the element with id="firstname"
element>element	html>body>input	Selects all <input> elements whose parent is <body> element, whose parent is <html>
:enabled	input:enabled	Selects every enabled <input> element
:hover	a:hover	Selects link on mouse hover
:focus	Input:focus	Selects the input element which has focus

WebDriver uses these CSS Selectors to identify the element. The WebDriver method that is used to identify an element by CSS Selector is *cssSelector*.

EXAMPLE 5.9 Consider the HTML code of 'firstName' edit box.

```
<input id="firstName" class="field" type="text" name="usrFirstName"
  value="" maxlength="30"/>
```

WebDriver code to identify this element using cssSelector method can be:

```
driver.findElement(By.cssSelector("#firstName")).sendKeys("Mark")
```

EXAMPLE 5.10 Consider the HTML code of the 'Cancel' button of Figure 5.3 is as follows:

```
<html>
...
<body>
...
<input type="submit" value="Cancel"/>
```

The CSS Selector attribute for the 'Cancel' button is: *html>body>input*

WebDriver code to click on the 'Cancel' button will be:

```
driver.findElement(By.cssSelector("html>body>input")).click
```

Note: Refer Chapter 6 for how to design CSS locator path for locating elements.

5.3.8 | XPath

XPath is based on tree representation of the HTML document. It provides the ability to navigate around the tree by selecting nodes.

EXAMPLE 5.11 Consider the HTML code of the 'firstName' edit box:

```
<html>
...
<body>
...
<table>
<tbody>
<tr>...</tr>
<tr>...</tr>
<tr>...</tr>
<tr>
<td>...</td>
<td>
<input id="firstName" class="field" type="text" name="usrFirstName"
  value="" maxlength="30"/>
</td>
```

For the code above, the XPath value for 'firstName' edit box element is:

```
html/body/table/tbody/tr[4]/td[2]/input
```

WebDriver uses the native XPath capability of the browser to identify an element. The method defined in WebDriver to recognize an element by its XPath is *XPath*. Below is the WebDriver code to identify element 'firstName' editbox:

```
driver.findElement(By.XPath("html/body/table/tbody/tr[4]/td[2]/
  input"))
```

Notes: 1. Refer Chapter 7 for how to design XPath for locating elements.

2. WebDriver has provided its' own implementation support for browsers which do not have native XPath support. This can lead to some unexpected behaviour while executing the same tests against various browsers. Table 5.5 lists the WebDriver drivers that support native XPath.

TABLE 5.5 | WebDriver's drivers support details

Driver	Tag and attribute names	Attribute values	Native XPath support
HTMLUnitDriver	Lower-cased	As they appear in HTML	Yes
InternetExplorerDriver	Lower-cased	As they appear in HTML	No
FirefoxDriver	Case insensitive	As they appear in HTML	Yes

Some Useful Tips

cssLocator and *XPath* value may change depending on where new elements are added to the HTML hierarchy tree though the actual element under test remain unchanged. Such continuous changes would make maintenance of tests time consuming and costly if CSSPath and XPath are not appropriately designed. CSS path and XPath generated by various browser add-ons are native paths which are least reliable. Readers are advised to develop a reliable CSS path and XPath. Details on how to design reliable CSS and XPath have been explained in detail in Chapters 6 and 7, respectively.

INTERVIEW QUESTIONS

1. What is an element?
2. What is HTML DOM?
3. Explain the commonly used attributes for below elements
   a) Button
   b) Edit box
   c) Link
   d) List box
4. Why 'id' attribute is considered the most reliable attribute for element identification?
5. Why using element attributes is to be given a priority for element identifcation over XPath and CSS path?
6. Develop the location identifier for locating below elements of amazon.com create new account page
   a) Email address edit box
   b) Password edit box
   c) Your account link
   d) Sign in button

6
CHAPTER
Locating Element Using CSS Selectors

Cascading Style Sheets (CSS) is a style sheet language that defines the presentation semantics (the look and formatting) of a HTML or XML document. For example, CSS describes fonts, colours, margins, height, width, background images and many other presentation semantics. The purpose of CSS is to separate the presentation information from the markup or content.

CSS defines a list of pattern-matching rules which determine which style is to be applied to elements in the DOM. These patterns are called *selectors*. If all rules in the pattern are satisfied for a certain element, then the selector matches the element. Browser applies the defined style to the matched element.

Selenium WebDriver uses the same principles of CSS selectors to identify an element in DOM. Webdriver has defined a 'cssSelector' method for identifying elements using style attribute of an element. In this chapter, we will discuss the various ways in which cssSelector() method can be used to identify an element in HTML DOM.

Figure 6.1 shows the account registration page of amazon site, we will be using Amazon.com webpages for illustration.

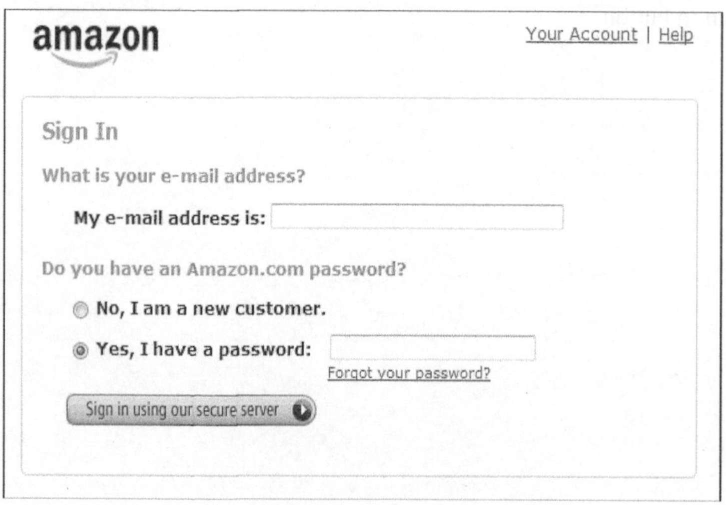

FIGURE 6.1 | New account creation page of amazon.com

The HTML code for the *email address* input field is as shown in Figure 6.2.

FIGURE 6.2 | HTML code of account creation page

6.1 | HOW TO FIND CSS STYLES OF AN ELEMENT

Various browser plugins are available to view CSS styles of an element. For Firefox browser, CSS Viewer can be used to find CSS style values of an element. The latest version of CSS Viewer can be downloaded from site https://addons.mozilla.org/en-US/firefox/addon/css-viewer/?src=api. Also, this plug-in is available in the CD that comes with this book. CSS Viewer 1.0.5 is the latest version available at the time of writing this book.

Follow the steps below to view CSS attributes of an element using CSS Viewer:

- Open Firefox browser.
- Navigate to the desired page, say amazon.com new account creation page.
- On Firefox browser, navigate Tools → CSS Viewer.
- Hover the mouse arrow over the element whose CSS styles are to be viewed. On mouse hover, CSS Viewer window opens that displays the CSS styles of the element. Suppose the requirement is to view the CSS styles of the amazon.com logo image. Figure 6.3 shows the CSS style attributes of the amazon.com logo image.

FIGURE 6.3 | Viewing CSS attributes of an element by using CSS Viewer

6.2 | HOW TO LOCATE ELEMENTS USING CSS ATTRIBUTES

CSS Attributes of an element can be used to uniquely locate the element in a web page. Firefox plug-in *Firepath* can be used to design CSS locators which can identify an element in the DOM tree. FirePath plug-in can be installed from site http://code.google.com/p/firepath/. This plug-in also helps to view/design XPath locator and Sizzle locator of an element. XPath locators are discussed in detail in the next chapter.

Follow the below steps to view the CSS locator path of an element.

- Open Firefox and then activate *Firebug* window by clicking on the bookmark .
- On *Firebug* window, click on the tab FirePath ▾. *Firepath* window opens.
- On *Firepath* window, select locator as *'CSS'* as shown in Figure 6.4.

FIGURE 6.4 | Firepath window

- To view CSS locator path of an element, click on the mouse icon and then point and click the arrow on the desired element. The relative CSS path of the element is displayed on the *Firepath* window as shown in Figure 6.5.

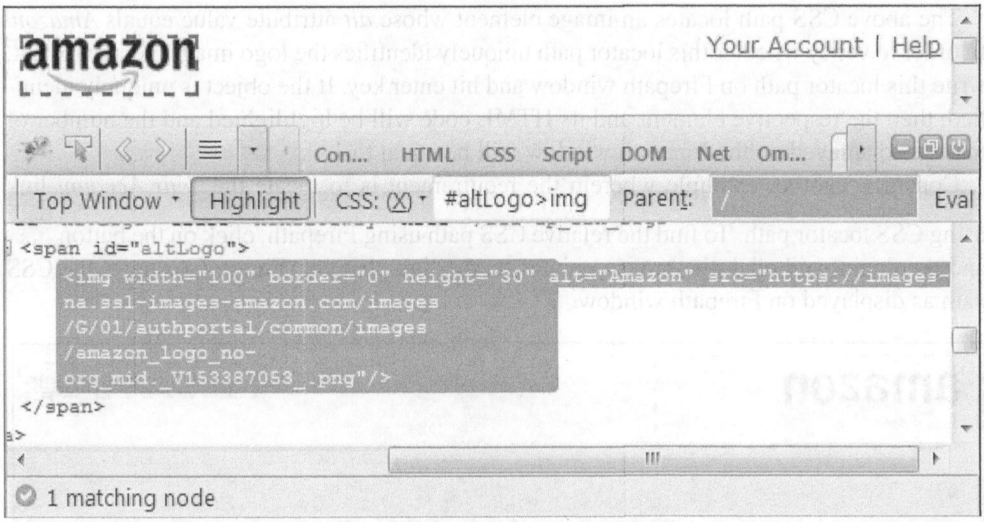

FIGURE 6.5 | Relative CSS path of amazon logo image

Suppose we want to find the CSS path of the amazon.com logo image. Figure 6.5 shows the relative CSS path of this image element as **#altLogo>img**. The respective image element is highlighted with blue square box on the web page. Also, the respective HTML code of the element is highlighted on the *Firepath* window as shown in Figure 6.5. The above relative CSS path can be made more reliable by specifying the tag name of the element. The tag name of the element with *id* attribute as *altLogo* is *span*. Thus, the new CSS path will now be **span#altLogo>img**. Write this CSS locator path on the *Firepath* window and see if it still recognizes the logo image element. If the element is recognized then the element and its HTML code will be highlighted. If no matching element (corresponding to the specified locator path) is found, *Firepath* displays the message "No matching nodes".

The CSS path displayed by Firepath is mostly not the most appropriate (reliable) identifier path of the element. The best way to design CSS locator path of an element is by using the HTML attributes of the element. Assume the HTML code of the logo image to be:

```
<img width="100" border="0" height="30" alt="Amazon" src="https://
  images-amazon.com/...amazon_logo_no-org_mid._V153387053_.png"
  style=""/>
```

The above HTML code describes the various attributes of the element such as its height, width, alt, src, etc. One or more of these attributes can be used to uniquely identify the logo image. One of the reliable attributes of the logo image is its *alt* attribute. CSS locator path of the logo image element using this *alt* attribute can be designed as:

```
img[alt='Amazon']
```

The above CSS path locates an image element whose *alt* attribute value equals *Amazon.* In order to verify whether this locator path uniquely identifies the logo image element or not, write this locator path on Firepath window and hit enter key. If the object is uniquely identified, then the respective element and its HTML code will be highlighted and the number of matches displayed on the Firepath window will be equal to 1.

Consider, another example wherein the requirement is to locate the *Your Account* link using CSS locator path. To find the relative CSS path using Firepath, click on the button 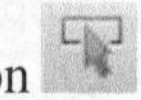 and then point and click the mouse pointer on the link element. Figure 6.6 shows the CSS path as displayed on Firepath window.

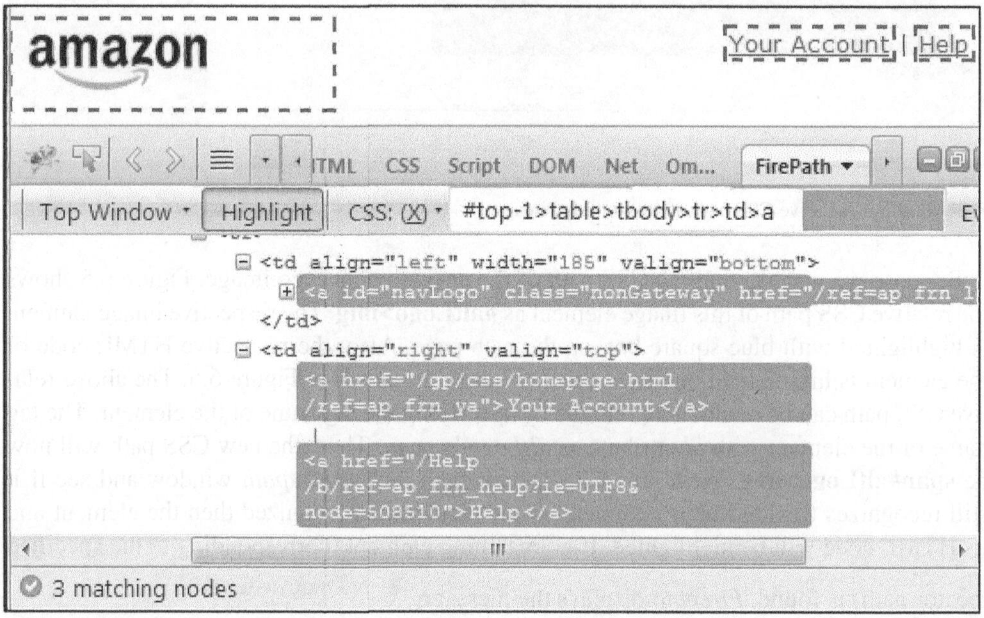

FIGURE 6. 6 | CSS path for your account link element as displayed in Firepath window

As evident from Figure 6.6, Firepath has not been able to uniquely locate the *Your Account* element. Firepath has designed a CSS locator path that matches the description of three elements – Amazon.com logo image, Your Account link element and Help link element. If the above CSS locator path is used in WebDriver code using method *findElement*, then it will locate the first matched element, that is, the Amazon logo image. And if, *findElements* method is used then it will return three elements. Now, let us try and see how we can use the HTML code of the *Your Account* link element to design a reliable and uniquely identifiable CSS path. Assume the HTML code of this link element to be:

```
<a href="/gp/css/homepage.html/ref=ap_frn_ya">Your Account</a>
```

The tag name of this element is *'a'* and its *href* attribute value is `/gp/css/homepage.html/ref=ap_frn_ya`. The CSS locator path of this element can be:

```
a[href='/gp/css/homepage.html/ref=ap_frn_ya']
```

Or,

```
a[href*='ap_frn_ya']
```

Above CSS locator path looks for an element on the web page whose tag name is *'a'* and whose *href* attribute value contains string *'ap_frn_ya'*.

Notes: 1. An easy way of finding HTML code of an element is by navigating through the highlighted code in the Firepath window. The idea is to find the HTML code of the element in the Firepath window and then use this HTML code to design the CSS locator path.

2. Always ensure CSS locator path uniquely identifies the element on the web page.

6.2.1 | Difference Between CSS and Sizzle

Sizzle is a js library on top of CSS3. This means Sizzle has few more methods such as :contains(text), :password, :first, :last, etc. However, currently Sizzle is baked into Selenium 1.0 but not in WebDriver.

6.3 | CSS SELECTOR METHODS

Table 6.1 shows the list of commonly used CSS Selector methods. First column of this table lists the selectors, second column illustrates an example usage of this selector and third column describes the outcome of the example illustrated.

TABLE 6.1 | CSS selector methods

Selector	Example	Example description
.class	.ap_col2_ap_left	Selects all elements with class="ap_col2_ap_left"
#id	#firstname	Selects the element with id="firstname"
*	*	Selects all elements
element	p	Selects all <p> elements
element,element	div,p	Selects all <div> elements and all <p> elements
element element	div p	Selects all <p> elements inside <div> elements
element>element	div>p	Selects all <p> elements where the parent is a <div> element

Selector	Example	Example description
element+element	div+p	Selects all <p> elements that are placed immediately after <div> elements
[attribute]	[attribute name]	Selects all elements with a target attribute
[attribute=value]	[attribute name=attribute value]	Selects all elements with attribute name="attribute value"
[attribute~=value]	[title~=MakeOrder]	Selects all elements with a title attribute containing the word "MakeOrder"
[attribute|=value]	[lang|=en]	Selects all elements with a lang attribute value starting with "en"
:link	a:link	Selects all unvisited links
:visited	a:visited	Selects all visited links
:active	a:active	Selects the active link
:hover	a:hover	Selects links on mouse over
:focus	input:focus	Selects the input element which has focus
:first-letter	p:first-letter	Selects the first letter of every <p> element
:first-line	p:first-line	Selects the first line of every <p> element
:first-child	p:first-child	Selects every <p> element that is the first child of its parent
:before	p:before	Insert content before the content of every <p> element
:after	p:after	Insert content after every <p> element
:lang(language)	p:lang(it)	Selects every <p> element with a lang attribute equal to "it" (Italian)
element1~element2	p~ul	Selects every <ul> element that are preceded by a <p> element
[attribute^=value]	a[src^="https"]	Selects every <a> element whose src attribute value begins with "https"
[attribute$=value]	a[src$=".pdf"]	Selects every <a> element whose src attribute value ends with ".pdf"
[attribute*=value]	a[src*="w3schools"]	Selects every <a> element whose src attribute value contains the substring "w3schools"
:first-of-type	p:first-of-type	Selects every <p> element that is the first <p> element of its parent
:last-of-type	p:last-of-type	Selects every <p> element that is the last <p> element of its parent

(continued)

TABLE 6.1 | *(continued)*

Selector	Example	Example description
:only-of-type	p:only-of-type	Selects every <p> element that is the only <p> element of its parent
:only-child	p:only-child	Selects every <p> element that is the only child of its parent
:nth-child(n)	p:nth-child(2)	Selects every <p> element that is the second child of its parent
:nth-last-child(n)	p:nth-last-child(2)	Selects every <p> element that is the second child of its parent, counting from the last child
:nth-of-type(n)	p:nth-of-type(2)	Selects every <p> element that is the second <p> element of its parent
:nth-last-of-type(n)	p:nth-last-of-type(2)	Selects every <p> element that is the second <p> element of its parent, counting from the last child
:last-child	p:last-child	Selects every <p> element that is the last child of its parent
:root	:root	Selects the document's root element
:empty	p:empty	Selects every <p> element that has no children (including text nodes)
:target	#news:target	Selects the current active #news element (clicked on a URL containing that anchor name)
:enabled	input:enabled	Selects every enabled `<input>` element
:disabled	input:disabled	Selects every disabled `<input>` element
:checked	input:checked	Selects every checked `<input>` element
:not(selector)	:not(p)	Selects every element that is not a <p> element
::selection	::selection	Selects the portion of an element that is selected by a user

6.4 | DESIGNING CSS LOCATOR PATHS

Section below describes in detail on how to design the CSS locator path using various attributes of the HTML element.

6.4.1 | Finding Elements Using Absolute Path

CSS absolute path refers to the absolute hierarchical location of the element with respect to the root node of the DOM. CSS absolute path describes the complete parent–child hierarchy of the element.

EXAMPLE 6.1 Develop absolute CSS path of the *Email Address* field of Figure 6.1.

Let us have a look at Figure 6.2 which shows the HTML code of the *Email Address* field. From Figure 6.1, the absolute tree hierarchy of the *Email Address* field is as follows:

```
html body div div div form div div span input#ap_email
```

Code below shows how to identify the *Email Address* field using JUnit code:

```
WebElement emailAddress = driver.findElement(By.cssSelector("html body
            div div div form div div span input"));
emailAddress.sendKeys("abc@google.com");
```

While creating CSS absolute path, space is provided between parent child elements. Also, the white spaces can be replaced with a greater than (>) separator.

EXAMPLE 6.2 Example shows how to define the absolute CSS path using '>' separator.

```
WebElement emailAddress = driver.findElement(By.cssSelector
            ("html>body>div> div>div>form>div>
            div>span>input"));
```

Using absolute CSS path for locating elements is not a good technique of element identification. The reason being its dependency on the complete tree hierarchy. Any change in the tree hierarchy such as addition or deletion of even a paragraph (<p>) element will cause a change in the absolute CSS path. Such changes will cause the scripts to fail and will require the element identification definition be changed in tests. Frequent such changes will not only impact regression run but will also result in high maintenance effort. To avoid this problem, we can use the relative CSS path of an element for element identification.

6.4.2 | Finding Elements Using Relative Path

Locator CSS path of an element can also be defined with respect to the position of other elements in the hierarchical tree. Since this path is relative to the position of another element, it is called *relative* path. Example below shows how to identify the first `<input>` element in the HTML DOM. For the Amazon.com account registration page as shown in Figure 6.1, the first `<input>` element is *Email Address* field.

EXAMPLE 6.3 Code shows how the first input field of a web page can be located.

```
WebElement emailAddress = driver.findElement(By.cssSelector("input"));
```

As we observe, above CSS path is not sufficient to recognize the other `<input>` elements of the web page say password field, radio buttons, etc. To solve this problem, we can also define the CSS path of an element using its attributes, say Class, Id, etc.

Note: In case multiple elements have the same element description, the element whose hierarchy in DOM tree is highest is recognized as the matched element by Webdriver.

6.4.3 | Finding Elements Using ID Selector

The ID attribute of an element can be used to uniquely locate an element in the DOM tree. The id attribute of an element is defined in CSS path by a preceding hash (#) sign.

EXAMPLE 6.4 The HTML code for the *Email Address* field as shown in Figure 6. 2.

```
<input id="ap_email" type="email" autocapitalize="off" autocorrect=
"off" tabindex="1"maxlength="128" size="30" value="" name="email"/>
```

As evident from the code, the value of attribute id is ap_email.Webdriver code to uniquely identify the element in the DOM tree using its *id* attribute will be:

```
WebElement emailAddress = driver.findElement(By.cssSelector
                          ("#ap_email"));
```

Above code will locate all the elements whose *id* attribute value is *ap_email*. In situations where two or more elements have the same *id* attribute, the above code may fail to uniquely identify the required element. To resolve this issue, we can specify the HTML tag of the element node along with its *id* description. The HTML tag of the *Email Address* field node is input. Therefore, the new CSS path for element identification will be:

```
WebElement emailAddress = driver.findElement(By.cssSelector
                          ("input#ap_email"));
```

Note: Ideally, id attribute of an element needs to be unique throughout the DOM tree.

6.4.4 | Finding Elements Using Class Selector

The *Class* attribute can be used to uniquely locate an element in the HTML DOM tree. The id attribute of an element is defined in CSS path by a preceding dot (.) sign.

EXAMPLE 6.5 Consider the HTML code of the *Password* field as shown in Figure 6.1.

```
<input id="ap_password" class="password" type="password"
  onkeypress="displayCapsWarning(event,'ap_caps_warning', this);"
  tabindex="2" size="20" maxlength="1024" name="password"/>
```

As evident from the code, the value of attribute *class* is *password.* Webdriver code to uniquely identify the element in the DOM tree using its *class* attribute will be:

```
WebElement emailAddress = driver.findElement(By.cssSelector
                          (".password"));
```

Above code will locate all the elements whose *class* attribute value is *password.* As we know, the *class* attribute value of two or more elements can be same. In such situations WebDriver may fail to locate the required element. To resolve this issue, we can specify the HTML tag of the element node along with its *class* description. The HTML tag of the *Password* field node is input. So the new CSS path for element identification will be:

```
WebElement emailAddress = driver.findElement(By.cssSelector
                            ("input.password"));
```

6.4.5 | Finding Elements Using Other Attributes Selector

Apart from *ID* and *Class* attribute, other element attributes such as *name, alt, tabindex,* etc., can also be used to locate the element.

EXAMPLE 6.6 Consider the HTML code of the *Password* field. This element can also be located using its *name* attribute as:

```
WebElement password = driver.findElement(By.cssSelector("[name=
                        password]"));
```

Above code will locate the first element whose *name* attribute value is *password.* Sometimes this description would not be sufficient to uniquely identify an element as *name* attribute value of two or more elements can be the same. To help uniquely identify an element, *html tag* of the element can also be used as one of its identification properties as shown below:

```
WebElement password = driver.findElement(By.cssSelector("input
                        [name=password]"));
```

Above code will locate the first `<input>` element whose *name* attribute value is *password.*

EXAMPLE 6.7 Alternatively, the *Password* element can also be identified in DOM tree using its *type* attribute.

```
WebElement password = driver.findElement(By.cssSelector("input
                        [type=password]"));
```

Above code will locate the first `<input>` element whose *type* attribute value is *password.*

EXAMPLE 6.8 Alternatively, the *Password* element can also be identified in DOM tree using its *tabindex* attribute.

```
WebElement password = driver.findElement(By.cssSelector("input
                        [tabindex='2']"));
```

Above code will locate the first `<input>` element whose *tabindex* attribute value is *2.*

EXAMPLE 6.9 Consider the HTML code of the button 

is

```
<input id="signInSubmit" width="201" type="image" height="22"
  border="0" value="Continue" tabindex="5" alt="Continue" onload="if
  (typeof uet == 'function') { uet('cf'); }" src="https://images-
  amazon.com/images/.../V192194766.gif"/>
```

The above element can also be identified using its *alt* attribute as

```
WebElement signIn = driver.findElement(By.cssSelector("input
                      [alt='Continue']"));
```

6.4.6 | Finding Elements Using Multiple Attributes Selector

In real-world scenario, one attribute may not be always sufficient enough to uniquely identify an element in a HTML page. In such situations, we can locate an element using multiple attributes. Example below demonstrates how to locate an element using multiple attribute values.

EXAMPLE 6.10 Consider for example, we need to uniquely identify the button 

of amazon.com create a new account page. Code below shows how to uniquely identify this element using more than one element attributes.

```
WebElement signIn = driver.findElement(By.cssSelector("input[id=
                      'signInSubmit'] [alt='Continue']"));
```

Above code locates an <input> element whose *id* attribute value is *signInSubmit* and *alt* attribute value is *Continue*. As evident from the HTML code of Example 6.1, the above code will locate the *SignIn* button.

EXAMPLE 6.11 Code below shows how to use more than two attributes to locate an element.

```
WebElement signIn = driver.findElement(By.cssSelector("input
                      [id='signInSubmit'] [alt='Continue']
                      [value='Continue']"));
```

Above code locates the *SignIn* button using three attributes *id*, *alt* and *value* attribute.

EXAMPLE 6.12 Alternatively, the *SignIn* button can also be uniquely located by using other element attributes such as *tabindex*, *size*, *height*, etc.

```
WebElement signIn = driver.findElement(By.cssSelector("input
                      [id='signInSubmit'][type='image']
                      [tabindex='5'][height='22']"));
```

Note: Attributes tabindex, height, size, width, etc., needs to be avoided for element identification. This is because the values of these attributes may vary from browser to browser. Also, these values can be changed by developer even in the absence of any valid change requirement.

6.4.7 | Finding Elements Using Attribute Name Selector

Webdriver provides the flexibility to locate elements using attribute names. This approach is bit different from the previous approach we just discussed. In previous approach, we were using the attribute values to identify an element. In this approach, we use attribute name to identify an element.

EXAMPLE 6.13 Let us consider a scenario wherein the requirement is to ensure that all `<input>` elements on amazon.com home page should have attribute *id* defined. The approach here will be to identify all `<input>` elements whose *id* attribute is not defined. This list can then be send to the developers for a code fix.

Code below shows how to find all `<input>`elements whose *id* attribute is defined.

```
List<WebElement> checkboxesWithIdAttribute = driver.findElements
  (By.cssSelector("input[id]"));
```

Now, the requirement was to locate all `<input>` elements whose *id* attribute is not defined. This can be achieved by using a Boolean not pseudo-class. The Webdriver code for the same will be

```
List<WebElement> checkboxesWithIdAttribute = driver.findElements
  (By.cssSelector("input:not([id])"));
```

EXAMPLE 6.14 Let us consider another scenario where there are five checkboxes (Figure 6.7) in a web page and we need to identify these checkboxes and select/deselect them.

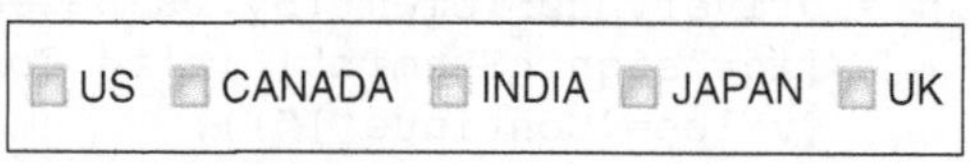

FIGURE 6.7 | Checkboxes

Suppose, the HTML code of these elements is:

```
<input type="checkbox" name="country" value="1"/>US
<input id="id1" type="checkbox" name="country" value="1"/>CANADA
<input id="id2" type="checkbox" name="country" value="1"/>INDIA
<input id="id3" type="checkbox" name="country" value="1"/>JAPAN
<input id="id4" type="checkbox" name="country" value="1"/>UK
```

Suppose, the requirement is to locate all checkboxes which has an *id* attribute. The Webdriver code for the same will be

```
List<WebElement> checkboxesWithIdAttribute = driver.findElements
  (By.cssSelector("input[type='checkbox'][id]"));
```

Again, suppose the requirement is to locate all checkboxes whose *id* attribute is not defined. This can be achieved by using a Boolean not pseudo-class. The Webdriver code for the same will be

```
List<WebElement> checkboxesWithNoIdAttribute = driver.findElements
  (By.cssSelector("input[type='checkbox']:not([id])"));
```

6.4.8 | Finding Elements Using Partial Match (Regular Expressions)

In real-life scenario, there are many instances where attribute values of the elements change dynamically. Every time the web page is opened, the specific elements attribute values change. Such elements whose attribute values change dynamically during run-time are called *dynamic elements*. One example would be ASP.NET applications where IDs are generated dynamically. Another example could be a page containing a list of recent five order numbers as link elements. Since the page will get updated with latest order numbers every time; the *linkText* attribute of order number link elements will change dynamically.

CSS selector provides the flexibility to locate elements matching partial attribute values. Table 6.2 explains the use of CSS partial match expressions:

TABLE 6.2 | Finding elements using partial match

Syntax	Objective	Example	Description
^=	Identify element whose attribute value **starts with**<string>	Input[id^= 'User']	Locate `<input>` element whose **id** attribute starts with **User**. For example elements with id value as – Username, UserName, User123, User_Name, etc.
$=	Identify element whose attribute value **ends with** <string>	Input[id$= 'User']	Locate `<input>` element whose **id** attribute starts with **User**. For example elements with id value as – firstUser, second_User, 1User, _User, etc.
*=	Identify element whose attribute value **contains**<string>	Input[id*= 'user']	Locate `<input>` element whose **id** attribute contains string **User**. For example elements with id value as – firstUser, second_UserName, 1User123, _User2, etc.

EXAMPLE 6.15 For Figure 6.1, write WebDriver code to identify the link element whose *href* attribute starts with '/gp/css/'

For Figure 6.1, there is only one link element 'Your Account' whose href attribute value starts with '/gp/css/'. The HTML code of this link element is:

```
<a href="/gp/css/homepage.html/ref=ap_frn_ya">Your Account</a>
```

Symbol '^' is used along with attribute name to locate elements whose attribute value starts with the specified string. Below is the WebDriver code to locate an element by looking for an element whose *href* attribute value starts with '/gp/css/'.

```
WebElement yaLink = driver.findElement(By.cssSelector("a[href^=
                    '/gp/css/']"));
```

EXAMPLE 6.16 For the example above, write code to find the link element whose *href* attribute value ends with string `'ap_frn_ya'`.

Symbol '$' is used along with attribute name to locate elements whose attribute value ends with the specified string. Below is the WebDriver code to locate an element by looking for an element whose *href* attribute value starts with string `'ap_frn_ya'`.

```
WebElement yaLink = driver.findElement(By.cssSelector("a[href^=
                    'ap_frn_ya']"));
```

EXAMPLE 6.17 For the example above, write code to find the link element whose *href* attribute value contains string `'homepage.html'`.

Symbol '*' is used along with attribute name to locate elements whose attribute value contains the specified string. Below is the WebDriver code to locate an element by looking for an element whose *href* attribute value contains string `'homepage.html'`.

```
WebElement yaLink = driver.findElement(By.cssSelector("a[href*=
                    'homepage.html']"));
```

6.4.9 | Finding Elements Using Pseudo-Class Selectors

Pseudo classes are used to add special effects to some selectors. Pseudo classes classify elements on characteristics other than their name, attributes or content. That is, on characteristics that cannot be deduced from the document tree. Pseudo elements create abstractions about the document tree which are beyond those specified by the document language. For example, document languages do not offer mechanisms to access the first letter or first line of an element's content. CSS pseudo elements allow style sheet designers to refer and apply style to this otherwise inaccessible content. Neither pseudo elements nor pseudo classes appear in the document source or DOM tree.

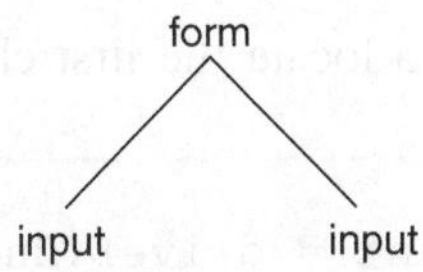

Selenium Webdriver provides the flexibility to access DOM elements using CSS pseudo class.

6.4.10 | Finding Elements Using Child ElementsPseudo Class

CSS Selectors provide various ways to locate a child element from parent element. Figure 6.8 shows a sample code of checkboxes in a website.

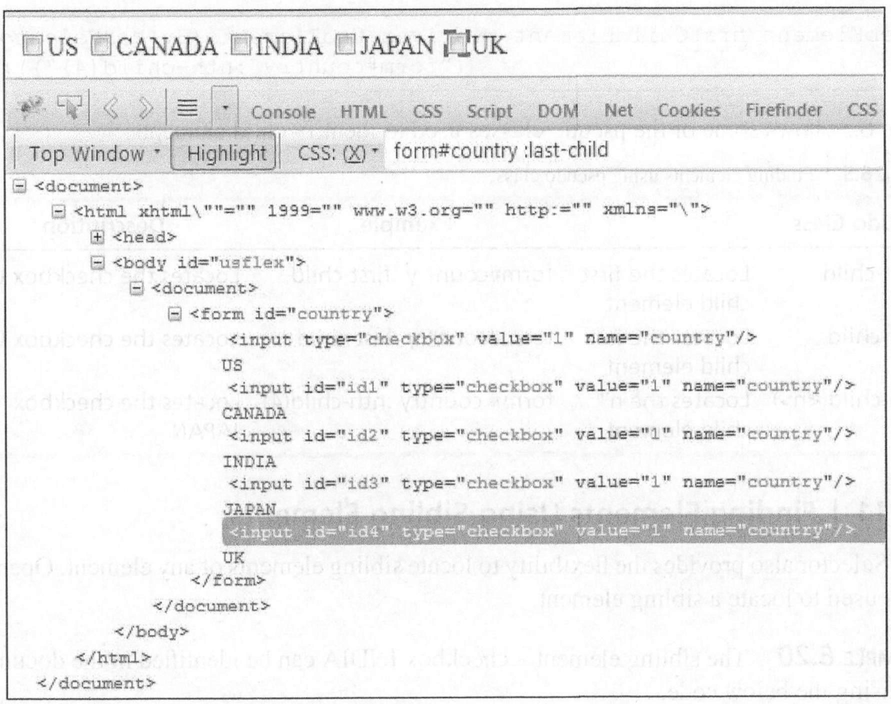

FIGURE 6. 8 | Sample code for checkboxes in a website.

We can locate the first element in this code using pseudo class :first-child. Let us assume the parent element in the code above to be

```
<form id="country">
```

Webdriver code to identify this element will be

```
WebElement parentElement = driver.findElements(By.cssSelector
                           ("form#country");
```

EXAMPLE 6.18 WebDriver code to locate the first child element (checkbox US) of the above parent element will be

```
WebElement firstChildElement = driver.findElements(By.cssSelector
                               ("form#country :first-child"));
```

Note: There is a white space between parent element class description value and symbol ":".

EXAMPLE 6.19 Pseudo class 'nth-child(<n>)' is used to find the nth child of any parent element. WebDriver code to find the 4th child element (checkbox JAPAN) of the above parent element will be:

```
WebElement firstChildElement = driver.findElements(By.cssSelector
                               ("form#country :nth-child(4)"));
```

Table 6.3 shows some of the pseudo classes used to identify child elements.

TABLE 6.3 | Finding elements using pseudo class

Pseudo Class		Example	Description
:first-child	Locates the first child element	form#country :first-child	Locates the checkbox US
:last-child	Locates the last child element	form#country :last-child	Locates the checkbox UK
:nth-child(<n>)	Locates the nth child element	form# country :nth-child(4)	Locates the checkbox JAPAN

6.4.11 | Finding Elements Using Sibling Elements

CSS Selector also provides the flexibility to locate sibling elements of any element. Operator '+' is used to locate a sibling element.

EXAMPLE 6.20 The sibling element – checkbox INDIA can be identified in the document tree using the below code.

```
WebElement firstChildElement = driver.findElements(By.cssSelector
                               ("form#country> input + input +
                               input)"));
```

In situations where a *tagname* changes dynamically during run-time, the *tagname* can be specified by '*'. For example, the above code can also be written as

```
WebElement firstChildElement = driver.findElements(By.cssSelector
                               ("form#country> input + * +
                               input)"));
```

6.4.12 | Finding Elements Using User Action Pseudo Class

CSS Pseudo class can be used to validate the user actions. For instance, CSS provides the flexibility to validate whether the clicked link appears in red colour or not. Another example would be validate the current element has focus or not.

Example 6.21 Consider the google search result page as shown in Figure 6.9. Suppose the requirement is to find all the links that has been unvisited (link colour = blue). The WebDriver code to find all unvisited link elements will be

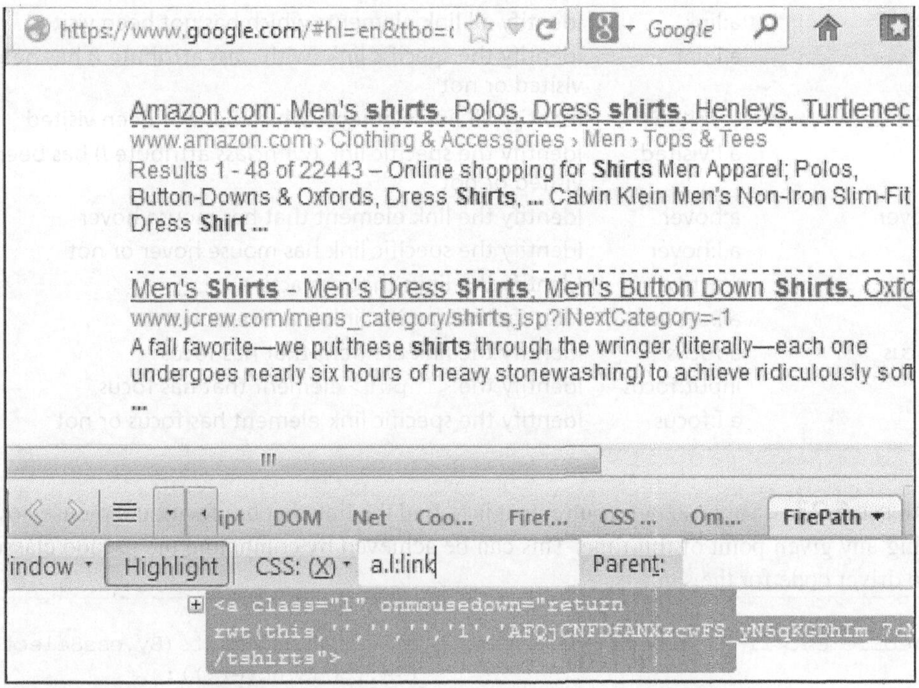

FIGURE 6. 9 | Google search page

```
List<WebElement> unvisitedLinks = driver.findElements(By.
                                  cssSelector("a:link"));
```

Example 6.22 Suppose the requirement is to find whether a specific link of Figure 6.1 has been visited or not. WebDriver code for the same will be

```
WebElement link;
      try{
            link = driver.findElement(By.cssSelector
                  ("a.l:link"));
```

```
        }catch (Exception e){
                System.out.println("Link has not visited");
        }
```

Table 6.4 shows some of the user action pseudo classes. First column of this table lists the pseudo classes, second column illustrates an example usage of this pseudo class and third column describes the outcome of the example illustrated.

TABLE 6. 4 | Finding elements using user-action pseudo class

Pseudo class	Example	Description
:link	a:link	Identify all link elements which has not been visited
	a.l:link	Identify the specific link (with *class* attribute *l*) has been visited or not
:visited	a:visited	Identify all link elements which has not been visited
	a.l:visited	Identify the specific link (with*class* attribute *l*) has been visited or not
:hover	a:hover	Identify the link element that has mouse hover
	a.l:hover	Identify the specific link has mouse hover or not
:active	a:active	Identify the links that are active
	a.l:active	Identify the specific link is active or not
:focus	a:focus	Identify the link element that has focus
	input:focus	Identify the `<input>` element that has focus
	a.l:focus	Identify the specific link element has focus or not

EXAMPLE 6.23 Suppose the requirement is to find the link that has focus and mouse hover during any given point of run-time. This can be achieved by combining the pseudo classes. Web driver code for the same is:

```
WebElement linkHasFocusAndIsActive = driver.findElements(By.cssSelector
                                          ("a:focus:hover"));
```

6.4.13 | Finding Elements Using UI State Pseudo Class

UI state pseudo classes are used to locate elements for various states such as enabled, disabled or checked. These classes can also be used to validate user action. For instance, validating whether a checkbox appears checked after clicking on it.

EXAMPLE 6.24 Let us suppose the requirement is to find out whether checkbox US shown in Figure 6.3 is checked or not. This validation can be done using checked pseudo class.

```
<input id="id1" type="checkbox" value="1" name="country"/>CANADA
```

WebDriver code for the same will be

```
WebElement checkbox;
try{
        driver.findElement(By.cssSelector("input#id1")).
         click();
        checkbox = driver.findElement(By.cssSelector
        ("input#id1:checked"))
        }catch (Exception e){
                System.out.println("checkboxis not checked");
        }
```

Table 6.5 describes the UI state pseudo classes. First column of this table lists the UI state Pseudo Classes, second column illustrates an example usage of this pseudo class and third column describes the outcome of the example illustrated.

TABLE 6.5 | Finding elements using UI state pseudo class

Pseudo class	Example	Description
:enabled	input:enabled	Locate all <input> elements which are enabled
:disabled	input:disabled	Locate all <input> elements which are disabled
:checked	input:checked	Locate all <input> elements which are checked

6.4.14 | Finding Elements Using JQuery Selectors

jQuery Selectors are one of the important features of jQuery library. These Selectors use familiar CSS syntax to allow page authors to quickly and easily identify any set of page elements to operate upon. Similar to CSS Selectors, jQuery Selectors allow us to identify HTML elements as a single element or a list of elements.

jQuery Selectors can be used in situations where CSS Selectors are not natively supported by the browsers. jQuery provides the `find()` method which can be used to search for desired elements. Javascript Executor class is used to execute jQuery's `find()` method inside Webdriver code.

Note: As of now, almost all the browsers support CSS3. Latest information on CSS support for various browsers is available at the site http://caniuse.com/#index

EXAMPLE 6.25 Find all the checkboxes which are selected for Figure 6.10.

FIGURE 6. 10 | Checkboxes in a web page

Suppose the HTML code of these elements is as follows:

```
<input id="id0" type="checkbox" value="1" name="country"/>US
<input id="id1" type="checkbox" value="1" name="country"/>CANADA
```

```
<input id="id2" type="checkbox" checked="true/" value="1"
  name="country"/>INDIA
<input id="id3" type="checkbox" value="1" name="country"/>JAPAN
<input id="id4" type="checkbox" checked="true/" value="1"
  name="country"/>UK
```

Code below shows how to find all the selected checkboxes in a webpage using jQuery Selectors.

```
@SuppressWarnings("unchecked")
@Test
public void testFindSelectedCheckboxes(){
        WebDriver driver = new FirefoxDriver();
        //Suppose the html file is kept in c:\temp directory
        driver.get("file:///C:/Temp/Checkbox.html");
        //Create an instance of Javascript Executor
        JavascriptExecutor js = (JavascriptExecutor) driver;
        /*
        * Identify all checkboxes which are selected by using
          jQuery find() method
        * find() method returns element in an array
        */
        List<WebElement> checkboxElements = (List<WebElement>)
          js.executeScript("return jQuery.find(':checked')");
        System.out.println("Selected Checkboxes Count=" + checkbox
          Elements.size());
}
```

However, it is required that that application under test (AUT) uses jQuery API for the above code to work. In case AUT does not use jQuery API, then jQuery library needs to be loaded to the page explicitly. This can be achieved by using the utility code shown below.

```
//load jQuery library if not already loaded
public void loadjQueryLibrary(WebDriver driver){
        if (!isjQueryLoaded(driver)) loadjQuery(driver);
}

//Verify jQuery library is loaded or not
private Boolean isjQueryLoaded(WebDriver driver){
        Boolean isjQueryLibraryLoaded;
        try{
                isjQueryLibraryLoaded = (Boolean)
                  ((JavascriptExecutor) driver).
                  executeScript("return jQuery()!=null");
```

```
        }catch (WebDriverException e) {
                isjQueryLibraryLoaded = false;
        }
        return isjQueryLibraryLoaded;
}

//load jQueryLibray 1.9.0
private void loadjQuery(WebDriver driver){
        ((JavascriptExecutor) driver).executeScript("var headID=" +
                "document.getElementByTagName(\"head\")[0];" +
                "varinjectorScript = document.createElement
                  ('script');" +
                "injectorScript.type = 'text/javascript';" +
                "injectorScript.src = 'http://ajax.googleapis.com/" +
                "ajax/libs/jquery/1.9.0/jquery.min.js';" +
                "headID.appendChild(newScript);");
}
```

loadjQueryLibrary() method loads the jQuery library if it is not already loaded by AUT. This method calls jQueryLoaded() method to verify whether jQuety library is loaded. If jQuery is not loaded, then it calls loadjQuery() method to load the jQuery library to the web page. In the code above, jQuery version 1.9.0 has been used. We can replace this version number with the latest version number to load the latest jQuery library files.

6.5 | CHECKING AN ELEMENTS CSS VALUE

Various styles are applied on the elements of the web page to make the web page look attractive and user-friendly. Developers add these styles from CSS. Sometimes, we may require to test whether respective styles have been correctly applied or not. For example, it may be required to verify the font family and font size of the text on a `<input>` button. Another example could be to verify the background colour of the button. WebDriver provides *getCSSValue()* method to read the style attributes of an element. Example below shows how to find the style attributes of a button.

EXAMPLE 6.26 Consider the 'Sign in' button on amazon.com account creation page. Write code to find the font family, font size, colour, width and height attributes of this button.

In order to verify the style attributes, we need to know the expected style attributes of the element. This can be found out from the respective developer or by using CSS Viewer plug-in. Figure 6.11 shows CSS style attributes of the sign in button element.

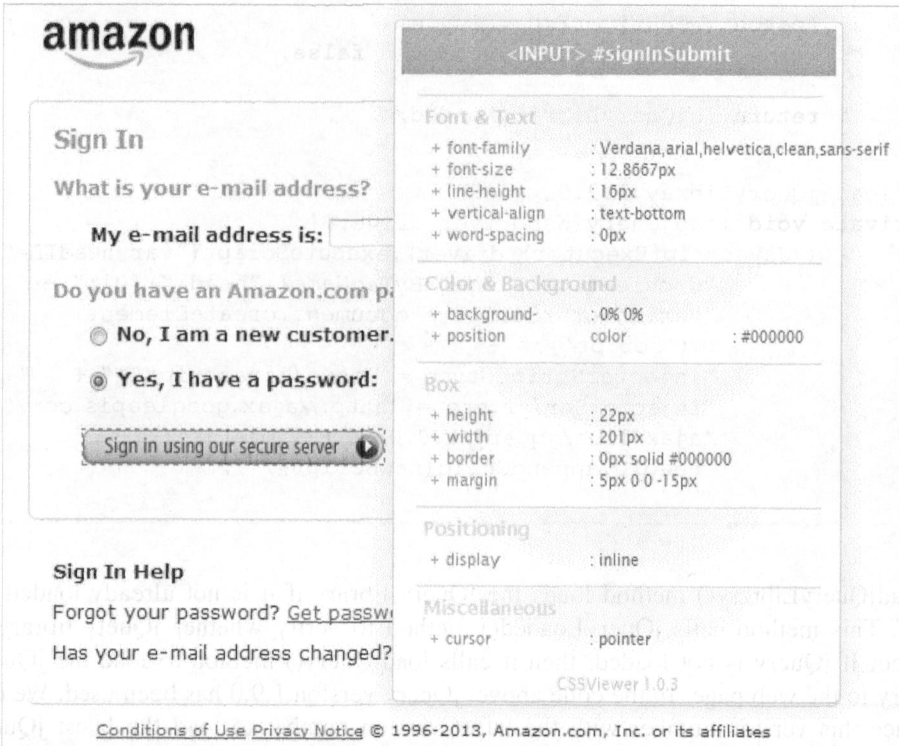

FIGURE 6. 11 | CSS Style attributes of 'Sign in' button

HTML code of the sign-in button is:

```
<input id="signInSubmit" width="201" type="image" height="22"
  border="0" value="Continue" tabindex="5" alt="Continue"
  onload="if (typeof uet == 'function') { uet('cf'); }"
  src="https://images-na.ssl-images-amazon.com/images/G/01/x-
  locale/common/buttons/sign-in-secure._V192194766_.gif"/>
```

WebDriver code to verify CSS style attributes is shown below:

```
WebElement signIn = driver.findElement(By.cssSelector
  ("input#signInSubmit"));
String fontFamily = signIn.getCssValue("font-family");
String fontSize = signIn.getCssValue("font-size");
String color = signIn.getCssValue("color");
String height = signIn.getCssValue("height");
String width = signIn.getCssValue("width");

Boolean isTrue = fontFamily.equalsIgnoreCase("Verdana,
  arial,helvetica,clean,sans-serif");
```

```
assertTrue("Failed: fontFamily", isTrue);
isTrue = fontSize.equalsIgnoreCase("12.8667px");
assertTrue("Failed: fontSize", isTrue);
isTrue = color.equalsIgnoreCase("rgba(0, 0, 0, 1)");
assertTrue("Failed: color", isTrue);
isTrue = height.equalsIgnoreCase("22px");
assertTrue("Failed: height", isTrue);
isTrue = width.equalsIgnoreCase("201px");
assertTrue("Failed: width", isTrue);
```

INTERVIEW QUESTIONS

1. What is CSS Selector? How it works?
2. How you will find CSS attributes of an element in Firefox and Chrome browser?
3. What is the difference between absolute CSS path and relative CSS path of an element?
4. You see a Selenium Developer using the same CSS path in code as it is displayed in Firebug. What you will advise him and why?
5. What is Pseudo Class CSS Selector?
6. What is the difference between Action class and UI state CSS selector?
7. Develop the CSS path for locating below elements of amazon.com create new account page
   a) Email address edit box
   b) Password edit box
   c) Your account link
   d) Sign in button

7 CHAPTER

Locating Element Using XPath

XPath is XML path language based on a tree representation of the XML document. It is a query language for selecting nodes from XML document. It provides the ability to navigate around the tree by selecting nodes using a variety of criteria.

Selenium WebDriver supports XPath for identifying elements in a web page. WebDriver uses native XPath capabilities wherever possible. For browsers that do not have native XPath support, WebDriver has provided its own implementation. However, this can lead to some unexpected behaviour unless we are aware of the differences in the various XPath engines which are given in Table 7.1.

TABLE 7.1 | Differences between various WebDriver XPath engines

Driver	Tag and attribute values	Attribute values	Native XPath support
HtmlUnitDriver	Lower-cased	As it appears in HTML	Yes
InternetExplorerDriver	Lower-cased	As it appears in HTML	No (IE8)
FirefoxDriver	Case insensitive	As it appears in HTML	Yes

Consider the following piece of HTML code:

```
<input type="text" name="username"/>
<INPUT type="text" name="password"/>
```

For the above HTML code, Table 7.2 shows the number of matches for various WebDriver drivers. The first column of the table specifies XPath expression while the rest of the columns specifies the number of element that would match the XPath description for various drivers.

TABLE 7.2 | Number of matches for various drivers

	Number of matches for		
XPath expression	HtmlUnitDriver	InternetExplorerDriver	FirefoxDriver
//input	1	2	2
//INPUT	0	2	0

Notes: 1. From IE9 onwards internet explorer has started supporting DOM Level 3 XPath specifications.

2. XPath is least preferred locator strategy because of its slow performance.

One important difference between XPath and CSS is XPath allows searching elements both backward and forward in the DOM tree, whereas CSS allows searching only in forward direction. That is, XPath allows locating a parent element from a child element, whereas CSS does not.

Consider the account creation page of amazon.com. We will use this page as application page under test throughout this chapter. Figure 7.1 shows the amazon.com new user account creation page.

FIGURE 7.1 | Account creation page of amazon.com

The HTML code for the *email address* input field is as shown in Figure 7.2.

7.1 | HOW TO LOCATE ELEMENTS USING XPATH

XPath of an element can be used to uniquely locate the element in a web page. Firefox plug-in *Firepath* can be used to design XPath locators which can identify an element in the DOM tree.

Follow the below steps to view the XPath locator path of an element:

- Open Firefox and then activate *Firebug* window by clicking on the bookmark .
- On *Firebug* window, click on the tab FirePath ▾. *Firepath* window opens.
- On *Firepath* window, select locator as '*XPath* as shown in Figure 7.3.
- To view XPath of an element, click on the mouse icon and then point and click the arrow on the desired element. The absolute XPath of the element is displayed on the *Firepath* window as shown in Figure 7.4.

FIGURE 7.2 | HTML code of account creation page

FIGURE 7.3 | Firepath window

In case we want to find the XPath of the amazon.com logo image. Figure 7.4 shows the absolute XPath of this image element as **html/body/div[1]/div[1]/div/table/tbody/tr/td[1]/a/span/img**. The respective image element is highlighted with blue square box on the web page. Also, the respective HTML code of the element is highlighted on the *Firepath* window as shown in Figure 7.4. The above absolute XPath is not a reliable mechanism to locate elements. This is because any addition or deletion of an element (even a label element) may change the absolute XPath of existing elements. Such continuous changes in the web pages will require continuous change in test scripts. This makes automation maintenance

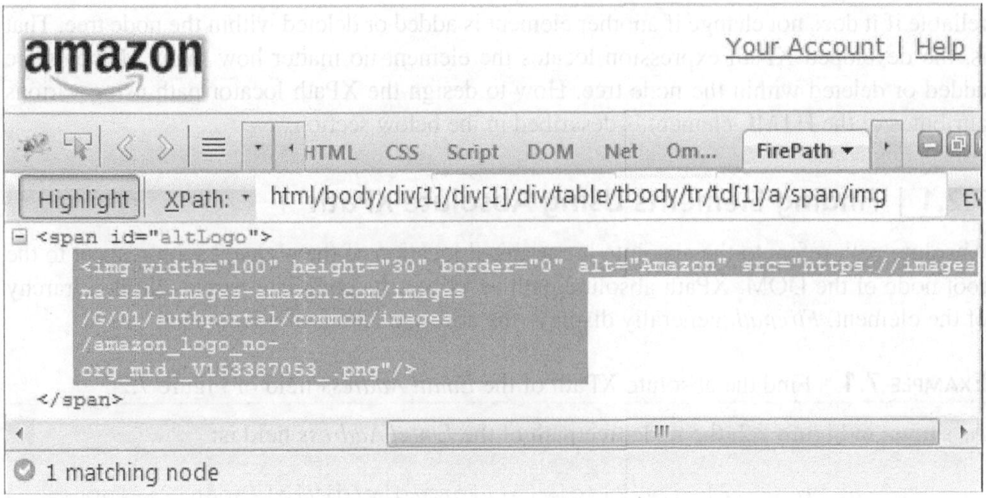

FIGURE 7.4 | Absolute XPath of Amazon logo image

difficult. In order to avoid this problem, relative XPath of an element is to be used. HTML code of the element can be used to design a relative XPath that uniquely identifies an element on the web page.

Assume the HTML code of the logo image to be:

```
<img width="100" border="0" height="30" alt="Amazon"
  src="https://images-amazon.com/...amazon_logo_no-org_
  mid._V153387053_.png" style=""/>
```

The above HTML code describes the various attributes of the element such as its height, width, alt, src, etc. One or more of these attributes can be used to uniquely identify the logo image. One of the reliable attributes of the logo image is its *alt* attribute. XPath of the logo image element using this *alt* attribute can be designed as:

```
//img[@alt='Amazon']
```

The above XPath locates an image element whose *alt* attribute value equals *Amazon.* In order to verify whether this locator path uniquely identifies the logo image element or not, write this locator path on Firepath window and hit Enter key. If the object is uniquely identified, then the respective element and its HTML code will be highlighted and the number of matches displayed on the Firepath window will be equal to 1.

7.2 | DESIGNING XPATH LOCATOR PATHS

As we learned in the last section that XPath expression developed by *Firepath* is not a reliable one. So, we need to develop a reliable XPath expression. XPath expressions are to be developed in a way that it relies on element attributes to locate the element. In scenarios, where element attributes are not sufficient to uniquely locate the element, attempt is made to minimize the dependency on node tree path to locate the element. A XPath expression is considered reliable if it does not change if another element is added or deleted within the node tree. That is, the developed XPath expression locates the element no matter how many elements are added or deleted within the node tree. How to design the XPath locator path using various attributes of the HTML element is described in the below section.

7.2.1 | Finding Elements Using Absolute XPath

Absolute path refers to the absolute hierarchical location of the element with respect to the root node of the DOM. XPath absolute path describes the complete parent–child hierarchy of the element. *Firepath* generally displays the absolute XPath of an element.

EXAMPLE 7.1 Find the absolute XPath of the *Email Address* field of Figure 7.2

As shown in Figure 7.2, the node tree path of the *Email Address* field is:

```
html/body/div[2]/div[2]/div[5]/form/div/div[3]/span[2]/input
```

WebDriver code to locate the element is:

```
WebElement emailAddress = driver.findElement(By.XPath("html/body/
  div[2]/div[2]/div[5]/form/div/div[3]/span[2]/input"));
```

WebDriver code to write to the email field is:

```
emailAddress.sendKeys("abc@google.com");
```

Note: Two html tags in XPath are separated by a '/' sign. Unlike CSS, index can be used to identify element tags. For example, as visible in Figure 7.2, between *form* node and *div* node there is only one *div* node so this has been represented as *.../form/div/...* However, between this *div* node and the next *div* node that contains the *Email Address*<input>there are three *div* elements, so the next node has been represented as *.../form/div/div[3]...* Similarly, between this *div* node and the next node (*span*) that contains the *Email Address* field, they are two *span* nodes. Thus, the next node has been located as *.../form/div/div[3]/span[2]...*

Locating elements using its absolute path has one drawback. The element identification is dependent on the node structure of the tree. The tree node structure can be under frequent changes depending upon the development work on the page. Even a small change such as introduction of new *div* element in the tree will result in change in the absolute XPath of the *Email Address* field. In order for the scripts to work, the XPath for the element in the scripts needs to be updated frequently as per the change. Such frequent changes will result in huge automation maintenance cost. Moreover, it will severely impact regression run executions because of high failures due to failed object identification. To solve this problem, we can use relative XPath of the elements.

7.2.2 | Finding Elements Using Relative XPath

An element can also be located in the DOM tree with respect to the position of other elements in the DOM tree. Since this path is relative to the position of another element, it is called *relative* path. For example, we can locate the *Email Address* field for Figure 7.2 using code:

```
WebElement emailAddress = driver.findElement(By.XPath("//input"));
```

Above code locates the first <input> element in the web page DOM tree.

EXAMPLE 7.2 Locate the first image element for Figure 7.1.

The HTML code of the first <img> element is:

```
<document>
<html xmlns="\"http://www.w3.org/1999/xhtml\"">
<head>
<body id="usflex">
<div id="ap_container">
<img alt="" style="display:none;" src="https://images-n...<document>
...
```

WebDriver code to identify the first image element of the above DOM tree is:

```
WebElement emailAddress = driver.findElement(By.XPath("//img"));
```

EXAMPLE 7.3 Locate the first link element of Figure 7.1.

HTML code for the first link element for Figure 7.1 is shown below. The first link element for Figure 7.1 is amazon logo. This link element has been highlighted in the code below.

```
<document>
<html xmlns="\"http://www.w3.org/1999/xhtml\"">
<head>
<body id="usflex">
<div id="ap_container">
<img alt="" style="display:none;" src="https://images-..."/>
<div id="wrapper">
<div id="topSlots">
<div id="top-1">
<table width="100%" cellspacing="0" cellpadding="0" border="0">
<tbody>
<tr>
<td align="left" width="185" valign="bottom">
<a id="navLogo" class="nonGateway" href="/ref=ap_frn_logo">
</td>
<td align="right" valign="top">
<a href="/gp/css/homepage.html/ref=ap_frn_ya">Your Account</a>
<a href="/Help/b/ref=ap_frn_help?ie=UTF8&node=508510">Help</a>
```

WebDriver code to identify this element in the above DOM tree is:

```
WebElement emailAddress = driver.findElement(By.XPath("//a"));
```

7.2.3 | Finding Elements Using Index with XPath

As we can observe in the example above, there are multiple links in the DOM tree but the WebDriver identifies the first link element it finds in the DOM tree. In order to locate other link elements in the DOM tree, position (index) of the element can be specified along with its *tag* name. For example, in the code above, location of link *Your Account* is second in the DOM tree. Thus, XPath expression //a[2] can be used to identify this link. Similarly, the position of link *Help* is third in the DOM tree. XPath expression //a[3] can be used to locate the *Help* link in the DOM tree.

EXAMPLE 7.4 Locate the *Password* field in Figure 7.1.

Password field is the second `<input>` field in the DOM tree. Thus, the XPath expression to identify this element will be //input[2]. WebDriver code to locate this element using its index value is:

```
WebElement emailAddress = driver.findElement(By.XPath("//input[2]"));
```

Note: Identifying elements using its index value is not a reliable method of locating elements. This is because, in case, one more input element is added between the `<input>` node of *Email Address* and *Password* field, then the scripts fail as //input[2] no longer points to the Password field.

7.2.4 | Finding Elements Using Attribute Values with XPath

As we observe, none of the above mechanisms are reliable way of locating elements. Reliability of XPath expression can be enhanced by using element attributes within the expression. Selenium WebDriver offers the flexibility to locate elements by using the attribute values of the element. For example, an element can be identified using its *id*, *class*, *type*, *alt*, *value*, *name,* etc., attribute values. '@' symbol is used to specify the attribute with the XPath.

EXAMPLE 7.5 Locate the *Email Address* field using its attribute values.

The HTML code for the *Email Address* field is:

```
<input id="ap_email" type="email" autocapitalize="off"
  autocorrect="off" tabindex="1" maxlength="128" size="30"
  value="" name="email"/>
```

The above HTML code defines the attributes *id, type, autocapitalize, autocorrect, tabindex, maxlength, size, value* and *name.* Any values of these attributes can be used to identify the *Email Address* element on the webpage.

Code below uses *id* attribute to identify the *Email Address* field.

```
WebElement emailAddress = driver.findElement(By.XPath("//input[@
  id='ap_email']"));
```

Alternatively, *Email Address* field can also be recognized using *name* attribute value

```
WebElement emailAddress = driver.findElement(By.XPath("//
  input[@name='email']"));
```

Alternatively, *Email Address* field can also be recognized using *type* attribute value

```
WebElement emailAddress = driver.findElement(By.XPath("//input[@
  type='email']"));
```

Similarly, the *Email Address* field can also be identified in web page using its other attribute values say *tabindex, size, maxlength,* etc. However, these are not reliable attributes for element identification. The reason being the value of *tabindex* can be changed by the developer anytime. Also, addition or deletion of new elements on the page can change the *tabindex* value. Other attributes are related to GUI look and feel attributes which are susceptible to change.

EXAMPLE 7.6 Locate the *Your Account* link as shown in Figure 7.1 using XPath locator

The HTML code of the *Your Account* link is:

```
<a href="/gp/css/homepage.html/ref=ap_frn_ya">Your Account</a>
```

The above HTML code defines the *href* attribute of the link element <a>. WebDriver code to locate this element using its *href* attribute value will be:

```
WebElement yourAccountLink = driver.findElement
  (By.XPath("//a[@ href='/gp/css/homepage.html/ref=ap_frn_ya']"));
```

EXAMPLE 7.7 Locate the image *Amazon* as shown in Figure 7.1 using XPath locator

The HTML code of the image is:

```
<img width="100" border="0" height="30" alt="Amazon"
  src="https://images-na.ssl.png"/>
```

The above HTML code defines the *alt, width, border, height* and *src* attributes of the image. WebDriver code to identify this element using its *alt* attribute will be:

```
WebElement amazonImage = driver.findElement
  (By.XPath("//a[@ alt='Amazon']"));
```

Note: Attributes *tabindex, height, size, width,* etc. need to be avoided for element identification. This is because the values of these attributes may vary from browser to browser. Also, these values can be changed by developer even in the absence of any valid change requirement.

7.2.5 | Finding Elements Using Multiple Attribute Values with XPath

In real-world scenario, one attribute may not be always sufficient enough to uniquely identify an element in a HTML page. In such situations, we can identify an element using multiple attribute values. The locator XPath is defined in such a way that it tries to locate the element by using more than one attribute values of the element. Example below demonstrates how to locate an element using multiple attribute values.

EXAMPLE 7.8 Locate the *Email Address* field element using multiple attribute values.

The HTML code for the *Email Address* field is:

```
<input id="ap_email" type="email" autocapitalize="off"
  autocorrect="off" tabindex="1" maxlength="128" size="30"
  value="" name="email"/>
```

WebDriver code to identify the element using its *id* and *name* attributes is:

```
WebElement emailAddress = driver.findElement(By.XPath("//input[@
  id='ap_email'][@name='email']"));
```

Also, WebDriver code to identify the element using its *id, name* and *type* attributes is:

```
WebElement emailAddress = driver.findElement(By.XPath("//input[@
  id='ap_email'] [@name='email'][@type='email'"));
```

EXAMPLE 7.9 Locate the third checkbox of Figure 7.5.

FIGURE 7.5 | Checkboxes

HTML code of the above checkboxes is:

```
<input id="id0" type="checkbox" value="1" name="country"/>US
<input id="id1" type="checkbox" value="1" name="country"/>CANADA
```

```
<input id="id2" type="checkbox" checked="true/" value="1"
  name="country"/>INDIA
<input id="id3" type="checkbox" value="1" name="country"/>JAPAN
<input id="id4" type="checkbox" checked="true/" value="1"
  name="country"/>UK
```

WebDriver code to identify the third checkbox using its *id, type* and *name* attribute will be:

```
WebElement checkbox = driver.findElement(By.XPath("//input[@
  type='checkbox'] [@id='id2'][@name='country'"));
```

7.2.6 | Finding Elements Using Partial Match of Attribute Values

(Use of Regular Expressions in Attribute Values)

In real-life scenario, there are many instances where attribute values of the elements change dynamically. For dynamic elements, every time the web page is opened, elements attribute values changes. Such elements whose attribute values change dynamically during run-time are called *dynamic elements*. One example would be *Order Confirmation Page* which displays order number message 'Order number is: 112345'. The complete string is dynamic as the order number will vary from one run to another. Another example could be a page displaying a list of recent five order numbers as link elements. Since the page will get updated with latest order numbers every time; the *linkText* attribute of order number link elements will change dynamically.

XPath, like CSS, provides the flexibility to locate elements matching partial attribute values. Table 7.3 explains the use of XPath partial match expressions:

TABLE 7.3 | XPath partial match expressions

Syntax	Objective	Example	Description
starts-with()	Identify element whose attribute value **starts with**<string>	Input[starts-with(@id, 'User')]	Locate `<input>` element whose *id* attribute value starts with text *User*. For example elements with id value as – Username, UserName, User123, User_Name, etc.
ends-with()	Identify element whose attribute value **ends with** <string>	Input[ends-with (@id, 'Name')]	Locate `<input>` element whose *id* attribute value ends with text *Name*. For example elements with id value as – firstUser, second_User, 1User, _User, etc.
contains()	Identify element whose attribute value **contains**<string>	Input[contains (@id, 'User')]	Locate `<input>` element whose *id* attribute contains string *User*. For example elements with id value as – firstUser, second_UserName, 1User123, _User2, etc.

EXAMPLE 7.10 Identify the order number link elements that is displayed on a web page as shown in Figure 7.6.

Order number	Date	Status
112453	07-Feb-2013	Shipped
110987	01-Jan-2013	Delivered
110567	31-Dec-2012	Delivered

FIGURE 7.6 | Dynamic link elements in a web page

Assume the HTML code of the link element 112453 is:

```
<a href="reforderID1=112453">112453</a>
<a href="reforderID2=110987">112453</a>
```

For the above link, method *linkText* to identify the link won't work as the text of the link will vary from one run to another. The *href* attribute of the link also cannot be used as it is, as it contains the order number. However, a partial match of *href* attribute value can be used to locate the link element. WebDriver code to identify this element can be:

```
WebElement orderNbr = driver.findElement(By.XPath("//a[starts-with(@
  href,'reforderID']"));
```

Note: Above code will locate the first link element that matches the attributes. In order to locate all elements that matches, method *findElements()* is to be used.

EXAMPLE 7.11 Find all the orders whose status is shipped in Figure 7.4.

Assume the HTML code of the shipped link is:

```
<a href="reforderID=112453/Details/Shipped">Shipped</a>
```

For the above HTML code, we observe that the end string of the *href* attribute is always 'shipped'. So this element can be identified using this string. WebDriver code to locate all *Shipped* links will be:

```
List <WebElement> shippedOrders = driver.findElements(By.XPath
("//a[contains(@href,Shipped]"));
```

EXAMPLE 7.12 Find all the order numbers displayed in Figure 7.4.

For the HTML code as discussed in Example 7.1, the WebDriver code to locate all order number link elements can be:

```
List<WebElement> orders = driver.findElements(By.XPath("//a[contains(@
  href,'reforderID']"));
```

EXAMPLE 7.13 Figure 7.7 shows an alert box which is opened on clicking button 'Open Alert Box'. Write code to click on the 'OK' button of alert box.

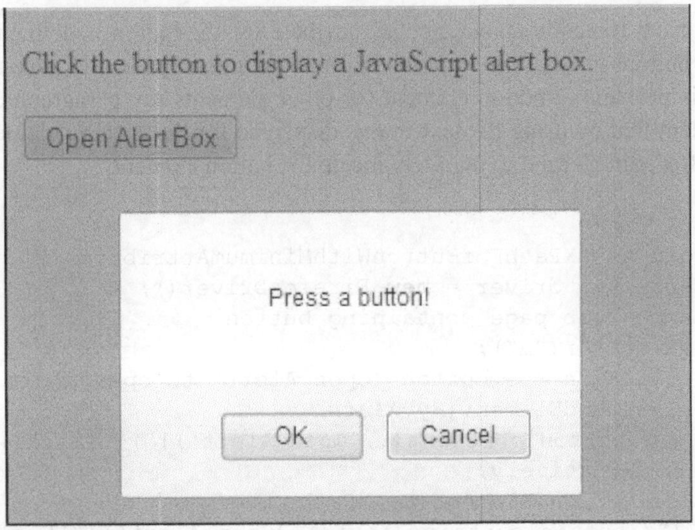

FIGURE 7.7 | XPath identifier for button

Assume HTML code of the page with button as shown below.

```
<!DOCTYPE html>
<html>
<body>
<p>Click the button to display a JavaScript alert box.</p>
<button onclick="functionShowAlertBox()">Open Alert Box</button>
<p id="alertBox"></p>
<script>
function functionShowAlertBox()
{
var x;
var r=confirm("Press a button!");
if (r==true)
  {
  x="You pressed OK!";
  }
else
  {
  x="You pressed Cancel!";
  }
document.getElementById("alertBox").innerHTML=x;
}
```

```
</script>
</body>
</html>
```

As evident from the code above, no 'id' attribute for the button is defined. If there are multiple such buttons in GUI, then it will be difficult to uniquely identify the button element. To resolve this problem, a button element (or other elements say paragraph element <p>) can also be identified by using the text that is displayed for the specific element. Here text 'Open Alert Box' can be used to uniquely locate the button element.

```
@Test
public void testXPathForButtonWithMinimumAttributes(){
        WebDriver driver = new FirefoxDriver();
        //open web page containing button
        driver.get("…");
        //click on the button 'Open Alert' to open alert box
        driver.findElement(By.XPath
          ("//button[contains(.,'Open Alert')]")).click();
        //Alternatively,
        //driver.findElement(By.XPath
          ("//button[contains(text(),'Open Alert')]")).click();

}
```

7.2.7 | Finding Elements Using Attribute Name with XPath

XPath provides the flexibility to locate elements using attribute names. This approach is bit different from the previous approach we just discussed. In the previous approach, we were using the attribute values to identify an element. In this approach, we would use attribute name to identify an element.

EXAMPLE 7.14 Find all the link elements whose *href* attribute is defined.

Code below shows how to find all <a> link elements whose *href* attribute is defined.

```
List<WebElement> elements = driver.findElements(By.XPath("//a[@
  href]"));
```

EXAMPLE 7.15 Find all the `<input>` elements whose *id* attribute is defined.

Code below shows how to find all `<input>` link elements whose *id* attribute is defined.

```
List<WebElement> elements = driver.findElements(By.XPath("//
  input[@id]"));
```

Example 7.16 Find all the elements whose *id* attribute is defined.

In order to locate all elements whose *id* attribute is defined, the tagname in the XPath can be replaced with '*' to denote all elements. Code below shows how to find all elements whose *id* attribute is defined.

```
List<WebElement> elements = driver.findElements(By.XPath("//*[@id]"));
```

7.2.8 | Finding Elements by Matching Any Attribute with a Value

XPath provides the flexibility to identify an element by matching any of the attributes of an element to an attribute value. For example, suppose requirement is to locate an `<input>` element whose any of the attribute values is 'password'. This can be achieved by replacing the attribute name with symbol '*' as shown below.

```
List<WebElement> elements = driver.findElements(By.XPath("//input[@*=
  'password']"));
```

Consider the HTML code below. The code contains 6 elements – 1 image element, 4 input elements and 1 link element.

```
<span id="amazonLogo">
<img width="100" border="0" height="30" alt="Amazon"
  src="https://img-amazon.png"/>
</span>
<input id="ap_email" type="email" autocapitalize="off"
  autocorrect="off" tabindex="1" maxlength="128" size="30"
  value="" name="email"/>
<input id="ap_password" class="password" type="password"
  tabindex="2" size="20" maxlength="1024" name="password"/>
<input id="checkbox1" type="checkbox" checked="true/" value="1"
  name="country"/>US
<input id="checkbox2" type="checkbox" checked="true/" value="1"
  name="country"/>UK
<a href="https://www.amazon.com/ap/forgotpassword">
  Forgot your password?</a>
```

Example 7.17 For the HTML code above, find the `<input>` element of whose attribute values is *ap_password*

The above HTML code has 4 input elements – 2 checkboxes and 2 text fields. The *Password* field has its *id* attribute value as *ap_password.* WebDriver code to locate this element is:

```
List element = driver.findElement(By.XPath("//input[@*=
  'ap_password']"));
```

The above code checks all the <input> elements and their attributes for any of their attribute values is *ap_password* and returns the matching element.

EXAMPLE 7.18 For the HTML code above, find an element any of whose attribute values is *ap_password*

The above HTML code has 6 elements – 1 image, 2 checkboxes 2 text fields and 1 link. The code below checks all the elements to see which element attribute value matches with value *ap_password* and then returns the matching element.

```
List element = driver.findElement(By.XPath("//*[@*='ap_password']"));
```

EXAMPLE 7.19 For the HTML code above, locate all the checkboxes

The above HTML code has two checkboxes. The *type* attribute value of both the checkboxes equals *checkbox*.

```
<input id="checkbox1" type="checkbox" checked="true/" value="1"
  name="country"/>US
<input id="checkbox2" type="checkbox" checked="true/" value="1"
  name="country"/>UK
```

WebDriver code to identify all checkboxes for above code can be:

```
List<WebElement> checkboxes = driver.findElements(By.XPath
  ("//*[@type='checkbox']"));
```

Alternatively,

```
List<WebElement> checkboxes = driver.findElements(By.XPath
  ("//*[@*='checkbox']"));
```

Also, we observe that the *name* attribute value of both the checkboxes equals *country*. This attribute value can also be used to locate these checkboxes.

```
List<WebElement> checkboxes = driver.findElements(By.XPath
  ("//*[@name='country']"));
```

7.2.9 | Finding Elements Using XPath Axis

An axis defines a node-set relative to the current node. An axis stores certain information about the context node or other nodes within the document tree. The information stored depends on the axis being used. For example, an axis called 'child' stores information about the children of the context node. Therefore, this axis can be used to select a child from the context node.

Consider the *Employee* table as shown in Figure 7.7. This table contains information about employee id, employee name and employee designation.

Employee ID	Employee Name	Designation
122768	Charles	Software Developer
122657	Joseph	Automation Developer

FIGURE 7.8 | Employee Web table in a web page

The HTML code of the above table is as shown below.

```
<html>
<body>
<table>
<tr>
<td>Employee ID</td>
<td>Employee Name</td>
<td>Designation</td>
</tr>
<tr>
<td>122768</td>
<td>Charles</td>
<td>
<input id="id1" type="text" name="designation"
  value="Software Developer"/>
</td>
</tr>
<tr>
<td>122657</td>
<td>Joseph</td>
<td>
<input id="id2"type="text" name="designation"
  value="Automation Developer"/>
</td>
</tr>
</table>
```

Figure 7.9 shows the DOM tree representation of the HTML elements.

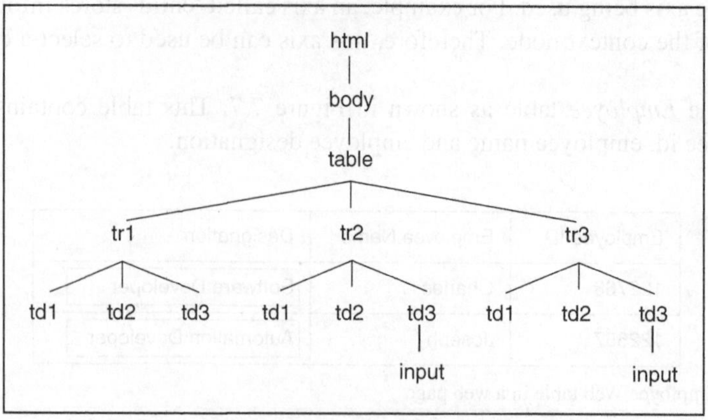

FIGURE 7.9 I DOM tree of the employee table

List of Axes

Figure 7.4 shows some of the XPath axes. There are many other axes which we can use within XPath expressions. Table 7.4 gives a list of the axes we can use with XPath.

TABLE 7.4 I XPath axes

Axis name	Description	Example	XPath expression
ancestor	Selects all ancestors (parent, grandparent,..) of the current node	Locates the row element which contains employee '122768' details (Or locate the parent element of the cell element '122768'. Parent element of this cell element is its row (row element)).	//td[text()='122768']/ancestor::tr. Alternatively, //td[contains(text(), '122768')]/ancestor::tr
		Locates the table which contains employee '122768' details	//td[text()='122768']/ancestor::table. Alternatively, //td[contains(text(), '122768')]/ancestor::table
ancestor-or-self	Selects all ancestors (parent, grandparent,..) of the current node and current node itself	Locates the row element which contains employee '122768' details	//td[text()='122768']/ancestor-or-self::tr
		Locates the table element which contains employee '122768' details	//td[text()='122768']/ancestor-or-self::table
		Locates the cell element which contains employee '122768' details	//td[text()='122768']/ancestor-or-self::td

(continued)

TABLE 7.4 | *(continued)*

Axis name	Description	Example	XPath expression
attribute	Selects all the attributes of the current node	Locates the *value* attribute of the <input> field *Designation*	//td[text()='122768']/attribute::value
child	Selects all children of the current node	Locates all <input> child elements of the cell row=3, column=3	//table//tr[3]/td[3]/child::input
descendant	Selects all descendants (children, grandchildren,...) of the current node	Locates all the rows of the table	//table/descendant::tr
		Locates the third row of the table	//table/descendant::tr[3]
		Locates all the cells of column 3 of the table	//table/descendant::tr/td[3]
		Locates all the cells of the table	//table/descendant::td
		Locates all <input> child elements of the cell row=3, column=3	//table/descendant::td/input
descendant-or-self	Selects all descendants (children, grandchildren,..) of the current node and current node itself	Locates all the rows of the table	//table/descendant-or-self::tr
		Locates the cell element which contains employee '122768' details	//td[text()='122768']/descendant-or-self::td
following	Selects all nodes in the document after the closing tag of the current node	Locates all cells after the cell containing value '122768'	//td[text()='122768']/following::td
		Locates all the rows after the row containing cell value '122768'	//td[text()='122768']/following::tr
following-sibling	Selects all siblings of the current node	Locates all the sibling cells of the cell containing value '122768'	//td[text()='122768']/following-sibling::td
parent	Selects the parent node of the current node	Locates the cell that contains the <input> element with *id* attribute value equal to *id1*	//input[@id='d1']/parent::td Or, //input[@id='d1']/parent::*
		Locates the cell that contains the <input> element with *'value'* attribute value equal to *'Automation Developer'*	//input[@value='Automation Developer']/parent::td
		Locates the row that contains value '122768'	//td[text()='122768']/parent::tr

Axis name	Description	Example	XPath expression
preceding	Selects all nodes that appear before the current node	Selects the row element that precedes the row containing value '122768'	//td[text()='122768']/ preceding::tr
		Selects all the cells of the row element that precedes the row containing value '122768'	//td[text()='122768']/ preceding::td Or, //td[text()='122768']/ preceding::*
preceding-sibling	Selects all the sibling nodes before the current node	Selects all the cells of row 2 that precedes the cell 3,3	//table//tr[3]//td[3]/ preceding-sibling::td

EXAMPLE 7.20 For Figure 7.1, locate the element that precedes the *Password* field

XPath axis *preceding* can be used to find the preceding element. To locate all the preceding element, symbol '*' can be with *preceding* axis. 'findElement' method can be used to locate the first preceding element. Let us suppose the element that precedes the *Password* field is the radio button. WebDriver code to locate this radio button can be:

```
WebElement radioElement = driver.findElement(By.XPath("//input[@
  id='ap_password']//preceding::*"));
```

EXAMPLE 7.21 For Figure 7.1, locate all the elements that precedes the *Password* field

There are many elements preceding the *Password* field element. They are radio buttons, text fields, label elements, images, etc. 'findElements' method can be used to locate more than one element. WebDriver code to locate all elements that precede the *Password* field can be:

```
List<WebElement> elements = driver.findElements(By.XPath("//
  input[@id='ap_password']//preceding::*"));
```

EXAMPLE 7.22 For Figure 7.1, locate all the `<input>` elements that precede the *Password* field.

HTML tag name can be specified with the XPath axis *preceding* to locate all the `<input>` elements that precede an element.

For Figure 7.1, there are three `<input>` elements that precede the *Password* field. They are: 2 radio buttons and 1 Email Address field. WebDriver code to locate all these elements can be:

```
List<WebElement> inputElements = driver.findElements(By.XPath("//
  input[@id='ap_password']//preceding::input"));
```

EXAMPLE 7.23 For Figure 7.1, locate all the radio buttons that precede the *Password* field.

The requirement of the above example is to locate all the <input> elements with tag name radio that precede the Password element. This can be done by defining the attributes of the preceding element in the *preceding* XPath axis of the example above. That is, attribute value "type=radio" is to be defined in the *preceding* axis definition of the XPath expression.

For Figure 7.1, there are 2 radio buttons that precede the *Password* field. WebDriver code to locate all these elements can be:

```
List<WebElement> radioElements = driver.findElements(By.XPath("//
  input[@id='ap_password']//preceding::input[@type='radio']"));
```

INTERVIEW QUESTIONS

1. What is XPath? When to use XPath for locating elements?
2. Which location mechanism is faster CSS or XPath? Why?
3. Give an example how will you locate a dynamic element using XPath locator.
4. Develop XPath expression for locating 'Sign In' button of amazon.com page or Figure 7.1.
5. What is XPath axis?
6. When to use XPath axis for locating elements?

8 CHAPTER

User Interface Map

Selenium WebDriver API uses locator information to find elements on the page. Defining the locator information in classes may result in duplication of element location information in various classes. Because of such duplication, it becomes increasingly difficult to maintain tests as the size of the test suite increases. Any change in element locator information requires updating of the element locator information in all the classes wherever it has been defined. Identifying classes which requires update and then updating them is a very time consuming and difficult task. In short, change identification and change implementation becomes a nightmare.

One way to solve this problem is to use Page Object Model framework (Agile Automation Framework). In this framework, each page is used as a reusable class. All the elements of the page are defined in the same page class without any duplication. In order to avoid locator information duplication within the page class, the locator information is defined at the top of the page using `@FindBy` method.

Another way to resolve this problem is to create a repository which defines locator information of all the elements. This element repository is termed as *Object* or *UI Map*. A user interface (UI) Map helps in creating one-point maintenance framework for elements' locator information.

UI Maps are easier to maintain. Maintaining all locator information in one place also helps to avoid duplication of elements' locator information. Whenever a change to a specific elements' locator information is required, it can be easily identified and changed in the UI Map. Making changes in one file is much simpler and easier rather than making changes in multiple files (class files or tests). Since changes are to be done in one file, change identification and change implementation is easier. Also, the UI Map can be version controlled.

8.1 | CREATING SELENIUM EXTENSION FOR UI MAP USING PROPERTIES FILE

In the following section, we will discuss how to extend Selenium WebDriver to develop a UI Map for amazon.com site login page. Firstly, a UI Map can be any flat file or *.properties* file. Locator information can be defined as key-value pairs in the UI Map file. This UI Map can be imported in all the page class files which need to interact with application front-end.

8.1.1 | Defining Locator Information in UI Map

Let us first create a UIMap.properties file. The locator information can be added to this file as key-value pairs. Assume the format for defining key-value pairs to be:

```
[element_logical_name] = [locator_attribute_name] :: [locator_
  attribute_value]
```

Now let us define the locator information for amazon.com login page.

```
login.username.txtbox=id::ap_email
login.password.txtbox=id::ap_password
login.signin.button=id::signInSubmit
```

8.2 | CREATING A UIMAP CLASS TO READ LOCATORS FROM UIMap.properties FILE

Now we will build a UIMap class to access locator information from properties file.

```
import java.io.IOException;
import java.io.InputStream;
import java.util.Properties;

import org.openqa.selenium.By;

public class UIMap {

       public enum locateElementBy{id, name, className, tagName,
              linkText, partialLinkText, cssSelector, XPath};

       Properties prop;

       public UIMap(String uimapLocation){
              prop = new Properties();
              InputStream uimapFile = getClass().getResourceAsStream
                            (uimapLocation);
              try {
                     System.out.print(uimapLocation);
                     prop.load(uimapFile);
                     uimapFile.close();
              } catch (IOException e){
                     e.printStackTrace();
              }
       }
```

```
//get attribute name (locator) and attribute value
private String[] getLocatorInfo(String elementLogicalName){
      String[] locator = new String[2];

      //get locator info using logical name as key
      String locatorInfo = prop.getProperty(elementLogica
                            lName);

      //get locator_attribute_name and locator_attribute_value
      locator[0] = locatorInfo.split("::")[0];
      locator[1] = locatorInfo.split("::")[1];
      return locator;
}

//get the locator instance
public By locateBy(String elementLogicalName){
   By by = null;

   //get locator information
   String[] locator = this.getLocatorInfo(elementLogicalName);
   String identifyBy = locator[0];
   String attributeValue = locator[1];

   //return an instance of By class depending on
     locator_attribute_name
   if (identifyBy.equalsIgnoreCase(locateElementBy.id.toString()))
                  by = By.id(attributeValue);
   else if (identifyBy.equalsIgnoreCase(locateElementBy.
         name.toString()))
                  by = By.name(attributeValue);
   else if (identifyBy.equalsIgnoreCase(locateElementBy.
         className.toString()))
                  by = By.className(attributeValue);
   else if (identifyBy.equalsIgnoreCase(locateElementBy.
         tagName.toString()))
                  by = By.tagName(attributeValue);
   else if (identifyBy.equalsIgnoreCase(locateElementBy.
         linkText.toString()))
                  by = By.linkText(attributeValue);
   else if (identifyBy.equalsIgnoreCase(locateElementBy.
         partialLinkText.toString()))
                  by = By.partialLinkText(attributeValue);
   else if (identifyBy.equalsIgnoreCase(locateElementBy.
         cssSelector.toString()))
                  by = By.cssSelector(attributeValue);
   else if (identifyBy.equalsIgnoreCase(locateElementBy.
         XPath.toString()))
                  by = By.XPath(attributeValue);
```

```
            else logger.info("locator attribute name not found in
                UIMap file");

            return by;
        }
}
```

8.2.1 | Creating a Sample Test

Now let us create a sample test that would use the UIMap properties file and UIMap class file to locate elements.

Following example opens amazon.com login page and then uses UIMap file to locate login page elements.

```
@Test
public void testUIMap() {
        WebDriver driver = new FirefoxDriver();
        //open amazon.com login page
        driver.get("https://www.amazon.com/ap/signin......");

        //get uiMap properties file
        UIMap uiMap = new
                UIMap("/com/webdriver/ElementRepository/UIMap.properties");

        //enter user name
        driver.findElement(uiMap.locateBy("login.username.txtbox")).
          sendKeys("abc@gmail.com");
        //enter password
        driver.findElement(uiMap.locateBy("login.password.txtbox")).
          sendKeys("password");
        //click on sign in button
        driver.findElement(uiMap.locateBy("login.signin.button")).click();
}
```

8.3 | CREATING SELENIUM EXTENSION FOR UI MAP USING CLASS FILE

In the example above, we observe that there is no intellisense for inputting location information. This problem can be solved by defining locator information in a class file. The locator information can be defined as variables inside this class. Then an instance of this class can be created in the class where locator information needs to be used.

8.3.1 | Defining Locator Information

Following code shows UIMapInfo class that stores locator information of all elements.

```
public class UIMapInfo {
  public enum loginPage{
        EmailIDTxtbox("id::ap_email"),
        PasswordTxtbox("id::ap_password"),
        SubmitBtn("id::signInSubmit");

        private String locator;

        loginPage(String locator) {
        this.locator = locator;
     }
     public String getLocator () {
        return this.locator;
     }
  }
}
```

Note: Enumeration is to be defined for various pages. Each enumeration defines the required locators of the page.

8.4 | CREATING A UIMAP CLASS TO READ LOCATORS FROM UIMapInfo CLASS

Next we need to write UIMap class that would read location attributes from UIMapInfo class.

```
public class UIMap {

      public enum locateElementBy{id, name, className, tagName,
                linkText, partialLinkText, cssSelector,
                XPath};

            //get attribute name (locator) and attribute value
            private String[] getLocatorInfo(String
              uiMapInfoLocator){
            String[] locator = new String[2];

            //get locator info using logical name as key
            String locatorInfo = uiMapInfoLocator;

            //get locator_attribute_name and locator_attribute_value
            locator[0] = locatorInfo.split("::")[0];
            locator[1] = locatorInfo.split("::")[1];
            return locator;
     }
```

```
        //get the locator instance
public By locateBy(String elementLogicalName){
        By by = null;

        //get locator information
        String[] locator = this.getLocatorInfo(elementLogic
          alName);
        String identifyBy = locator[0];
        String attributeValue = locator[1];

        //return an instance of By class depending on locator_
          attribute_name
        if (identifyBy.equalsIgnoreCase(locateElement
           By.id.toString()))
                by = By.id(attributeValue);
        else if (identifyBy.equalsIgnoreCase(locateElement
              By.name.toString()))
                by = By.name(attributeValue);
        else if (identifyBy.equalsIgnoreCase(locateElement
              By.className.toString()))
                by = By.className(attributeValue);
        else if (identifyBy.equalsIgnoreCase(locateElement
              By.tagName.toString()))
                by = By.tagName(attributeValue);
        else if (identifyBy.equalsIgnoreCase(locateElement
              By.linkText.toString()))
                by = By.linkText(attributeValue);
        else if (identifyBy.equalsIgnoreCase(locateElement
              By.partialLinkText.toString()))
                by = By.partialLinkText(attributeValue);
        else if (identifyBy.equalsIgnoreCase(locateElement
              By.cssSelector.toString()))
                by = By.cssSelector(attributeValue);
        else if (identifyBy.equalsIgnoreCase(locateElement
              By.XPath.toString()))
                by = By.XPath(attributeValue);
        else logger.info("locator attribute name not found in
             UIMap file");

        return by;
    }
}
```

8.4.1 | Creating a Sample Test

Now let us create a sample test that would use the UIMap properties file and UIMap class file to locate elements.

Following example opens amazon.com login page and then uses UIMap file to locate login page elements.

```
@Test
public void testUIMap1() {
        WebDriver driver = new FirefoxDriver();
        //open amazon.com login page
        driver.get("https://www.amazon.com/ap/signin.......");

        //get uimap
        UIMap1 uimap = new UIMap1();
        //enter user name
        driver.findElement(uimap.locateBy(UIMapInfo.loginPage.
          EmailIDTxtbox.getLocator())).sendKeys("abc@gmail.com");
        driver.findElement(uimap.locateBy(UIMapInfo.loginPage.
          PasswordTxtbox.getLocator())).sendKeys("password");
        driver.findElement(uimap.locateBy(UIMapInfo.loginPage.
          SubmitBtn.getLocator())).click();
}
```

While writing the above code in eclipse, we can observe that we can select the appropriate locator using eclipse intellisense when we use a dot (.) operator on UIMapInfo class as shown in Figures 8.1 and 8.2.

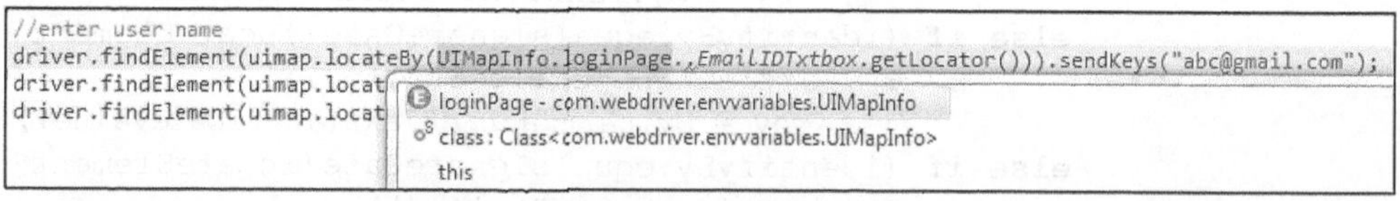

FIGURE 8.1 | Eclipse intellisense for selecting locator

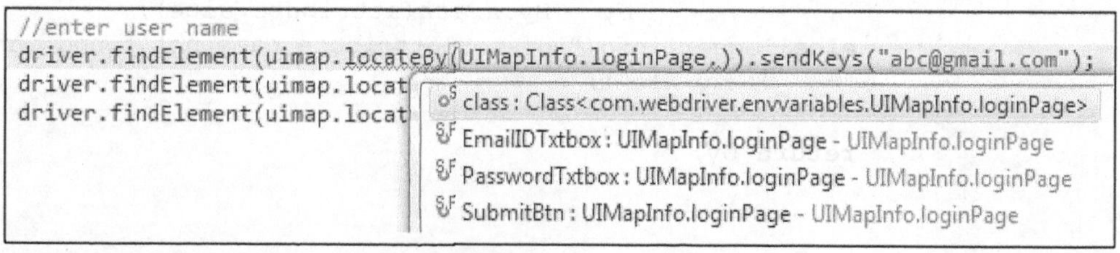

FIGURE 8.2 | Eclipse intellisense for selecting locator

9

CHAPTER

Working with Browsers

A web browser is a software application that allows users to retrieve, present and traverse information resources on the World Wide Web. An information resource is identified by a Uniform Resource Identifier (URI). The information may be a web page, image, audio, video or any other content. The first web browser was invented in 1990 by Sir Tim Berners-Lee. It was called WorldWideWeb (no spaces) and was later renamed as Nexus. There are various browsers available in the market as of now. These include internet explorer, chrome, firefox, safari, opera, etc. This chapter describes how to use WebDriver methods to simulate user actions on a firefox browser.

9.1 | INTRODUCTION

WebDriver supports multiple browsers for test execution. At the time of writing of the book, it supports Google Chrome 12; Internet Explorer 6,7,8,9 (both 32 bit and 64 bit); Firefox 3, 4, 5, 6, 7, 8, . . . 22, 23 and Opera 11.5+

- **Open Firefox Browser:** WebDriver provides `FirefoxDriver()` class to open a new Firefox browser session. Following code shows how to create an instance of `FirefoxDriver()` and open www.google.com site.

```
//create an instance of firefox driver
WebDriver driver = new FirefoxDriver();
//Open google.com site
driver.get("http://www.google.com");
```

- **Open Chrome Browser:** WebDriver provides `ChromeDriver()` class to open a new Chrome browser session. Following code shows how to create an instance of `ChromeDriver()` and open www.google.com site.

```
//create an instance of chrome driver
WebDriver driver = new ChromeDriver();
//Open google.com site
driver.get("http://www.google.com");
```

- **Open Internet Explorer Browser:** WebDriver provides *InternetExplorerDriver()* class to open a new IE browser session. Following code shows how to create an instance of *InternetExplorerDriver()* and open www.google.com site.

```
//create an instance of internet explorer driver
WebDriver driver = new InternetExplorerDriver();
//Open google.com site
driver.get("http://www.google.com");
```

9.2 | WEBDRIVER BROWSER METHODS

WebDriver provides a variety of methods to simulate user actions on a browser. Some of those methods are described below.

9.2.1 | get

Loads a new page in the current browser window. This is achieved using HTTP GET operation. This method blocks the WebDriver test execution until the page load is complete.

syntax	void get(java.lang.String url)
parameters	url - URL of the site to navigate to
returns	void

EXAMPLE 9.1 Write WebDriver code to open Firefox browser and navigate to http://www.google.com site

Following code shows how to launch a new Firefox browser session and open google.com site in this browser

```
//create an instance of firefox driver
WebDriver driver = new FirefoxDriver();
//Open google.com site
driver.get("http://www.google.com");
```

9.2.2 | getCurrentUrl

Returns the current URL of the browser page

syntax	java.lang.String getCurrentUrl()
parameters	
returns	URL of the page currently loaded in the browser

EXAMPLE 9.2 Write code to open Firefox browser, navigate to google.com site and then verify that the current page is google.com site

```
WebDriver driver = new FirefoxDriver();
//Open google.com site
String openURL = "http://www.google.com";
```

```
driver.get(openURL);
//get current url
String currentURL = driver.getCurrentUrl();
//is current url a google.com site
Boolean isCurrentURLCorrect = currentURL.equalsIgnoreCase(openURL);
//pass test if condition is true else fail the test and exit current
  test
//execution
Assert.assertTrue("Google page is not loaded. Expected:" + openURL + "::
  Actual:" + isCurrentURLCorrect , isCurrentURLCorrect);
```

9.2.3 | getTitle

Returns the title of the current web page

syntax	java.lang.String getTitle()
parameters	
returns	The title of the current web page, with leading and trailing whitespace stripped, or null if one is not already set

Example 9.3 Write code to open Firefox browser, navigate to google.com site and verify that the current page title is correct or not.

```
String googlePageTitle = "google.com - Google Search";
//Open google.com site
driver.get("http://www.google.com");
//get current url
String currentPageTitle = driver.getTitle();
//is current page title correct
Boolean isCurrentPageTitleCorrect= currentPageTitle.equalsIgnore
  Case(googlePageTitle);
//pass test if condition is true else fail the test and exit
  current test
//execution
Assert.assertTrue("Google page is not loaded. Expected:" +
  googlePageTitle + ":: Actual:" + currentPageTitle, isCurrent
  PageTitleCorrect);
```

9.2.4 | findElements

Finds all the matched elements in the current page. This method continuously tries to identify the elements till zero or more elements are found or timeout time is reached, whichever happens first.

syntax	`java.util.List<WebElement> findElements(By by)`
parameters	`by - The locating mechanism to use`
returns	`The list of all matched elements or an empty list if no match is found`

EXAMPLE 9.4 Find all the link elements of a web page.

All the link elements have tag name 'a'. Therefore, method *tagName* can be used to identify all link elements in a web page. WebDriver code to locate all link elements of a page is shown below:

```
List<WebElement> linkElements = driver.findElements(By.tagName("a"));
```

Note: Interface `WebDriver.Timeouts` is to be used to configure the timeout time of element recognition.

9.2.5 | findElement

Finds the first matched WebElement in the current web page. This method continuously tries to identify the element till the element is found or timeout time is reached, whichever happens first. If no matched element is found till timeout time, then it returns an exception. This method implicitly waits to identify the element until the configured timeout is reached.

syntax	`WebElement findElement(By by)`
parameters	`by - The locating mechanism to use`
returns	`The first matched WebElement, else throws NoSuchElementException if no matched element is found`

EXAMPLE 9.5 Find the first link element of a web page

All the link element have tag name as 'a'. Therefore, method *tagName* can be used to identify all link elements in a web page. WebDriver code to locate the first link element of a page is shown below:

```
WebElement linkElements = driver.findElement(By.tagName("a"));
```

Note: Interface `WebDriver.Timeouts` is to be used to configure the timeout time of element recognition.

9.2.6 | getPageSource

Returns the page source of the last loaded page. The page source returned is a representation of the underlying DOM. It may not be formatted or escaped in the same way as the response sent from the server.

syntax	java.lang.String getPageSource()
parameters	
returns	The page source of the current page

EXAMPLE 9.6 Write code to open google.com page and retrieve its page source

```
driver.get("http://www.google.com");
//get page source
String pageSource = driver.getPageSource();
```

Note: If the page is modified after page reload (e.g. page refresh after selecting some list box options), then there is no guarantee that the returned page source text is of the reloaded page. WebDriver documentation can be referenced to know the exact behaviour of the specific driver.

9.2.7 | navigate

Simulates browser back, forward, refresh and navigate to options.

syntax	WebDriver.Navigation navigate()
parameters	
returns	A WebDriver.Navigation that allows the selection of what to do next

This method allows WebDriver test scripts to simulate user interactions with browsers such as navigating to specific URL, clicking on browser back or forward button, clicking on browser refresh button, etc. Table 9.1 describes the various browser navigation methods.

TABLE 9.1 | Browser navigation methods

Method	Description	Example
back()	Simulates user click on browser Back button	`driver.navigate().back()`
forward()	Simulates user click on browser Forward button	`driver.navigate().forward()`
refresh()	Simulates user click on browser Refresh button	`driver.navigate().back()`
to(<URL>)	Simulates user click on browser Go button after specifying the URL	`driver.navigate().to(<URL>)`

EXAMPLE 9.7 Suppose user opens amazon.com site and then navigates to google.com site. Then user clicks on the browser back button to navigate back to the amazon.com site. Write a WebDriver code for the same.

navigate.to() method can be used to navigate to another web page while *navigate().back()* method can be used to simulate user click on browser Back button.

```
WebDriver driver = new FirefoxDriver();
driver.get("http://www.amazon.com");
//navigate to google.com on the same browser
driver.navigate().to("http://www.google.com");
//click on browser back button
driver.navigate().back();
```

9.2.8 | getWindowHandles

Returns all browser windows of the WebDriver instance.

syntax	java.util.Set<java.lang.String> getWindowHandles()
parameters	
returns	A set of window handles which can be used to iterate over all the open windows

EXAMPLE 9.8 Suppose user opens amazon.com login page and then clicks on the link *Conditions of use* which opens another browser page *Amazon.com Help: Conditions of use* as shown in Figure 9.1. Write a code to find the page title of both of these browser windows.

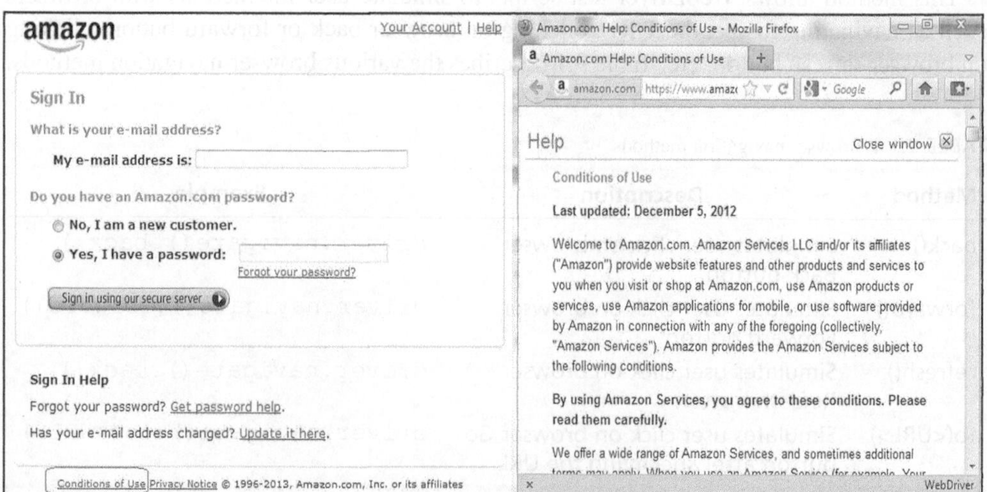

FIGURE 9.1 | Amazon.com login page and terms and conditions page

```
WebDriver driver = new FirefoxDriver();
//open amazon.com site
driver.get("http://www.amazon.com");
//navigate to login page
driver.findElement(By.id("nav-your-account")).click();
//click on the link - conditions of use.
//this opens another browser window.
driver.findElement(By.linkText("Conditions of Use")).click();
//get the browser windows open
Set<String> openedBrowserHandles = driver.getWindowHandles();
//print the page title name of all open browsers
for(String browserHandle:openedBrowserHandles){
      String browserTitle = driver.switchTo().
        window(browserHandle).getTitle();
      System.out.println("Browser Title:"+browserTitle);
}
```

9.2.9 | getWindowHandle

Returns the current active browser window of the WebDriver instance.

syntax	java.lang.String getWindowHandle()
parameters	
returns	Returns the currently active window handle. This can be used to switch to this browser at a later time when more than one browsers are open

EXAMPLE 9.9 Suppose user opens amazon.com login page and then clicks on the link *Conditions of use* which opens another browser page *Amazon.com Help: Conditions of use* as shown in Figure 9.2. Write code to retrieve the page title of the new browser session and then switch back the driver context to the previous browser session.

```
WebDriver driver = new FirefoxDriver();
//open amazon.com site
driver.get("http://www.amazon.com");
//navigate to login page
driver.findElement(By.id("nav-your-account")).click();
//get the window handle of the current browser session
String firstBrowserHandle = driver.getWindowHandle();
//click on the link - conditions of use.
//this opens another browser window.
driver.findElement(By.linkText("Conditions of Use")).click();
//get the browser windows open
Set<String> openedBrowserHandles = driver.getWindowHandles();
//print the page title name of all open browsers
```

```
for(String browserHandle:openedBrowserHandles){
      String browserTitle = driver.switchTo().window(browserHandle).
        getTitle();
      System.out.println("Browser Title:"+browserTitle);
}
//switch focus to the previous browser session
driver = driver.switchTo().window(firstBrowserHandle);
```

Figure 9.2 shows the output of above code as seen on Eclipse console window.

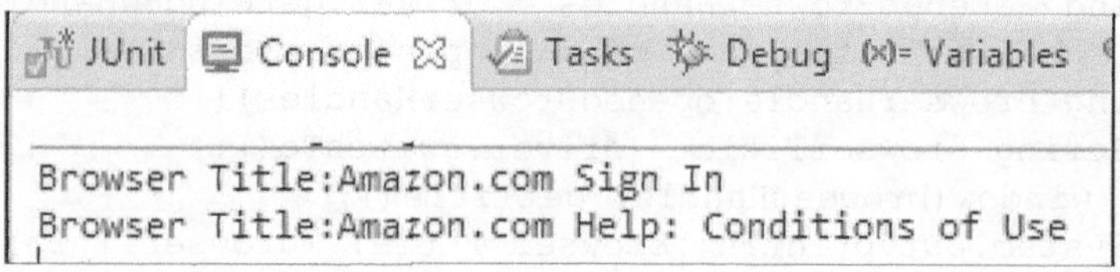

FIGURE 9.2 | Eclipse console tab

9.2.10 | switchTo

Switches focus of the driver instance to a specific browser or frame when multiple browsers/ frames are associated with the driver instance.

syntax	`WebDriver.TargetLocator switchTo()`
parameters	
returns	A TargetLocator which can be used to switch driver instance focus to a specific frame or window

WebDriver provides the flexibility to switch driver instance focus to any of the browser windows or frames associated with the driver instance. Table 9.2 lists some of the methods associated with `switchTo()` method to switch driver instance focus.

TABLE 9.2 | Methods associated with `switchTo()` method to switch driver instance focus

Method	Description	Example
window(<Window Name>)	Switches the driver instance focus to the window with the specified name	`driver.switchTo().window("Google - Search")`
activeElement()	Switches the driver instance focus to the element that has focus. If no element on the web page has focus then the driver instance focus is set to the body element.	`driver.switchTo().activeElement()`

(continued)

TABLE 9.2 | *(continued)*

Method	Description	Example

alert()	Switches the focus of the driver instance to the alert box. The alert box can be accepted or dismissed.	`driver.switchTo().alert().accept()`
		Or,
		`driver.switchTo().alert().dismiss()`

frame(<Name or Id Or Index Or WebElement>)	Switches the focus of the driver instance to a frame using either its' name, id or index attribute.	`driver.switchTo().frame(<frameIndex>)`
		Or,
		`driver.switchTo().frame(<frameName>)`
		Or,
		`driver.switchTo().frame(<frameID>)`
		Or,
		`driver.switchTo().frame(<WebElement>)`

defaultContent()	Switches the focus of the driver instance to the first frame on the page, or the main document when a page contains iframes	`driver.switchTo().defaultContent();`

Example 9.10 Suppose user opens amazon.com login page and then clicks on the link *Conditions of use* which opens another browser page *Amazon.com Help: Conditions of use* as shown in Figure 9.3. Write code to close the newly opened browser window and then switch driver context to the previously opened browser page.

```
WebDriver driver = new FirefoxDriver();
//open amazon.com site
driver.get("http://www.amazon.com");
//navigate to login page
driver.findElement(By.id("nav-your-account")).click();
//get the window handle of the current browser session
String firstBrowserHandle = driver.getWindowHandle();
//click on the link - conditions of use.
//this opens another browser window.
driver.findElement(By.linkText("Conditions of Use")).click();
//get the browser windows open
Set<String> openedBrowserHandles = driver.getWindowHandles();
//switch driver context to the latest opened browser window
for(String browserHandle:openedBrowserHandles){
    driver = driver.switchTo().window(browserHandle);
```

```
}
//close the last opened browser
driver.close();
//switch focus to the previous browser session
driver = driver.switchTo().window(firstBrowserHandle);
```

Example 9.11 Write code to switch browser context using browser index value when multiple browsers are opened.

A method can be written that takes browser index as input parameter and then switches driver focus to that browser. Method `switchToByIndex` takes WebDriver instance and browser index value as input parameters. This method iterates through all the open browser windows to find the matching browser index. Once the matching browser index is found, it switches WebDriver driver instance focus to the matched browser and then returns this driver instance.

```
@Test
public void testSwitchBrowserByIndex(){
        WebDriver driver = new FirefoxDriver();
        driver.get("http://www.amazon.com");
        driver.findElement(By.id("nav-your-account")).click();
        //click on the link - conditions of use
        //this opens another browser window.
        driver.findElement(By.linkText("Conditions of Use")).click();
        //set the current driver instance context to second browser
        //browser opened first has index value=0
        driver = this.switchToByIndex(driver, 1);
        System.out.println(driver.getTitle());
}
private WebDriver switchToByIndex(WebDriver driver, int index){
        int browserIndex=0;
        //get the browser windows open. First browser has index value=0
        Set<String> windowHandles = driver.getWindowHandles();
        for(String browserHandle:windowHandles){
                browserIndex = browserIndex + 1;
                if (browserIndex==index){
                        driver = driver.switchTo().window(browserHandle);
                        break;
                }
        } return driver;
}
```

Figure 9.3 shows the output of above code as visible on Eclipse console window.

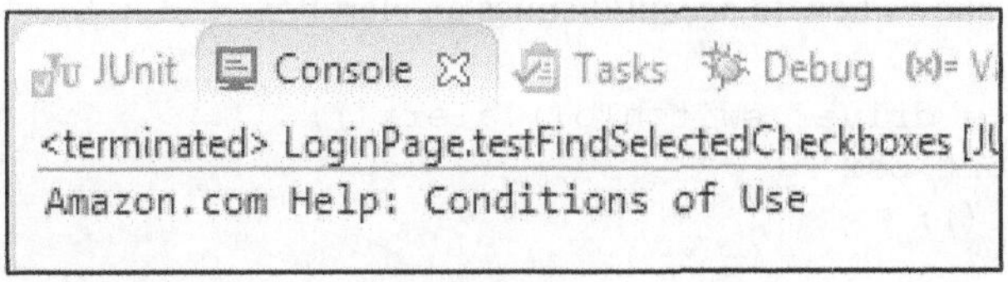

FIGURE 9.3 | Eclipse console tab

Note: Browser which is opened first has index value=0, browser opened next has value =1 and so on.

EXAMPLE 9.12 Write code to switch browser context using browser page title name when multiple browsers are opened.

This can be achieved by writing a method that iterates over all the browsers to find the browser that matches the specified browser page title and switches the driver focus to the matched browser. Method mentioned in the above example can be modified as shown below to implement the same.

```
private WebDriver switchToByPageTitle(WebDriver driver, String
        pageTitle){
    //get the browser windows open. First browser has index value=0
    Set<String> windowHandles = driver.getWindowHandles();
    for(String browserHandle:windowHandles){
        String currentPageTitle =
            driver.switchTo().window(browserHandle).getTitle();
        if (currentPageTitle.contains(pageTitle)) {
            driver = driver.switchTo().window(browserHandle);
            break;
        }
    }
    return driver;
}
```

EXAMPLE 9.13 Consider the alert boxes shown in Figure 9.4. Write code to accept/dismiss these alert boxes

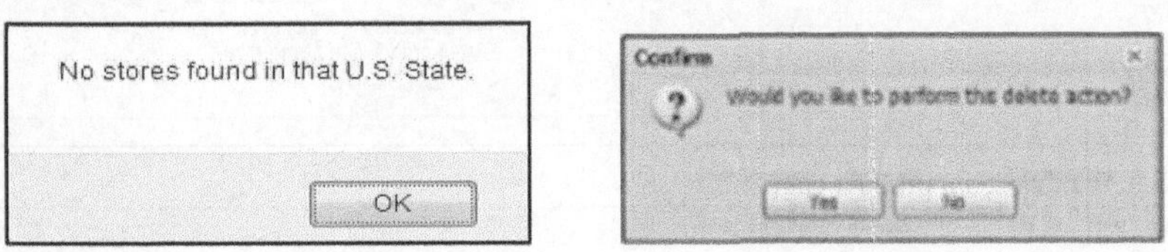

FIGURE 9.4 | (a) Alert box 1 and (b) Alert box 2

Following code shows how to accept/dismiss an alert box.

```
Alert alert = driver.switchTo().alert();
//accept alert box
alert.accept();

//dismiss alert box
//alert.dismiss();
```

EXAMPLE 9.14 Suppose on walmart.com user searches store availability of a product as shown in Figure 9.5. Figure 9.5 shows the product page. Users can specify the zipcode to locate stores that has this product. On clicking on *Find* button on this page, a frame opens which shows the list of stores available in that area. Figure 9.6 shows this frame. Write WebDriver code to switch driver instance context to this frame.

Assume HTML code of the frame is:

```
<iframe id="mpi_iframe" src="about:blank" name="mpi_iframe"
style="display:none"></iframe>
```

FIGURE 9.5 | Walmart.com product page

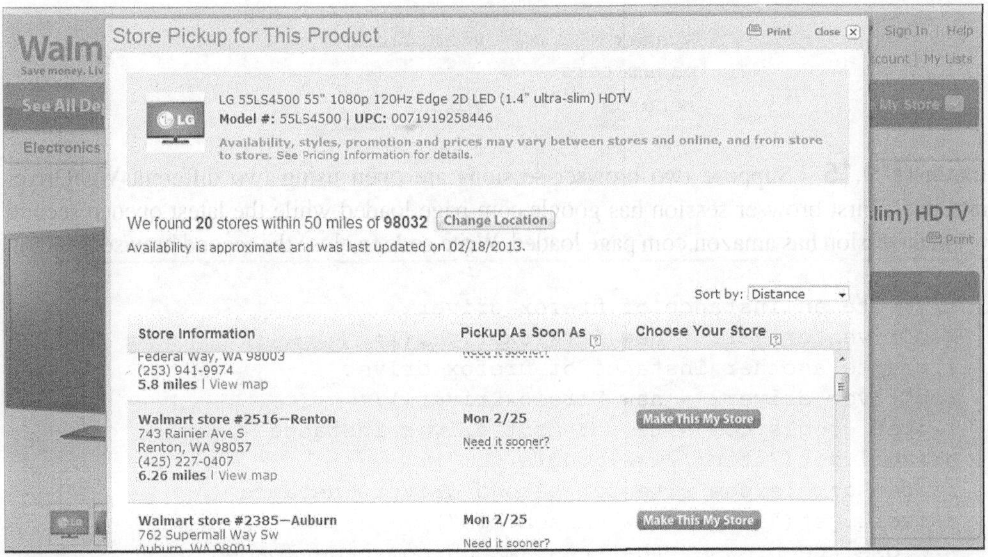

FIGURE 9.6 | Walmart.com store locator frame

WebDriver code to switch driver instance context to this frame is:

```
WebDriver driver = new FirefoxDriver();
//open product page
driver.get(“http://www.walmart.com/ip/LG-55LS4500-55-1080p-
  120Hz-Edge-2D-LED-1.4-ultra-slim-HDTV/21693004”);
//enter the zipcode to locate stores
driver.findElement(By.cssSelector(“input#s2s_zip”)).sendKeys(“98032”);
//click on the find stores button
driver.findElement(By.id(“SPUL_OVERLAY_LINK”)).click();
//switch driver instance context to the frame using frame name
driver = driver.switchTo().frame(“mpi_iframe”);
//Alternatively,frame id can also be used
//driver = driver.switchTo().frame(“mpi_iframe”);

//Alternatively,frame index can also be used. Index value starts with 0
//driver = driver.switchTo().frame(0);
```

9.2.11 | Close

Closes the current browser window. Closes the browser session, if it is the last browser window that is open.

syntax	void close()
parameters	
returns	void

EXAMPLE 9.15 Suppose two browser sessions are open using two different WebDriver instances. First browser session has google.com page loaded while the latest opened second browser session has amazon.com page loaded. Write code to close the second browser session.

```
//create an instance of firefox driver
WebDriver driver1 = new FirefoxDriver();
//create another instance of firefox driver
WebDriver driver2 = new FirefoxDriver();
//open google.com site for first driver instance
driver1.get("http://www.google.com");
//open google.com site for second driver instance
driver2.get("http://www.amazon.com");
//close the browser that has amazon.com page loaded
driver2.close();
```

9.2.12 | quit

Quits the driver instance and closes all browser windows associated with it.

syntax	void quit()
parameters	
returns	void

EXAMPLE 9.16 Write code to open google.com site and then close the browser session.

```
WebDriver driver = new FirefoxDriver();
driver.get("http://www.google.com");
//quit the current driver instance and close all the associated
  browsers
driver.quit();
```

9.2.13 | manage

Gets the *Option* interface.

syntax	WebDriver.Options manage()
parameters	
returns	An option interface

Options interface provides methods to manage various browser options such as fetching cookie details, adding cookies, deleting cookies, setting WebDriver timeouts, etc. Table 9.3 shows the various methods of the *Options* interface.

TABLE 9.3 | Various methods of the *Options* interface

Method	Description	Return Type
addCookies(Cookie cookie)	Add a specific cookie	void
deleteAllCookies()	Delete all cookies for the current browser session	void
deleteCookie(Cookie cookie)	Delete a cookie from the browser's 'cookie jar'	void
deleteCookieNamed(<cookie name>)	Delete the specific cookie	void
getCookieNamed(<cookie name>)	Get a cookie with a given name	Cookie
getCookies()	Get all cookies for the current browser session	Java.util.Set<Cookie>
ime()	Returns the interface for controlling IME engines to generate complex-script input	WebDriver.ImeHandler
timeouts()	Returns the interface for managing driver timeouts.	WebDriver.Timeouts

Chapter 14 describes in detail all the cookie-related methods discussed above.

Method `timeouts()` mentioned in the above table is used allows user to specify WebDriver timeout time, page load timeout time and script timeout time. These have been described in detail in Chapter 15.

9.3 | MAXIMIZING THE BROWSER WINDOW

WebDriver provides *maximize()* method to maximize the browser window. This method is defined in the *window* interface of the *driver* class. Following code shows how to maximize the browser window.

```
WebDriver driver = new FirefoxDriver();
driver.manage().window().maximize();
```

The *window* interface also provides methods to get/set the browser window size, state, etc.

INTERVIEW QUESTIONS

1. Write code to open amazon.com site against Chrome browser.
2. Which method you will use to retrieve browser URL and title of the page?
3. List browser navigation methods.
4. How will you automate user actions against a page frame?
5. Does WebDriver provides flexibility to define browser settings (such as add-ons to load) before launching the browser? Specify the interface which offers this feature.

10 CHAPTER

Working with Browser Elements

A web application consists of many elements such as the text box, buttons, list box, links, radio buttons and checkbox. WebDriver provides methods `findElement` and `findElements` to locate elements on a web page. Table 10.1 shows some of the standard elements.

TABLE 10.1 Page elements

Text Box
Button
Link
Image
Checkbox
Radio Button
List Box
Web Table
Frame

Figure 10.1 shows the account registration page of amazon.com site. We will use amazon.com account registration page for explanation throughout this chapter. WebDriver code to open this page is

```
WebDriver driver = new FirefoxDriver();
driver.get("http://www.amazon.com");
//click on sign in link
driver.findElement(BylinkText("Sign in")).click();
//get the Email Address field element
WebElement emailAddressElement = driver.findElement(By.id
  ("ap_email"));
```

10.1 | WORKING WITH TEXT BOX

Text boxes are the input field elements of a web page.

FIGURE 10.1 | Create new account page of amazon.com site

EXAMPLE 10.1 Write WebDriver code to enter text 'abc@gmail.com' in the *Email Address* field.

FIGURE 10.2 | Text box element

Consider the HTML code of the *Email Address* input field is:

```
<input id="ap_email" type="email" autocapitalize="off" autocorrect=
  "off" tabindex="1" maxlength="128" size="30" value=""
  name="email"/>
```

WebDriver code to enter text on the *Email Address* field can be:

```
driver.findElement(By.id("ap_email")).sendKeys("abc@gmail.com");
```

Alternatively,

```
emailAddressElement.sendKeys("abc@gmail.com");
```

10.1.1 | WebDriver Methods for Text Box Element

WebDriver provides various methods to clear text box field, enter text to input field, retrieve input field attribute values, etc. Some of these methods are described below.

sendKeys

This method simulates typing into an element which may set its value.

Syntax: `void sendKeys(CharSequence... keysToSend)`

EXAMPLE 10.2 Write WebDriver code to enter text 'abc@gmail.com' in the *Email Address* field.

```
driver.findElement(By.id("ap_email")).sendKeys("abc@gmail.com");
```

clear

This method clears the values of the text element

Syntax: `void clear()`

EXAMPLE 10.3 Write WebDriver code to clear the text entered on the *Email Address* by the example mentioned above.

```
driver.findElement(By.id("ap_email")).clear();
```

getText

This method retrieves the *innertext* of the element without any leading or trailing whitespace. It returns a String object.

Syntax: `String getText()`

EXAMPLE 10.4 User enters some text say 'abc@gmail.com' on the *Email Address* field. Write code to retrieve the value of this text field.

```
//enter text to the Email Address field
driver.findElement(By.id("ap_email")).sendKeys("abc@gmail.com");
//retrieve the value of the Email Address field
String emailFieldValue = driver.findElement(By.id("ap_email")).getText();
System.out.println("Email field value:" + emailFieldValue);
//Output:: Email field value: abc@gmail.com
```

getTagName

The method retrieves the tag name of the element. It returns a String object.

Syntax: `String getTagName()`

EXAMPLE 10.5 Write code to retrieve the tag name of the *Email Address* field element.

```
//get Email Address field element
WebElement emailAddressElement = driver.findElement(By.id("ap_
  email"));
//get tag name of the Email Address element
String emailFieldTagName = emailAddressElement.getTagName();
System.out.println("Email field tag name:" + emailFieldTagName);
//Output:: Email field tag name:input
```

getLocation

This method retrieves the (x, y) coordinates of the element. It returns *Point* object.

Syntax: `Point getLocation()`

EXAMPLE 10.6 Write code to retrieve the (x, y) coordinates of the *Email Address* field element.

```
//get the Point location object of Email Address field
Point point = emailAddressElement.getLocation();
System.out.println("X coordinate:" + point.x);
//Output:: X coordinate:417
System.out.println("Y coordinate:" + point.y);
//Output:: Y coordinate:143
```

getSize

This method retrieves the height and width of the element. It returns Dimension object.

Syntax: `Dimension getSize()`

EXAMPLE 10.7 Write code to retrieve the height and width of the *Email Address* field element.

```
//get the Dimension object of Email Address field
Dimension dimension = emailAddressElement.getSize();
System.out.println("Height:" + dimension.height);
//Output::Height:18
System.out.println("Width:" + dimension.width);
//Output::Width:234
```

getCSSValue

This method retrieves the CSS values of the element. It returns a *String* object. Figure 10.3 shows the CSS values of the *Email Address* field element.

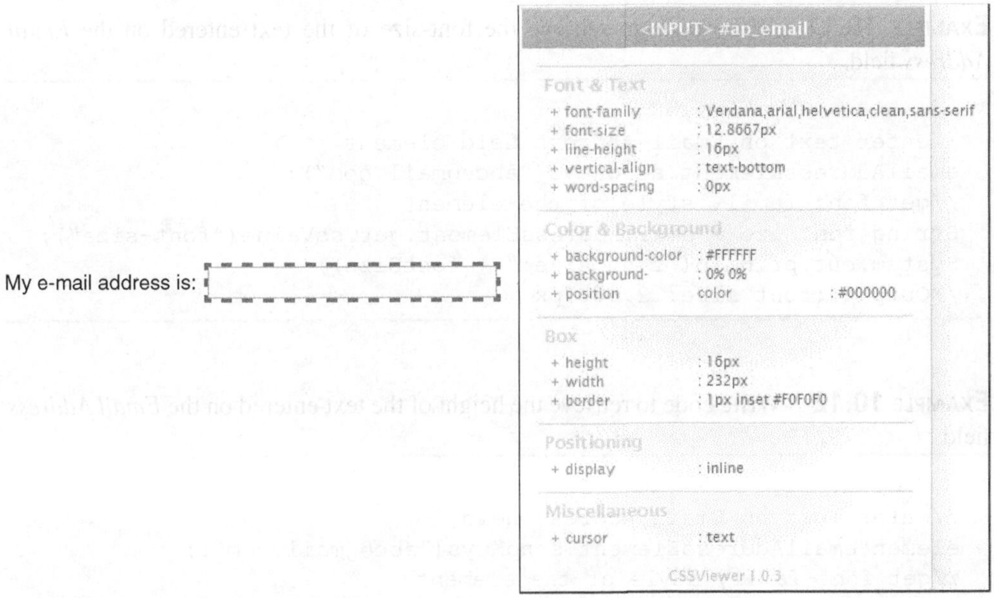

FIGURE 10.3 | CSS styles of *Email Address* input element

EXAMPLE 10.8 Write code to find the colour of the *Email Address* field element.

```
//get color of the element
String color = emailAddressElement.getCssValue("color");
System.out.println("Color:" + color);
//Output::Color:rgba(0, 0, 0, 1)
```

EXAMPLE 10.9 Write code to find the background colour of the *Email Address* field element.

```
//get background color of the element
String bgcolor = emailAddressElement.getCssValue("background-color");
System.out.println("Background color:" + bgcolor);
//Output::Background color:rgba(255, 255, 255, 1)
```

EXAMPLE 10.10 Write code to retrieve the font-family of the text entered on the *Email Address* field.

```
//enter text on Email Address field element
emailAddressElement.sendKeys("abc@gmail.com");
//get font-family style of the element
String fontFamily = emailAddressElement.getCssValue("font-family");
System.out.println("font family:" + fontFamily);
//Output::font family:Verdana,arial,helvetica,clean,sans-serif
```

EXAMPLE 10.11 Write code to retrieve the font-size of the text entered on the *Email Address* field.

```
//enter text on Email Address field element
emailAddressElement.sendKeys("abc@gmail.com");
//get font-family style of the element
String fontSize = emailAddressElement.getCssValue("font-size");
System.out.println("font size:" + fontSize);
//Output::font size:12.8667px
```

EXAMPLE 10.12 Write code to retrieve the height of the text entered on the *Email Address* field.

```
//enter text on Email Address field
elementemailAddressElement.sendKeys("abc@gmail.com");
//get font-family style of the element
String height = emailAddressElement.getCssValue("height");
System.out.println("Height:" + height);
//Output::Height:16px
```

getAttribute

This method retrieves the attribute value of the given attribute. It returns String object.

Syntax: `String getAttribute(String)`

Suppose the HTML code of the *Email Address* field element is:

```
<input id="ap_email" type="email" autocapitalize="off" autocorrect="off"
  tabindex="1" maxlength="128" size="30" value="" name="email"/>
```

EXAMPLE 10.13 Write code to retrieve attribute values of the various attributes of the *Email Address* field element.

```
//retrieve text value entered on the Email Address field
String valueBefore = emailAddressElement.getAttribute("value");
System.out.println("value before entering any text:" + valueBefore);
//Output::value before entering any text:

//enter text to Email Address field
emailAddressElement.sendKeys("webdriver@gmail.com");
```

```
//retrieve text value entered on the Email Address field
String valueAfter = emailAddressElement.getAttribute("value");
System.out.println("value after entering text:" + valueAfter);
//Output::value after entering text:webdriver@gmail.com

//retrieve 'id' attribute value of the element
String id = emailAddressElement.getAttribute("id");
System.out.println("id:" + id); //Output::id:ap_email
//retrieve 'name' attribute value of the element
String name = emailAddressElement.getAttribute("name");
System.out.println("name:" + name); //Output::name:email
//retrieve 'type' attribute value of the element
String type = emailAddressElement.getAttribute("type");
System.out.println("type:" + type); //Output::type:email
//retrieve 'tabindex' attribute value of the element
String tabIndex = emailAddressElement.getAttribute("tabindex");
System.out.println("tabIndex:" + tabIndex); //Output::tabIndex:1
//retrieve 'autocorrect' attribute value of the element
String autocorrect = emailAddressElement.getAttribute("autocorrect");
System.out.println("autocorrect:"+autocorrect);//Output::autocorrect:off
//retrieve 'size' attribute value of the element
String size = emailAddressElement.getAttribute("size");
System.out.println("fontsize:" + size); //Output::size:30
//retrieve 'maxlength' attribute value of the element
String maxlength = emailAddressElement.getAttribute("maxlength");
System.out.println("color:" + maxlength); //Output::maxlength:128
```

isDisplayed

This method helps find out whether the element is displayed on the GUI or not. It returns a Boolean value. It returns *true* if element is displayed, else returns *false*.

Syntax: `Boolean isDisplayed()`

```
//is Email Address field element displayed
Boolean isElementDisplayed = emailAddressElement.isDisplayed();
System.out.println("Is element displayed:" + isElementDisplayed);
//Output::Is element displayed:true
```

isEnabled

This method helps find out whether the element is enabled on the GUI or not. It returns a Boolean value. It returns *true* if element is enabled, else returns *false*.

Syntax: `Boolean isEnabled()`

```
//is Email Address field element enabled
Boolean isElementEnabled = emailAddressElement.isEnabled();
System.out.println("Is element enabled:" + isElementEnabled);
//Output::Is element enabled:true
```

10.2 | WORKING WITH BUTTONS

WebDriver provides various methods to simulate user action on button element. Suppose, there exists a button 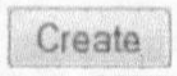 on a web page. On user click on this button, the web page form gets submitted. Assume HTML code of this button to be:

```
<input id="createOrder" type="button" tabindex="1" name="create"
  value="Create"/>
```

10.2.1 | WebDriver Methods for Text Box Element

Described below are some of the WebDriver methods to simulate user action on web page buttons.

Click

This method simulates user click on a button. If button click causes a new page to load, then this method blocks script execution till new page has loaded.

EXAMPLE 10.14 Write code to click on the *Create* button

```
driver.findElement(By.id("createOrder")).click();
```

Or,

```
WebElement button = driver.findElement(By.id("createOrder"));
  button.click();
```

Submit

This method submits the form if the current element is a form or an element within a form. It implies it simulates the same user action as user click on any button that submits the form.

EXAMPLE 10.15 Write code to click on the *Create* button to submit the form.

```
driver.findElement(By.id("createOrder")).submit();
```

Or,

```
WebElement button = driver.findElement(By.id("createOrder"));
  button.submit()
```

10.2.2 | Other WebDriver Methods for Button Element

Table 10.2 describes rest of the WebDriver methods for the button element.

TABLE 10.2 WebDriver methods to work with button element

Method	Description/Example	Output
getTagName()	Returns the tag name of the element. `String tagName = button.getTagName()`	input

getLocation()	Returns x, y coordinates of the element.
	`Point point = button.getLocation()`
	`System.out.println(point.x + "," + point.y)`
		330,200

getSize()	Returns height and width of the element.
	`Dimension dimension = button.getSize()`
	`System.out.println(dimension.height + "," + point.width)`
		22,201

getCSSValue (<style name>)	Returns the specified style of the element. `String bgColor = button.getCssValue ("background-color")`	rgba(240, 240, 240, 1)
getAttribute (<attribute name>)	Returns the attribute value of the given attribute. `String name = button.getAttribute("name")`	create
isDisplayed()	Returns 'true' if element is visible on GUI, else returns 'false'. `Boolean isVisible = button.isDisplayed()`	true
isEnabled()	Returns 'true' if element is enabled, else returns 'false', `Boolean isEnabled = button.isEnabled()`	true

10.3 | WORKING WITH LINK

WebDriver provides various methods to simulate user action on link element and to capture link element properties. Consider the *Forgot your password?* link element shown in Figure 10.1. Suppose the HTML code of this link is:

```
<a href="https://www.amazon.com/ap/forgotpassword...">Forgot
  your password?</a>
```

10.3.1 | WebDriver Methods for Link Element

Described below are some of the methods to simulate user action on link elements and to capture its attribute values.

Click

This method simulates user click on a link element. If a mouse-click on the link causes a new page to load, then this method blocks script execution till new page has loaded.

EXAMPLE 10.16 Write a code to click on the Forgot your password? link element.

```
driver.findElement(By.linkText("Forgot your password?")).click();
Or,
WebElement link = driver.findElement(By.linkText("Forgot your
  password?")); link.click();
```

10.3.2 | Other WebDriver Methods for Link Element

Table 10.3 describes rest of the WebDriver methods for the link element.

TABLE 10.3 WebDriver methods to work with link element

Method	Description/Example	Output
getTagName()	Returns the tag name of the element. `String tagName = link.getTagName()`	`a`

getLocation()	Returns x, y coordinates of the element.
	`Point point = link.getLocation()`
	`System.out.println(point.x + "," + point.y)`
		`463,256`

getSize()	Returns height and width of the element.
	`Dimension dimension = link.getSize()`
	`System.out.println(dimension.height + "," + point.width)`
		`13,130`

getCSSValue (<style name>)	Returns the specified style of the element. `String bgColor = link.getCssValue ("color")`	`rgba(0, 75, 145, 1)`
getAttribute (<attribute name>)	Returns the attribute value of the given attribute. `String name = link.getAttribute ("href")`	`https://www.amazon.com/ap/forgot password...`
isDisplayed()	Returns 'true' if element is visible on GUI, else returns 'false'. `Boolean isVisible = link.isDisplayed()`	`true`
isEnabled()	Returns 'true' if element is enabled, else returns 'false', `Boolean isEnabled = link.isEnabled()`	`true`

10.4 | WORKING WITH IMAGES

WebDriver provides various methods to simulate user actions on image element and to capture image element properties. Consider the image amazon element shown in Figure 10.1. Suppose the HTML code of this image element is:

```
<img width="100" border="0" height="30" alt="Amazon" src="https:
 //images-amazon.png">
```

10.4.1 | WebDriver Methods for Image Element

Some of the methods to simulate user action on image elements and to capture its attribute values are described below.

Click

This method simulates user click on an image element. If a mouse-click on the image causes a new page to load, then this method blocks script execution till new page has loaded.

EXAMPLE 10.17 Write code to click on the *amazon* image element.

```
driver.findElement(By.XPath("//img[@alt='Amazon']")).click();

Or,

WebElement image = driver.findElement(By.XPath("//img[@alt='Amazon']"));
  image.click();
```

10.4.2 | Other WebDriver Methods for Image Element

Table 10.4 describes rest of the WebDriver methods for the image element.

TABLE 10.4 WebDriver methods to work with image element

Method	Description/Example	Output
getTagName()	Returns the tag name of the element. `String tagName = image.getTagName()`	`img`

getLocation()	Returns x, y coordinates of the element.
	`Point point = image.getLocation()`
	`System.out.println(point.x + "," + point.y)`
		`227,18`

getSize()	Returns height and width of the element.
	`Dimension dimension = image.getSize()`
	`System.out.println(dimension.height + "," + point.width)`
		`30,100`

(continued)

TABLE 10.4 | *(continued)*

Method	Description/Example	Output
getCSSValue (<style name>)	Returns the specified style of the element. `String bgColor = image.getCssValue ("color")`	`rgba(0, 75, 145, 1)`
getAttribute (<attribute name>)	Returns the attribute value of the given attribute. `String name = image.getAttribute("href")`	`https://images-amazon.png`
isDisplayed()	Returns 'true' if element is visible on GUI, else returns 'false'. `Boolean isVisible = image.isDisplayed()`	`true`
isEnabled()	Returns 'true' if element is enabled, else returns 'false', `Boolean isEnabled = image.isEnabled()`	`true`

10.5 | WORKING WITH CHECKBOX

WebDriver provides various methods to select/deselect checkbox and retrieve its various attributes. Consider the checkboxes shown in Figure 10.4.

FIGURE 10.4 | Checkbox element

Suppose HTML code of the checkboxes is:

```
<input id="id0" type="checkbox" value="1" name="country"/>US
<input id="id1" type="checkbox" value="1" name="country"/>CANADA
<input id="id2" type="checkbox" checked="true/" value="1"
  name="country"/>INDIA
<input id="id3" type="checkbox" value="1" name="country"/>JAPAN
<input id="id4" type="checkbox" checked="true/" value="1"
  name="country"/>UK
```

10.5.1 | WebDriver Methods for Checkbox Element

Described below are some of the methods to simulate user action on checkbox elements and to capture its attribute values.

Click

This method simulates user click on a checkbox element. A click can select a checkbox, if not already selected. If a checkbox is already selected, then execution of click method on it will deselect the checkbox.

EXAMPLE 1.18 Write code to select checkbox *US*

```
driver.findElement(By.id("id0")).click();
Or,
WebElement checkbox = driver.findElement(By.id("id0"));
checkbox.click();
```

isSelected

This method helps to find out whether checkbox is selected or not. It returns *true*, if checkbox is selected else, returns *false.*

EXAMPLE 1.19 Write code to select checkbox *US* if it is not selected.

```
//find is checkbox checked
Boolean isCheckboxSelected = checkbox.isSelected();
//select the checkbox if not already checked
if(!isCheckboxSelected) checkbox.click();
```

EXAMPLE 1.20 Write code to select all the checkboxes of Figure 10.3.

```
WebDriver driver = new FirefoxDriver();
List<WebElement> checkboxes = driver.findElements(By.name("country"));
//Alternatively,
//List<WebElement> checkboxes = driver.findElements(By.type
  ("checkbox"));
for (int i=0;i<checkboxes.size();i++){
      if (!checkboxes.get(i).isSelected()){
            checkboxes.get(i).click();
      }
}
```

10.5.2 | Other WebDriver Methods for Checkbox Element

Table 10.5 describes rest of the WebDriver methods for the checkbox element.

TABLE 10.5 WebDriver methods to work with checkbox element

Method	Description/Example	Output
getTagName()	Returns the tag name of the element. `String tagName = checkbox.getTagName()`	`input`

getLocation()	Returns x, y coordinates of the element.
	`Point point = checkbox.getLocation()`
	`System.out.println(point.x +","+ point.y)`
		`12,12`

(continued)

TABLE 10.5 | *(continued)*

Method	Description/Example	Output

getSize()	Returns height and width of the element.
	`Dimension dimension = checkbox.getSize()`
	`System.out.println(dimension.height + "," + point.width)`
		`13,13`

getCSSValue (<style name>)	Returns the specified style of the element. `String bgColor = checkbox.getCssValue ("background-color")`	`rgba(255, 255, 255, 1)`
getAttribute (<attribute name>)	Returns the attribute value of the given attribute. `String name = checkbox.getAttribute ("value")`	`1`
isDisplayed()	Returns 'true' if element is visible on GUI, else returns 'false'. `Boolean isVisible = checkbox.isDisplayed()`	`true`
isEnabled()	Returns 'true' if element is enabled, else returns 'false', `Boolean isEnabled = checkbox.isEnabled()`	`true`

10.6 | WORKING WITH RADIO BUTTONS AND RADIO GROUP

10.6.1 | WebDriver Methods for Radio Button Element

WebDriver provides various methods to select a radio button and retrieve its attributes values. We can select a radio button using *click()* method. The state of the radio button (selected or not) can be found out using isSelected() method.

Consider the radio buttons shown in Figure 10.5.

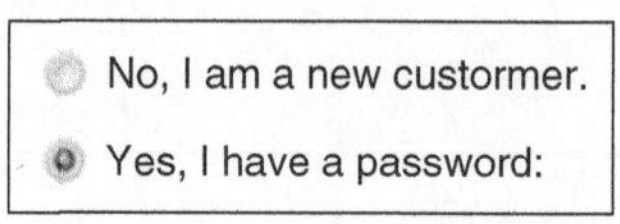

FIGURE 10.5 | Radio button element

Assume HTML code of these radio buttons to be:

```
<input id="ap_signin_create" type="radio" tabindex="6" value="1"
  name="create"/>No, I am a new customer.
<input id="ap_signin_existing" type="radio" tabindex="7" value="0"
  checked="checked" name="create"/>Yes, I have a password:
```

Click

This method simulates user click on a radio button element.

Example 1.21 Suppose a new user navigates to the amazon account registration page and then clicks on the radio button *No, I am a New Customer*. Write code to simulate user click on this radio button.

```
driver.findElement(By.id("ap_signin_create)).click();
//Alternatively, we can also use value attribute to locate the
  radio buttons
//driver.findElement(By.XPath("//input[@value='1')).click();

Or,

WebElement radioBtnNewUsr = driver.findElement(By.id("ap_signin_
  create"));
radioBtnNewUsr.click();
```

isSelected

This method helps to find out whether a radio button element is selected or not. It returns *true*, if radio button is selected else, returns *false*.

Example 1.22 Suppose an existing user navigates to the amazon account registration page and clicks on the radio button *No, I am a New Customer*. Then, again the user clicks on the radio button *Yes, I have a password:*. Write code to simulate user click on these radio buttons. Also, find the state of these radio buttons.

```
WebElement radioBtnNewUsr = driver.findElement(By.id("ap_signin_
  create"));
WebElement radioBtnOldUsr = driver.findElement(By.id("ap_signin_
  existing"));
//select new user radio button
radioBtnNewUsr.click();
//select existing user radio button
radioBtnOldUsr.click();
//find if the new user radio button is selected
Boolean isNewUsrRadioBtnSelected = radioBtnNewUsr.isSelected()
//Output:: false
//find if the old user radio button is selected
Boolean isOldUsrRadioBtnSelected = radioBtnNewUsr.isSelected()
//Output:: true
```

10.6.2 | Other WebDriver Methods for Radio Button Element

Table 10.6 describes the rest of the WebDriver methods for the checkbox element.

TABLE 10.6 WebDriver methods to work with radio button element

Method	Description/Example	Output
getTagName()	Returns the tag name of the element. `String tagName = radioBtnNewUsr.getTagName()`	input

getLocation()	Returns x, y coordinates of the element.
	`Point point = radioBtnNewUsr.getLocation()`
	`System.out.println(point.x + "," + point.y)`
		258,212

getSize()	Returns height and width of the element.
	`Dimension dimension = radioBtnNewUsr.getSize()`
	`System.out.println(dimension.height + "," + point.width)`
		13,13

getCSSValue (<style name>)	Returns the specified style of the element. `String bgColor = radioBtnNewUsr.getCssValue("background-color")`	rgba(255, 255, 255, 1)
getAttribute (<attribute name>)	Returns the attribute value of the given attribute. `String name = radioBtnNewUsr.getAttribute("value")`	1
isDisplayed()	Returns 'true' if element is visible on GUI, else returns 'false'. `Boolean isVisible = radioBtnNewUsr.isDisplayed()`	true
isEnabled()	Returns 'true' if element is enabled, else returns 'false', `Boolean isEnabled = radioBtnNewUsr.isEnabled()`	true

10.6.3 | Working with Radio Group

Instead of locating a specific radio button, we can also work with a group of radio buttons. This can be achieved by retrieving a list of radio buttons (*WebElements*) which are in a specific radio group. *findElements*() method can be used to retrieve all radio buttons.

Example 1.23 Write WebDriver code to select the *No, I am a New Customer* radio button of Figure 10.5 by its *value* attribute.

```
List<WebElement> radioGroup = driver.findElements(By.name("create"));
//value of radio button No, I am a New Customer is '1'. Select
  this radio button.
this.selectByValue(radioGroup, "1")
```

Described below is method *selectByValue* which selects a radio button by its value (attribute). It takes list of radio group elements and the (value of) radio button to select. The code identifies the button with the specified value and selects the identified radio button.

```
public void selectByValue(List<WebElement> radioGroup, String value){
        for (WebElement radioBtn:radioGroup){
                if (radioBtn.getAttribute("value").equalsIgnoreCase
                   (value)){
                        radioBtn.click();
                        assertTrue(radioBtn.isSelected());
                        break;
                }
        }
}
```

EXAMPLE 1.24 Write WebDriver code to select the *No, I am a New Customer* radio button of Figure 10.5 by its index value.

The radio group for Figure 10.4 contains two radio buttons. Assume index value of first radio button to be '0' and of second radio button to be '1'. Therefore, index value of the radio button *No, I am a New Customer* is zero. Below is the WebDriver code to click on this button.

```
List<WebElement> radioGroup = driver.findElements(By.name("create"));
//index value of radio button No, I am a New Customer is '1'
this.selectByIndex(radioGroup, 0)

public void selectByIndex(List<WebElement> radioGroup, int index){
        for (int i=0;i<radioGroup.size();i++){
                if (i==index){
                        radioGroup.get(i).click();
                        assertTrue(radioGroup.get(i).isSelected());
                        break;
                }
        }
}
```

10.7 | WORKING WITH DROPDOWN AND LIST BOX

WebDriver supports simulating user action on Dropdown and List controls using Select class instead of WebElement class. The Select class provides various methods and properties to interact with dropdowns and list boxes.

10.7.1 | Working with Dropdown

Consider the *Shipping Page* of amazon.com. It has a *Country* dropdown as shown in Figure 10. 6.

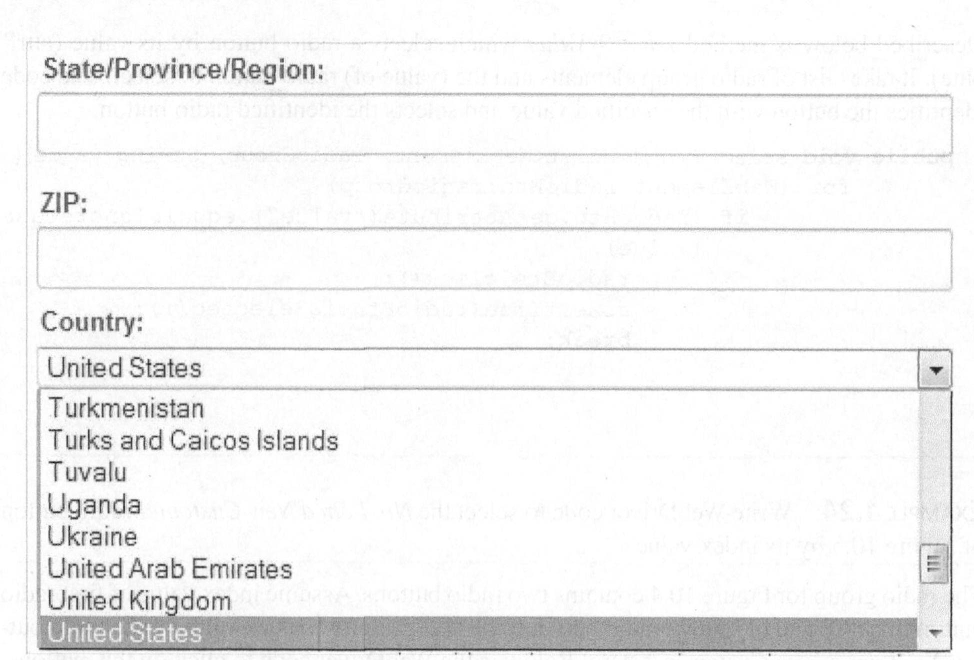

FIGURE 10.6 | Dropdown element

Assume HTML code of this dropdown to be:

```
<select id="enterAddressCountryCode" class="enterAddressFormField"
  name="enterAddressCountryCode">
<option value="">--</option>
<option value="AF">Afghanistan</option>
<option value="AX">Aland Islands</option>
<option value="AL">Albania</option>
...
<option value="UA">Ukraine</option>
<option value="AE">United Arab Emirates</option>
<option value="GB">United Kingdom</option>
<option value="US">United States</option>
...
</select>
```

WebDriver code to select option *United States* from the above dropdown is:

```
Select countryDropdown =
      new Select(driver.findElement(By.id("enterAddressCountryCode")));
countryDropdown.selectByVisibleText("United States");
```

Some of the methods to simulate user action on dropdowns are described below.

selectByVisibleText

This method selects the option from the list whose visible text value matches the specified string. This string is the same text that is visible to the user in the dropdown list.

Syntax: `void selectByVisibleText(String)`

EXAMPLE 1.25 User navigates to the *Shipping Page* of the amazon.com and adds a shipping address. Write WebDriver code to select country as *United States* as shown in Figure 10.6.

Select method can be used to select the visible list option *United States* from this list control.

```
//get country element
WebElement country = driver.findElement(By.id("enterAddressCountry
  Code"));
Select countryDropdown = new Select(country);
//select the visible text option United States
countryDropdown.selectByVisibleText("United States");
```

selectByValue

This method selects the option from the list whose (elements) value matches the specified string.

Syntax: `void selectByValue(String)`

EXAMPLE 1.26 User navigates to the *Shipping Page* of the amazon.com and adds a shipping address. Write WebDriver code to select country as *United States* by using the <option> tag attribute value *US* as shown in Figure 10.6.

Method *selectByValue* can be used to select a list option by its attribute value. *The* <option> tag value for *United States* list option is *US*. WebDriver code to select a list option by its value attribute is shown below.

```
//get country element
WebElement country = driver.findElement(By.id("enterAddressCountry
  Code"));
Select countryDropdown = new Select(country);
//select the list option whose 'value' attribute value is US
countryDropdown.selectByValue("US");
```

selectByIndex

This method selects the option from the list whose position in the list element matches the specified integer value.

Syntax: `void selectByIndex(int)`

EXAMPLE 1.27 User navigates to the *Shipping Page* of the amazon.com and adds a shipping address. Write WebDriver code to select country as *United States* by specifying the position of the option *United States* as shown in Figure 10.6.

Method *selectByIndex* can be used to select a list option by specifying its position in the list. As shown the HTML code of Figure 10.6, Afghanistan is the first option, followed by Aland Islands, Albania, etc. The index value for these options starts with '0' and goes on as 0,1,2,3.... Therefore, the index value for Albania will be 2. Assume the index value of *United States* in the list is 88. WebDriver code to select a list option by its *value* attribute is shown below.

```
//get country element
WebElement country = driver.findElement(By.id("enterAddressCountry
  Code"));
Select countryDropdown = new Select(country);
//select the list option whose index is 88
countryDropdown.selectByIndex(88);
```

Note: This method may not work as expected in scenarios where list box is dynamic, i.e., its options change from time to time.

getFirstSelectedOption

This method returns the first selected option webelement.

Syntax: `WebElement getFirstSelectedOption()`

EXAMPLE 1.28 Write code to find the list option selected in the above example

```
//get country element
WebElement country = driver.findElement(By.id("enterAddressCountry
  Code"));
Select countryDropdown = new Select(country);
//select the list option whose index is 88
countryDropdown.selectByIndex(88);
WebElement firstSelectedElement = countryDropdown.getFirstSelected
  Option();
System.out.println("First Selected Option:" + firstSelectedElement.
  getText());
//Output::First Selected Option:United States
```

getOptions

This method returns all the option elements for a list.

Syntax: `List<WebElement> getOptions()`

EXAMPLE 1.29 Write code to find all the list option elements for the list shown in Figure 10.5.

```
//get all the option elements of the list box
List<WebElement> options = countryDropdown.getOptions();
System.out.println("Count of Options:" + options.size());
//Output::count of Options:92
//get various attribute values of the element at index 88
System.out.println("Text value:" + options.get(88).getText());
//Output::Text value:United States
System.out.println("value attribute:" +
                options.get(88).get Attribute("value"));
//Output::Text value:US
System.out.println("Text value:" + options.get(88).getAttribute("text"));
//Output::Text value:United States
```

10.7.2 | Working with List Control with Multi-select Option

The Select class of WebDriver can be used to simulate user actions on list control with multi-select options as well. Figure 10.7 shows a multi-select list control. This list control allows users to search various models of cars. User can search for one or more models of cars by selecting one or more option from this list box.

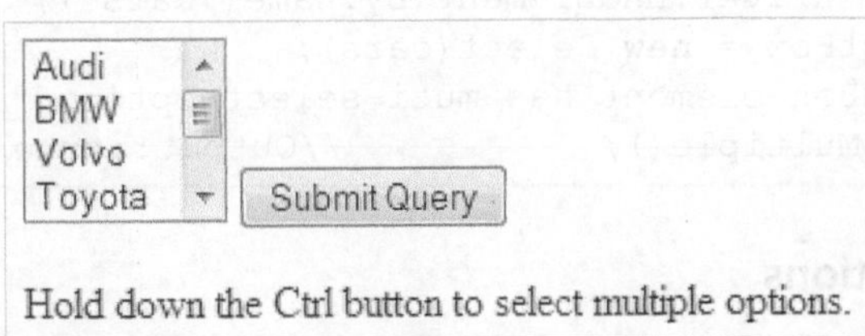

FIGURE 10.7 | List box element

The HTML code of the above list control is:

```
<form action="form_action.asp">
       <select multiple="" name="cars">
              <option value="audi">Audi</option>
              <option value="bmw">BMW</option>
              <option value="volvo">Volvo</option>
              <option value="toyota">Toyota</option>
              <option value="hyundai">Hyundai</option>
              <option value="honda">Honda</option>
       </select>
```

```
    <input type="submit"/>
</form>
<p>Hold down the Ctrl button to select multiple options.</p>
```

WebDriver code for this list box element:

```
//get cars element
WebElement cars = driver.findElement(By.name("cars"))
Select carsListBox = new Select(cars);
```

The methods described in the above section 'Working with Dropdown' can be used to select the various options or retrieve the attribute value of any option element. Described below are some more methods to work with multi-select list controls.

isMultiple

This method finds out whether the list box control is multi-select or not. It returns *true,* if the list box control is multi-select else returns false.

Syntax: `Boolean isMultiple()`

EXAMPLE 1.30 Write a code to find out whether the list box specified in Figure 10.7 is multi-select or not.

```
//get cars element Web
Element cars = driver.findElement(By.name("cars"))
Select carsListBox = new Select(cars);
//get carsListBox element has muti-select option
carsListBox.isMultiple();              //Output::true
```

getAllSelectedOptions

This method returns all the option elements which are selected in a list box.

Syntax: `List<WebElement> getAllSelectedOptions()`

EXAMPLE 10.31 For the list box shown in Figure 10.7, user selects options 'Audi' and 'Toyota'. Write code find the options selected for this list box control.

```
//select option Audi
carsListBox.selectByVisibleText("Audi");
//select option Toyota
carsListBox.selectByVisibleText("Toyota");
//get all selected options
List<WebElement> selectedOptions = carsListBox.getAllSelected
  Options();
System.out.println("Count of options selected:" + selected
  Options.size());
```

```
//Output:: Count of options selected:2
System.out.println("Selected option 1:" + selectedOptions.get(0).
  getText());
//Output:: Selected option 1:Audi
System.out.println("Selected option 2:" + selectedOptions.
  get(1).getText());
//Output:: Selected option 2:Toyota
```

deselectByVisibleText

This method deselects the specified selected option from the list whose (elements) text value matches the specified string.

Syntax: `void deselectByVisibleText(String)`

EXAMPLE 10.32 For the list box shown in Figure 10.6, user selects options 'Audi' and 'Toyota'. Write code to deselect option 'Toyota' from the list of selected options.

```
//select option Audi
carsListBox.selectByVisibleText("Audi");
//select option Toyota
carsListBox.selectByVisibleText("Toyota");
//get all selected options
List<WebElement> selectedOptions = carsListBox.getAllSelected
  Options();
System.out.println("Count of options selected:" + selectedOptions.
  size());
//Output:: Count of options selected:2
//deselect option 'Audi'
carsListBox.deselectByVisibleText("Audi");
//get all selected options
selectedOptions = carsListBox.getAllSelectedOptions();
System.out.println("Count of options selected:" + selectedOptions.
  size());
//Output:: Count of options selected:1
//deselect option 'Toyota'
selectedOptions.get(0).deselectByVisibleText("Toyota");
System.out.println("Count of options selected:" + selected
  Options.size());
//Output:: Count of options selected:0
```

deselectByValue

This method deselects the option from the list whose (elements) value matches the specified string.

Syntax: `void deselectByValue(String)`

Example 1.33 For the list box shown in Figure 10.7, user selects options 'Audi' and 'Toyota'. Write code to deselect option 'Toyota' from the list of selected options using option elements *value* attribute.

```
//select option Audi
carsListBox.selectByVisibleText("Audi");
//select option Toyota
carsListBox.selectByVisibleText("Toyota");
//get all selected options
List<WebElement> selectedOptions = carsListBox.getAllSelectedOptions();
System.out.println("Count of options selected:" + selectedOptions.
  size());
//Output:: Count of options selected:2
//deselect option 'Audi'
carsListBox.deselectByValue("audi");
//get all selected options
selectedOptions = carsListBox.getAllSelectedOptions();
System.out.println("Count of options selected:" + selectedOptions.
  size());
//Output:: Count of options selected:1
//deselect option 'Toyota'
selectedOptions.get(0).deselectByValue("toyota");
System.out.println("Count of options selected:" + selectedOptions.
  size());
//Output:: Count of options selected:0
```

deselectByIndex

This method deselects the option from the list whose position in the list element matches the specified integer value.

Syntax: `void deselectByIndex(int)`

Example 1.34 For the list box shown in Figure 10.7, user selects options 'Audi' and 'Toyota'. Write code to deselect option 'Toyota' from the list of selected options using its index value.

```
//select option Audi
carsListBox.selectByVisibleText("Audi");
//select option Toyota
carsListBox.selectByVisibleText("Toyota");
//get all selected options
List<WebElement> selectedOptions = carsListBox.getAllSelected
  Options();
System.out.println("Count of options selected:" + selectedOptions.
  size());
//Output:: Count of options selected:2
//deselect option 'Audi'
```

```
carsListBox.deselectByIndex(0);
//get all selected options
selectedOptions = carsListBox.getAllSelectedOptions();
System.out.println("Count of options selected:" + selectedOptions.
  size());
//Output:: Count of options selected:1
//deselect option 'Toyota'
selectedOptions.get(0).deselectByIndex(3);
System.out.println("Count of options selected:" + selectedOptions.
  size());
//Output:: Count of options selected:0
```

deselectAll

This method deselects all the selected options in a list box.

Syntax: `void deselectAll()`

EXAMPLE 1.35 For the list box shown in Figure 10.7, user selects options 'Audi' and 'Toyota'. Write code to deselect all the selected options.

```
//select option Audi
carsListBox.selectByVisibleText("Audi");
//select option Toyota
carsListBox.selectByVisibleText("Toyota");
//get all selected options
List<WebElement> selectedOptions = carsListBox.getAllSelected
  Options();
System.out.println("Count of options selected:" + selected
  Options.size());
//Output:: Count of options selected:2
//deselect all the selected options
carsListBox.deselectAll();
//get all selected options
selectedOptions = carsListBox.getAllSelectedOptions();
System.out.println("Count of options selected:" + selected
  Options.size());
//Output:: Count of options selected:0
```

10.7.3 | Other WebDriver Methods for List Box Element

WebElement class can also be used to work on list boxes. In order to select any option from list box, first step is to find all elements of the list box with tag name as option and execute a click method on the specific option element which needs to be selected.

```
//get list box element
WebElement country = driver.findElement(By.id("enterAddress
  CountryCode"));
```

```
//get all elements with tagname=option for the list box element
List<WebElement> options = country.findElements(By.tagName
("option"));
//select option United States in the list (select by index)
options.get(88).click();
WebElement option = options.get(88);
option.getAttribute("value")          //Output::US
```

All the methods defined in Table 10.5 are applicable to this option element.

10.8 | WORKING WITH WEB TABLES

Selenium WebDriver provides a generic WebElement class to work with various GUI elements of a web page. It also provides helper classes to work with list box element. However, WebDriver has no build-in support for web tables or <table> elements. Chapter 11 describes in detail on developing a helper class implementation for web tables.

10.9 | WORKING WITH POP-UP WINDOWS

Pop-up windows often appear on a web page when a web page is submitted. Its general purpose is to confirm user that the intended operation has been performed or to warn user that the intended operation cannot be performed because of some error. It is also used in situations where re-confirmation of user is required for performing the intended operation, say funds transfer. Chapter 12 describes in detail how to work with these pop-up windows.

10.10 | WORKING WITH FRAMES

Frames allow a visual HTML browser to be split into multiple sections, each of which can show a different document. This helps lower bandwidth use, as repeating parts of a layout can be used in one frame, while variable content is displayed in another. An iframe allows displaying another HTML document in a frame. Chapter 13 discusses in detail on how to work with various frames.

INTERVIEW QUESTIONS

1. What are page elements?
2. Write code to retrieve the text entered in the text box.
3. Write code to retrieve the text entered for a label element say text displayed for label element 'Sign In Help' in Figure 10.1.
4. Write code to de-select a selected checkbox.
5. Write code to select a radio button shown in Figure 10.1 by its
   a) value
   b) index
6. Write code to retrieve all the list options displayed for a list box for Figure 10.7.

11
CHAPTER

Working with Web Tables

Web tables are elements on a web page whose tag name value is <table>. Rows of the web table have tag name <tr> while columns of the table are represented with tag name <td>. Figure 11.1 shows *Employee* web table.

Employee ID	Employee Name	Designation
122768	Charles	Software Developer
122657	Joseph	Automation Developer

FIGURE 11. 1 | Employee web table

Selenium Webdriver provides a generic WebElement class to work with various elements on a web page. It also provides helper classes such as Select to work with list box elements. However, there is no built-in class to support web tables.

In this chapter, we will learn how to implement a helper class for web table element to simulate user actions on a web table and to read web table data. Using this class we can perform various operations on web table.

11.1 | LOCATING WEB TABLE

Assume the HTML code of the web table shown in Figure 11.1 to be

```
<table border="1" name="employee">
      <tr>
            <td>Employee ID<td>
            <td>Employee Name<td>
            <td>Designation<td>
      </tr>
....
```

The above HTML code defines two attributes of the web table – *border* and *name*. The *name* attribute can be used to uniquely locate the table element on the web page. Following is the WebDriver code to identify the above web table using its *name* attribute.

```
WebElement tableEmployee = driver.findElement(By.
                    name("employee"));
```

In some applications, it may happen that developer may not define any of the attributes of the table. In such scenario, the web table HTML code may look like as shown below:

```
<table>
        <tr>
                <td>Employee ID<td>
                <td>Employee Name<td>
                <td>Designation<td>
        </tr>
....
```

As evident from the HTML code above, none of the attributes of the table element has been defined. For the scenario above, *XPath* or *css* path of the element can be used to locate the element. For example, the above table can be located by its *XPath* using the code below:

```
WebElement tableEmployee = driver.findElement(By.XPath("//table"));
```

This table can also be located using its *css* path as shown below:

```
WebElement tableEmployee = driver.findElement(By.
                           cssSelector("table"));
```

In situations where there exists more than one table on a web page, index value of the table can be used to identify the table during run-time. But using index values to locate an element is not a reliable method of element identification. A more appropriate approach would be to use design XPath to locate the table by using reference of any of its previous or next elements.

Suppose there exists a link element named *Edit* at the top of the *Employee* table as shown in Figure 11.2.

Edit

Employee ID	Employee Name	Designation
122768	Charles	Software Developer
122657	Joseph	Automation Developer

FIGURE 11. 2 | Employee table followed by a link element

From Figure 11.2, the element next to the *Edit* link element is the table element. XPath to locate the table element next to the Edit element can be:

```
WebElement tableEmployee = driver.findElement(By.XPath("//a[@
                           name="Edit"]/following-
                           sibling::table"));
```

11.2 | LOCATING WEB TABLE USING COLUMN NAMES

The above method of locating elements is a better approach as compared to the approach of locating elements using elements index value. However, the above method has one drawback. The above method will fail if properties of 'Edit' button changes or one more table element is inserted between the current table element and the 'Edit' button element. Again, it is not a very good automation practice to code element identification attributes with reference to other elements. This can make it difficult to track the changes to be done when some element attribute changes. That is, the maintenance effort of the tests may increase with this approach. A more reliable way of locating table elements is by using the column name attributes of the table. By locating elements using the column names limit the impact of change to the respective table element only. In this case, change of attributes of 'Edit' button or insertion of table elements between the 'Employee' table and 'Edit' button will not cause a failure in locating the 'Employee' table. The identification attributes, in this case, are not dependent on any other element. This helps make changes to test easier when a change occurs to the table element attributes.

Following code shows how to locate a table using its column names. Code below first retrieves the column attributes (names) of all the tables of the web page and then checks which table matches the expected column names. The matched table is considered the identified table element.

Note: Separator ";" is being used to distinguish between two column names.

```
@Test
public void testTableByColumnName(){
        WebDriver driver = new FirefoxDriver();
        driver.get("http://..../Employee Table.html");
        WebElement tableEmployee = this.findTableByColumnName
          (driver, "Employee ID;Employee Name;Designation");
        //get total number of rows
        int rowCount = table.findElements(By.tagName("td")).
          Size();
        //Output::3
}

//find table with the given column names
public WebElement findTableByColumnName(WebDriver driver,
  String columnNames) throws NoSuchElementException{
        //get all table elements
        List<WebElement> tables = getTables(driver);
        //find the table element which has the given column
          names
        WebElement table = getTableWithColumnNames(columnNames,
          tables);
        if (table==null) throw new NoSuchElementException("No
          such table found.");
                return table;
}

//get table with the given column names
private WebElement getTableWithColumnNames(String
  expectedColumnNames, List<WebElement> tables){
        WebElement table=null;
        for (int i=0;i<tables.size();i++){
```

```
                String actualColumnNames = getColumnNames(tables.
                  get(i));
                Boolean isMatch = isColumnNamesMatch(expectedCol
                  umnNames, actualColumnNames);
                if (isMatch) {
                        table = tables.get(i) ;
                        break;
                }
        }
        return table;
}

//get column names of the table
private String getColumnNames(WebElement table){
        String columnNames = null;
        WebElement firstRow = table.findElement(By.tagName("tr"));
        List<WebElement> columns = table.findElements(By.
          tagName("td"));
        for (int columnCount=0;columnCount<columns.
          size();columnCount++){
                columnNames = columnNames + ";" + columns.
                  get(columnCount).getText().trim();
        }
        return columnNames;
}

//is current column name matches with the expected table
  column names
private Boolean isColumnNamesMatch(String expectedColumns,
  String actualColumns){
        Boolean isMatched=false;
        actualColumns = actualColumns.toLowerCase();
        expectedColumns = expectedColumns.toLowerCase();
        if (actualColumns!="" && actualColumns.contains
          (expectedColumns)){
                isMatched = true;
        }
        return isMatched;
}

//get all tables
private List<WebElement> getTables(WebDriver driver){
        return driver.findElements(By.tagName("table"));
}
```

Above code searches through all the table elements to find the table element whose column name field matches with the given column names. In scenarios where some of the column names change dynamically, the above code can be modified to identify such dynamic tables as well. The expected column names can be defined as regular expression string and method `isColumnNamesMatch` can be modified to find the regular expression match of the column names. Following code shows the modified method `isColumnNamesMatch` to identify table elements whose column names changes dynamically.

```
//compare the column names against regular expression string
of column names
private Boolean isColumnNamesMatch(String regexExpectedColumns,
  String actualColumns){
      Boolean isMatched=false;
      actualColumns = actualColumns.toLowerCase();
      regexExpectedColumns = regexExpectedColumns.
        toLowerCase();
      if (actualColumns!="" && actualColumns.matches
        (regexExpectedColumns)){
             isMatched = true;
      }
      return isMatched;
}
```

Code below shows how to locate a dynamic web table one whose column name changes during run time. Assume the column names are 'Employee Name<Type>', Employee ID <Type>, Designation, where value of 'Type' can be Manager, Sr. Manager, Associate, etc. The regular expressions to identify a dynamic web table needs to use the static content of the dynamic column names to locate the table. In this case, 'Employee name' , 'Employee ID' and Designation are static contents. We can use below regular expressions to locate this dynamic table:

String regexColumnName = "Employee name.*;Employee ID.*;Designation".
WebElement tableEmployee = **this**.findTableByColumnName
(driver, regexColumnName);

Method 'testTableByColumnName' shows how to use develop the code to locate a dynamic table.

```
@Test
public void testTableByColumnName(){
      WebDriver driver = new FirefoxDriver();
      driver.get("file:///C:/Users/Dynamic%20
        Table.html");
      String regexColumnName = "Employee.*;Employee.*;.*"
      //Or, String regexColumnName = ".*Employee ID.*"
      WebElement tableEmployee = this.findTableByColumnName
        (driver, regexColumnName);
      //get total number of rows
      int rowCount = table.findElements(By.tagName("td")).
        Size();
      //Output::3
}
```

In certain scenarios, it may happen that some column names are completely dynamic. An example would be column name that displays order number. In this case, static content of the other column names can be used to locate the table. Suppose we have a table whose column names are *<sequence nbr>, Employee id, Employee name, Designation* where sequence number is a dynamic number value. Regular expression string to locate this table can be:

```
String regexColumnName = ".*;Employee Name;Employee ID;
Designation"
```

There could also be situations where in some of the columns of the table gets added or removed dynamically. The above code can be used to locate such dynamic tables as well. Consider the column names of such a dynamic table is: *Employee ID; <Employee Type>;Employee Name, Designation.* Here, column <Employee Type> is dynamic in nature and sometimes appears and sometimes not. So the column names when this field does not appears in table would be *'Employee ID, Employee Name and Designation'*.

Regular expression to locate this dynamic table can be:

```
String regexColumnName = "Employee ID.*;.*Employee Name.*;.*"
WebElement tableEmployee = this.findTableByColumnName
(driver, regexColumnName);
```

Notes: 1. Locating elements with reference to other elements to be used only if other reliable methods of identifying elements have failed.

2. Locating table name using its column names to be used only in scenarios where no attributes say name, class ,etc., of the table is defined.

11.3 | LOCATING ROWS AND CELLS OF A WEB TABLE

Rows and cells of the web table can be retrieved by retrieving the <tr> and <td> elements of the web table.

EXAMPLE 11.1 Write WebDriver code to find the total number of rows in the web table shown in Figure 11.1.

Tag name <tr> is used to represent a row in a web table. Total number of rows in a web table can be found by finding the total number of elements which has tag name <tr> for table element. Following is the web driver code to find the total number of rows in *Employee* web table.

```
//find total number of rows
int rowCount = tableEmployee.findElements(By.tagName("tr")).
  size();
System.out.print("Row count:" + rowCount); //Output::Row
  count:3
```

EXAMPLE 11.2 Write WebDriver code to find the total number of columns for the first row in the web table shown in Figure 11.1.

Tag name <td> is used to represent a column in a web table. Total number of columns in a row of a web table can be found by finding the total number of elements which has tag name

<td> for the specific row element <tr>. Below is the web driver code to find the total number of columns in the first row of *Employee* web table.

```
//find all row elements
List<WebElement> rows = tableEmployee.findElements(By.tagName
  ("tr"));
//find all column elements in the first row
List<WebElement> columns = rows.get(0).findElements(By.tagName
  ("td")); //find total number of columns in the first row
int columnCount = columns.size();
System.out.print("Column count:" + columnCount);//Output::
  Column count:3
```

EXAMPLE 11.3 Write WebDriver code to find the value of cell (2,2) of the web table shown in Figure 11.1.

getText() method can be used to retrieve the *text* attribute of any cell element. Following code shows how to retrieve the text value of cell (2,2)

```
//find all row elements
List<WebElement> rows = tableEmployee.findElements(By.tagName
  ("tr"));
//find all column elements in the first row
List<WebElement> columns = rows.get(1).findElements(By.tagName
  ("td"));
//find total number of columns in the first row
String cellValue22= columns.get(1).getText();
System.out.print("Value of cell(2,2):" + cellValue22);
//Output::Value of cell(2,2):Charles
```

Table 11.1 shows how to use XPath axes to locate various attributes of the table shown in Figure 11.2.

TABLE 11. 1 | Using XPath axes to locate various table attributes

Axis Name	Description	Example	XPath Expression
ancestor	Selects all ancestors (parent, grandparent,..) of the current node	Locate the row element which contains employee '122768' details	//td[text()='122768']/ ancestor::tr. Alternatively, //td[contains(text(),'122768')]/ ancestor::tr
		Locate the table which contains employee '122768' details	//td[text()='122768']/ ancestor::table. Alternatively, //td[contains(text(),'122768')]/ ancestor::table

(*continued*)

TABLE 11. 1 | *(continued)*

Axis Name	Description	Example	XPath Expression
ancestor-or-self	Selects all ancestors (parent, grandparent,..) of the current node and current node itself	Locate the row element which contains employee '122768' details	//td[text()='122768']/ ancestor-or-self::tr
		Locate the table element which contains employee '122768' details	//td[text()='122768']/ ancestor-or-self::table
		Locate the cell element which contains employee '122768' details	//td[text()='122768']/ ancestor-or-self::td
attribute	Selects all the attributes of the current node	Locate the *value* attribute of the <input> field *Designation*	//td[text()='122768']/ attribute::value
child	Selects all children of the current node	Locate all <input> child elements of the cell row=3, column=3	//table//tr[3]/td[3]/ child::input
descendant	Selects all descendants (children, grandchildren,...) of the current node	Locate all the rows of the table	//table/descendant::tr
		Locate the third row of the table	//table/descendant::tr[3]
		Locate all the cells of column 3 of the table	//table/descendant::tr/ td[3]
		Locate all the cells of the table	//table/descendant::td
		Locate all <input> child elements of the cell row=3, column=3	//table/descendant::td/ input
descendant-or-self	Selects all descendants (children, grandchildren,..) of the current node and current node itself	Locate all the rows of the table	//table/descendant-or-self::tr
		Locate the cell element which contains employee '122768' details	//td[text()='122768']/ descendant-or-self::td
following	Selects all nodes in the document after the closing tag of the current node	Locate all cells after the cell containing value '122768'	//td[text()='122768']/ following::td
		Locate all the rows after the row containing cell value '122768'	//td[text()='122768']/ following::tr

TABLE 11. 1 | *(continued)*

Axis Name	Description	Example	XPath Expression
following-sibling	Selects all siblings of the current node	Locate all the sibling cells of the cell containing value '122768'	//td[text()='122768']/following-sibling::td

parent	Selects the parent node of the current node	Locate the cell that contains the `<input>` element with *id* attribute value equal to *id1*	//input[@id='d1']/parent::td
			Or,
			//input[@id='d1']/parent::*

		Locate the cell that contains the `<input>` element with *'value'* attribute value equal to *'Automation Developer'*	//input[@value='Automation Developer']/parent::td
		Locate the row that contains value '122768'	//td[text()='122768']/parent::tr
preceding	Selects all nodes that appear before the current node	Select the row element that precedes the row containing value '122768'	//td[text()='122768']/preceding::tr

		Select all the cells of the row element that precedes the row containing value '122768'	//td[text()='122768']/preceding::td
			Or,
			//td[text()='122768']/preceding::*

preceding-sibling	Selects all the sibling nodes before the current node	Select all the cells of row 2 that precedes the cell 3,3	//table//tr[3]//td[3]/preceding-sibling::td

Note: It is always advisable to avoid use of index in location identifiers to locate cell values. Instead retrieve all the desired cell elements and loop through them to find the desired element.

11.4 | LOCATING CHILD ELEMENTS OF A WEB TABLE

Working with tables that contain only data is relatively easy. However, most often we come across tables that have elements inside its cells. One example is the *Employee* table as shown in Figure 11.1. This table has `<input>` elements in cells (2,3) and (3,3).

EXAMPLE 11.4 Write code to enter text 'WebDriver' to the element in cell (2,3)

<input> element in cell (2,3) can be located by executing the *findElement* method on cell element (2,3)

```
//find all row elements
List<WebElement> rows = tableEmployee.findElements(By.tagName
  ("tr"));
//find all column elements of the first row
List<WebElement> columns = rows.get(1).findElements(By.tagName
  ("td"));
//find the input element of the cell (2,3)
WebElement inputElement = columns.get(2).findElement(By.tagName
  ("input"));
```

Alternatively, suppose the HTML code of the input element of cell (2,3) is:

```
<input id="d1" type="text" value="Software Developer" name=
  "designation"/>
```

WebDriver code to locate this element in cell (2,3) can be:

```
WebElement inputElement = columns.get(2).findElement(By.name
  ("designation"));
inputElement.sendKeys("WebDriver");
```

Alternatively, *XPath* locator can also be used to locate this element

```
WebElement inputElement = columns.get(2).findElement(By.XPath
  ("//input[@name='designation']"));
```

Alternatively,

```
WebElement inputElement = columns.get(2).findElement(By.XPath
  ("//input[@value='Software Developer']"));
```

Alternatively, XPath can be designed to directly retrieve the required element using XPath axis. The following code locates the child input element of the following sibling element of element whose value is 'Charles'.

```
WebElement inputElement = tableEmployee.findElement(By.XPath("//
  td[contains(text(),'Charles')] /following-sibling::td//input
  [@name='designation']"));
```

11.5 | LOCATING DYNAMIC CHILD ELEMENTS OF A WEB TABLE

Dynamic web tables are tables with dynamic child elements. For example, consider the 'Cancel Ticket' table shown in Figure 11.3.

	Ticket Number	Passenger Name	Date	Email
☑	2365467	Joseph Mathew	03/26/2013	jmathew@gmail.com
☐	2365466	John Graham	03/26/2013	jgraham@gmail.com
☐	2365465	Rayn Mathew	03/26/2013	rmathew@gmail.com

Cancel Ticket

FIGURE 11. 3 | Dynamic web table for cancelling booked tickets

This above table shows the details of the ticket booked by a passenger and provides the option to cancel a ticket. Fields *Ticket Number* and *Email* are dynamic elements as their values can change from one run to another. This is because once a ticket is cancelled the above table would get refreshed and would show new list of tickets that can be cancelled. The *Email* field is also dynamic as it would change from one ticket number to another. Now the question arises how to automate (perform user actions using code) dynamic tables. One example of user action on this dynamic table could be to click on the *Email* link of the passenger say 'Joseph'. This can be achieved by first locating the *Email* field cell element of the passenger 'Joseph'. Next step would be to find the child link element of this cell element. Once this dynamic element is located, *click* method can be executed on it to simulate a user click on this link.

Assume HTML code of the table and 'Cancel Ticket' button to be:

```
<table>
      <tr>
            <td></td>
            <td>Ticket Number</td>
            <td>Passenger Name</td>
            <td>Date</td>
            <td>Email</td>
      </tr>
      <tr>
            <td>
              <input id="2365467" type="checkbox" checked=
                "true" value="1"/>
            </td>
            <td>2365467</td>
            <td>Joseph Mathew</td>
            <td>03/26/2013</td>
            <td>
                       <a id="email" alt="Email" href="javascri
                         pt:sendemail();">jmathew@gmail.com</a>
            </td>
      </tr>
```

```
......
......
<a class="button primary" href="javascript:cancelTicket();">Ca
ncel Ticket</a>
```

As per the HTML code, no specific attributes (say name, class) of the table has been defined. In such scenarios, one option to locate the table could be index value of the table in the page. But as we know, index is not a reliable element identification mechanism. In order to uniquely identify the table, the best approach would be to locate the <table> element that precedes the *'Cancel'* button element. XPath for locating the <table> element which precedes 'cancel' button element can be:

```
XPath = //a[@class='button primary']/preceding::table
```

WebDriver code to locate the `<table>` element using this XPath is:

```
WebElement cancelTicketTable = driver.findElement(By.XPath
  ("//a[@class='button primary']/preceding::table"));
//Alternatively, this table can also be located by using
column name attributes as shown below:
String regexColumnName = ".*Ticket Number; Passenger Name;.*"
WebElement cancelTicketTable = this.findTableByColumnName
  (driver, regexColumnName);
```

EXAMPLE 11.5 Write WebDriver code to click on the 'Email' link of the order number '2365467'.

WebDriver code to click on the *'Email'* link of the order number '2365467' can be:

```
//find all rows
List<WebElement> rows = cancelTicketTable.findElements(By.
  tagName("tr"));
//find row count
int rowCount = rows.size();
//find the row which has order number 2365467
int rowNum=0;
for (int i=1;i<=rowCount;i++){
List<WebElement> columns = rows.get(i-1).findElements(By.tagName
  ("td"));
       for (int j=1;j<columns.size();j++){
              if (columns.get(j-1).getText().contains("2365467")){
                     rowNum = i;
                     break;
              }
       }
```

```
        if (!(rowNum==0)) break;
  }
  //locate the Email link element of a given row
  List<WebElement> columns = rows.get(rowNum).findElements(By.
    tagName("td"));
  WebElement emailLink = columns.get(4).findElement(By.tagName
    ("a"));
  //click on the Email link element
  emailLink.click();
```

11.6 | CREATING AN EXTENSION CLASS FOR WEB TABLES

Selenium Webdriver provides a generic WebElement class to work with various elements on a web page. It also provides helper classes such as Select to work with list box elements. However, there is no built-in class to support web tables. In this section, we will learn how to implement a helper class for web table.

Let us implement the web table extension class with WebTable.java. The steps to implement a WebTable class are described as follows:

1. Create a WebTable class and its constructor. The constructor would accept web table element object as input parameter. Also, write getter and setter methods as shown below:

```
import java.util.List;

import org.openqa.selenium.By;
import org.openqa.selenium.WebElement;

public class WebTable {
        public WebElement webTable;
        //Constructor for webTable class
        public WebTable(WebElement webTable){
                this.setWebTable(webTable);
        }
        //getter property method
        public WebElement getWebTable(){
                return webTable;
        }
        //setter property method
        public void setWebTable(WebElement webTable){
                this.webTable = webTable;
        }
```

2. Now add methods to retrieve all row elements and all column elements as shown below:

```
        /*
        * @Desc: get all row elements
```

```
* @return List<WebElement> row elements
*/
public List<WebElement> getRowElements(){
	return this.webTable.findElements(By.tagName
	   ("tr"));
}
/*
* @Desc: get all column elements of the given row
* @return List<WebElement> column elements of the
  given row
*/
public List<WebElement> getColumnElements(int rowIndex){
	List<WebElement> rows = this.getRowElements();
	List<WebElement> columns = rows.get(rowIndex).
	  findElements(By.tagName("td"));
	return columns;
}
```

3. Add methods to retrieve total number of rows and columns of the table as shown by the following code:

```
/*
* @Desc: get total row count of table
* @return int row count
*/
public int getRowCount(){
	List<WebElement> rows = this.getRowElements();
	return rows.size();
}
/*
*@Desc: get total column count of first row of the table
*@return: int column count
*/
public int getColumnCount(){
	return this.getColumnElements(0).size();
}
/*
*@Desc: get total column count of the given row of the
  table
*@param: row number
*@return: int column count
*/
public int getColumnCount(int rowNum){
	return this.getColumnElements(rowNum).size();
}
```

4. Add method to find the cell which contains specific data.

```
/*
*@Desc: get cell-ordinates of the cell which
contains the given data
*@param: compareMethod. Acceptable values: 0=case-
  insensitive compare;1=case-sensitive compare
*@return: int[] cell ordinates
*/
public int[] getCellWithData(String cellData, int
  compareMethod){
      int[] cell = new int[2];
      Boolean bFlag=false;
      List<WebElement> rows = this.getRowElements();
      for (int i=1;i<=rows.size();i++){
      List<WebElement> columns = this.
        getColumnElements(i-1);
      for (int j=1;j<=columns.size();j++){
             String cellValue = columns.get(j-1).
               getText();
             switch(compareMethod){
             case 0:
                    if (cellValue.equalsIgnoreCase
                      (cellData)){
                          cell[0] = i;
                          cell[1] = j;
                          bFlag = true;
                          break;
                    }
                    break;
             case 1:
                    if (cellValue.contentEquals
                      (cellData)){
                          cell[0] = i;
                          cell[1] = j;
                          bFlag = true;
                          break;
                    }
                    break;
             }
             if (bFlag) break;
         }
}
return cell;
}
```

5. Add method to find the data contained in a specific cell.

```
/*
 *@Desc: get cell data of the given cell
 *@param: rowIndex row number of the cell
 *@param: columnIndex column number of the cell
 *@return: String cell data
 */
public String getCellData(int rowIndex, int
 columnIndex){
      List<WebElement> rows = this.getRowElements();
      List<WebElement> columns = this.
       getColumnElements(rowIndex-1);
      return columns.get(columnIndex-1).getText();
}
```

6. Add method to find the element contained in a specific cell.

```
/*
 *@Desc: get element which is contained in the given
  cell
 *@param: rowIndex row number of the cell
 *@param: columnIndex column number of the cell
 *@param: elementTagName tag name of the element
  present in the cell
 *@param: elementIndex index value of the element.
 * specify 0 if only one element of the specific
   tagName exists
 * else, specify the exact index value
 *@return: WebElement web element
 */
public WebElement getCellElement(int rowIndex, int
 columnIndex, String elementTagName, int elementIndex){
            List<WebElement> rows = this.
            getRowElements();
            List<WebElement> columns = this.
            getColumnElements
              (rowIndex-1);
            List<WebElement> elements = columns.
            get(columnIndex-1).findElements(By.
            tagName(elementTagName));
            return elements.get(elementIndex);
      }
}
```

EXAMPLE 11.6 Write WebDriver code to retrieve all rows and columns of the table shown in Figure 11.3.

```
//XPath to locate web table
String tableXPath = "//a[@class='button primary']/
  preceding::table";
// create an instance of the WebTable class using the table
  element
WebTable table = new WebTable(driver.findElement(By.XPath
   (tableXPath))) ;
// find all row elements of the table
List<WebElement> rows = table.getRowElements();
// find all column elements of the first row of the table
List<WebElement> columns = table.getColumnElements(0);
```

EXAMPLE 11.7 Write WebDriver code to retrieve the total row count and column count of the table shown in Figure 11.3.

```
// find total number of rows of the table
int tableRowCount = table.getRowCount();   //Output::4
// find total number of columns of the table
int tableColumnCount = table.getColumnCount();   //Output::5
// find total number of columns of row-3 of the table
int tableColumnCount = table.getColumnCount(2); //Output::5
```

EXAMPLE 11.8 Write WebDriver code to find the cell which contains order number 2365467 and email id jmathew@gmail.com

```
// find table cell which contains order number 2365467
int[] cell1 = table.getCellWithData("2365467",0); //
  Output::2,2
// find table cell which contains email id jmathew@gmail.com
int[] cell2 = table.getCellWithData(jmathew@gmail.com,1); //
  Output::2,5
// Alternatively,(case-insensitive compare)
int[] cell3 = table.getCellWithData(JMmathew@gmail.com,0); //
  Output::2,5
```

EXAMPLE 11.9 Write WebDriver code to find the data contained in the cell 2,2 and 2,5.

```
// find data contained in the cell 2,2
String cellData22 = table.getCellData(2,2)//Output::2365467
// find data contained in the cell 2,5
String cellData22 = table.getCellData(2,5)//Output::jmathew@
  gmail.com
```

EXAMPLE 11.10 Write WebDriver code to find the element contained in the cell 2,1 and 2,5.

```
// find the first checkbox element contained in the cell 2,1
WebElement checkBox = table.getCellElement(2, 1, "input", 0);
// find the first link element contained in the cell 2,5
WebElement emailLink = table.getCellElement(2, 5, "a", 0);
```

INTERVIEW QUESTIONS

1. What are various ways to locate a static web table?
2. What is a dynamic web table?
3. What are the various ways to uniquely locate a dynamic web table?
4. Write code to locate a dynamic table.
5. Write code to retrieve the contents of cell (2,1) of Figure 11.1.
6. Write code to find the cell ordinates which contain string 'jmathew' for the table shown in Figure 11.1.
7. Write code to enter text 'Developer' to the text element of the cell (2,3) of the table of Figure 11.1.

12 CHAPTER

Working with Popup Windows

Pop-ups are generally new web browser windows usually generated by JavaScript using cross-site scripting (XSS). Pop-up windows often appear on a web page when a web page is submitted. Its general purpose is to confirm user that the intended operation has been performed or to warn user that the intended operation cannot be performed because of some error. It is also used in situations where re-confirmation of user is required for performing the intended operation, say funds transfer. Selenium WebDriver provides methods to switch driver context between various open windows. Once driver context is switched to the specific window, desired action can be taken on it. In WebDriver, pop-up windows can be handled by switching driver context to the pop-up window and then accepting or cancelling pop-up window. Once pop-up window is closed, driver context is be switched back to the main window.

The pop-up window can be located by using its either *name* attribute or window handle. WebDriver provides method driver.switchTo().window(<name orwindowhandle>) to locate a pop-up window and then switch driver context to this pop-up window.

12.1 | IDENTIFYING A POP-UP WINDOW BY ITS NAME

Suppose on clicking on 'Submit Order' button on a web page, a pop-up window is thrown. User has the option to either confirm the order or cancel it from the pop-up window as shown in Figure 12.1.

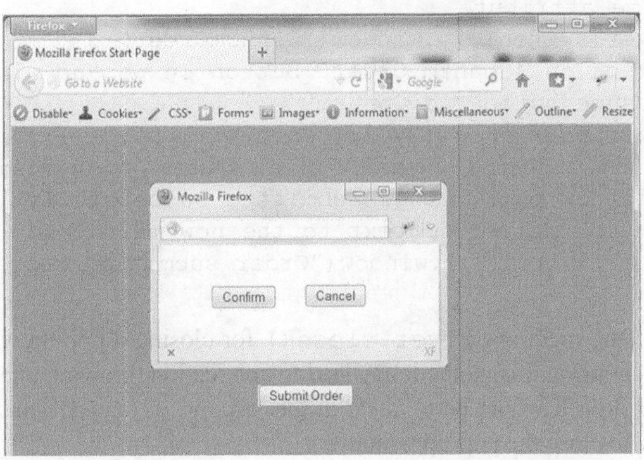

FIGURE 12.1 | Pop-up window

Assume HTML code of the 'Submit Order' button to be:

```
<button id="orderbutton"
onclick="window.open("confirmorder.html","ConfirmOrder","width=300,
  height=100");">Submit Order</button>
```

WebDriver code below shows how to switch driver context to the pop-up window and click on the 'Confirm' button. Code below first shows how to cancel a pop-up window and then shows how to accept a pop-up window.

```
@Test
public void testIdentifyPopupWindowUsingName(){
    WebDriver driver = new FirefoxDriver();
    driver.get("..............");
    ... ... ... ...
    ... ... ... ...
    //get windowhandle of current window
    String parentWindowHandle = driver.getWindowHandle();
    //click on submit order button
    driver.findElement(By.id("orderbutton")).click();
    //switch driver context to the pop-up window using its
      name attribute
    driver.switchTo().window("ConfirmOrder");
    //verify pop-up window title name. Assume title=Confirm Order
    assertTrue(driver.getTitle().equals("Confirm Order"));
    //Close the pop-up window
    driver.close();
    //switch driver context back to main page using
      windowhandle
    driver.switchTo().window(parentWindowHandle);
    //click on submit order button again
    driver.findElement(By.id("orderbutton")).click();
    //switch driver context to the pop-up window using its
      name attribute
    driver.switchTo().window("ConfirmOrder");
    //click on 'Confirm Order' button on pop-up window.
    //Assume button id=Confirm
    driver.findElement(By.id("Confirm")).click();
    //Assume clicking on confirm order causes pop-up window to close
    //and new page 'Order submitted successfully' to open
    //switch driver context to the new main page
    driver.switchTo().window("Order submitted successfully");
}
```

Notes: 1. Avoid using method `driver.close()` for closing a pop-up window. Closing a pop-up by using this method may lead to application throwing unexpected errors. A better approach would be to click on the 'accept' or 'cancel' button of the pop-up window to close the pop-up window.

2. The `driver.switchTo().window()` method throws NoSuchElementException if it fails to locate the desired pop-up window. The test code needs to handle this error in order to develop a robust and reliable test.

12.2 | IDENTIFYING A POP-UP WINDOW BY ITS WINDOW HANDLE ID AND TITLE

Most often developers do not define the *name* attribute of pop-up window. In such scenarios, window handle id can be used to locate pop-up windows. But this value is dynamic and varies from one run session to another. In case multiple pop-up windows are open, it would become difficult to identify the desired pop-up window. To solve this problem, *title* attribute of the pop-up window can be used along with window handle attribute to uniquely locate a pop-up window.

For example, consider user click on 'Contact Us' link of a website opens two windows – one for contacting using phone number and other for contacting using chat. Assume title of the chat window to be 'Chat with us'. Following code shows how to identify this window among multiple open windows.

```
@Test
public void testIdentifyPopupWindowUsingName(){
       WebDriver driver = new FirefoxDriver();
       driver.get("...............");
       ... ... ... ...
       ... ... ... ...
       //get windowhandle of current window
       String parentWindowHandle = driver.getWindowHandle();
       //click on contact us button. This opens two more windows.
       driver.findElement(By.linkText("Contact Us")).click();
       //switch to window with title 'Chat with us'
       driver = this.switchToWindowWithTitle("Chat with us");
       //switch to the parent window
       driver.switchTo().window(parentWindowHandle);
}

private WebDriver switchToWindowWithTitle(WebDriver driver,
  String windowTitle){
       //get window handles of all open windows
       Set<String> openWindowsHandles = driver.getWindowHandles();
       //identify window with desired title and switch driver
         context to it
       for (String openWindowHandle : openWindowsHandles ){
              try{
                     if (driver.switchTo().window(openWindowHandle).
                       getTitle().equals(windowTitle)){
                            driver.switchTo().window
                              (openWindowHandle);
                            break;
                     }
              }catch (NoSuchElementException e){
                     e.printStackTrace();
              }
```

```
        }
        //return the driver instance whose context is set to
          the desired pop-up
        //window
        return driver;
    }
```

12.3 | IDENTIFYING A POP-UP WINDOW BY ITS CONTENTS

In certain applications, developers neither define the *name* attribute nor *title* attribute of the pop-up page. This makes it difficult to uniquely locate the pop-up window during run-time. This becomes more complex when multiple such pop-up windows are open. To solve this problem, pop-up windows are to be recognized by the contents displayed on the pop-up page.

EXAMPLE 12.1 Consider the web pages shown in Figure 12.2. It shows two pop-up windows: *Conditions of Use* and *Privacy Notice*. Assume neither *name* nor *title* attribute of these pop-windows have been defined. Write WebDriver code to locate *Conditions of Use* pop window by its contents and then close it.

FIGURE 12.2 | Two pop-up windows

```
@Test
public void testLocatePopupWindowUsingContents(){
        String contentsOfConditionsOfUsePage = "Conditions of Use";
        String contentsOfPrivacyNoticsPage = "Amazon.com Privacy
          Notice";
        WebDriver driver = new FirefoxDriver();
        driver.get("https://www.amazon.com/ap/signin...");
        //get windowhandle of current window
        String parentWindowHandle = driver.getWindowHandle();
        //click on link Conditions of Use
        driver.findElement(By.linkText("Conditions of Use")).click();
        //click on link Privacy Notice
        driver.findElement(By.linkText("Privacy Notice")).click();
        //get window handles of all open browser pages
        Set<String> allOpenWindows = driver.getWindowHandles();
        //Locate Conditions Of Use pop-up window by its content and
          then close
        //it
        for (String wndHandle:allOpenWindows){
                driver = driver.switchTo().window(wndHandle);
                if(driver.getPageSource().contains
                  (contentsOfConditionsOfUsePage)) {
                        driver.close();
                        break;
                }
        }
        //switch driver context back to main page using
          windowhandle
        driver = driver.switchTo().window(parentWindowHandle);
}
```

Note: Method getPageSource retrieves all the contents of the web page. Use of this method needs to be avoided as far as possible as it may lead to wrong validations. It may happen that the contents visible on page source are never visible on the web page. Thus in this case, a validation on the basis of page source contents proves to be a wrong validation. Page source contents of a web page can be viewed by doing a Right Mouse Click on the page and then selecting option – View Page Source.

12.4 | HANDLING JAVASCRIPT ALERT WINDOWS

Web developers also use JavaScript alerts to inform users of any form of submit errors, warnings, to confirm form submit, getting user response, etc. Automated tests need to simulate the user interaction with these alert boxes to automate various test cases.

Figure 12.3 shows a generic JavaScript alert box.

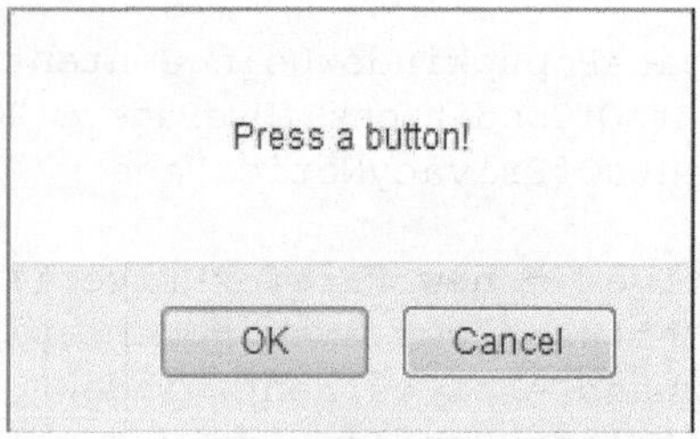

FIGURE 12.3 | JavaScript alert box

Selenium WebDriver provides an Alert class for working with JavaScript alerts. Method `switchTo()` to be used to switch driver context to the alert box before any user action can be taken on it.

```
Alert alert = driver.switchTo().alert()
```

Note: Method `driver.switchTo().alert()` throws NoAlertPresentException if no alert box is found during run-time.

Note: Handling NoAlertPresentException exception helps build a robust code.

Described as follows are some of the methods of Alert class.

- **`accept()`** : This method clicks on the 'OK' button of the alert box. Following code shows how to accept an alert box.

```
driver.switchTo().alert().accept();
```

- **`dismiss()`** : This method clicks on the 'Cancel' button of the alert box. Following code shows how to dismiss an alert box.

```
driver.switchTo().alert().dismiss();
```

- **`getText()`** : This method retrieves the text displayed on the alert box. Following c ode shows how to retrieve the text displayed on alert box.

```
driver.switchTo().alert().getText(); //Output::Press a button!
```

- **`sendKeys()`** : This method writes the specified text string on the alert prompt box. Following code shows how to write desired text on the edit box of the alert prompt box.

```
driver.switchTo().alert().sendKeys("some text");
```

Assume HTML code of the alert box is as shown below.

```
<!DOCTYPE html>
<html>
<body>
<p>Click the button to display a JavaScript alert box.</p>
<button onclick="functionShowAlertBox()">Open Alert Box</button>
<p id="alertBox"></p>
<script>
function functionShowAlertBox()
{
var x;
var r=confirm("Press a button!");
if (r==true)
  {
  x="You pressed OK!";
  }
else
  {
  x="You pressed Cancel!";
  }
document.getElementById("alertBox").innerHTML=x;
}
</script>
</body>
</html>
```

EXAMPLE 12.2 Write code to retrieve the text displayed on the alert box and to accept the alert box.

Method `getText()` can be used to retrieve the text displayed on the alert box and method `accept()` can be used to accept the alert box.

```
@Test
public void testAlertBox(){
        WebDriver driver = new FirefoxDriver();
        //open web page containing alert box
        driver.get("…");
        //get windowhandle of current window
        String parentWindowHandle = driver.getWindowHandle();
        //click on the button 'Open Alert Box' to open alert box
        driver.findElement(By.XPath("//button[contains
          (.,'Open Alert')]")).click();
        //switch driver context to alert box
        Alert alert = driver.switchTo().alert();
        //get text displayed on the alert box
        System.out.println(alert.getText());//Press a button!
```

```
        //click on the 'OK' button of alert box
        alert.accept();
        //switch driver context back to main page using windowhandle
        driver = driver.switchTo().window(parentWindowHandle);
}
```

EXAMPLE 12.3 Write code to dismiss alert box of Figure 12.3.

```
@Test
public void testAlertBox(){
        WebDriver driver = new FirefoxDriver();
        //open web page containing alert box
        driver.get("…");
        //get windowhandle of current window
        String parentWindowHandle = driver.getWindowHandle();
        //click on the button 'Open Alert Box' to open alert box
        //Note: also partial text match can be used to locate
          the element using
        //contains() method
        driver.findElement(By.XPath("//button[contains
          (.,'Open Alert')]")).click();
        //switch driver context to alert box
        Alert alert = driver.switchTo().alert();
        //click on the 'Cancel' button of alert box
        alert.dismiss();
        //switch driver context back to main page using windowhandle
        driver = driver.switchTo().window(parentWindowHandle);
}
```

12.5 | HANDLING A PROMPT BOX ALERT

Prompt box is an alert box with an option of user input. User is required to enter some text in the edit box of the alert window before accepting or cancelling the prompt box. Figure 12.4 shows a prompt box.

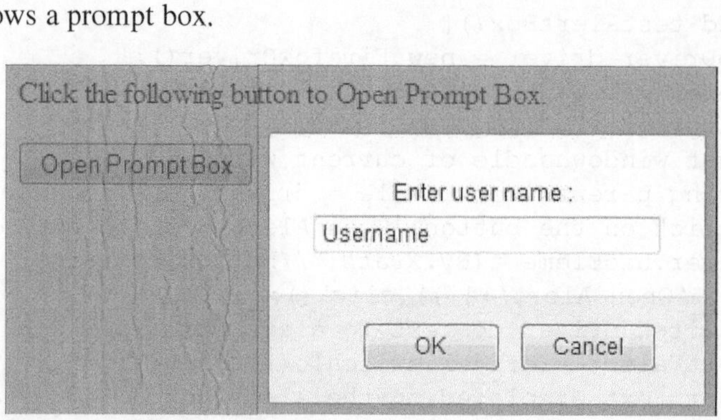

FIGURE 12.4 | Prompt box

EXAMPLE 12.4 Write WebDriver code to enter some text on the prompt box and then accept the prompt box.

Assume HTML code of the prompt box to be:

```
<!DOCTYPE html>
<html>
<head>
<script type="text/javascript">
<!--
function openPromptBox(){
  var enteredVal = prompt("Enter user name : ", "Username");
  alert("You have entered : " + enteredVal );
}
//-->
</script>
</head>
<body>
<p>Click the following button to Open Prompt Box. </p>
<form>
<input type="button" value="Open Prompt Box" onclick="openPromptBox();"/>
</form>
</body>
</html>
```

Method `sendKeys()` can be used to write a text string to prompt box and method `accept()` can be used to accept the alert box.

```
@Test
public void testPromptBox(){
        WebDriver driver = new FirefoxDriver();
        //open web page containing alert box
        driver.get("…");
        //get windowhandle of current window
        String parentWindowHandle = driver.getWindowHandle();
        //click on the button 'Open Prompt Box' to open prompt box
        driver.findElement(By.XPath("//input[@value='Open
          Prompt Box']")).click();
        //switch driver context to alert box
        Alert alert = driver.switchTo().alert();
        //enter some text string on the prompt box
        alert.sendKeys("Some Text");
        //click on the 'OK' button of alert box
        alert.accept();
        //switch driver context back to main page using windowhandle
        driver = driver.switchTo().window(parentWindowHandle);
}
```

INTERVIEW QUESTIONS

1. How will you locate a pop-up window and simulate user-click on 'Accept' button on pop-up window?
2. How will you automate a alert box?
3. How will you locate pop-up windows which does not have 'name' or 'title' attribute?
4. How will you automate a prompt box?

13 CHAPTER

Working with Frames

A frame is part of the web page or browser window which loads and displays content independent of its container. The elements that are inside a frame may or may not come from the same site as other elements of content on display. Frames allow developers to present HTML pages in multiple views. Multiple views to help to keep the other views as is, while one view is being scrolled.

For example, consider the Java docs page shown in Figure 13.1. It has three frames.

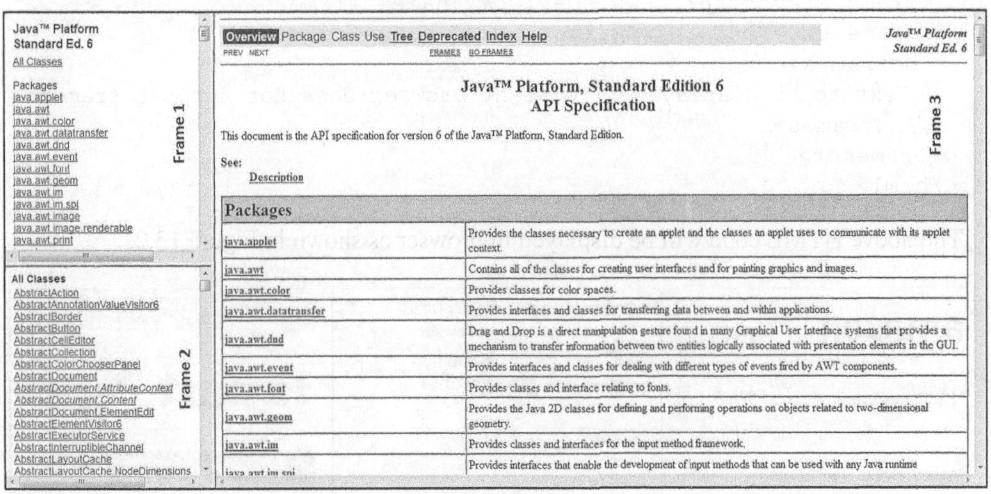

FIGURE 13.1 | Web page containing three frames

Assume HTML code of the above web page to be:

```
<html>
  <head>
  <frameset onload="top.loadFrames()" title="" cols="21%,79%">
    <frameset onload="top.loadFrames()" title="" rows="53%,47%">
      <frame title="All Packages" name="packageListFrame" src="overview-frame.html">
      <frame title="All classes and interfaces (except non-static nested types)" name="packageFrame" src="allclasses-frame.html">
    </frameset>
    <frame scrolling="yes" title="Package, class and interface descriptions" name="classFrame" src="overview-summary.html">
        <!DOCTYPE html PUBLIC "-//W3C//DTD HTML 4.01 Transitional//EN" "http://www.w3.org/TR/html4/loose.dtd">
      <html>
    </frame>
    <noframes> <H2> Frame Alert</H2> <P> This document is designed to be viewed using the frames feature. If you see this message,
    non-frame-capable web client. <BR> Link to<A HREF="overview-summary.html">Non-frame version.</A> </noframes>
  </frameset>
</html>
```

HTML 4.0 standards defines two different forms of frames. First one is the *frame* element used inside *frameset* container and the second one is the *iframe* element used within the body of the document.

13.1 | FRAMESET AND FRAME

A HTML 4 document which would normally contain a *head* and a *body* may instead contain a *head* and *frameset*. Both *body* and *frameset* cannot co-exist in the same HTML document. The attributes *rows* and *cols* define the dimensions of the frame. It is either specified in percentage or pixels. Inside the *frameset*, a number of *frames* can be defined. In the HTML code below *src* defines the target links of these frames. Sometimes developers use *<noframe>* element so that some message can be displayed to the user if frames are disabled in the browser. Example below shows how *frameset* and *frame* elements are used in a browser.

```
<html>
<frameset cols="33%, 33%, 33%">
  <frame src="http://www.amazon.com" name="frame1" id="frameid1">
  <frame src="http://www.ebay.com" name="frame2">
  <frame src="http://www.kmart.com" name="frame3">
  <noframes>
    Text to be displayed if current browser does not support frames
  </noframes>
</frameset>
</html>
```

The above HTML code will be displayed in browser as shown in Figure 13.2.

FIGURE 13.2 | Frameset element containing three frame elements

13.2 | IFRAME

The *iframe* element is used within a normal HTML body. Attributes of the *iframe* element are defined similar to the *frame* element. Figure 13.3 shows jQueryUI.com site which uses *iframe* element inside the *<body>* element of the HTML document.

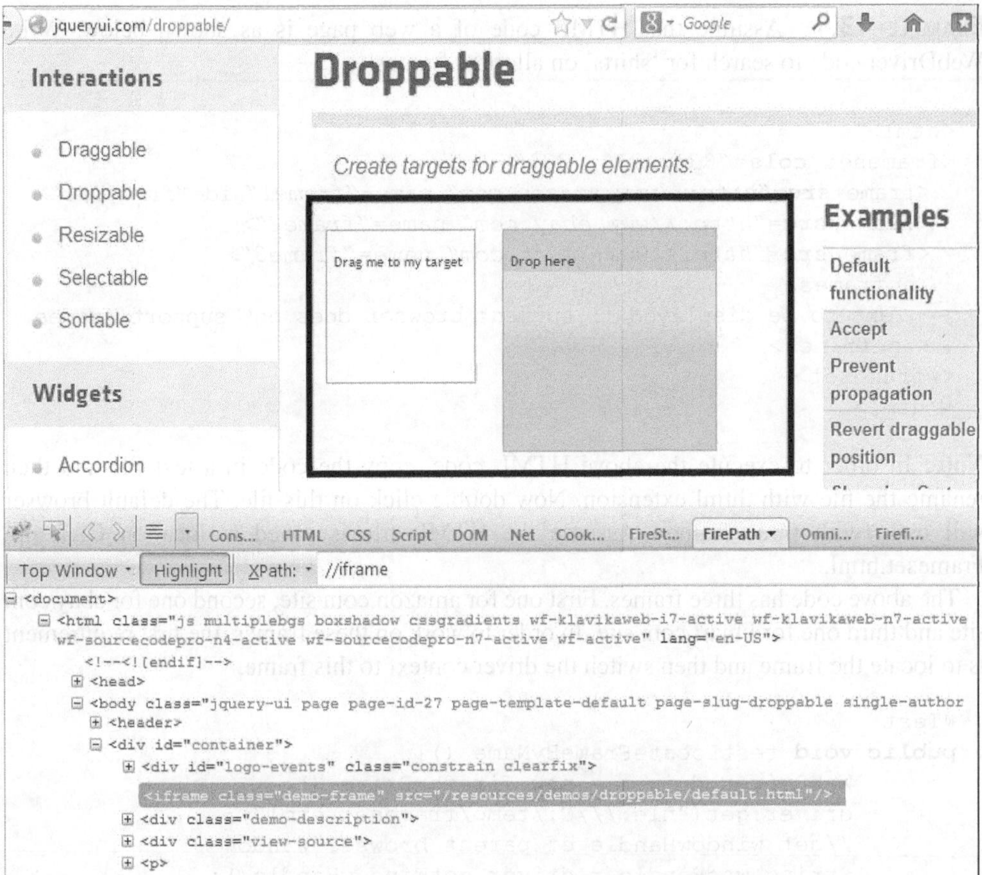

FIGURE 13.3 | iframe element inside <body> element of the web page document

13.3 | WORKING WITH FRAMESET AND FRAME

Selenium WebDriver provides four ways of locating a *frame* element – index, name, id or the frame element itself. That is, a frame can be located in a page by using its index value, or name attribute, or *id* attribute or *frame* element itself.

13.3.1 | Locating Frame Using *name* Attribute

Attribute *name* of the frame element can be used to locate the frame element.

EXAMPLE 13.1 Assume that HTML code of a web page is as shown below. Write WebDriver code to search for 'shirts' on all three frames.

```
<html>
<frameset cols="33%, 33%, 33%">
  <frame src="http://www.amazon.com" name="frame1" id="frameid1">
  <frame src="http://www.ebay.com" name="frame2">
  <frame src="http://www.kmart.com" name="frame3">
  <noframes>
    Text to be displayed if current browser does not support frames
  </noframes>
</frameset>
</html>
```

Note: In order to execute the above HTML code, copy the code in a text file and then rename the file with .html extension. Now double click on this file. The default browser will open with three frames. Assume the HTML file is saved at location C:\Temp\Frameset.html.

The above code has three frames. First one for amazon.com site, second one for ebay.com site and third one for kmart.com site. In order to work on these frames, the first requirement is to locate the frame and then switch the driver context to this frame.

```
@Test
public void testLocateFrameByName (){
        WebDriver driver = new FirefoxDriver();
        driver.get("file:///C:/temp/frameset.html");
        //get windowHandle of parent browser window
        String wndHandle = driver.getWindowHandle();

        //frame1 is amazon.com site. 'name' attribute of this
          frame is 'frame1'
        //switch driver context to the first frame
        driver = driver.switchTo().frame("frame1");
        //search for shirts
        //Assume 'id' attribute of search box is-'twotabsearchtextbox'
        driver.findElement(By.id("twotabsearchtextbox")).
          sendKeys("shirts");
        driver.findElement(By.id("twotabsearchtextbox")).
          sendKeys(Keys.ENTER);

        //switch driver context to parent window
        driver = driver.switchTo().window(wndHandle);
        //frame2 is ebay.com site. 'name' attribute of this
          frame is 'frame2'
        //switch driver context to the second frame
        driver = driver.switchTo().frame("frame2");
        //search for shirts
        //Assume 'id' attribute of search box is-'gh-ac'
```

```
        driver.findElement(By.id("gh-ac")).sendKeys("shirts");
        driver.findElement(By.id("gh-ac")).sendKeys(Keys.ENTER);
        //switch to parent window
        driver = driver.switchTo().window(wndHandle);
        //frame3 is kmart.com site. 'name' attribute of this
          frame is 'frame3'
        //switch driver context to the third frame
        driver = driver.switchTo().frame("frame3");
        //search for shirts
        //Assume 'id' attribute of search box is-'keyword'
        driver.findElement(By.id("keyword")).sendKeys("shirts");
        driver.findElement(By.id("keyword")).sendKeys(Keys.ENTER);
}
```

Note: Try to execute the above code by removing the code which switches the driver context back to the parent window. We will observe the test fails with error 'NoSuchFrameException'. This is because switch from one frame to another frame directly is not allowed. Only switching from parent window to a frame and vice-versa is allowed. Method `driver.switchTo().defaultContent()` can also be used to switch driver context back to the parent window.

13.3.2 | Locating Frame Using *id* Attribute

Attribute *id* of the frame element can be used to locate the frame element.

Example 13.2 Consider the HTML code of the example above. Write WebDriver code to locate first frame using its *id* attribute.

HTML code of the first frame is:

```
<frame src="http://www.amazon.com" name="frame1" id="frameid1">
```

The *id* attribute value of the above frame is *frameid1*. Code below show how to locate a frame using its *id* attribute.

```
@Test
public void testLocateFrameById() {
        WebDriver driver = new FirefoxDriver();
        driver.get("file:///C:/Temp/frameset.html");
        //switch driver context to frame 1 using its 'id' attribute
        driver = driver.switchTo().frame("frameid1");
        //search for shirts
        driver.findElement(By.id("twotabsearchtextbox")).
          sendKeys("shirts");
        driver.findElement(By.id("twotabsearchtextbox")).
          sendKeys(Keys.ENTER);
}
```

13.3.3 | Locating Frame Using *index* Value

Index value of the frame can also be used to locate the frame. The index value starts with 0 and goes on to 0, 1, 2....

EXAMPLE 13.3 Re-write the code of the section 'Locating frame using *name* attribute' to locate all the frames by their index value.

```
@Test
public void testLocateFrameByIndex() {
    WebDriver driver = new FirefoxDriver();
    driver.get("file:///C:/temp/frameset.html");

    //index value of frame1 amazon.com site is 0
    driver = driver.switchTo().frame(0);
    //search for shirts
    driver.findElement(By.id("twotabsearchtextbox")).
      sendKeys("shirts");
    driver.findElement(By.id("twotabsearchtextbox")).
      sendKeys(Keys.ENTER);

    //switch to parent window
    driver.switchTo().defaultContent();
    //index value of frame2 ebay.com site is 1
    driver = driver.switchTo().frame(1);
    //search for shirts
    driver.findElement(By.id("gh-ac")).sendKeys("shirts");
    driver.findElement(By.id("gh-ac")).sendKeys(Keys.ENTER);

    //switch to parent window
    driver.switchTo().defaultContent();
    //index value of frame2 kmart.com site is 2
    driver = driver.switchTo().frame(2);
    //search for shirts
    driver.findElement(By.id("keyword")).sendKeys("shirts");
    driver.findElement(By.id("keyword")).sendKeys(Keys.ENTER);
}
```

13.3.4 | Locating Frame Using *frame* Element

It is also possible to locate the frame element first and then switch WebDriver instance context to this frame element. Code below shows an implementation of the same.

EXAMPLE 13.4 Re-write code of the section '*Locate frame using name* attribute' to locate frame element first and then switch driver context to this frame element.

```
@Test
public void testLocateFrameByFrameElement() {
        WebDriver driver = new FirefoxDriver();
        driver.get("file:///C:/temp/frameset.html");

        //locate frame 1
        WebElement frame1 = driver.findElement(By.id("frameid1"));
        //switch driver context to frame1
        driver = driver.switchTo().frame(frame1);
        //search for shirts
        driver.findElement(By.id("twotabsearchtextbox")).
          sendKeys("shirts");
        driver.findElement(By.id("twotabsearchtextbox")).
          sendKeys(Keys.ENTER);
        //switch to parent window
        driver = driver.switchTo().defaultContent();
        //locate frame 2
        WebElement frame2 = driver.findElement(By.name("frame2"));
        driver = driver.switchTo().frame(frame2);
        //search for shirts
        driver.findElement(By.id("gh-ac")).sendKeys("shirts");
        driver.findElement(By.id("gh-ac")).sendKeys(Keys.ENTER);

        //switch to parent window
        driver = driver.switchTo().defaultContent();
        //locate frame 2
        WebElement frame3 = driver.findElement(By.name("frame3"));
        driver = driver.switchTo().frame(2);
        //search for shirts
        driver.findElement(By.id("keyword")).sendKeys("shirts");
        driver.findElement(By.id("keyword")).sendKeys(Keys.ENTER);
}
```

There could be scenarios where frame attributes are dynamic and none of the frame attributes can be relied upon to uniquely locate the frame element. In such scenarios, all the frames of the web document can be retrieved using findElements method. The list of frame elements so found can be used to switch driver context to various frames. Code below shows an example illustration of the same.

```
@Test
public void testLocateFrameByFrameElements() {
        WebDriver driver = new FirefoxDriver();
        driver.get("file:///C:/temp/frameset.html");
```

```
        //locate all frames on the apge document
        List<WebElement> allFrames = driver.findElements
          (By.tagName("frame"));

        //switch driver context to frame1
        driver = driver.switchTo().frame(allFrames.get(0));
        //search for shirts
        driver.findElement(By.id("twotabsearchtextbox")).
          sendKeys("shirts");
        driver.findElement(By.id("twotabsearchtextbox")).
          sendKeys(Keys.ENTER);

        //switch to parent window
        driver = driver.switchTo().defaultContent();
        //locate frame 2
        driver = driver.switchTo().frame(allFrames.get(1));
        //search for shirts
        driver.findElement(By.id("gh-ac")).sendKeys("shirts");
        driver.findElement(By.id("gh-ac")).sendKeys(Keys.ENTER);

        //switch to parent window
        driver = driver.switchTo().defaultContent();
        //locate frame 2
        driver = driver.switchTo().frame(allFrames.get(2));
        //search for shirts
        driver.findElement(By.id("keyword")).sendKeys("shirts");
        driver.findElement(By.id("keyword")).sendKeys(Keys.ENTER);
}
```

13.3.5 | Locating Frame Using *frame* Contents

In the example above, it can be observed that in list *allFrames*, we do not know which index value of *allFrames* contains which page. Suppose the developer changes the code of the above page to:

```
<html>
<frameset cols="33%, 33%, 33%">
  <frame src="http://www.ebay.com" name="frame1" id="frameid1">
  <frame src="http://www.amazon.com" name="frame2">
  <frame src="http://www.kmart.com" name="frame3">
  <noframes>
    Text to be displayed if current browser does not support frames
  </noframes>
</frameset>
</html>
```

In this case, the above code will fail as it will expect amazon.com site at index zero. In order to ensure we are working on the right frame, the contents of the frame can be used to locate the right frame element.

EXAMPLE 13.5 Write WebDriver code to locate frame containing amazon.com site by identifying the frame which has URL www.amazon.com.

```
@Test
public void testLocateFrameByFramePageURL() {
        WebDriver driver = new FirefoxDriver();
        driver.get("file:///C:/temp/frameset.html");
        driver = this.switchToFrameWithURL(driver, "www.amazon.com");
        //search for shirts
        driver.findElement(By.id("twotabsearchtextbox")).
          sendKeys("shirts");
        driver.findElement(By.id("twotabsearchtextbox")).
          sendKeys(Keys.ENTER);

}
//switch driver focus to a frame which has the given URL
private WebDriver switchToFrameWithURL(WebDriver driver,
  String URL){
        List<WebElement> allFrames = driver.findElements
          (By.tagName("frame"));
        for (int i=0;i<allFrames.size();i++){
                driver = driver.switchTo().frame(allFrames.get(i));
                String url = driver.getCurrentUrl();
                if (url.contains(URL)) break;
        }
        return driver;
}
```

EXAMPLE 13.6 Write WebDriver code to locate frame containing amazon.com site by identifying the frame whose page contents contains value 'amazon'.

```
@Test
public void testLocateFrameByFrameContents() {
        WebDriver driver = new FirefoxDriver();
        driver.get("file:///C:/Users/Rajeev/Desktop/frameset.html");
        driver = this.switchToFrameWithContents(driver, "amazon");
        //search for shirts
        driver.findElement(By.id("twotabsearchtextbox")).
          sendKeys("shirts");
```

```
        driver.findElement(By.id("twotabsearchtextbox")).
          sendKeys(Keys.ENTER);
    }

    //switch driver focus to a frame whose page source contains
    //the specified key strings
    private WebDriver switchToFrameWithContents(WebDriver driver,
      String contents){
          List<WebElement> allFrames = driver.findElements
            (By.tagName("frame"));
          for (int i=0;i<allFrames.size();i++){
                driver = driver.switchTo().frame(allFrames.get(i));
                String frameContents = driver.getCurrentUrl();
                if (frameContents.contains(contents)) break;
          }
          return driver;
    }
```

Note: The `driver.getTitle()` method can also be used to search the frame by its title. Frame title is defined in the HTML code with title attribute as shown below.

```
<frame title="All Packages" name="packageListFrame"
src="overview-frame.html">
```

13.4 | WORKING WITH IFRAME

HTML provides the flexibility to the developers to embed external documents or documents from another website by using the <iframe> tag. Various social media widgets and websites can be easily embedded in the web applications using <iframe> tag. Once embedded it appears as a link. For example, facebook like link of a facebook page can be embedded in any site the code as shown below.

```
<iframe scrolling="no" frameborder="0"
src="http://www.facebook.com/plugins/like.php?href=http%3A%2F%2Fwww.
  facebook.com/QTPBook&layout=button_count&show_faces=false&width=
  450&action=like&colorscheme=light&height=20" style="border:none;
  overflow:hidden; height:20px;" allowtransparency="true">
```

Note: To execute the above HTML code, copy the code in notepad and save it as .html file. Then double click on the file to open the HTML file in default browser window. Figure 13.4 shows how the above code renders on browser.

FIGURE 13.4 | Embedding facebook like link on a web page using <iframe>

Once a user hits on this link he will be directed to facebook login page. On successful login, the facebook like count of the page will increase by 1.

Working with frame created by <iframe> tag is very similar to working with frame created by <frameset> and <frame> tag.

EXAMPLE 13.7 Write web driver code to click on the facebook like link shown in Figure 13.4.

Assume the above HTML code is saved at location c:\temp\iframe.html

```
@Test
public void testIFrame() {
        WebDriver driver = new FirefoxDriver();
        driver.get(“file:///C:/temp/iframe.html”);
        //get the iframe element
        WebElement iframe = driver.findElement(By.tagName(“iframe”));
        //switch driver focus to iframe
        driver.switchTo().frame(iframe);
        //click on facebook like button
        driver.findElement(By.id(“u_0_0”)).click();

}
```

INTERVIEW QUESTIONS

1. What is the difference between frame and frameset?
2. Write code to search for text ‘shoes’ for all the frames shown in Figure 13.2.
3. Which is a better way of locating a frame – using frame index value, frame attributes or frame element?
4. How will you locate a frame using frame contents?

14
CHAPTER

Working with Cookies

A cookie is a piece of information sent from a website (server) and stored in the user's web browser (client machine) while a user is browsing a website. It is stored as a text file on the client machine. When the user browses the same website again, the stored information is sent to the website to notify it of the user's previous activities. The most common use of cookie is to store user session information. For example, a cookie might contain the following string:

Session-id = 53427908

Most of the websites, for example amazon.com, uses this technique. Whenever a user launches amazon.com site, a session id is created. The website stores session-id along with other user activity information in the server. Then, this session-id is send to the users' browser. Browser stores this information as text file on the users' machine. The session-id is, thereafter, used in all communication between users' browser and the website. This session-id helps to uniquely identify the user and uniquely track its activity on the site.

14.1 | HOW TO VIEW COOKIES IN FIREFOX BROWSER

Firefox add-on 'Web Developer' can be used to view browser cookie information. This add-on can be downloaded from site http://chrispederick.com/work/web-developer/. This add-on can also be installed on Chrome browser. Refer the steps below to view cookie information on Firefox browser:

- Open Firefox browser
- Navigate to amazon.com site and add an item to cart.
- Select option *Cookies → View Cookie Information* from the *Web Developer* menu as shown in Figure 14.1
- The cookie information window opens as shown in Figure 14.2. This window contains all information related to cookies such as total number of cookies, cookie name, cookie value, cookie expiry date, host site that stored this cookie, etc.

Notes: 1. For Chrome and IE browsers, the browser developer tools also provide the cookie information. These tools can also be used to verify the cookie details.

2. Firebug add-on *FireStorage Plus!* can also be used to view cookie details.

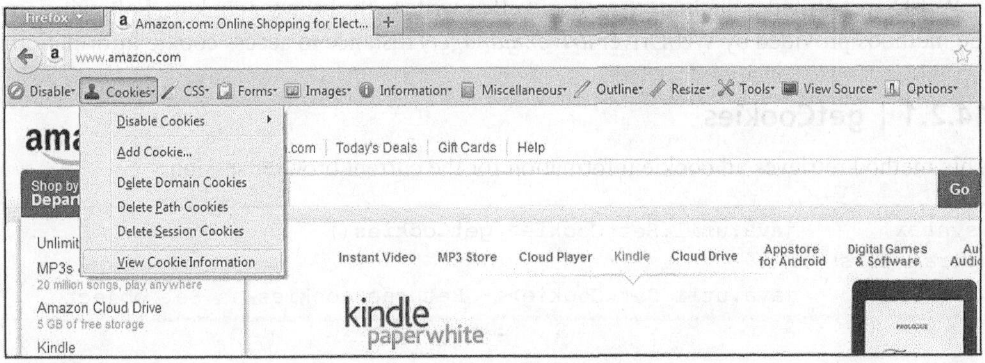

FIGURE 14. 1 | Viewing cookie information using Web Developer add-on

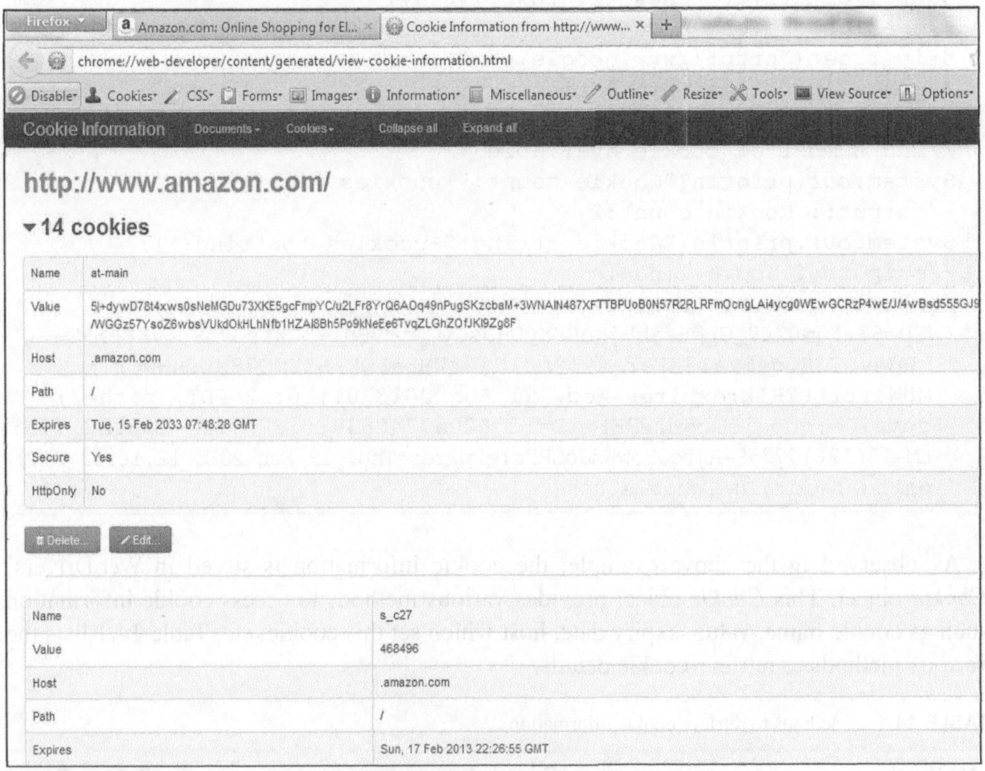

FIGURE 14. 2 | Cookies of amazon.com home page

14.2 | WEBDRIVE METHODS FOR COOKIE OBJECT

In test automation, we are required to validate the cookie information to ensure cookies are being correctly set on the users' browser. It may lead to bad user experience if cookies are not being correctly set.

WebDriver provides methods to read as well as write to the browser cookies. Following are the methods provided by WebDriver *driver.manage()* instance to access cookie information:

14.2.1 | getCookies

This method retrieves all cookie information for the current browser session.

syntax	java.util.Set<Cookie> **getCookies**()
parameters	
returns	java.util.Set<Cookie> - Returns cookies as Set object

EXAMPLE 14.1 Write code to read cookie values when user opens google.com page

```
WebDriver driver = new FirefoxDriver();
//open google.com page
driver.get("http://www.google.com");
//get all cookies information
Set<Cookie> cookies = driver.manage().getCookies();
//find number of cookie available
System.out.println("Cookie count:"+cookies.size());
//output:: Cookie count:2
System.out.println("Cookie string:"+cookies.toString());
//output of above line is
//output:: Cookie string:
[NID=67=Iqm02I8_GpW6aabRjUoDZXyDHPsCyCwjdRBnl15UXfs0v5EoJ7K8PXRT--
  _RdevSFIB0qe8VaI3XFsr-4Do9btTCj7rWM8sFQEkSZTmO78dLrHNwCr
  MfiWciriLPYRIk;expires=Wed, 21 Aug 2013 01:16:12 PDT; path=/;
  domain=.google.com,PREF=ID=1d0620a77408362f:FF=0:TM=1361261773:
  LM=1361261773:S=Ajfc9HoWFsJoNRFs;expires=Thu, 19 Feb 2015 12:16:12 PST;
  path=/; domain=.google.com]
```

As observed in the above example, the cookie information is stored in WebDrivers' *Cookie* object. This *Cookie* object provides various methods to access cookie information such as cookie name, value, expiry date, host which set this cookie, etc. Table 14.1 lists the various methods to retrieve cookie details.

TABLE 14.1 | Methods to retrieve cookie information

Method	Description	Return Type
toString()	Returns the complete cookie string	String
getDomain()	Returns host site name	String
getPath()	Returns cookie path	String
getName()	Returns cookie name	String

(continued)

TABLE 14.1 | *Continued*

getValue()	Returns cookie value	String
getExpiry()	Returns cookie expiry date	Date
isSecure()	Returns true if cookie is a secured cookie, else returns false	Boolean

EXAMPLE 14.2 Write a code to read the cookie details of all cookies when user opens google.com page

```
WebDriver driver = new FirefoxDriver();
//open amazon.com page
driver.get("http://www.amazon.com");
//open google.com page
driver.navigate().to("http://www.google.com");
//get cookie value
cookies = driver.manage().getCookies();
System.out.println("Cookie string:"+cookies.toString());
//output of above line is
//output:: Cookie string:
[NID=67=Iqm02I8_GpW6aabRjUoDZXyDHPsCyCwjdRBnll5UXfs0v5EoJ7K8PXRT--
  _RdevSFIB0qe8VaI3XFsr-4Do9btTCj7rWM8sFQEkSZTmO78dLrHNwCr
  MfiWciriLPYRIk;expires=Wed, 21 Aug 2013 01:16:12 PDT; path=/;
  domain=.google.com,PREF=ID=1d0620a77408362f:FF=0:TM=1361261773:
  LM=1361261773:S=Ajfc9HoWFsJoNRFs; expires=Thu, 19 Feb 2015
  12:16:12 PST; path=/; domain=.google.com]
//read all cookie values in the above cookie object
System.out.println("Domain, Path, Name, Value, Expiry, IsSecure");
for(Cookie cookie: cookies){
            System.out.println("Cookie string:" + cookie.toString());
       System.out.println(cookie.getDomain() + "," +
         cookie.getPath() + "," + cookie.getName() + "," +
         cookie.getValue() + "," + cookie.getExpiry() + "," +
         cookie.isSecure());
}
```

The above *cookies* object has two cookies – NID and PREF. Table 14.2 shows output of the above code:

TABLE 14.2 | Output of code Example 14.2

Domain	Path	Name	Value	Expiry	IsSecure
Cookie string:NID=67=Iqm02I8_GpW6aabRjUoDZXyDHPsCyCwjdRBnll5UXfs0v5EoJ7K8PXRT--_RdevSFIB0qe8VaI3XFsr-4Do9btTCj7rWM8sFQEkSZTmO78dLrHNwCrMfiWciriLPYRIk;expires=Wed, 21 Aug 2013 01:16:12 PDT; path=/; domain=.google.com					

Domain	Path	Name	Value	Expiry	IsSecure
.google .com	/	NID	67=Iqm02I8_GpW6aabRjUoDZXy DHPsCyCwjdRBnll5UXfs0v5Eo J7K8PXRT--_RdevSFIB0qe8VaI3XFsr-4Do9btTCj7rWM8sFQEkSZTmO78 dLrHNwCrMfiWciriLPYRIk	Wed Aug 21 01:16:12 PDT 2013	false
Cookie string:PREF=ID=1d0620a77408362f:FF=0:TM=1361261773:LM=1361261773: S=Ajfc9HoWFsJoNRFs; expires=Thu, 19 Feb 2015 12:16:12 PST; path=/; domain=.google.com					
.google .com	/	PREF	ID=1d0620a77408362f:FF=0:TM=13 61261773:LM=1361261773: S=Ajfc9HoWFsJoNRFs	Thu Feb 19 00:16:12 PST 2015	false

14.2.2 | getCookieNamed

This method retrieves cookie details of the specified cookie.

syntax	Cookie getCookieNamed(java.lang.String name)
parameters	java.lang.String name - name of the cookie to be retrieved
returns	Cookie - returns cookie object

Example 14.3 Write a code to read PREF cookie details for the example explained above.

```
WebDriver driver = new FirefoxDriver();
driver.get("http://www.google.com");
//get PREF cookie
Cookie cookie = driver.manage().getCookieNamed("PREF");
System.out.println("Cookie string:" + cookie.toString());
//output::Cookie string:
PREF=ID=1d0620a77408362f:FF=0:TM=1361261773:LM=1361261773:
  S=Ajfc9HoWFsJoNRFs;
expires=Thu, 19 Feb 2015 12:16:12 PST; path=/; domain=.google.com
System.out.println("Cookie domain:" + cookie.getDomain());
//output::Cookie domain: .google.com
System.out.println("Cookie path:" + cookie.getPath());
//output::Cookie path:/
System.out.println("Cookie name:" + cookie.getName());
//output::Cookie name:PREF
System.out.println("Cookie value:" + cookie.getValue());
```

```
//output::Cookie value:
ID=1d0620a77408362f:FF=0:TM=1361261773:LM=1361261773:
  S=Ajfc9HoWFsJoNRFs
System.out.println("Cookie expiry date:" + cookie.getExpiry());
//output::Cookie expiry date: Thu Feb 19 00:16:12 PST 2015
```

14.2.3 | deleteCookie

This method deletes a cookie from the browser's 'cookie jar'.

syntax	void deleteCookie(Cookie cookie)
parameters	Cookie - cookie object
returns	void

Example 14.4 Write a code to delete the PREF cookie for the above example.

```
WebDriver driver = new FirefoxDriver();
driver.get("http://www.google.com");
//get cookie count
int cookieCount = driver.manage().getCookies().size();
System.out.println("Cookie count after add to cart:" + cookieCount);
//Output:: Cookie count after add to cart:2
//get PREF cookie
Cookie cookie = driver.manage().getCookieNamed("PREF");
//delete PREF cookies
driver.manage().deleteCookie(cookie);
//get cookie count after PREF cookie delete
cookieCount = driver.manage().getCookies().size();
System.out.println("Cookie count after PREF cookie delete:" +
  cookieCount);
//Output:: Cookie count after PREF cookie delete:1
```

14.2.4 | deleteCookieNamed

This method deletes the cookie which has the specified name.

syntax	void deleteCookieNamed(java.lang.String name)
parameters	java.lang.String name - name of the cookie to be deleted
returns	void

Example 14.5 Write a code to delete the cookie named PREF for the above example.

```
WebDriver driver = new FirefoxDriver();
driver.get("http://www.google.com");
//get cookie count
int cookieCount = driver.manage().getCookies().size();
System.out.println("Cookie count after add to cart:" + cookieCount);
```

```
//Output:: Cookie count after add to cart:2
//delete PREF cookies
driver.manage().deleteCookieNamed("PREF");
//get cookie count after PREF cookie delete
cookieCount = driver.manage().getCookies().size();
System.out.println("Cookie count after PREF cookie delete:" +
  cookieCount);
//Output:: Cookie count after PREF cookie delete:1
```

14.2.5 | deleteAllCookies

This method deletes all cookies for the current domain.

syntax	void deleteAllCookies()
parameters	
returns	void

EXAMPLE 14.6 User opens amazon.com site, adds an item to cart and then deletes the cookies. Then he refreshes the browser. The test requirement is to verify after deleting cookies, amazon.com site does not shows any item in cart.

```
//create an instance of firefox driver
WebDriver driver = new FirefoxDriver();
//open amazon product page for xbox 360
driver.get("http://www.amazon.com/Xbox-360-4GB-Console/dp/
  B003O6JKLC");
//add to cart
driver.findElement(By.name("submit.add-to-cart"));
//get cookie count
int cookieCount = driver.manage().getCookies().size();
System.out.println("Cookie count after add to cart:" + cookieCount);
//output:: Cookie count after add to cart:6
//delete all cookies
driver.manage().deleteAllCookies();
//get cookie count after deleting cookies
cookieCount = driver.manage().getCookies().size();
System.out.println("Cookie count after deleting cookies:" +
  cookieCount);
//output:: Cookie count after deleting cookies:0
```

14.2.6 | addCookie

This method adds the specified cookie to the browser cookie.

syntax	void addCookie(Cookie cookie)
parameters	Cookie - The cookie to be added to the browser cookie
returns	void

EXAMPLE 14.7 User opens google.com and the deletes PREF cookie. Write a code to add new cookie PREFERENCE to the cookie object.

```
WebDriver driver = new FirefoxDriver();
driver.get("http://www.google.com");
int cookieCount = driver.manage().getCookies().size();
System.out.println("Cookie count before new cookie add:" +
  cookieCount);
//define PREFERENCE cookie details
Calendar cal = new GregorianCalendar();
int year = 2070;
int month = 6;
int day = 7;
int hour = 10;
int minute = 26;
int second = 47;
cal.set(year, month, day, hour, minute, second);
Date expiry = cal.getTime();
String name = "PREFERENCE";
String value = "ID=1d0620a77408362f:FF=0:TM=1361261";
String domain = "www.google.com";
String path = "/";
//add PREFERENCE cookie
Cookie cookie = new Cookie(name, value, domain, path, expiry);
driver.manage().addCookie(cookie);
cookieCount = driver.manage().getCookies().size();
System.out.println("Cookie count after new cookie add:" +
  cookieCount);
//get cookie named PREFERENCE
Cookie newCookie = driver.manage().getCookieNamed("PREFERENCE");
//get cookie name
System.out.println("Cookie name:" + newCookie.getName());
//get cookie value
System.out.println("Cookie name:" + newCookie.getValue());
```

INTERVIEW QUESTIONS

1. Explain how to read various cookie attributes such as expiry date, location, description, domain etc. from the stored cookie information.
2. Explain the various WebDriver methods to read cookie information.
3. Write code to write new cookie information to the browser cookie.
4. Write code to add new cookie information to browser that automatically adds an item to amazon.com site cart.
5. Write code to delete cookie information.

15 CHAPTER

Synchronization

Synchronization points are used in Selenium WebDriver to keep the code execution speed in sync with the application under test response time. The reason being WebDriver executes the code statements in a fraction of second while it may take more than a second for the application to respond. Depending on server load, database volume, network speed and code performance, the application response varies from time to time. Since the page/element may take time to load, by that time WebDriver will throw an element not found exception and will fail the tests. Code synchronization is used in these scenarios to pause WebDriver code execution till the application under test (AUT) responds or a timeout occurs. Synchronization code helps halt WebDriver execution until the object is not loaded into the application. As soon as the object is properly loaded, Webdrive code execution starts.

15.1 | WHEN TO USE SYNCHRONIZATION

Synchronization code to be used to pause WebDriver test execution till the page has properly loaded. Following are the three instances where synchronization statements are a must:

- *When a new web page loads* like clicking on a link, element opens new page.
- *When the existing page reloads* because of some user action like click on refresh button or refine search by price range on amazon.com site.
- *When the page attributes or page elements changes* because of some user action like selecting an option in the list box causes new elements (options) to be displayed on the page.
- *When a user action causes some file to load from server and open automatically* like opening of an excel file after clicking on a button.

15.2 | SYNCHRONIZATION METHODS

There are various ways to synchronize the WebDriver test with the application response time. One way could be to pause test execution till a given time. This is called *implicit wait.* Another way could be to pause the test execution till a condition is true say page title attains a specific value. This is called *explicit wait.* WebDriver also provides the flexibility to develop customized synchronization statements. Following are the synchronization methods that can be used in WebDriver:

- Implicit wait
- Explicit wait
- Customized wait

Note: Synchronization statements should never throw the code in indefinite wait or indefinite code loop.

15.2.1 | Implicit Wait

Selenium WebDriver provides an implicit wait for synchronizing tests as per application response time. When implicit wait is implemented in tests, the WebDriver halts test execution till the time element is found or a timeout occurs, whichever happens first. WebDriver continuously polls HTML DOM for the element presence before timing out after the specified timeout time. If WebDriver is not able to locate the element or elements within the specified time then it times out and throws `NoSuchElementException`. The default implicit timeout time for WebDriver is zero. This implies if Webdriver is not able to locate the element or elements in the first attempt, then it times out and throws an exception.

The implicit timeout time can be modified by using the Timeouts interface. The Timeouts interface provides an implicitly `Wait ()` method. This method defines the time WebDriver can wait and poll for the elements presence before timing out. Once defined, the implicit wait is set for the lifetime of the WebDriver's object instance. However, implicit wait may slow down test execution as it will wait for the each element appearing in the DOM and thereby increase the overall execution time.

Configuring Implicit Wait Timeout Time

Implicit timeout time specifies the amount of time the driver should wait when searching for an element if it is not immediately present. When searching for a single element, the driver polls the page until the element has been found, or timeout occurs. On timeout,WebDriver throws NoSuchElementException. When searching for multiple elements, the driver polls the page until at least one element has been found or timeout occurs. Following code shows how to set the implicit wait time to 10 seconds.

```
driver.manage().timeouts().implicitlyWait(10, TimeUnit.SECONDS)
```

The implicit wait time can specified in units of nanosecond, millisecond, second, minute, hour, etc.

Configuring Page Load Wait Timeout Time

Page load time specifies the amount of time to wait for a page load to complete before throwing an error. If the timeout is negative, WebDriver page load time is indefinite, i.e., WebDriver waits indefinetely for the page to load. In this case, if the AUT hangs, timeout never occurs. It is always advisable to use a positive value of timeout time. Following code shows how to configure page load wait time to 5000 milliseconds.

```
driver.manage().timeouts().pageLoadTimeout(5000, TimeUnit.
  MILLISECONDS)
```

EXAMPLE 15.1 Write WebDriver code which sets the implicit wait time to 1 second and page load time to 5 seconds before opening amazon.com site.

```
WebDriver driver = new FirefoxDriver();
//set page load timeout time to 5 second
driver.manage().timeouts().pageLoadTimeout(5, TimeUnit.SECONDS);
//set implicit timeout time to 1 second
driver.manage().timeouts().implicitlyWait(1, TimeUnit.SECONDS);
//open amazon.com
driver.get("http://www.amazon.com");
//navigate to page today's deals
driver.findElement(By.linkText("Today's Deals")).click();
```

Configuring Script Timeout Time

Script timeout time specifies the amount of time to wait for an asynchronous script to finish execution before throwing an error. If the timeout is negative, then the script will be allowed to run indefinitely. Executing Javascript code against a browser is an example of asynchronous script. In this case, WebDriver has no way to know when JavaScript code has completed execution. And if Webdrive starts code execution before JavaScript code execution is complete, the test will fail. A solution approach to this problem would be to estimate the execution time of JavaScript code and set the *script timeout time* to be same including some safe margin time. Following code shows how to configure script timeout time to 2 minutes.

```
driver.manage().timeouts().setScriptTimeout (2, TimeUnit.MINUTES)
```

EXAMPLE 15.2 Write code to execute an asynchronous JavaScript which pauses test execution for 2 seconds where script timeout time is 5 seconds.

```
@Test
public void testAsyncWaitWith2sec(){
        WebDriver driver = new FirefoxDriver();
        driver.manage().timeouts().setScriptTimeout(5, TimeUnit.
          SECONDS);
        long start = System.currentTimeMillis();
        //JavaScript executes a windows command to pause
          execution for 2 seconds
        ((JavascriptExecutor) driver).executeAsyncScript(
             "window.setTimeout(arguments[arguments.length - 1],
             2000);");
            System.out.println(
                 "Elapsed time: " + (System.currentTimeMillis() -
                 start));
}
Output:: Elapsed time: 2020
```

The above test can wait for maximum 5 seconds for the JavaScript to complete execution. The JavaScript takes 2 seconds to complete execution and send back the response. After initiating JavaScript code execution, the test enters a pause state where it continuously polls for a response from the JavaScript. The maximum time it can poll, for the above test, is 5 seconds. For the case above, it receives the response from JavaScript after 2.02 seconds (less than 5 seconds). Hence, the script executes fine.

```
@Test
public void testAsyncWaitWith6sec(){
      WebDriver driver = new FirefoxDriver();
      driver.manage().timeouts().setScriptTimeout(5, TimeUnit.
        SECONDS);
      long start = System.currentTimeMillis();
        ((JavascriptExecutor) driver).executeAsyncScript(
                        "window.setTimeout(arguments[arguments.
                          length - 1], 6000);");
            System.out.println(
                        "Elapsed time: " + (System.
                          currentTimeMillis() - start));

}
Output:: Script fails
```

The above test has script timeout time=5 seconds, whereas JavaScript execution time (wait time for the above)=6 seconds. Since, in the above case the script does not receive any response within 5 seconds, it times out and fails. Exception handler code is to be written to handle such exceptions and throw meaningful error to user.

Suppose we have a requirement where we would like to execute an external script, dll or jar file where time taken to execute an external code does not impacts currents test execution. In this scenario, we can use method executeScript as shown below. Example below executes a JavaScript code that throws a pop-up window. In this case, the test code is not dependent on whether JavaScript code executes perfectly or not or when it completes execution. Therefore, in this case even though timeout occurs the test passes.

EXAMPLE 15.3 Write JavaScript code which throws an alert pop-up box.

```
@Test
public void testExecuteTestIndependentScript() {
      WebDriver driver = new FirefoxDriver();
      driver.manage().timeouts().setScriptTimeout(1, TimeUnit.
        SECONDS);
      long start = System.currentTimeMillis();
      System.out.println("Start time:" + start);
      ((JavascriptExecutor) driver).executeScript(
              "alert(\"Waiting for user
                intervention\"),5000;");
```

```
    long end = System.currentTimeMillis();
    System.out.println("End time: " +end);
    long elapsedTime =end - start;
    System.out.println("Elapsed time: " +elapsedTime);
}

Output:: Start time:1366342945886
         End time: 1366342945977
         Elapsed time: 91
```

In the above test, the test script executes the JavaScript file but does not wait for it to complete its execution. As soon as the JavaScript statement is executed, it starts to execute the next line of code. The JavaScript when executed throws an alert pop-up box and waits for 5 seconds for the user to respond. Thus, even when the JavaScript execution is still in progress, the test execution completes.

Note: Increasing the implicit wait timeout should be used judiciously as it can increase test execution time, especially when used with slower location strategies like XPath.

EXAMPLE 15.4 Write a code to inject an XMLHttpRequest and wait for the result.

```
Object response = ((JavascriptExecutor) driver)
  .executeAsyncScript(
      "var callback = arguments[arguments.length - 1];" +
      "var xmlReq = new XMLHttpRequest();" +
      "xmlReq.open('GET', '/resource/jsonData.json', true);" +
      "xmlReq.onreadystatechange = function() {" +
      " if (xmlReq.readyState == 4) {" +
      " callback(xmlReq.responseText);" +
      " }" +
      "}" +
      "xmlReq.send();");
JSONObject json = new JSONObject((String) response);
assertEquals("apple", json.getString("Fruit"));
```

15.2.2 | Explicit Wait

Explicit wait provides an option to write custom code or conditions for wait before proceeding further in the code. Explicit wait provides a better control over test flow when compared to implicit wait. An explicit wait can be used when synchronization is required for a specific step (line of code) in the test. Selenium WebDriver provides WebDriverWait and ExpectedCondition classes for implementing an explicit wait.

The ExpectedCondition class provides a set of predefined conditions to wait before proceeding further in the code.

EXAMPLE 15.5 Write WebDriver code that synchronizes with new web page opened by verifying the title of the page.

Method ExpectedConditions.titleContains() can be used to implement an explicit wait on page title. This method will pause Selenium execution until the title of the page equals the specified title name or timeout occurs, whichever happens first.

Following code opens amazon.com page as shown in Figure 15.1 and then clicks on the 'Sign In' link. Method WebDriverWait and ExpectedConditions.titleContains() have been used to pause Selenium execution until title of the page attains the specific value or timeout occurs.

```
@Test
public void testExplicitlWaitOnTitle(){
       WebDriver driver = new FirefoxDriver();
       //open amazon.com site
       driver.get("https://www.amazon.com");
       //click on sign-in link
       driver.findElement(By.id("nav-signin-text")).click();
       //create an instance of WebDriverWait and set
         timeout=10seconds
       WebDriverWait wait =new WebDriverWait(driver,10);
       //Wait until the title of page contains string 'SignIn' of
       //10 seconds is reached
       wait.until(ExpectedConditions.titleContains("Sign In"));

}
```

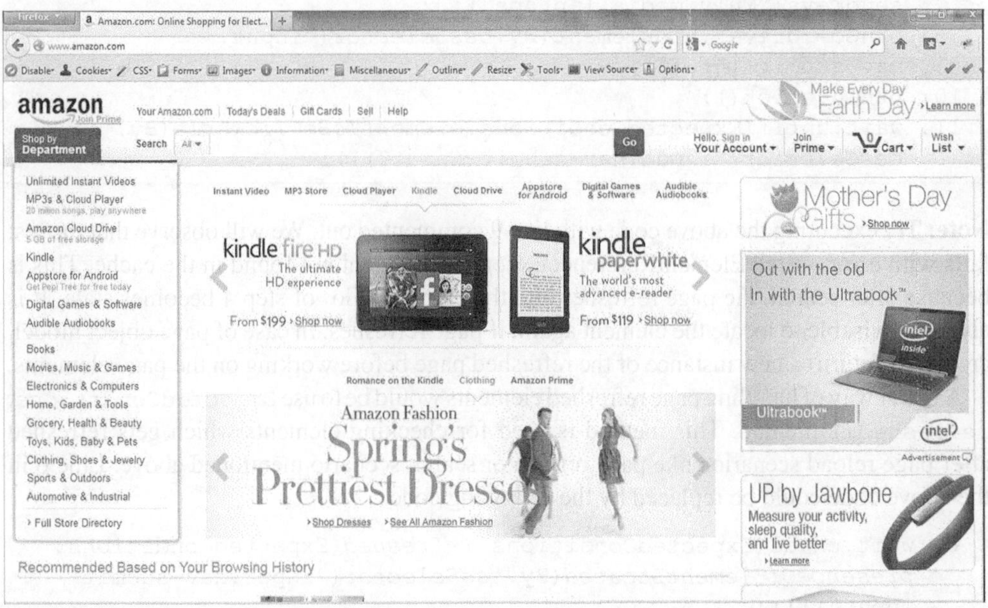

FIGURE 15. 1 | Amazon.com home page

EXAMPLE 15.6 Write WebDriver code to synchronize WebDriver code until an element is clickable in UI.

Method *ExpectedConditions.elementToBeClickable* () can be used to pause Selenium execution until an element is clickable.

Following code shows how to synchronize WebDriver test until a button element is clickable in UI.

```
1. WebDriver driver = new FirefoxDriver();
   //open amazon.com site
2. driver.get("https://www.amazon.com");
   //search for 'laptops'
3. driver.findElement(By.id("twotabsearchtextbox")).
   sendKeys("laptops");
   //click on webelement Go button
4. WebElement btnGo= driver.findElement(By.cssSelector("input.
   nav-submit-input"));
5. btnGo.click();
   //wait until Go button is clickable or timeout occurs which-
   ever happens first
6. WebDriverWait wait =new WebDriverWait(driver,10);
   wait.until(ExpectedConditions.elementToBeClickable(By.
   cssSelector("input.nav-submit-input")));
   //search for 'Multimedia laptops'
7. driver.findElement(By.id("twotabsearchtextbox")).clear();
8. driver.findElement(By.id("twotabsearchtextbox")).
   sendKeys("Multimedia laptops");
9. btnGo= driver.findElement(By.cssSelector("input.
   nav-submit-input"));
10. btnGo.click();
11. wait.until(ExpectedConditions.elementToBeClickable(By.
   cssSelector("input.nav-submit-input")));
```

Note: Try executing the above code with line 9 commented out. We will observe that the test fails with error – StaleElementReferenceException.Element not found in the cache. This is because after search, the page refreshes and the element 'Go' of step 4 becomes stale. It is always advisable to locate the element again, if page refreshes. In case of page object model, create (or return) a new instance of the refreshed page before working on the page elements.

A better way of handling page refreshed elements would be to use `ExpectedConditions.refreshed()` method. This method is used for checking elements which gets refreshed after page reload scenarios like page refresh or search scenario mentioned above. Line 6 in the above code could be replaced by the following code.

```
6. wait.until(ExpectedConditions.refreshed(ExpectedConditions.
   presenceOfElementLocated(By.cssSelector("input.nav-submit-
   input"))));
```

Table 15.1 shows the various methods of ExpectedConditions that can be used for test synchronization:

TABLE 15.1 | Various methods of ExpectedConditions that can be used for test synchronization

Method	Description
alertIsPresent()	Expect alert window exists
elementSelectionStateToBe(By locator, boolean selected)	Expect the element selection to be as specified, selected or deselected
elementSelectionStateToBe(WebEleme nt element, boolean selected)	Expect the element selection to be as specified, selected or deselected
elementToBeClickable(By locator)	Expect the element is clickable
elementToBeSelected(By locator)	Expect the element is selected
elementToBeSelected(WebElement element)	Expect the element is selected
frameToBeAvailableAndSwitchToIt(java. lang.String frameLocator)	Expect the frame available for switching to it
invisibilityOfElementLocated(By locator)	Expect element is either invisible or not present on the DOM
invisibilityOfElementWithText(By locator, java.lang.String text)	Expect an element with the specified text is either invisible or not present on the DOM
not(ExpectedCondition<?> condition)	Check with the logical opposite condition of the given condition
presenceOfAllElementsLocatedBy(By locator)	Check that there is at least one element present on a web page
presenceOfElementLocated(By locator)	Check that an element is present on the DOM of a page
refreshed(ExpectedCondition<T> condition)	Wrapper for a condition, which allows for elements to update by redrawing
stalenessOf(WebElement element)	Wait until an element is no longer attached to the HTML DOM
textToBePresentInElement(By locator, java. lang.String text)	Check if the given text is present in the specified element.
textToBePresentInElementValue(By locator, java.lang.String text)	Check if the specified text is present in the specified elements value attribute
titleContains(java.lang.String title)	Check that the title contains a case-sensitive substring
titleIs(java.lang.String title)	Check the title of a page
visibilityOf(WebElement element)	Check that an element, known to be present on the DOM of a page, is visible.
visibilityOfElementLocated(By locator)	Check that an element is present on the DOM of a page and is visible

15.2.3 | Customized Wait

Selenium WebDriver provides the flexibility to build custom-expected conditions by using the ExpectedConditions class. This helps to design synchronization statements for a wide variety of test conditions.

EXAMPLE 15.7 Write synchronization code using customized wait statements to pause test execution until 'Go' button is visible on the amazon.com search page after a product item is searched.

```
@Test
public void testCustomizedPageRefreshWait(){
    WebDriver driver = new FirefoxDriver();
    //open amazon.com site
    driver.get("https://www.amazon.com");
    //search for 'laptops'
    driver.findElement(By.id("twotabsearchtextbox")).
      sendKeys("laptops");
    WebElement btnGo = driver.findElement(By.cssSelector
      ("input.nav-submit-input"));
    btnGo.click();
    //Set timeout time=3seconds
    //Expected condition is expecting a 'Go' button element
      is returned after page refresh
    try{
            WebElement refreshedGoBtn = (new WebDriverWait
               (driver,3))
                       .until(new ExpectedCondition<WebElement>
                         (){
                            @Override
                            public WebElement apply(WebDriver
                               driver){
                                  return driver.findElement
                                    (By.cssSelector("input.
                                    nav-submit-input"));
                            }
                       });
    }catch(NoSuchElementException e){
            fail("Go button not found after page refresh");
    }catch(TimeoutException e){
            fail("Go button not found till 3 seconds after
              page refresh");
    }
    //search for 'Multimedia laptops'
    driver.findElement(By.id("twotabsearchtextbox")).clear();
```

```
driver.findElement(By.id("twotabsearchtextbox")).
    sendKeys("Multimedia laptops");
  refreshedGoBtn.click();
}
```

Customized wait or synchronization statements can be implemented in various ways by using custom ExpectedCondition class. Following are some common examples of customized synchronization statements.

Waiting for Element's Visibility

Developers may code GUI elements to be invisible to the user unless a specific user action is taken. In such situation, it is required the test script waits till the element is visible on the page before taking any user action on it. Synchronization statements can be written using ExpectedCondition class that pauses Selenium execution till the element is visible in HTML DOM.

```
//Pause test execution till element is visible or timeout is
   reached whichever
//occurs first. Timeout time is 5seconds
Boolean isElementVisible =
      (new WebDriverWait(driver,5)).until(new
        ExpectedCondition<Boolean>(){
             public Boolean apply(WebDriver d){
                    return d.findElement(By.id("id")).
                         isDisplayed();
             }
      });
```

Waiting for Element's Attribute Value Update

Depending on user action taken on GUI elements, attribute values of elements can change. For example, specific links may get enabled for certain users depending on user's right. Another example can be 'previous' button getting enabled only on certain pages where user can navigate back to the previous page. Code below synchronizes test code till 'readonly' attribute of an element is updated to 'true'.

```
Boolean isDisabled =
      (new WebDriverWait(driver,5)).until(new
        ExpectedCondition<Boolean>(){
             public Boolean apply(WebDriver d){
                    return d.findElement(By.id("id2")).
                          getAttribute("readonly").
                            contains("true");
             }
      });
```

Waiting for DOM Events

DOM events such as opening of an excel file on click of a button requires test code to wait till the file is opened before it can be read. These DOM events may be using a JavaScript framework such as jQuery for AJAX and content manipulation. For example, jQuery is used to load a big JSON file asynchronously on the page. The test script needs to wait till jQuery loads the file before this file can be read. Following code shows the synchronization statement for pausing the test code till jQuery has loaded the file or is active.

```
Boolean isFileLoaded =
        (new WebDriverWait(driver,5)).until(new
          ExpectedCondition<Boolean>(){
        public Boolean apply(WebDriver d){
                JavascriptExecutor js = (JavascriptExecutor) d;
                return (Boolean) js.executeScript("return
                  jQuery.active==0"));
        });
```

INTERVIEW QUESTIONS

1. Why is code synchronization essential?
2. Explain the code synchronization features of Selenium WebDriver.
3. What is the difference between implicit wait and explicit wait?
4. User open Amazon.com site and searches for item say shirts. Write webdriver code for the same with appropriate synchronization statements.
5. In an application, when user selects an option in a list box, the page refreshes and loads new elements on the page. Which synchronization statement you will user to ensure WebDriver code pauses till new elements of the page is loaded properly?
6. An automation developer has written a code that searches for two items. First it searches for 'shirts' and then searches for 'shoes'. When the automation code is executed, the automation developer observes that the code throws stale element exception when search for 'shoes'. Explain where is the problem in the code and how will you resolve this problem.

16 CHAPTER

Checkpoints

Test case automation requires automation of the business flow and validation of the results. Validation of the results helps to decide whether a bug exists in the application or not. There are many reasons which can cause a test to fail. Few include mismatch of expected data to actuals, mismatch in expected business flow, change in page elements attributes, unhandled exception thrown by tests, etc. Absence of validation points or checkpoints may result in higher analysis time. In order to ensure quick analysis of failed tests it is extremely important to include checkpoints at appropriate places in the test. These checkpoints help to easily identify the exact point where a bug exists in the application under test. Various types of checkpoints can be implemented in Selenium to compare the expected and actual results. *Assert* statements can be used to compare the expected and actual values. Java library file slf4j.jar can be used to report failure reasons, expected and actual results in the result logs.

16.1 | ASSERTIONS

There are generally two to three types of failures for which a test can fail. They are as follows:

1. Test failure because of mismatch of expected data and actual data
2. Test failure because of mismatch of expected business flow and actual business flow
3. Test failure because of unhandled exception caused by the test like NoElementFoundException and NullPointException.

It is important that tests exit execution at the first point of failure especially in the cases 2 and 3 above. Most of the times test execution beyond the point of first failure results in NoElementFoundException at each and every line of code. Execution of lines of code beyond first point of failure results in unnecessary loss of execution time. Also, lot of failures in test report makes it hard and time consuming to identify the root cause of test failure. It is always recommended to exit the execution of the specific test at its very first point of failure. However, there could be exceptions to this. For example in scenarios where the requirement is to compare data of two excel files, it is good to continue execution till all data is compared and then finally publish the pass/fail results of compared data.

Assertions can be used to exit test execution of the test at its point of failure. Assertions compare the expected to actual results. If the two does not match, then it exits execution of the specific test. Only failed assertions are recorded in test result logs. Assert methods can be used directly as `Assert.assertEquals(...)`. However, code readability is good if they are referenced through static import:

```
import static org.junit.Assert.*;
...
assertEquals(...);
```

Note: Ensure assertions are enabled during run-time. If assertion is not enabled then none of the assertion statement will get executed during run-time.

Consider the login page of amazon.com as shown in Figure 16.1.

FIGURE 16.1 | Attribute checkpoint

EXAMPLE 16.1 Write checkpoint code to verify whether *Sign In* button is enabled or not.

Assume the HTML code for the *Sign In* button to be:

```
<input id="signInSubmit" width="201" type="image" height="22"
  border="0" value="Continue" tabindex="5" alt="Continue"
  onload="if (typeof uet == 'function') {et('cf');}" src=
  "https://images-na.ssl-images-V192194766_.gif"/>
```

WebDriver code to check whether *Sign In* button is enabled or not is shown in Figure 16.2. Figure 16.2 also shows the test execution results of the test when checkpoint condition passed. As shown below, no assert statements are logged in test result logs if checkpoint passes. If assertion statement passes, then the test continues executing the next line of code. The console tab in Figure 16.2 shows output of line 19 and line 22.

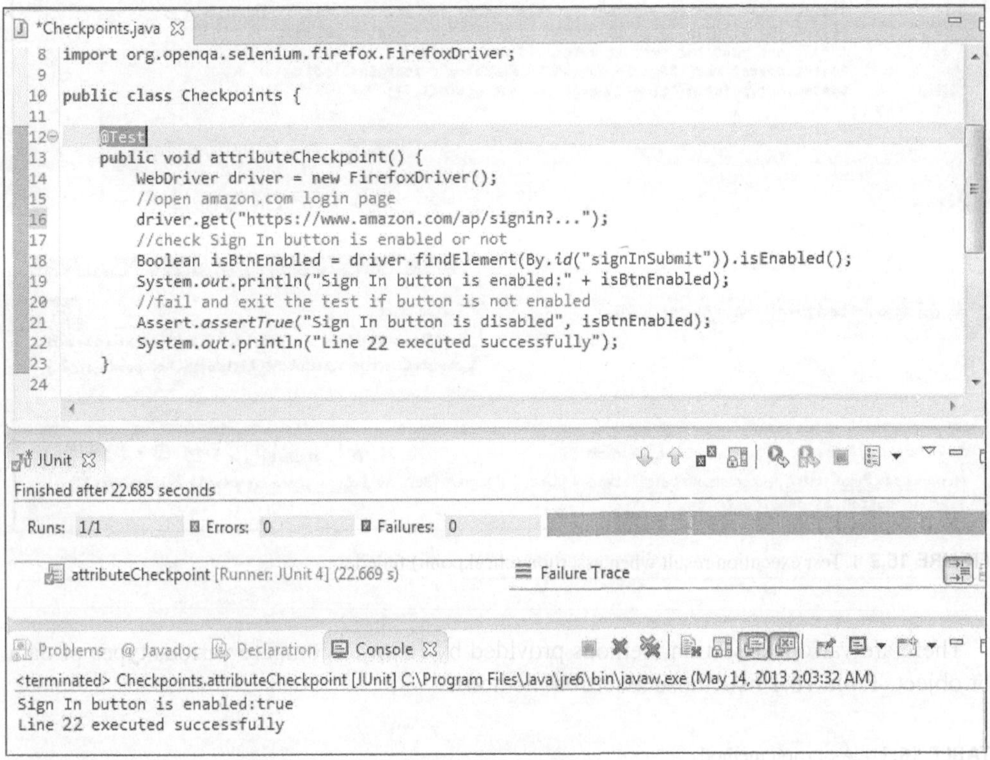

FIGURE 16.2 | Test results when assertion (checkpoint) passed

Assume a bug where in 'Sign In' button is disabled and hence user is not able to click on this button. Thus when the above test will be executed, it will fail. Figure 16.3 below shows the test execution results when the assertion failed ,i.e, the 'Sign In' button was disabled. As eveident from Figure 16.3 test exited after point of failure. Hence, line 22 never got executed. This is the reason why the console tab in Figure 16.3 shows output till line 19 only.

FIGURE 16.3 | Test execution result when assertion (checkpoint) failed

There are various assertion methods provided by JUnit to compare various types of data or object. Table 16.1 lists those assertion methods.

TABLE 16.1 | Assertion methods

Method	Description
`assertArrayEquals(byte[] expecteds, byte[] actuals)`	Asserts that two byte arrays are equal. If not an assertion error is thrown.
`assertArrayEquals(char[] expecteds, char[] actuals)`	Asserts that two char arrays are equal. If not an assertion error is thrown.
`assertArrayEquals(int[] expecteds, int[] actuals)`	Asserts that two int arrays are equal. If not an assertion error is thrown.
`assertArrayEquals(long[] expecteds, long[] actuals)`	Asserts that two long arrays are equal. If not an assertion error is thrown.
`assertArrayEquals(Object[] expecteds, Object[] actuals)`	Asserts that two object arrays are equal. If not an assertion error is thrown.

Method	Description
assertArrayEquals(**short**[] expecteds, **short**[] actuals)	Asserts that two short arrays are equal. If not an assertion error is thrown.
assertArrayEquals(**String** msg, **byte**[] expecteds, **byte**[] actuals)	Asserts that two byte arrays are equal. If they are not, an AssertionError is thrown with the given message.
assertArrayEquals(**String** msg, **char**[] expecteds, **char**[] actuals)	Asserts that two char arrays are equal. If they are not, an AssertionError is thrown with the given message.
assertArrayEquals(**String** msg, **int**[] expecteds, **int**[] actuals)	Asserts that two int arrays are equal. If they are not, an AssertionError is thrown with the given message.
assertArrayEquals(**String** msg, **long**[] expecteds, **long**[] actuals)	Asserts that two long arrays are equal. If they are not, an AssertionError is thrown with the given message.
assertArrayEquals(**String** msg, **Object**[] expecteds, **Object**[] actuals)	Asserts that two object arrays are equal. If they are not, an AssertionError is thrown with the given message.
assertArrayEquals(**String** msg, **short**[] expecteds, **short**[] actuals)	Asserts that two short arrays are equal . If they are not, an AssertionError is thrown with the given message.
assertEquals(**double** expected, **double** actual)	Asserts that two double or floats are equal. If they are not, an AssertionError is thrown.
assertEquals(**double** expected, **double** actual, double delta)	Asserts that two doubles or floats are equal to within a positive delta. If they are not, an AssertionError is thrown. If the expected value is infinity then the delta value is ignored.NaNs are considered equal: assertEquals(Double.NaN, Double.NaN, *) passes
assertEquals(**long** expected, **long** actual)	Asserts that two longs are equal. If they are not, an AssertionError is thrown.
assertEquals(**Object**[] expecteds, **Object**[] actuals)	Asserts that two object arrays are equal. If they are not, an AssertionError is thrown.
assertEquals(**Object** expected, **Object** actual)	Asserts that two objects are equal. If they are not, an AssertionError is thrown.
assertEquals(**String** msg, **double** expected, **double** actual)	Asserts that two doubles or floats are equal. If they are not, an AssertionError is thrown with the given message.

(continued)

TABLE 16.1 | *(continued)*

Method	Description
assertEquals(String msg, **double** expected, **double** actual, **double** delta)	Asserts that two doubles or floats are equal to within a positive delta. If they are not, an AssertionError is thrown with the given message. If the expected value is infinity then the delta value is ignored. NaNs are considered equal: assertEquals(Double.NaN, Double.NaN, *) passes
assertEquals(String msg, **long** expected, **long** actual)	Asserts that two long are equal. If they are not, an AssertionError is thrown with the given message.
assertEquals(String msg, **Object**[] expecteds, **Object**[] actuals)	Asserts that two object arrays are equal. If they are not, an AssertionError is thrown with the given message.
assertEquals(String msg, **Object** expected, **Object** actual)	Asserts that two objects are equal. If they are not, an AssertionError is thrown with the given message.
assertFalse(boolean condition)	Asserts that a condition is false. If it isn't it throws an AssertionError.
assertFalse(String msg, **boolean** condition)	Asserts that a condition is false. If it isn't it throws an AssertionError with the given message.
assertNotNull(Object object)	Asserts that an object isn't null. If it is an AssertionError is thrown.
assertNotNull(String msg, **Object** object)	Asserts that an object isn't null. If it is an AssertionError is thrown with the given message.
assertNotSame(Object unexpected, **Object** actual)	Asserts that two objects do not refer to the same object. If they do refer to the same object, an AssertionError is thrown.
assertNotSame(String msg, **Object** unexpected, **Object** actual)	Asserts that two objects do not refer to the same object. If they do refer to the same object, an AssertionError is thrown with the given message.
assertNull(Object object)	Asserts that an object is null. If it isn't an AssertionError is thrown.
assertNull(String msg, **Object** object)	Asserts that an object is null. If it isn't an AssertionError is thrown with the given message.
assertSame(Object unexpected, **Object** actual)	Asserts that two objects refer to the same object. If they are not the same, an AssertionError without a message is thrown.

Method	Description
`assertSame(String msg, Object unexpected, Object actual)`	Asserts that two objects refer to the same object. If they are not the same, an AssertionError with the given message is thrown.

`assertThat(String reason, T actual, org.hamcrest.Matcher<T> Matcher)`	Asserts that actual satisfies the condition specified by matcher. If not, an AssertionError is thrown with the reason and information about the matcher and failing value.
	Example:
	:
	assertThat("Help! Integers don't work", 0, is(1)); // fails:
	// failure message:
	// Help! Integers don't work
	// expected: is <1>
	// got value: <0>
	assertThat("Zero is one", 0, is(not(1))) // passes

`assertThat(T actual, org.hamcrest.Matcher<T> Matcher)`	Asserts that actual satisfies the condition specified by matcher. If not, an AssertionError is thrown with information about the matcher and failing value.
	
	Example:
	assertThat(0, is(1)); // fails:
	// failure message:
	// expected: is <1>
	// got value: <0>
	assertThat(0, is(not(1))) // passes

`assertTrue(boolean condition)`	Asserts that a condition is true. If it isn't it throws an AssertionError without a message.
`assertTrue(String msg, boolean condition)`	Asserts that a condition is true. If it isn't it throws an AssertionError with the given message.
`fail()`	Fails a test with no message.
`fail(String msg)`	Fails a test with the given message.

16.2 | TYPES OF CHECKPOINT

A checkpoint or verification point is used to verify the actual run-time results against the expected results. It helps to decide the pass/fail status of the test case being executed. Checkpoints can also be used as decision nodes to decide the logical flow of the code.

Table 16.2 lists various types of checkpoints that can be implemented using Selenium WebDriver.

TABLE 16.2 | Types of checkpoints

Checkpoint type	Description	Example
Attribute Checkpoint	Checks attribute values of elements such as checked, enables, tagname, value, etc.	Check whether a checkbox is selected or not
Text Checkpoint	Validates whether an expected text appears on the page or not	Check whether message 'Transaction successful' appears on the page or not
Image Checkpoint	Validates image attribute values such as source file location, width, height, etc.	Check if the logo image 'amazon.com' has the same source location on all amazon pages
Bitmap Checkpoint	Compares expected image against run-time image pixel by pixel	Check if an image is properly displayed on a page
Table Checkpoint	Validates the contents of a web table	Check the amount displayed on the table is correct
Database Checkpoint	Validates the contents of database	Check whether amount has been deducted from the payee account after funds transfer
XML Checkpoint	Checks the contents of XML document	Check tag values of XML
File Checkpoint	Checks the contents of file say text file, word file, excel file, json file, etc.	Check if specific text appears in a text file or not.

16.2.1 | Attribute Checkpoint

Attribute checkpoint verifies the attribute value of an element. For example, it can be used to verify whether a button is enabled on the screen or not, checkbox is selected or not, an element is displayed to the user or not, etc.

EXAMPLE 16.2 Write a code to verify checkbox 'US' in Figure 16.4 is selected or not.

FIGURE 16.4 | Checkboxes

Assume HTML code of the checkbox US to be:

```
<input id="id0" type="checkbox" value="1" name="country"/>
```

WebDriver code to verify whether checkbox 'US' is selected or not is:

```
Boolean isSelected = driver.findElement(By.id("id0")).isSelected();
//fail the test if checkbox is selected (Throws assertion
  error if condition
//is not false)
assertFalse("checkbox is selected", is Selected);
```

Example 16.3 Consider the login page of amazon.com as shown in Figure 16.1. Write a code to verify the *href* attribute of the link Forgot your password?

Assume HTML code of the link to be:

```
<a href="https://www.amazon.com/ap/forgotpassword? ...homepage.
  html">Forgot your password?</a>
```

WebDriver code to verify href attribute of the forgot password link is shown below.

```
String expectedHref = "https://www.amazon.com/ap/forgotpassword?...
  homepage.html";
String href = driver.findElement(By.linkText("Forgot your password?")).
  getAttribute("href");
//fail the test if href value does not matches (Throws assertion
  error if
//expected value does not matches actual value)
assertEquals("Link HRef attribute is InCorrect",expectedHref,
  href);
```

Example 16.4 Write code to find the font attribute of the text **No, I am a new customer.** displayed on amazon.com login page.

Assume HTML code of this element to be:

```
<label for="ap_signin_create_radio">No, I am a new customer.
   </label>
```

The CSS attributes of the element as viewed in CSSViewer is shown in Figure 16.5.

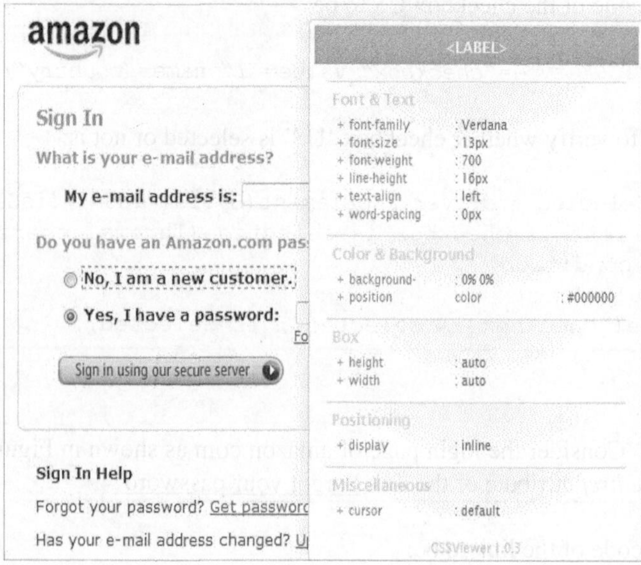

FIGURE 16.5 | CSS attributes of the element

WebDriver code to check the font attribute of this element is:

```
String actualFontFamily = driver.findElement(By.cssSelector
  ("span.ap_col2.bold.ap_radio_label")),getCSSValue("font-family");
//fail the test if Font value does not matches
assertEquals("Incorrect Font", "Verdana", actualFontFamily);
```

Also, code below can be used to retrive the textual content of the label element "No, I am a new customer:".

```
String actualText = driver.findElement(By.cssSelector("span.
   ap_col2.bold.ap_radio_label")).getText();
//fail the test if text value does not matches
assertEquals("Incorrect label text", "No, I am new customer:",
   actualText);
```

16.2.2 | Text Checkpoint

Text Checkpoint verifies whether or not correct text is displayed on the page. For example, after submitting an order, a text checkpoint can be implemented to verify the order submitted successfully message. Text checkpoints can also be implemented to verify the warning messages displayed on the page when user submits a form with invalid data.

Suppose an automated tests needs to be written that verifies the error message displayed to the user on invalid input of user credentials.

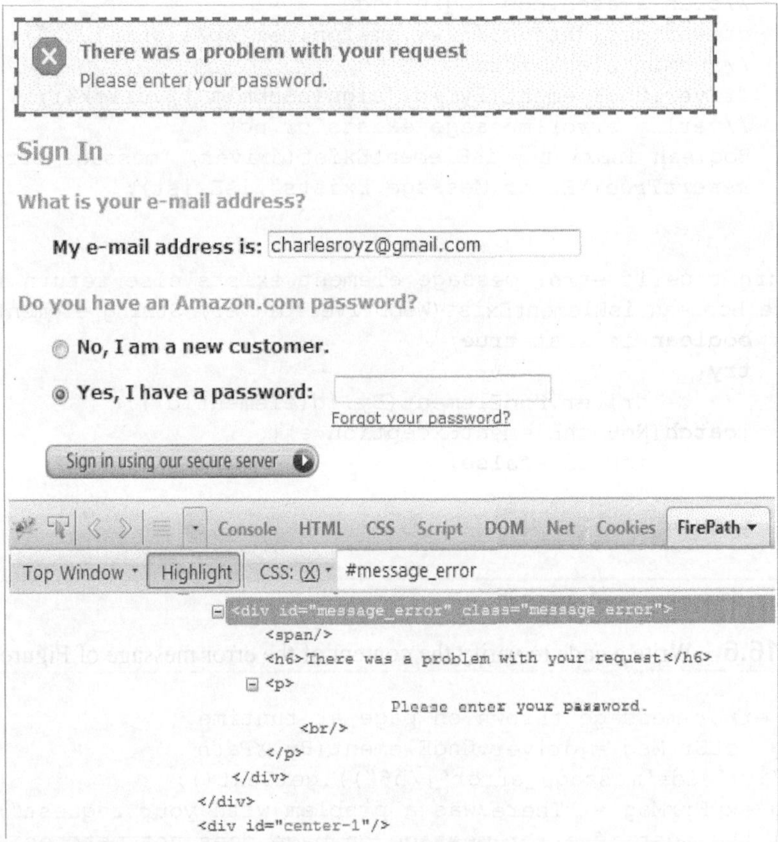

FIGURE 16.6 | Text checkpoint to verify page warning message

Suppose the HTML code of the warning message displayed in Figure 16.1 is as follows:

```
<div id="message_error" class="message error">
<span/>
        <h6>There was a problem with your request</h6>
        <p>     Please enter your password.
                <br/>
        </p>
</div>
```

EXAMPLE 16.5 Write a code to verify that an error message exists.

```
@Test
public void textCheckpoint() {
        WebDriver driver = new FirefoxDriver();
```

```
        //open amazon.com login page
        driver.get("https://www.amazon.com/ap/signin?...");
        //submit blank form
        driver.findElement(By.id("signInSubmit")).click();
        //verify error message exists or not
        Boolean isExist = isElementExist(driver, "message_error");
        assertTrue("Error Message Exists",isExist);

}
//return true if error message element exists else return false
private Boolean isElementExist(WebDriver driver, String elementId){
        boolean isExist=true;
        try{
                driver.findElement(By.id(elementId));
        }catch(NoSuchElementException e){
                isExist=false;
        }
        return isExist;
}
```

EXAMPLE 16.6 Write a code to verify the content of the error message of Figure 16.6.

```
//get error message thrown on page at runtime
String actErrMsg = driver.findElement(By.XPath
  ("//div[@id='message_error']/h6")).getText();
String expErrMsg = "There was a problem with your request";
//fail the test if error message on page does not matches
  expected error
//message
assertEquals("Incorrect error message",expErrMsg,actErrMsg);
```

Alternatively, text checkpoint code can also be applied by verifying whether an element with specified text value exists or not. Below code will look for an element whose text value matches text value 'There was a problem with your request'.

```
driver.findElement(By.XPath("//div[@id='message_error']/
  h6[contains(text(), 'There was a problem with your request')]"));
```

The above code will throw `NoSuchElementException` if specified element is not found. It is always advisable to handle such exceptions and log some meaningful error messages to result log.

```
@Test
public void textCheckpoint() {
        WebDriver driver = new FirefoxDriver();
        //open amazon.com login page
        driver.get("https://www.amazon.com/ap/signin?...");
```

```
        //submit blank form
        driver.findElement(By.id("signInSubmit")).click();
        //verify error message exists or not
        Boolean isExist = isElementExist(driver, "//div[@
          id='message_error']/h6[contains(text(), 'There was
          a problem with your request')]");
        assertTrue("Invalid Error Message",isExist);

}
//return true if the element with the specified XPath exists
private Boolean isElementExist(WebDriver driver, String elementXPath){
        boolean isExist=true;
        try{
                driver.findElement(By.XPath(elementXPath));
        }catch(NoSuchElementException e){
                isExist=false;
        }
        return isExist;
}
```

Note: Partial text match can also be done using the same 'contains' statement above.

```
driver.findElement(By.XPath("//div[@id='message_error']/
  h6[contains(text(), 'was a problem with your')]"));
```

16.2.3 | Image Checkpoint

Image checkpoint verifies image properties such as source file location, width, height, etc. In test automation, certain times we need to verify whether the *src* attribute of the image adheres to the standard coding practices or not. That is, the *src* attribute value follows a specific path pattern or not.

Consider the amazon.com image shown in Figure 16.7. Assume HTML code of this image to be:

```
<img width="100" height="30" border="0" alt="Amazon" src="https:
  //images-na.ssl-images-amazon.com/V153387053_.png" style=""/>
```

Figure 16.7 shows the CSS attributes of the image.

EXAMPLE 16.7 Write WebDriver code to verify the *src* attribute of the image shown in Figure 16.7.

```
@Test
public void attributeCheckpoint() {
        WebDriver driver = new FirefoxDriver();
        //open amazon.com login page
        driver.get("https://www.amazon.com/ap/signin ");
```

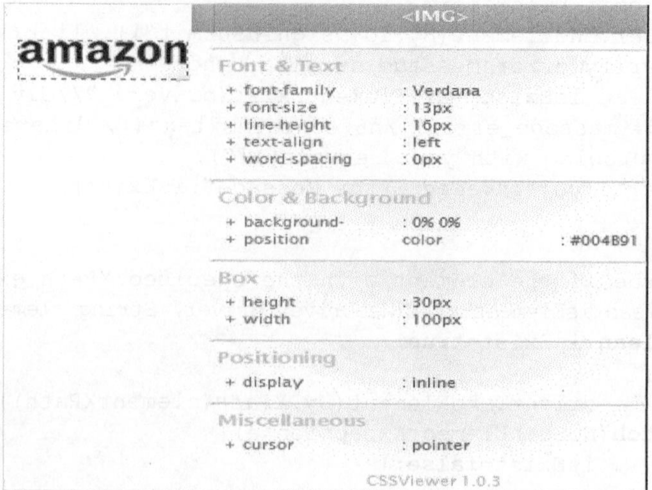

FIGURE 16. 7 | CSS attributes of image.

```
//get src attribute of the \amazon.com image
String actualSrc = driver.findElement(By.XPath
  ("//img[@alt='Amazon']")).getAttribute("src");
String expSrcPattern = "https://images-na.ssl-images-
  amazon.com/";
//fail the test if the src attribute of the image does
  not follows
//expected path pattern
assertTrue("Incorrect src path", actualSrc.
  contains(expSrcPattern));
}
```

EXAMPLE 16.8 Write WebDriver code to verify the css attribute *height* of the image shown in Figure 16. 7.

Following code shows how to find the CSS attribute of an image.

```
String cssHeight = driver.findElement(By.XPath
  ("//img[@alt='Amazon']")).getCssValue("height")
//Output::30px
```

16.2.4 | Bitmap Checkpoint

Bitmap checkpoint compares two images pixel by pixel to verify both the images are same. Refer Chapters 20 and 21 for bitmap checkpoint.

16.2.5 | Table Checkpoint

Table checkpoint is used to verify table data. There are various test scenario which require table contents to be verified against expected data.

EXAMPLE 16.9 Consider the table shown in Table 16.2. Write a code to verify employee name is 'Charles' for employee id 122768.

Employee ID	Employee Name	Designation
122768	Charles	Software Developer
122657	Joseph	Automation Developer

Assume the HTML code of the table to be:

```
<table>
    <tbody>
        <tr>
            <td>Employee ID</td>
            <td>Employee Name</td>
            <td>Designation</td>
        </tr>
        <tr>
            <td>122768</td>
            <td>Charles</td>
            <td>
                <input id="d1" type="text" value="Software Developer"
                  name="designation"/>
            </td>
        </tr>
        <tr>
            <td>122657</td>
            <td>Joseph</td>
            <td>
                <input id="d2" type="text" value="Automation
                  Developer" name="designation"/>
            </td>
        </tr>
    </tbody>
</table>
```

WebDriver to verify table data is as below:

```
@Test
public void tableCheckpoint() {
        WebDriver driver = new FirefoxDriver();
        //load page containing the table
        driver.get("...");
        //get table with the table fields Employee ID...
        //(refer chapter 'Working with WebTables' for the below
          method)
        WebElement table = driver.findTableByColumnName
          (driver, "Employee ID;Employee Name;Designation");
        //get cell ordinates which contains data '122768'
        //(refer chapter 'Working with WebTables' for the below
          method)
        int[] cell = table.getCellWithData("122768",0);
        //get cell data of the specified cell
        //(refer chapter 'Working with WebTables' for the below
          method)
        String cellData = table.getCellData(cell[0],cell[1]);
        //fail the test if cell data value is not 'Charles'
        assertEquals("Employee name is wrong","Charles",cellData);
}
```

Note: Refer to Chapter 11 for how to work with web tables.

16.2.6 | Database Checkpoint

Database checkpoint verifies the contents of the database. It can be used to verify the page data against database data. It can also be used whether or not the database fields are correctly updated after some UI operation or batch job execution. Refer to Chapter 24 for how to code database checkpoint.

16.2.7 | XML Checkpoint

XML Checkpoint verifies the data content of XML documents in XML files or in web pages. Refer to Chapter 25 for how to code database checkpoint.

16.2.8 | File Checkpoint

File checkpoint verifies the data of the files. For example, verifying the total amount in the order confirmation receipt. It can also be applied to continuously monitor the application logs for any exception. Refer to Chapter 22 for how to code file checkpoint.

INTERVIEW QUESTIONS

1. What is a checkpoint?
2. Why checkpoints are essential for writing any test code?
3. Name various types of checkpoint.
4. For an application, order number is displayed on order confirmation page. Explain how will you capture this order number from the web page.
5. What is the difference between image checkpoint and bitmap checkpoint?

17
CHAPTER
Data-driven Testing

Testing is often repetitive involving same test case to be executed against a variety of test data sets. Hardcoding such test data in the test scripts results in unnecessary re-writing same lines of code for various tests. Such code redundancy not only increases the automation development effort but also the maintenance effort. This problem can be solved by parameterizing the tests to receive the test data input from the test data files. This is called *Data-driven Testing.*

In data-driven testing, test scripts are coded to interact with the test data files for test input data and expected output data. *Test input data* refers to the data that exists in the data files and is used to define the code logic or to fill up forms of GUI. For example, username and password data can be saved as test input data in flat files and the same can be used to login to AUT when tests are running. *Test output data* refers to the data that is outcome of the test script execution and is to be updated in the test data files. For example, order number generated by the AUT while placing an order. Test scripts need to save this data to the test data files to ensure testers can track what went wrong in case the test failed.

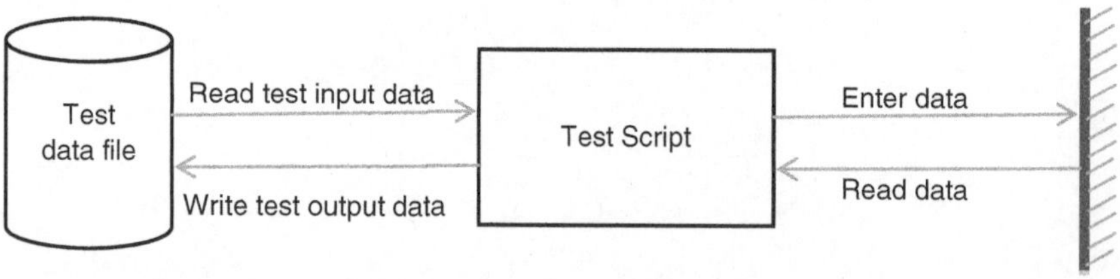

17.1 | BENEFITS OF DATA-DRIVEN TESTING

- **Reduced code redundancy:** Parameterization of data inside test scripts eliminates the need of duplicating tests for executing them against variety of test data set.
- **Reduced test development effort/cost:** Data driving tests helps execute the same tests against multiple sets of data. This eliminates the need to write multiple test scripts thereby reducing the test development effort.
- **Reduced test maintenance effort/cost:** In case test data needs to be changed or updated, the same can be easily done by modifying the test data files. This eliminates the need to modify automated tests.

Test data can be defined in a notepad file, comma separated file, MS Excel or any database. Code is to be written to read and write data to test data files. This code is used to read and write data to test data files from test scripts wherever required. Another way of data driving tests is to use the JUnit framework.

17.2 | DATA DRIVING TEST USING JUNIT

JUnit framework is commonly used to create tests using Selenium WebDriver in Java. JUnit provides *Parametrized* class to data drive the tests. The features of this class can be used to parameterize the tests data within the tests.

In order to parameterize the tests, first we need to create a class which contains all the test data. Annotations `@RunWith` and `@Parameters` is used to parameterize a test in JUnit. Annotation `@RunWith` is used to indicate that the class contains parameterized test data. Annotation @ `Parameters` is used to define the test data. When the test is executed, JUnit executes the test against every instance of data defined in the test data section.

Figure 17.1 shows how to parameterize a test using JUnit parameterization feature. Annotations `@RunWith` has been used at the top of the class and annotation `@Parameters` has been used to the above method that defines test data. The *Console* section of Figure 17.1

NewFile.html | EnvVariables.properties | TestJUnitParameterization.java

```
package com.webdriver.tests;

import java.util.Arrays;[..]

@RunWith(value = Parameterized.class)
public class TestJUnitParameterization {
    private int paramNumber;

    public TestJUnitParameterization(int paramNumber) {
        this.paramNumber = paramNumber;
    }

    @Parameters
    public static Collection testData() {
        return Arrays.asList(new Object[][]{{1},{2},{3},{4} });
    }

    @Test
    public void testParameterization(){
        System.out.println("Parameterized number is :" + paramNumber);
    }
}
```

Console | JUnit

```
<terminated> TestJUnitParameterization [JUnit] C:\Program Files\Java\jre6\bin\javaw.exe (Jun 20, 2013
Parameterized number is :1
Parameterized number is :2
Parameterized number is :3
Parameterized number is :4
```

FIGURE 17.1 | Data-driven testing using JUnit parameterization

shows the execution results. It contains four rows signifying the same test was executed against four different sets of data.

Note: Executing a parameterized test by selecting the specific test method throws *unrooted error*. For example, if we try to execute the test *'testParametrization'* by doing a Right Click and then Selecting Run, then the test will fail with error *unrooted error*. To avoid this error, always execute the test from class level. For example, the above case executes the test by selecting class *'TestJUnitParameterization'* (Select class *TestJUnitParameterization'* → Right Click → Run As → JUnit).

EXAMPLE 17.1 Consider the Google currency converter page shown below in Figure17.2. Write WebDriver code using JUnit parameterization framework to automate the following tests:

(a) Verify currency conversion for USD to INR
(b) Verify currency conversion for AUD to INR
(c) Verify currency conversion for USD to EUR

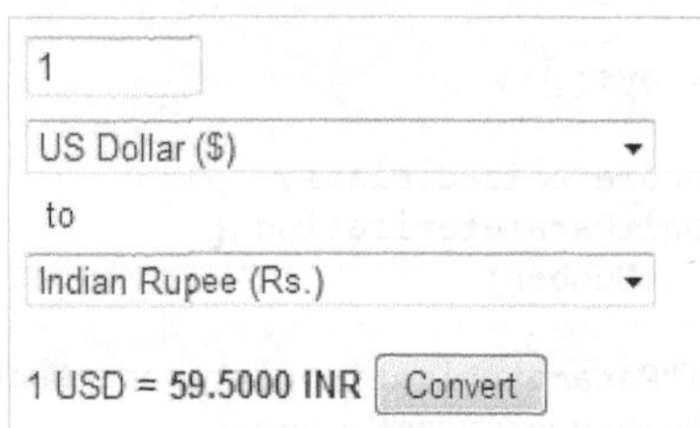

FIGURE 17.2 | Google currency converter page

It is evident from the above tests that test case flow remains the same while the test data varies. JUnit parameterization can be used to parameterize the test data. Following code shows how to automate the above test.

```
@RunWith(value = Parameterized.class)
public class TestJUnitParameterization1 {

       private long convertAmt;
       private String fromCurrency;
       private String toCurrency;
       public static WebDriver driver;

       public TestJUnitParameterization1(long convertAmt,
         String fromCurrency, String toCurrency){
              this.convertAmt = convertAmt;
              this.fromCurrency = fromCurrency;
              this.toCurrency = toCurrency;
       }
```

```
@Parameters
public static Collection<Object []> testData() {
    Object[][] testData = new Object[][]{
                {1,"USD","INR"},
                {1,"AUD","INR"},
                {1,"USD","EUR"}
    };
    return Arrays.asList(testData);
}
@BeforeClass
public static void setUp(){
        driver= new FirefoxDriver();
        driver.get("http://www.google.com/finance/
          converter");
}
@Test
public void testCurrencyConverter(){
        WebDriver driver= new FirefoxDriver();
        driver.get("http://www.google.com/finance/
          converter");
        //enter conversion amount
        String conversionAmt = String.
          valueOf(convertAmt);
        driver.findElement(By.name("a")).clear();
        driver.findElement(By.name("a")).
          sendKeys(conversionAmt);
        //select convert from currency option
        Select fromCurrencySelect =
          new Select(driver.findElement(By.name("from")));
        fromCurrencySelect.selectByValue(fromCurrency);
        //select covert to currency option
        Select toCurrencySelect =
          new Select(driver.findElement(By.name("to")));
        toCurrencySelect.selectByValue(toCurrency);
        //click on convert button
        driver.findElement(By.XPath(
          "//input[@value='Convert']")).click();
        //capture the conversion amount
        String convertedAmt = driver.findElement(By.XPath(
          "//div[@id='currency_converter_result']/
            span")).getText();
        System.out.println(conversionAmt + fromCurrency +
          "=" + convertedAmt);
}
```

```
        @AfterClass
        public static void tearDown(){
                driver.quit();
        }
}
```

Figure 17.3 shows the multiple iteration test results and output of the above code.

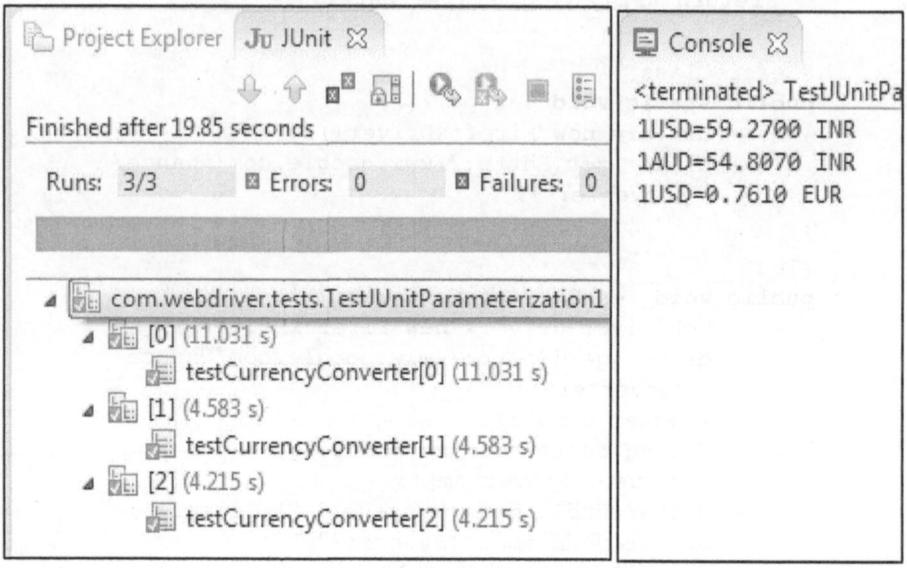

FIGURE 17.3 | JUnit execution results tab and Eclipse console tab with execution results

Note: JUnit parameterization is a quick way of developing use and throw tests. This method should not be used for actual test development. This is because in this method the test data is hard-coded within the test. Moreover, no other test can re-use this data. Maintaining the test data which is duplicated and maintained in various tests is very difficult.

17.3 | DATA DRIVING TEST USING CSV FILE

In the above code, we observe the test data is hard-coded within the test and hence cannot be re-used in other tests. This makes test data maintenance very difficult and resource intensive. This is the reason why this method of test data parameterization is to be avoided while developing tests. A better approach is to maintain test data in flat files, for example, CSV(comma separated value) file. This helps to build one-point maintenance for test data.

Comma separated value (CSV) file is a file which contains tabular data in plain-text form. The first row contains the table field names while the rest of the columns contain table data. Two sets of data (or two columns) within a row is separated by comma (‘,’). The extension name of a comma separated file is *csv*. Figure 17.4 shows an example of CSV file containing login data.

```
Amount, From Currency, To Currency
1,INR,USD
1,INR,AUD
10,USD,EUR
```

FIGURE 17.4 | CurrencyConverter.csv File

Assume *CurrencyConverter.csv* is stored in eclipse at location *"/com/webdriver/testdata/CurrencyCoverter.csv"*. Figure 17.5 shows the location of the CSV file as viewed in Eclipse *Project Explorer* tab.

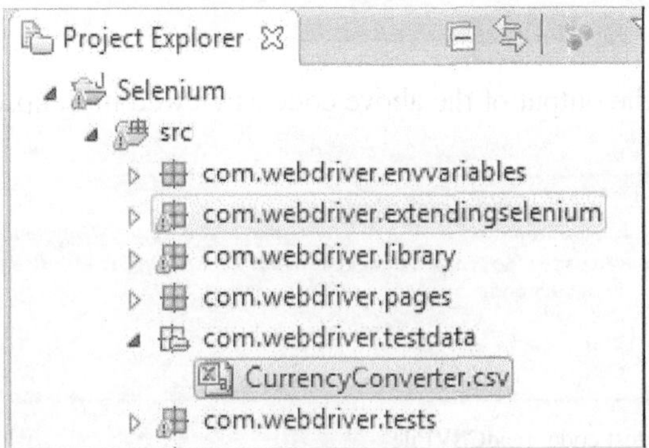

FIGURE 17.5 | Location of file CurrencyConver.csv in Eclipse

Following code shows how to read the above CSV file using Java code.

```
@Test
public void readCSVFile() {
        String rowData;
        String testDataPath = “/com/webdriver/testdata/
          CurrencyConverter.csv”;
        //get the absolute path of the file in hard drive
        String filepath = getClass().getResource(testDataPath).
          getFile();
        System.out.println(“Absolue file path:” + filepath);

        try{
               //read csv file
               BufferedReader br =
                 new BufferedReader(new FileReader(filepath));
               //read file till end of file is reached
               while((rowData = br.readLine()) != null){
```

```
                //read each value(column value) in the
                  line(row)
                String[] columnData = rowData.split(",");
                for (String data:columnData){
                        System.out.print(data + "\t");
                }
                System.out.print("\n");
            }
            //close file
            br.close();
        }catch(FileNotFoundException e){
            e.printStackTrace();
        }catch (IOException e) {
            e.printStackTrace();
        }
    }
```

Figure 17.6 shows the output of the above code as viewed in Eclipse *console* tab.

```
Console  JUnit
<terminated> DataDrivenTesting.readCSVFromEclipse [JUnit] C:\Program Files\Java\jre6\bin\javaw.exe (Jun 21, 2013 10:17:36 PM)
Absolue file path:/F:/workspaces/Selenium/bin/com/webdriver/testdata/CurrencyConverter.csv
Amount  ToCurrency      FromCurrency
1       INR             USD
1       INR             AUD
10      USD             EUR
```

FIGURE 17.6 | Output of test code 'readCSVFile'

In test automation, it is always advisable to create a reusable method that can be called to read various CSV files. This helps build a robust and reusable framework which in turn minimizes development and maintenance cost and effort.

As we observe from the code above, during test execution we require specific row data from the CSV file. But the code above reads and returns the complete data set defined in the CSV file. In order to return specific data from the CSV file, we would need to differentiate between different rows of data in the data set. One way this can be achieved is to define a unique key to all the rows. The Java code can read through all the data to identify the specific key and then return row with this key. Figure 17.7 shows the test data file with a unique key defined.

```
Key, Amount, From Currency, To Currency
1,1,INR,USD
2,1,INR,AUD
3,10,USD,EUR
```

FIGURE 17.7 | Test data file with unique key for each row

The *key* value (1,2,3...) can be used to retrieve specific row of data from the CSV file. Though this method helps easy development of tests, maintenance of test is still a problem. This is because using key values (1,2,3...) makes code less readable. It is difficult to understand which type of test data the specific test is using when looking at these key values. A better approach would to use *key names* for each row of data. The *keyName* to be defined in a way that makes it unique for a given data set and also conveys the type of test data it is referring to. Figure 17.8 shows test data CSV file with *keyName* defined for each row.

```
Key, KeyName,Amount, From Currency,To Currency
1,1INR2USD,1,INR,USD
2,1INR2AUD,1,INR,AUD
3,10USD2EUR,10,USD,EUR
```

FIGURE 17.8 | Test data file with unique key name for each row

Following code shows how read data from CSV file using *KeyName* and *field* name attributes.

```
public class CSVFile {

       String csvAbsoluteFilepath="";

       public CSVFile(String csvFilepath){
              csvAbsoluteFilepath =
                 getClass().getResource(csvFilepath).getFile();
       }
       public String getData(String keyName, String field){
                            return this.readCSV(keyName, field);
       }

       public String getData(int key, String field){
                return this.readCSV(String.valueOf(key), field);
       }

       private String readCSV(String key, String field){
              int fieldPosition = getFieldPosition(field);
              int keyPosition = getKeyPosition(key);

              String data=null;
              try{
                     int rowNum=-1;
                     BufferedReader br = new BufferedReader(
                        new FileReader(csvAbsoluteFilepath));
                     //read first line which defines field names
                     String rowData= br.readLine();
                     while(rowData != null ){
```

```
                    rowNum = rowNum + 1;
                    //read key and keyName field
                     values to find the
                    //row number position
                     of the key
                    if (rowNum==keyPosition){
                     String[] columnData = rowData.
                       split(",");
                     for (int j=0;j<columnData.
                       length;j++){
                          if (j==fieldPosition){
                               data = columnData[j];
                               rowData = null;
                               break;
                          }
                     }
                    }
                    if (rowData!=null) rowData=
                    br.readLine();
               }
               //close file
               br.close();
               }catch(FileNotFoundException e){
                    e.printStackTrace();
               }catch (IOException e) {
                    e.printStackTrace();
               }
          return data.trim();
     }

     private int getFieldPosition(String field){
          int fieldPosition = -1;
          try{
               BufferedReader br = new BufferedReader(
                new FileReader(csvAbsoluteFilepath));
               //read first line which defines field names
               String rowData=br.readLine();
               //iterate through all
               data of first row to find
               //the position of
               the given 'field'
               String[] columnData = rowData.split(",");
               for (int i=0;i<columnData.length;i++){
                    if (columnData[i].
                    equalsIgnoreCase(field)){
                         fieldPosition = i;
                         break;
```

```
                        }
                    }
                    //close file
                    br.close();
            }catch(FileNotFoundException e){
                    e.printStackTrace();
            }catch (IOException e) {
                    e.printStackTrace();
            }
            return fieldPosition;
    }

    private int getKeyPosition(String key){
            int keyPosition=-1;

            try{
                    BufferedReader br = new BufferedReader(
                       new FileReader(csvAbsoluteFilepath));
                    //read first line which defines field names
                    String rowData= br.readLine();
                    while(rowData != null ){
                        keyPosition = keyPosition + 1;
                        //read key and keyName field values
                          to find the
                        //row number position of the key
                        String[] columnData = rowData.
                        split(",");
                        for (int j=0;j<2;j++){
                          if (columnData[j].
                            equalsIgnoreCase(key)){
                                rowData = null;
                                break;
                          }
                        }
                        if (rowData!=null) rowData=
                        br.readLine();
                    }

                    //close file
                    br.close();
            }catch(FileNotFoundException e){
                    e.printStackTrace();
            }catch (IOException e) {
                    e.printStackTrace();
            }
            return keyPosition;
    }
}
```

Following code shows how to use the *CSVFile* class to read data from any a CSV file.

```
@Test
public void readCSVFile1(){
        CSVFile csv =
          new CSVFile("/com/webdriver/testdata/
              CurrencyConverter.csv");
        System.out.println(csv.getData(1, "Amount"));//
          Output::1
        System.out.println(csv.getData("10USD2EUR",
          "Amount"));//Output::10
}
```

Note: The CSV file path should not be hardcoded in the tests as shown above. It is good to save the location path of test data files as environment variables in EnvVariables.properties files. The test script should always refer this variable.

Example 17.2 Consider the Google currency converter page shown in Figure 17.2. Write WebDriver code to automate the following tests. Assume test data is stored in a CSV file as shown in Figure 17.4.

(a) Verify currency conversion for USD to INR
(b) Verify currency conversion for AUD to INR
(c) Verify currency conversion for USD to EUR

```
public class DataDrivenTesting {
        public static WebDriver driver;
        public static CSVFile csv;

        @BeforeClass
        public static void setUp(){
                csv =
                         new CSVFile("/com/webdriver/testdata/
                           CurrencyConverter.csv");
                driver= new FirefoxDriver();
                driver.get("http://www.google.com/finance/converter");
        }

        @Test
        public void testCurrencyConverter(){
                for (int i=1;i<=3;i++){
                         String conversionAmt = csv.getData(i, "Amount");
                         String fromCurrency = csv.getData
                           (i, "FromCurrency");
                         String toCurrency = csv.getData
                           (i,   "ToCurrency");
                         this.currencyConverter(conversionAmt,
                           fromCurrency, toCurrency);
                }
        }
```

```
    public void currencyConverter(String conversionAmt,
                String fromCurrency, String toCurrency){
            //enter conversion amount
            driver.findElement(By.name("a")).clear();
            driver.findElement(By.name("a")).
              sendKeys(conversionAmt);

            //select convert from currency option
            Select fromCurrencySelect =
              new Select(driver.findElement(By.name("from")));
            fromCurrencySelect.selectByValue(fromCurrency);

            //select covert to currency option
            Select toCurrencySelect =
              new Select(driver.findElement(By.name("to")));
            toCurrencySelect.selectByValue(toCurrency);

            //click on convert button
            driver.findElement(By.XPath("//input[@
              value='Convert']")). click();

            //capture the conversion amount
            String convertedAmt = driver.findElement(By.XPath(
              "//div[@id='currency_converter_
                result']/span")).getText();
            System.out.println(
                     conversionAmt + fromCurrency + "=" +
                       convertedAmt);

    }
    @AfterClass
    public static void tearDown(){
            driver.quit();
    }
}
```

Figure 17.9 shows the output of the above code.

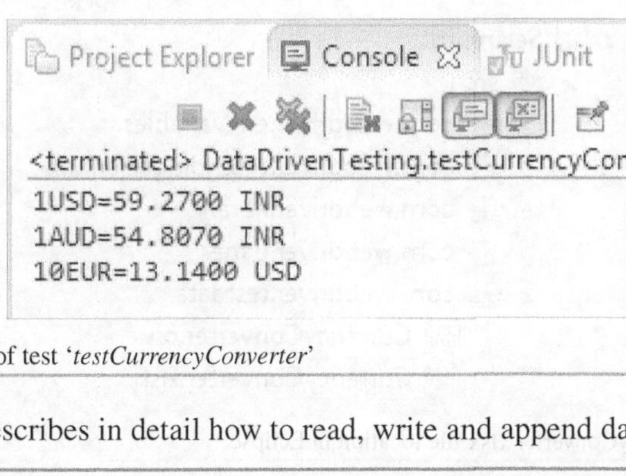

FIGURE 17.9 | Output of test '*testCurrencyConverter*'

Note: Chapter 22 describes in detail how to read, write and append data to CSV files

17.4 | DATA DRIVING TEST USING EXCEL DB

One drawback of CSV file is that the complete file needs to be loaded in memory before it can be read. If the file size is huge then there can be memory issues during run-time. Another drawback of CSV file is that it can only be read sequentially. If the data size is huge and last rows of data needs to be read then it will take more time to read the required data. This can slow down the test execution. One effective way to overcome this problem is use of MS Excel files to store data. MS Excel is a more user-friendly tool to store test data in the form of tables. MS Excel can be read in two days either as worksheet or as database. Reading MS Excel as worksheet has same problems as CSV. Therefore, it is always recommended to read MS Excel as database. SQL queries can be used to read any data from MS Excel database. Accessing data from MS Excel using SQL queries is much more reliable and faster than reading test data.

Note: Refer Chapter 23 for details on how MS Excel sheets can be used as database.

Figure 17.10 shows the currency conversion test data stored in a MS Excel file named *CurrencyConverter*.xls.

	A	B	C	D	E
1	Key	KeyName	Amount	FromCurrency	ToCurrency
2	1	1INR2USD	1	INR	USD
3	2	1INR2AUD	1	INR	AUD
4	3	10USD2EUR	10	USD	EUR

CurrencyConversion / Sheet2 / Sheet3

FIGURE 17.10 | Test data file CurrencyConverter.xlsx

Assume the above file is saved at location `com/webdriver/testdata` in Eclipse as shown in Figure 17.11.

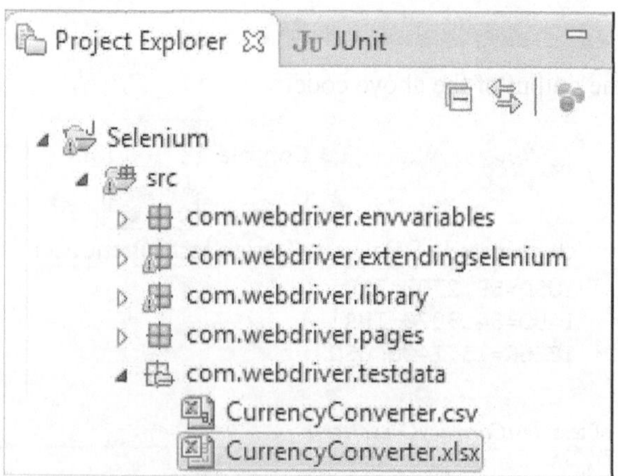

FIGURE 17.11 | CurrencyConverter.xlsx file location in Eclipse

Following code shows *ExcelDB* class. This class has a public method *executeQuery()*. This method takes *sql* as input parameter and executes this *sql* against MS Excel database. The results data obtained is returned by this method as *ArrayList*.

```
import java.sql.Connection;
import java.sql.DriverManager;
import java.sql.ResultSet;
import java.sql.ResultSetMetaData;
import java.sql.SQLException;
import java.sql.Statement;
import java.util.ArrayList;

public class ExcelDB {
        public String excelFilepath;
        public int rowCount;
        public int columnCount;
        public Connection conn;
        public Statement stmt;
        public ResultSet resultSet;

        public ExcelDB(String filepath){
                excelFilepath = filepath;
        }

        /**
         * @desc: execute a sql query against excel database
         * @param sql sql query
         * @return sql query results as ArrayList
         */
        public ArrayList<Object> executeQuery(String sql){
                ResultSet resultSet = this.executeSql(sql);
                ArrayList<Object> recordSet = resultSetToArrayLi
                  st(resultSet);
                closeConnection();
                return recordSet;
        }

        //execute the sql query and return ResultSet object
        private ResultSet executeSql(String sql){
                String absolutePath = getAbsoluteFilepath
                  (excelFilepath);
                conn = getConnection(absolutePath);
                ResultSet resultSet = executeQueryOnExcel
                  (conn, sql);
                return resultSet;
        }
```

```
//get the absolute path of the excel file
private String getAbsoluteFilepath(String excelFilepath){
        String filepath =
                getClass().getResource(excelFilepath).
                  getFile();
        filepath = filepath.replaceFirst("/", "");
        return filepath;
}

//get connection object
private Connection getConnection(String excelFilepath){
        String username="";
        String password="";
        try {
                Class.forName("sun.jdbc.odbc.
                  JdbcOdbcDriver");
                String connString="jdbc:odbc:DRIVER={
                  Microsoft Excel Driver (*.xls, *.xlsx,
                    *.xlsm,
                   *.xlsb)};DBQ="+excelFilepath+"";
                conn = DriverManager.getConnection(
                  connString, username,password);
        } catch (ClassNotFoundException e) {
                e.printStackTrace();
        } catch (SQLException e) {
                e.printStackTrace();
        }
        return conn;
}

//execute the sql query and return ResultSet object
private ResultSet executeQueryOnExcel(Connection
  conn,String sql){
        try {
                      stmt = conn.createStatement();
         stmt.execute(sql);
                      resultSet = stmt.getResultSet();
                } catch (SQLException e) {
                e.printStackTrace();
        }
return resultSet;
}

//store ResultSet object data to an ArrayList
private ArrayList<Object> resultSetToArrayList(ResultSet
  resultSet){
```

```
            ArrayList<Object> recordSet = new
              ArrayList<Object>();
            ArrayList<String> records = new
              ArrayList<String>();

            int rowCntr=0;
            int colCntr;
            this.setColumnCount(resultSet);

            try{
              if (resultSet != null){
                     while(resultSet.next()){
                       for (colCntr=0;colCntr<columnCount;colCntr++){
                          records.add(resultSet.
                             getString(colCntr+1));
                       }
                       rowCntr= rowCntr + 1;
                       recordSet.add(records);
                     }
              }
            }catch(SQLException e) {
                       e.printStackTrace();
            }
            rowCount = rowCntr;
            return recordSet;
    }

    //get total number of rows of data returned by the sql query
    public int getRowCount(){
            return rowCount;
    }

    //get total columns of data returned by the sql query
    public int getColumnCount(){
            return columnCount;
    }

    //set total number of columns of data returned by the sql query
    private void setColumnCount(ResultSet resultSet){
            ResultSetMetaData rsmd;
            try {
                     rsmd = resultSet.getMetaData();
                     columnCount = rsmd.getColumnCount();
                  } catch (SQLException e) {
                     e.printStackTrace();
            }
    }
```

```
        //close the DB connection
        private void closeConnection(){
                try {
                                stmt.close();
                                conn.close();
                        } catch (SQLException e) {
                        e.printStackTrace();
                }
        }
}
```

Notes: 1. The above code may fail if both MS Excel and JRE are not of the same bit version. For example, trying to connect to MS Excel 32-bit with JRE 64-bit will throw an exception. If MS Excel is 32-bit, then JRE should also be 32-bit and if MS Excel is 64-bit, then JRE should also be 64-bit. A simple way of finding whether a program is 32-bit or 64-bit is to look for the installation directory of the file. A program is 64-bit if it is installed at location '*C:\Program Files*' while it is 32-bit if it is installed at location '*C:\Program Files (x86)*' for Win 7 OS.

2. The above code may also fail if MS Excel driver is not installed. Appropriate MS Excel driver can be downloaded from Microsoft site for MS Excel 2010, it can be downloaded for site http://www.microsoft.com/en-in/download/details.aspx?id=13255

Example 17.3 Write code to retrieve all test data from file *CurrencyConverter.xlsx* as shown in Figure 17.11.

An instance of the *ExcelDB* class is to be created and method *executeQuery* is to be called to retrieve data from MS Excel database file.

```
@Test
public void testDataDrivenTestingExcelDB() {
        String excelFilepath = "/com/webdriver/testdata/
          CurrencyConverter.xlsx";
        String sql = "select * from [CurrencyConversion$]";
        ExcelDB excelDB = new ExcelDB(excelFilepath);
        ArrayList<Object> resultSet = excelDB.executeQuery(sql);
        System.out.println("Row Count:" + excelDB.
          getRowCount());
        System.out.println("Column Count:" + excelDB.
          getColumnCount());
        for (int i=0;i<excelDB.getRowCount();i++){
          for (int j=0;j<excelDB.getColumnCount();j++){
            System.out.print(((ArrayList<?>)resultSet.get(i)).
              get(j) + "\t");
          }
          System.out.print("\n");
        }
}
```

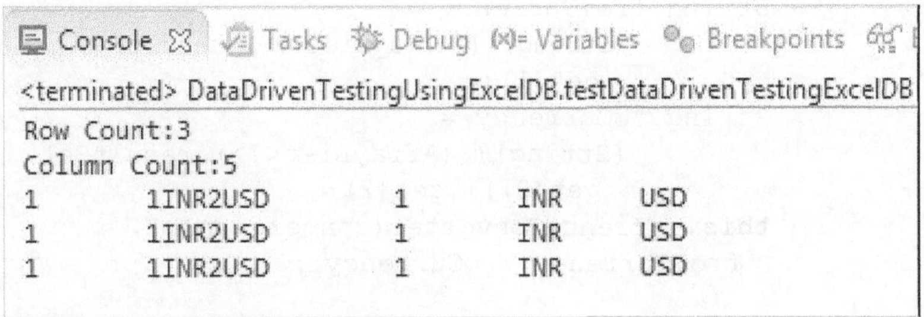

FIGURE 17.12 | Output of Example 17.3

Output of the above code is shown in Figure 17.12.

EXAMPLE 17.4 Consider the Google currency converter page shown below in Figure 17.2. Write WebDriver code to automate the below tests. Assume test data is stored in a MS Excel file as shown in Figure 17.10.

(a) Verify currency conversion for USD to INR
(b) Verify currency conversion for AUD to INR
(c) Verify currency conversion for USD to EUR

```
public class DataDrivenTestingUsingExcelDB {
	public static WebDriver driver;
	public static ExcelDB excelDB;

	@BeforeClass
	public static void setUp(){
		excelDB = new
ExcelDB("/com/webdriver/testdata/CurrencyConverter.xlsx");
		driver= new FirefoxDriver();
		driver.get("http://www.google.com/finance/converter");
	}

	@Test
	public void testCurrencyConverter(){
		ArrayList<Object> resultSet;
		//retrieve test data using key value
		String sql = "Select Amount,FromCurrency,
		  ToCurrency from
			[CurrencyConversion$] where Key='1'";
		resultSet = excelDB.executeQuery(sql);
		String conversionAmt =
			(String)(((ArrayList<?>) resultSet.
			  get(0))).get(0);
```

```
        String fromCurrency =
                (String)(((ArrayList<?>) resultSet.get(0))).
                 get(1);
        String toCurrency =
                (String)(((ArrayList<?>) resultSet.
                 get(0))).get(2);
        this.currencyConverter(conversionAmt,
         fromCurrency, toCurrency);

        //retrieve test data using keyname
        sql = "Select Amount,FromCurrency,ToCurrency from
                [CurrencyConversion$] where
                 KeyName='1INR2AUD'";
        resultSet = excelDB.executeQuery(sql);
        conversionAmt =
                (String)(((ArrayList<?>) resultSet.
                 get(0))).get(0);
        fromCurrency =
                (String)(((ArrayList<?>) resultSet.
                 get(0))).get(1);
        toCurrency = (String)(((ArrayList<?>) resultSet.
         get(0))).get(2);
        this.currencyConverter(conversionAmt,
         fromCurrency, toCurrency);

        //retrieve test data using keyname
        sql = "Select Amount,FromCurrency,ToCurrency from
                [CurrencyConversion$] where
                 KeyName='10USD2EUR'";
        resultSet = excelDB.executeQuery(sql);
        conversionAmt =
                (String)(((ArrayList<?>) resultSet.
                 get(0))).get(0);
        fromCurrency =
                (String)(((ArrayList<?>) resultSet.
                 get(0))).get(1);
        toCurrency = (String)(((ArrayList<?>) resultSet.
         get(0))).get(2);
        this.currencyConverter(conversionAmt,
         fromCurrency, toCurrency);
    }

    public void currencyConverter(
         String conversionAmt, String
           fromCurrency, String toCurrency){
```

```
                //refer the code of this class from the Example
                 under
                //section Data Driving Test using CSV File
                ............
                .........  .
        }
        @AfterClass
        public static void tearDown(){
                driver.quit();
        }
}
```

INTERVIEW QUESTIONS

1. What is data-driven testing?
2. What are the advantages of data-driving tests?
3. What are the various ways of data-driving tests?
4. Which is a better approach of data-driven testing – JUnit parameterization, CSV file or Excel DB? Why?
5. Explain how will you read data from Excel File.
6. Explain some challenges you faced while trying to read data from Excel DB file.

18
CHAPTER

Test Results

Test results are a very important component of test automation. Test results help decide whether test script has passed or failed and if failed the reason of failure. Test results should be detailed enough to help track the actions performed by the test, test data used and the exact pass and fail points. Test results to help in quick and easy tracking the root cause of test failure. A test can fail either because of a problem in test code or a bug. Test results should have appropriate comments (logs) which helps in quick and easy analysis of test results. Test results are to be user-friendly enough to be analyzed by any manual tester or business analyst. Test results to embed a screenshot of the application taken at the point of test failure. This helps to understand the state of the application under test (AUT) when test failure occurred.

18.1 | LOGGING COMMENTS TO TEST RESULTS

There are two ways of incorporating log comments in test results: assert statements and logger statements.

18.1.1 | Assert Statements

Assert statements are to be used when the requirement is to publish the results and exit the test at the very point of test failure. An example could be using assert statements to compare the expected amount to be debited from an account and the actual amount debited from the account for interbank money transfer test. In this situation, assert statements will compare the expected to actuals and if they do not match it will publish the mismatched results along with appropriate information and then will exit the test execution. Assert statements have been discussed in detail in chapter 'Checkpoints'.

18.1.2 | Logger Statements

Logger statements are to be used when the requirement is to publish any relevant information to the test result logs. For example, for a test that test interbank money transfer, information such as debtor account number, creditor account number, money transferred etc. are very important information for test result analysis. In case of test failure, this information will help in quick identification of the reason of test failure. An important piece of information for test results is the test steps. If the test results do not have test steps then it becomes very hard to replicate the test failure manually. Suppose for the interbank money transfer scenario, a user can hit on the 'Funds Transfer' link from Home page, Account page and Account details page. Suppose test fails while clicking on the 'Funds Transfer' link on Home page. In the absence of test steps a tester would not know the steps test executed before it failed. He might try to replicate the defect from Account Details page but he will not be able to, as defect exists on Home page. This increases the analysis time and hence the automation cost. It is extremely important to log the test steps in test results. An easier way of achieving so could be to write English like test statements of test steps just before executing a test. An advisable approach would be to develop an automation framework that logs every user action to the test results. This may make the test logs lengthy but goes a long mile in reducing the analysis time. In today's agile world where daily go-live to production is an expectation, it reduces regression time to couple of hours. Thereby reducing test analysis time to an hour or so. This makes it extremely important to generate test results that are self-explanatory and helps pin-point exact cause of test failure.

In order to log comments in test logs, we can use the logger library files provided by slf4j.org. Slf4j jar files can be downloaded from the site: http://www.slf4j.org/download.html. Once downloaded, the zipped files are to be unzipped. The unzipped jar files are then to be imported to the Java Build Path of the project.

Below is the simple JUnit code to publish text 'Hello World!' to the test results.

```
import org.slf4j.Loggcr;
import org.slf4j.LoggerFactory;
import org.junit.Test;

public class TestResults {
        @Test
        public void testSlf4jLogger() {
                Logger logger = LoggerFactory.getLogger(getClass());
                logger.info(“Hello World!!!”);
                int i=2;
                logger.info(“Hello World ” + i + “!!!”);
        }
}
```

Figure 18.1 shows the output of the above code as visible in Eclipse *console* tab.

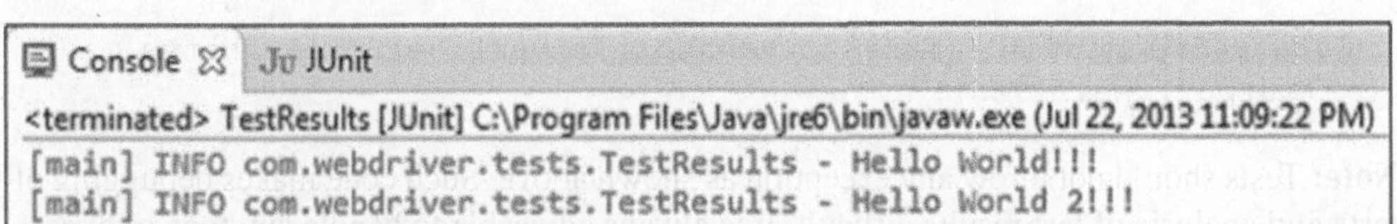

FIGURE 18.1 | Logging comments in test results

18.2 | CAPTURING AUT SCREENSHOT DURING RUN-TIME

In test automation screenshots are an effective way of analyzing what caused the tests to fail during run-time. Automation framework is to be designed in a way that it captures screenshot of the active screen at the very point of test failure.

Selenium WebDriver provides *TakesScreenshot* interface to capture screenshots of the active screen while tests are executing. This interface allows capturing screenshots of the entire page, current active window, visible part of the page or the complete desktop depending on the type of browser. It also allows the flexibility to covert the captured image to base64 data or raw bytes. Base64 or raw bytes can be used to compare two images by their pixels. This is generally used when we need to implement bitmap checkpoint.

EXAMPLE 18.1 Write code to capture image of the amazon.com home page during run-time and log the path of the screenshot to test results.

Code below shows how to capture screenshot of the page during run-time.

```
@Test
public void testCaptureScreenshot(){
        Logger logger = LoggerFactory.getLogger(getClass());
        WebDriver driver = new FirefoxDriver();
        driver.get("http://www.amazon.com/");
        //take screenshot
        File screenshot =
            ((TakesScreenshot)driver).getScreenshotAs(OutputType.FILE);
        //save screenshot file to c:\temp directory
        String errScreenshotPath = "c:\\temp\\screenshot.png";
        FileUtils.copyFile(screenshot, new File(errScreenshotPath));
        Logger.info(errScreenshotPath);
}
```

Figure 18.2 shows the screenshot image captured by the above code.

For Base64 string use code:

```
File screenshot = ((TakesScreenshot)driver).getScreenshotAs
  (OutputType.BASE64);
```

For BYTES use code:

```
File screenshot = ((TakesScreenshot)driver).getScreenshotAs
  (OutputType.BYTES);
```

Note: Tests should not throw any exception as shown above. Such code makes debugging of tests and analysis of test results difficult. It is always advisable to handle any type of exception thrown by the test code.

FIGURE 18.2 | screenshot.png

18.3 | RECORDING VIDEO OF TEST RUN

Videos of test run execution prove to be useful for quick analysis of failed tests. While tests are executing unattended, videos of test run can be captured and saved. Test run videos help in understanding how things went during test execution by capturing application or script errors or successes. Videos help to find out how AUT responded to a test execution. And if test failed, what user actions caused the test to fail.

Test run video help reduce analysis time of failed tests by helping to easily track the test failure repro steps.

Selenium WebDriver does not have any out of box support for capturing test run videos. However, this can be achieved by using Java-Screen-Recorder.

Java-Screen-Recorder is an open source platform independent screen capture and playback application. It produces high quality screen recordings using an internal lossless compression algorithm. The extension name of the recorded video files is '.cap'. The recordings can be played back by a screen player application. Java-Screen-Recorder also provides the option to convert the '.cap' file to the QT movie format, using the included screen converter application. Also, the output video can be post-processed to other formats, using a video conversion tool such as 'ffmpeg'.

Java-Screen-Recorder is licensed under the MIT License. It can be downloaded from site: http://code.google.com/p/java-screen-recorder/downloads/list. It consists of three jar files:

1. screen_recorder.jar
2. screen_player.jar
3. screen_converter.jar

The screen recorder, player and converter tools are all self-contained jar files. These tools require only the Java Runtime Environment for execution. These tools operate independently of any other external software codecs and libraries, to provide true platform independent video capture.

The steps to import the jar file to Eclipse workspace are as follows:

1. Download the application from site: http://code.google.com/p/java-screen-recorder/downloads/list
2. Unzip the files
3. Import files screen_recorder.jar and screen_converter.jar to an existing project Java Build Path.

18.3.1 | Screen Recorder

Screen Recorder is used for recording videos of screen. To run screen recorder manually, execute the following command.

```
java -jar screen_recorder.jar
```

The screen cursor can optionally be changed to white, using the option:

```
java -jar screen_recorder.jar -white_cursor
```

18.3.2 | Screen Player

Screen player is used for playing the captured screen videos (.cap). To run screen player, execute the following command:

```
java -jar screen_player.jar
```

18.3.3 | Screen Converter

Screen converter is a tool to convert screen recordings to the QuickTime movie format, which can then be post-processed to other formats using a video conversion tool such as ffmpeg.

To run the screen converter, execute the following command:

```
java -jar screen_converter.jar <screen_cap_file.cap>
```

In order to capture screen videos of individual tests, we would require to start/stop the screen recordings programmatically. Code below uses how to capture the screen video of a simple test method. The test below opens a google page and does a google search.

```
import java.io.FileNotFoundException;
import java.io.FileOutputStream;
import java.text.DateFormat;
import java.text.SimpleDateFormat;
```

```
import java.util.Calendar;

import org.junit.After;
import org.junit.Before;
import org.junit.Test;
import org.openqa.selenium.By;
import org.openqa.selenium.WebDriver;
import org.openqa.selenium.firefox.FirefoxDriver;
import com.wet.wired.jsr.recorder.DesktopScreenRecorder;
import com.wet.wired.jsr.recorder.JRecorder;
import com.wet.wired.jsr.recorder.ScreenRecorder;

public class ScreenVideoRecorder {
    ScreenRecorder recorder;
    WebDriver driver;
    @Test
    public void testVideoScreenCapture() {
        //capture video for
        // open google page and do a google search
        driver = new FirefoxDriver();
        driver.get("http://www.google.com");
        driver.findElement(By.name("q")).sendKeys("Java
          ScreenRecorder");
        driver.findElement(By.id("gbqfb")).click();
    }

    @Before
    public void setUp(){
        //file path where video is to be saved
        String videoFileName = "c:\\temp\\" + this.get
          UniqueNbr() + ".cap";
        FileOutputStream oStream = null;
           try {
              oStream = new FileOutputStream(videoFil
                eName);
        } catch (FileNotFoundException e) {
              e.printStackTrace();
        }
        JRecorder jrecorder = new JRecorder();
        recorder = new DesktopScreenRecorder(oStream,
          jrecorder);
        //start video recording
        recorder.startRecording();

    }
```

```
        @After
        public void tearDown(){
                driver.quit();
                //stop video recording
                recorder.stopRecording();
        }

        //get a unique number-datetime
        private String getUniqueNbr(){
                DateFormat dateFormat = new SimpleDateFormat
                  ("ddMMyyyy_HHmmss");
                Calendar cal = Calendar.getInstance();
                return dateFormat.format(cal.getTime());
        }
}
```

INTERVIEW QUESTIONS

1. What is the importance of logging test steps or failure reason?
2. Write code to capture screenshot of a web page at runtime.
3. Which Java API can be used to log comments?
4. What is the difference between JUnit assert statement and SLF4J logger statement?

19 CHAPTER

Advanced User Interactions

Selenium WebDriver Advanced User Interaction API allows users to simulate complex keyboard and mouse events such as pressing multiple keys at the same time, mouse drag and drop operations, holding a key and then performing some mouse operation, etc.

19.1 | ACTION BUILDER

Selenium WebDriver provides Actions class to simulate complex keyboard and mouse events. The actions class implements the builder pattern to create a composite action. A composite action can contain one or more keyboard or mouse actions.

EXAMPLE 19.1 Consider the following figures. Figure 19.1 shows amazon.com page with no mouse hover. When user hovers the mouse on the menu items, sub-menu links shows up as shown in Figure 19.2. Figure 19.2 shows the sub-menu links when user hovers the mouse on the item 'Unlimited Instant Videos'. Write WebDriver code to click on the link 'Learn More About Amazon Prime' as shown in Figure 19.2.

FIGURE 19.1 | Amazon.com page with no mouse hover

FIGURE 19.2 | Sub-menu links on mouse hover

Assume HTML code of the element 'Shop by Department' to be:

```
<a id="" class="nav_a nav-button-outer nav-menu-active nav-
shop-all-button nav-button-outer-open" alt="Shop By Department"
href="javascript:void(0)" style="display: inline;">
```

Assume HTML code of the menu item 'Unlimited Instant Videos' to be:

```
<li id="nav_cat_0" class="nav_first nav_pop_li nav_cat nav_hover
  nav_active">Unlimited Instant Videos</li>
```

Assume HTML code of the link 'Learn More About Amazon Prime' to be:

```
<div id="nav_subcats">
<div id="nav_subcats_0" class="nav_browse_subcat nav_super_cat"
  data-nav-promo-id="instant-video" style="display: block;">
<img class="nav_browse_promo" src="http://g-ecx.images-
  amazon.com/images/G/01/img12/digital/flyout/AIV_GNO-
  Flyout_TrueBloodS5._V384305703_.png" usemap="#nav_imgmap_
  instant-video"
  style="bottom: -24px; right: -20px; width: 500px; height: 495px;"/>
<ul class="nav_browse_ul nav_browse_cat_ul">
<li class="nav_pop_li nav_browse_cat_head">Unlimited Instant
  Videos</li>
<li class="nav_first nav_taglined nav_subcat_link nav_pop_li">
<li class="nav_subcat_link nav_pop_li">
<a class="nav_a nav_item" href="/gp/prime/signup/ref=...">Learn
More About Amazon Prime</a>
</li>
<li class="nav_taglined nav_subcat_link nav_pop_li nav_divider_
before">
<li class="nav_taglined nav_subcat_link nav_pop_li">
```

```
<li class="nav_taglined nav_subcat_link nav_pop_li">
</ul>
</div>
<div id="nav_subcats_1" class="nav_browse_subcat nav_super_cat"
data-nav-promo-id="mp3" style="display: none;">
```

WebDriver code to click on the link 'Learn More About Amazon Prime' is shown below:

```
@Test
public void testAdvancedUserInteractions() {
      WebDriver driver = new FirefoxDriver();
      //open amazon.com page
      driver.get("http://www.amazon.com");
      //create an instance of Actions class
      Actions builder = new Actions(driver);
      WebElement shopByDeptt = driver.findElement(By.XPath
        ("//a[@alt='Shop By Department']"));

      //build the action events
      //1. Move mouse on element 'Shop By Department'
      //2. Click on this element to show menu links
      //3. Move mouse to element 'Unlimited Instant Videos' (Figure 19.1)
      //4. Click on this element to show sub-menu links (Figure 19.2)
      //5. Move mouse to link 'Learn More...' (Figure 19.2)
      //6. Click on this link
      Action mouseHoverAndClick = builder.moveToElement
        (shopByDeptt)
            .click()
            .moveToElement(driver.findElement(By.id("nav_cat_0")))
            .click()
            .moveToElement(driver.findElement(By.XPath("//div[@
              id='nav_subcats_0']// a[contains(text(),'Learn
              More About Amazon Prime')]")))
            .click()
            .build();
      mouseHoverAndClick.perform();
      //print current url
      System.out.println(driver.getCurrentUrl());
      //Output:: http://www.amazon.com/gp/prime/signup/...
}
```

19.2 | METHODS

Action builder class provides a list of methods to simulate various keyboard and mouse events. Table 19.1 lists some of those methods:

TABLE 19.1 Action Builder Class Methods

Method	Description
click()	Clicks on the current mouse location
click(WebElement onElement)	Clicks in the middle of the specified element. Equivalent to: Actions.moveToElement(onElement).click()
clickAndHold()	Clicks (without releasing) at the current mouse location
clickAndHold(WebElement onElement)	Clicks (without releasing) in the middle of the given element.
release()	Releases the depressed left mouse button at the current mouse location
release(WebElement onElement)	Releases the depressed left mouse button, in the middle of the given element
contextClick()	Performs a context-click at the current mouse location
contextClick(WebElement onElement)	Performs a context-click at middle of the specified element. First performs a mouseMove to the location of the element.
doubleClick()	Performs a double-click at the current mouse location
doubleClick(WebElement onElement)	Performs a double-click at middle of the specified element
dragAndDrop(WebElement source, WebElement target)	Performs click and hold at the location of the source element, moves the location to the target element and then release the mouse
dragAndDropBy(WebElement source, int xOffset, int yOffset)	Performs click and hold at the location of the source element, moves by the given offset and then release the mouse
keyDown(Keys theKey)	Perform user action of key press and hold of the specified key
keyDown(WebElement element, Keys theKey)	Sets focus on the specified element and then performs user action of key press and hold of the specified key. Equivalent to: Actions.click(element).sendKeys(theKey)
keyUp(Keys theKey)	Performs a key release user action
keyUp(WebElement element, Keys theKey)	Sets focus on the specified element and then performs a key release user action
moveToElement(WebElement toElement)	Moves the mouse to the middle of the specified element. The element is scrolled into view and its location is calculated using getBoundingClientRect.
moveToElement(WebElement toElement, int xOffset, int yOffset)	Moves the mouse to an offset from the top-left corner of the element. The element is scrolled into view and its location is calculated using getBoundingClientRect.

(continued)

TABLE 19.1 I *(continued)*

Method	Description
moveByOffset(int xOffset, int yOffset)	Moves the mouse from its current position (or 0,0) by the given offset. If the coordinates provided are outside the viewport (the mouse will end up outside the browser window) then the viewport is scrolled to match.
sendKeys(CharSequence... keysToSend)	Sends keys to the active element
sendKeys(WebElement element, CharSequence... keysToSend)	Sends keys to the specified element. Equivalent to: Actions.click(element).sendKeys(keysToSend)
wait()	Performs a wait
wait(long timeout)	Performs a wait for the specified time
wait(long timeout, int nanos)	Performs a wait for the specified time
build()	Generates a composite action of all user actions. Also resets the internal builder state, so subsequent calls to build() will contain fresh sequences.
perform()	Performs the composite action

EXAMPLE 19.2 Consider Figure 19.3. User has the option to drag the text 'Drag and Drop Me' to the rectangular box. Write code to simulate this user action using *clickAndHold* method.

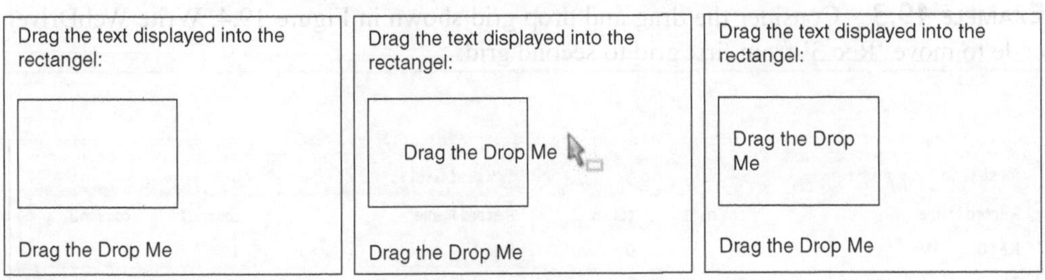

FIGURE 19.3 I Dragging the text and dropping it to the text box

This user action can be simulated using `clickAndHold` and `release` method. Code below shows the code to automate this scenario.

```
@Test
public void testClickHoldReleaseMouse() {
        WebDriver driver = new FirefoxDriver();
        //open site
        driver.get("….");
        //create an instance of Actions class
```

```
        Actions builder = new Actions(driver);
        WebElement dragText = driver.findElement(By.
          id("draggableText"));
        WebElement dropArea = driver.findElement(By.
          id("droppableArea"));
        //build the action events
        //1. Left click mouse on link element and hold
        //2. Move mouse to the text box element
        //3. Release mouse
        Action mouseClickHoldRelease = builder.
          clickAndHold(dragText)
              .moveToElement(dropArea)
              .release()
              .build();
        mouseClickHoldRelease.perform();

        //Alternatively,
        //mouseClickHoldRelease = builder.clickAndHold(dragText)
        //            .release(dropArea)
        //            .build();
        //mouseClickHoldRelease.perform();

        //Alternatively,
        // builder.dragAndDrop(dragText, dropArea).build().perform();
}
```

Example 19.3 Consider the drag and drop grid shown in Figure 19.4. Write WebDriver code to move 'Rec 3' from first grid to second grid.

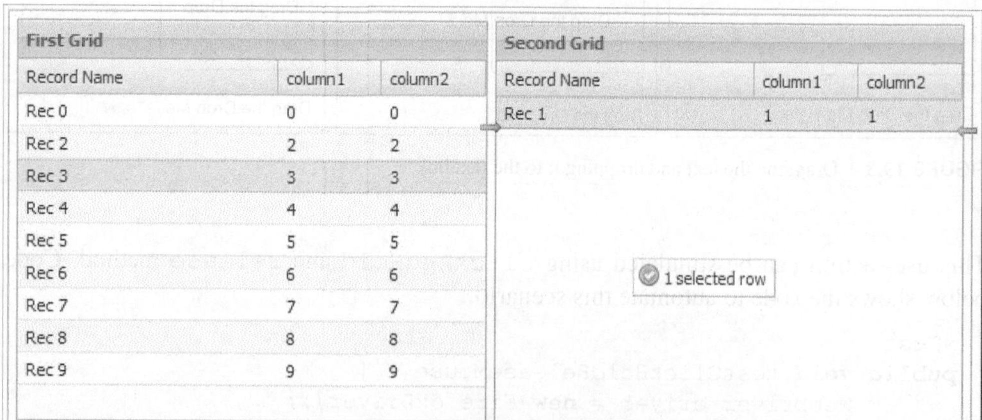

FIGURE 19.4 | Drag and drop grid

Assume HTML code of the first grid to be:

```
<div id="firstGrid" class="x-component" tabindex="-1" ...>
<table class="x-grid-table" cellspacing="0" cellpadding="0">
<tbody>
<tr>
<tr class="x-grid-row">
<tr class="x-grid-row x-grid-row-alt">
... ....
```

Assume HTML code of second grid is:

```
<div id="secondGrid" class="x-component" tabindex="-1" ...>
<table class="x-grid-table" cellspacing="0" cellpadding="0">
<tbody>
<tr>
<tr class="x-grid-row">
<tr class="x-grid-row x-grid-row-alt">
```

Following code shows simplest WebDriver code to drag elements from the first grid and drop it to the second grid.

```
@Test
public void testDragAndDrop(){
        WebDriver driver = new FirefoxDriver();
        driver.get("....");
        WebElement firstGridTableRec3 =
          driver.findElement(By.XPath("//div[@id='firstGrid']//
          table//tr[3]"));
        WebElement secondGrid = driver.findElement(By.
          id("secondGrid"));
        Actions builder = new Actions(driver);
        builder.dragAndDrop(firstGridTableRec3, secondGrid).
          perform();
}
```

Note: In the code above table row 3 has been accessed directly using XPath. Above code is just a simple illustration. Any dependency of element identification on index is to be avoided. A good approach would be to locate the table element and then iterate through the rows till the expected row is found and then desired user action is taken on it.

EXAMPLE 19.4 Consider Figures 19.5 and 19.6. Double click on the paragraph shown in Figure 19.5 displays some text on the page as shown in Figure 19.6. Write a code to simulate double click user action.

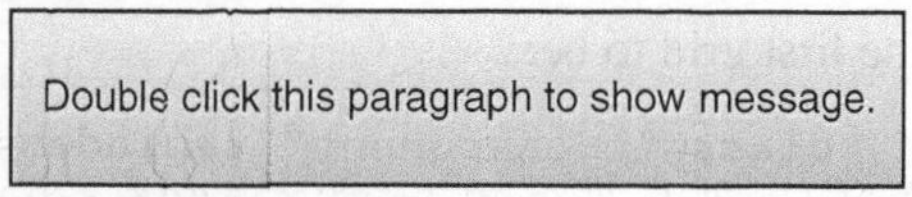

FIGURE 19.5 | Before double click

FIGURE 19.6 | After double click

Assume HTML code of the page to be:

```
<!DOCTYPE html>
<html>
<head>
<script>
function myFunction(){
document.getElementById("dblclick").innerHTML="Hello World!!!";
}
</script>
</head>
<body>
<p ondblclick="myFunction()">Double click this paragraph to
display message</p>
<p id="dblclick"></p>
</body>
</html>
```

WebDriver code to double click on the element is shown below:

```
@Test
public void testDoubleClick(){
        WebDriver driver = new FirefoxDriver();
        //assume file is saved at path: c:\temp\doubleclick.html
        driver.get("file:///C:/Temp/doubleclick.html");
        //locate element to be double clicked
        WebElement element = driver.findElement(By.XPath
          ("//p[contains(text(),'Double click')]"));
        //double click on the element
        Actions builder = new Actions(driver);
        builder.doubleClick(element).perform();
}
```

19.3 | COPYING CONTENTS TO/FROM CLIPBOARD

In test automation, certain times it is required to copy text to or from clipboard. Java provides *Clipboard* class to read/write data to clipboard. Consider the employee table shown below. Write code to copy cell(2,2) data to clipboard. Then, from clipboard, paste this data to cell(2,3).

Employee ID	Employee Name	Designation
122768	Charles	Software Developer
122657	Joseph	Automation Developer

FIGURE 19.7 | Employee table

```
@Test
public void testClipboard(){
    WebDriver driver = new FirefoxDriver();
    driver.get("file:///C:/Users/Rajeev/Desktop/dad.html");
    //For the table method used below refer chapter
      'Working with WebTables'
    WebElement table = findTableByColumnName(driver,
      "Employee ID; Employee Name;Designation") ;
    String name = table.getCellData(2,2);
    //get input element inside cell(2,3)
    WebElement textBox = getCellElement(2,3,"input",0);

    //get an instance of Clipboard class
    Toolkit toolkit = Toolkit.getDefaultToolkit();
    Clipboard clipboard = toolkit.getSystemClipboard();
    //get an instance of Clipboard class
    Toolkit toolkit = Toolkit.getDefaultToolkit();
    Clipboard clipboard = toolkit.getSystemClipboard();

    //copy contents of cell(2,2) to clipboard
    this.setClipboard(clipboard, name);

    //read clipboard data
    String clipboardData = this.getClipboard(clipboard);
    System.out.print("Clipboard Data:" + clipboardData);
    //Output::Clipboard Data:Charles
    //paste clipboard data to the textbox element at cell(2,3)
    textBox.sendKeys(clipboardData);
}

//copy contents to clipboard
private void setClipboard(Clipboard clipboard, String data){
```

```
        StringSelection textForCliboard = new
          StringSelection(data);
        clipboard.setContents(textForCliboard, null);
    }
    //get clipboard contents
    private String getClipboard(Clipboard clipboard){
        String clipboardData = null;
        Transferable clipboardContents = clipboard.
          getContents(null);
        Boolean isClipboardHasText = (clipboardContents!=null) &&
          clipboardContents.isDataFlavorSupported(DataFlavor.
            stringFlavor);
        if (isClipboardHasText){
                try {
                            clipboardData = (String)clipboardContents.
                              getTransferData(DataFlavor.
                                stringFlavor);
                } catch (UnsupportedFlavorException e) {
                            e.printStackTrace();
                } catch (IOException e) {
                            e.printStackTrace();
                }
        }
        return clipboardData;
    }
```

EXAMPLE 19.5 Write code to copy contents of cell(2,2) using key event CRTL+C. Write the contents of clipboard to the text box in cell(2,3). Action Builder class can be used to simulate complex keyboard events. Key event CTRL+C is used to copy contents to clipboard. Code below shows how to copy contents to clipboard:

```
Actions builder = new Actions(driver);
builder.keyDown(Keys.CONTROL)
       .sendKeys("C")
       .keyUp(Keys.CONTROL)
       .build();
builder.perform();
```

WebDriver code to automate the above scenario is shown by the code below:

```
//get cell (2,1) element
WebElement cell21 = driver.findElement(By.XPath("//table[@
id='prodTable2']//tr[2]//td[1]"));
//get cell (2,1) element
WebElement cell23 = driver.findElement(By.XPath("//table[@
id='prodTable2']//tr[2]//td[3]"));
```

```
//copy cell (2,1) contents and paste it to cell(2,3)
//create an instance of Action Builder class
Actions builder = new Actions(driver);
//1. Double click on cell(2,1) to select the cell contents
//2. Use key event CRTL+C to copy selected contents
//3. Click on cell(2,3)
//4. Use key event CTRL+V to paste contents
builder.doubleClick(cell21)
      .keyDown(Keys.CONTROL)
      .sendKeys("C")
      .keyUp(Keys.CONTROL)
      .click(cell23)
      .keyDown(Keys.CONTROL)
      .sendKeys("V")
      .keyUp(Keys.CONTROL)
      .build();
builder.perform();
```

19.4 | EXECUTING JAVASCRIPT CODE

Selenium WebDriver provides the flexibility to execute JavaScript code within the browser window. This feature is essentially useful to test the pages using JavaScript. For example, JavaScript can be used to execute analytics JavaScript code for web analytics testing.

Selenium WebDriver API provides `JavascriptExecutor` interface to execute JavaScript code within the browser window. Example below shows how to use `JavascriptExecutor` interface. The following code finds out the title of the page and the total links it contains by executing JavaScript code within browser window.

```
@Test
public void testJavascriptExecutor(){
      WebDriver driver = new FirefoxDriver();
      driver.get("http://www.amazon.com");
      //get instance of JavascriptExecutor class
      JavascriptExecutor je = (JavascriptExecutor) driver;
      //get page title
      String pageTitle = (String) je.executeScript("return
        document.title");
      assertEquals("Page title is wrong","Amazon.com:
        …",pageTitle);

      //get total number of links on the page
      long linkCount = (Long)je.executeScript
             ("var linkCount=document.getElementsByTagName('A');
               return linkCount.length");
      assertEquals("Total link count is wrong",281,linkCount);
}
```

Casting WebDriver instance to `JavascriptExecutor` interface helps execute JavaScript code from Selenium WebDriver.

```
JavascriptExecutor je = (JavascriptExecutor) driver;
```

The `JavascriptExecutor` interface provides `executeScript` method to execute JavaScript code within the browser window.

```
long linkCount = (Long)je.executeScript
        ("var linkCount=document.getElementsByTagName('A');
                return linkCount.length");
```

The `executeScript` method is to be typecasted to the return type of the JavaScript code. For instance in example above, the return type of JavaScript code is *Long*. So the method `executeScript` has been type casted to *Long*.

19.5 | CAPTURING SCREENSHOTS

In test automation, screenshots are an effective way of analysing what caused the tests to fail during run-time. Automation framework is to be designed in a way that it captures screenshot of the active screen at the very point of test failure.

Selenium WebDriver provides *TakesScreenshot* interface to capture screenshots of the active screen while tests are executing. This interface allows capturing screenshots of the entire page, current active window, visible part of the page or the complete desktop depending on the type of browser. It also allows the flexibility to covert the captures image to base64 data or raw bytes. Base64 or raw bytes can be used to compare two images by their pixels. This is generally used when we need to implement bitmap checkpoint.

EXAMPLE 19.6 Write code to capture image of the complete amazon.com home page during run-time.

Following code shows how to capture screenshot of the page during run-time.

```
@Test
public void testCaptureScreenshot(){
        WebDriver driver = new FirefoxDriver();
        driver.get("http://www.amazon.com/");
        //take screenshot
        File screenshot = ((TakesScreenshot)driver).
          getScreenshotAs(OutputType.FILE);
              //save screenshot file to c:\temp directory
        FileUtils.copyFile(screenshot, new File("c:\\temp\\
          screenshot.png"));
}
```

Figure 19.8 shows the screenshot image captured by the above code.

FIGURE 19.8 | screenshot.png

For Base64 string use code:

```
File screenshot = ((TakesScreenshot)driver).
  getScreenshotAs(OutputType.BASE64);
```

For BYTES use code:

```
File screenshot = ((TakesScreenshot)driver).
  getScreenshotAs(OutputType.BYTES);
```

Note: Tests should not throw any exception as shown above. Such code makes debugging of tests and analysis of test results difficult. It is always advisable to handle any type of exception thrown by the test code.

INTERVIEW QUESTIONS

1. Which WebDriver class is used to simulate user mouse click events?
2. Name some of the methods of Action Builder class.
3. Write code to click on the link 'Your Video Library' of Figure 19.1.
4. Which Java API will you use to copy contents to clipboard?
5. Users opens amazon.com site and copes textual content of link element 'Today's Deals' to clipboard. Next, the user pastes the clipboard contents to search box and hits enter key. Write code to automate this scenario.

20 CHAPTER

Extending Selenium

Selenium WebDriver provides highly flexible and robust API to build a scalable test automation framework. Selenium features and commands can be customized to develop an automation framework that suits the project needs. This chapter explains how to extend the Selenium WebDriver API to build a highly reusable and stable framework.

In this chapter, we will discuss how to build an extension for jQuery UI control. Also we will discuss how to build an extension for easy automation of web tables, object maps and image comparisons. These extensions can be used as an example for implementing support for any third party or custom controls used in the application under test.

Extensions are to be developed in a way that supports encapsulation of framework, i.e., it hides the framework technical complexities from the tests. This reduces both development and maintenance efforts.

20.1 | CREATING EXTENSION FOR JQUERY UI WIDGET

jQuery UI is a Javascript user-interface library to build interactive web applications. It provides abstractions for low-level interaction and animation, advance effects and high level themeable widgets. It is a free open source software licensed under the MIT license.

Interactions	Widgets
• Draggable • Droppable • Resizable • Selectable • Sortable	• Accordion • Autocomplete • Button • Datepicker • Dialog • Menu • Progressbar • Slider • Spinner • Tabs • Tooltip
Effects	**Utilities**
• Add Class • Color Animation • Effect • Hide • Remove Class • Show • Switch Class • Toggle • Toggle Class	• Position • Widget Factory

FIGURE 20.1 jQuery UI Widgets

The widgets mentioned above are build using a number of low-level HTML elements, such as DIVs, lists, input tags, etc. Though Selenium WebDriver recognizes these elements individually, it is always advisable to build extendable support for Selenium to recognize these controls as native jQuery widgets. The developed support can then be used to perform native operations supported by jQuery framework. This helps to ease test development and maximize code reusability. In the section, we will learn how to automate widgets *Datepicker* and *Tabs*.

20.2 | CREATING AN EXTENSION CLASS FOR JQUERY DATEPICKER WIDGET

Datepicker widget allows users to select dates. Figure 20.2 shows a *Datepicker* widget. This datepicker widget can be used for various purposes such as selecting date of birth, date of courier pickup, appointment date, etc. In this section, we will try to develop an extension class that helps to set date using this widget.

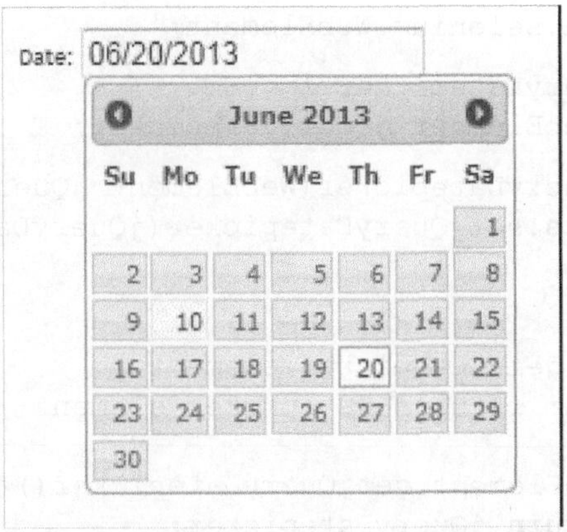

FIGURE 20.2 | Datepicker widget

Assume HTML code of the Datepicker element to be:

```
<div id="ui-datepicker-div" class="ui-datepicker
   ui-widget ui-widget-content ui-helper-clearfix ui-corner-
   all" style="position: absolute; top: 32px; left: 35px;
   z-index: 1; display: block;">
```

Assume HTML code of the element (for selecting previous months) to be:

```
<a class="ui-datepicker-prev ui-corner-all" title="Prev"
   data-event="click" data-handler="prev">
```

Assume HTML code of the element (for selecting future months) to be:

```
<a class="ui-datepicker-next ui-corner-all ui-state-hover
   ui-datepicker-next-hover" title="Next" data-event="click"
   data-handler="next">
```

Assume HTML code of date element to be:

```
<table class="ui-datepicker-calendar">
<thead>
<tr>
<th class="ui-datepicker-week-end">
<span title="Sunday">Su</span>
</th>
...
```

The following code shows how to extend Selenium to build customized functions for simulating user actions on datepicker widget.

```
package com.webdriver.extendingselenium;
import java.util.Calendar;
import java.util.List;

import org.openqa.selenium.By;
import org.openqa.selenium.WebElement;

public class JQueryDatepicker {
        private WebElement jQueryDatepicker;

        public JQueryDatepicker(WebElement jQueryDatepicker) {
                this.setjQueryDatepicker(jQueryDatepicker);
        }

        /*
         * @desc: get Datepicker element
         * @return: returns Datepicker element
         */
        public WebElement getjQueryDatepicker(){
                return jQueryDatepicker;
        }

        /*
         * @desc: set Datepicker element
         */
        public void setjQueryDatepicker(WebElement
           jQueryDatepicker){
                this.jQueryDatepicker = jQueryDatepicker;
        }

        /*
         * @desc: select specific date from Datepicker widget
         * @param: Datepicker element
         * @param: Date to select as Calendar object
         */
        public void selectDate(Calendar calendar){
                this.selectMonthYear(calendar);
```

```
        this.selectDayDate( calendar);
    }
    /*
     * @desc: selects day of the specified date
     * @param: Datepicker element
     * @param: Date to select as Calendar object
     */
    public void selectDayDate(Calendar calendar){
        //get date
        int day = calendar.get(Calendar.DAY_OF_MONTH);
        //get date webtable element
        List<WebElement> tableCells = jQueryDatepicker.
          findElements( By.XPath("//table//tbody//td"));
        for (int i=0;i<tableCells.size();i++){
                if (tableCells.get(i).getText().
                  equals(String.valueOf(day))){
                      tableCells.get(i).click();
                      break;
                }
        }
    }

    /*
     * @desc: selects month and year of the specified date
     * @param: Datepicker element
     * @param: Date to select as Calendar object
     */
    public void selectMonthYear(Calendar calendar){
        //get difference in months between todays date
          and the specified date
        int monthDiff = this.getMonthDiff(calendar);
        if (monthDiff<0){
                this.setFutureMonthYear(Math.
                  abs(monthDiff));
        }
        else {
                this.setPastMonthYear(Math.
                  abs(monthDiff));

        }
    }
    //get difference in months between todays date and the
      specified date
    private int getMonthDiff(Calendar calendar){
        Calendar currentDate = Calendar.getInstance();
        int currentMonths = currentDate.get(Calendar.
          YEAR)*12 + currentDate.get(Calendar.MONTH);
```

```
            int calendarMonths = calendar.get(Calendar.
              YEAR)*12 + calendar.get(Calendar.MONTH);
            return (currentMonths-calendarMonths);
        }

        //select the specified month/year by clicking on the
          element multiple times
        private void setFutureMonthYear(int diffMonth){
            WebElement next;
            for (int i=0;i<=diffMonth;i++){
                    next = jQueryDatepicker.findElement(
                      By.XPath("//a[@title='Next']"));
                    next.click();
            }
        }
        //select the specified month/year by clicking on the
          element multiple times
        private void setPastMonthYear(int diffMonth){
            WebElement prev;
            for (int i=0;i<=diffMonth;i++){
                    prev = jQueryDatepicker.findElement(
                      By.XPath("//a[@title='Prev']"));
                    prev.click();
            }
        }
}
```

It is advisable to build all extension codes in a separate library or utility package and the same can be imported in all the tests. If the reusability spans to multiple automation projects then a jar of the package is to be created. This jar file can be imported in all the projects wherever required.

Example 20.1 Website jqueryui.com/datepicker has a datepicker widget as shown in Figure 20.1. The datepicker element is inside a frame. Write a code to set the date to 29/4/2015 from the datepicker widget.

The following code shows how to use the above developed selenium extender to easily set dates.

```
@Test
public void testJQueryDatepicker() {
        WebDriver driver = new FirefoxDriver();
        driver.get("http://jqueryui.com/datepicker/");

        //switch to the frame that contains this Datepicker widget
        driver = driver.switchTo().frame(driver.findElement(
          By.XPath("//iframe")));
```

```
        //suppose date to be selected is 29-Apr-2015
        Calendar cal = Calendar.getInstance();
        cal.set(2015, 4, 29);

        //get select data text box
        WebElement dateTextBox = driver.findElement(
          By.cssSelector(“input#datepicker”));

        //activate datepicker widget
        dateTextBox.sendKeys(“”);

        //get datepicker element
        WebElement datepicker = driver.findElement(By.id(“ui-
          datepicker-div”));

        //get an instance of jQueryDatepicker extension class
        JQueryDatepicker jQueryDatepicker = new
          JQueryDatepicker(datepicker);
        //set date in datepicker widget
        jQueryDatepicker.selectDate(cal);
    }
```

20.3 | CREATING AN EXTENSION CLASS FOR JQUERYUI TAB

jQueryUI Tab is used for implementing a single content area with multiple panels. Each panel is associated with a header in a list. Figure 20.3 shows a jQuery UI Tab widget.

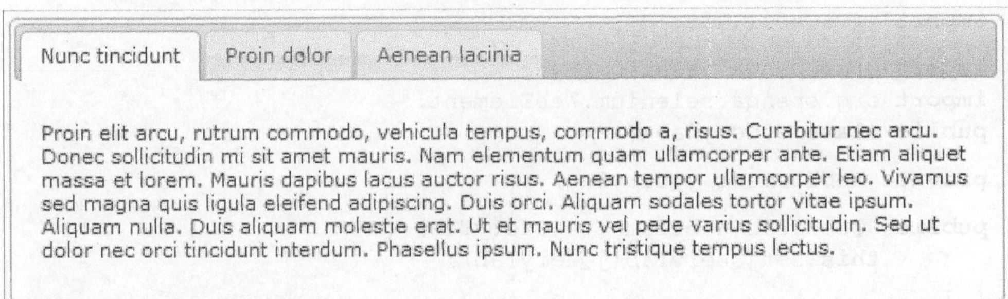

FIGURE 20.3 | jQuery UI Tab Widget

Let us assume HTML code of the widget to be:

```
<div id=”tabs” class=”ui-tabs ui-widget ui-widget-content
    ui-corner-all”>
```

Assume HTML code of tabs to be:

```
<ul class=”ui-tabs-nav ui-helper-reset ui-helper-clearfix
    ui-widget-header ui-corner-all” role=”tablist”>
```

```
<li class="ui-state-default ui-corner-top ui-tabs-active
    ui-state-active ui-state-hover" role="tab" tabindex="0"
    aria-controls="tabs-1" aria-labelledby="ui-id-1" aria-
    selected="true">
<a id="ui-id-1" class="ui-tabs-anchor" href="#tabs-1"
    role="presentation" tabindex="-1">Nunc tincidunt</a>
</li>

<li class="ui-state-default ui-corner-top" role="tab"
    tabindex="-1" aria-controls="tabs-2" aria-labelledby="ui-
    id-2" aria-selected="false">
<a id="ui-id-2" class="ui-tabs-anchor" href="#tabs-2"
    role="presentation" tabindex="-1">Proin dolor</a>
</li>
<li class="ui-state-default ui-corner-top" role="tab"
    tabindex="-1" aria-controls="tabs-3" aria-labelledby="ui-
    id-3" aria-selected="false">
<a id="ui-id-3" class="ui-tabs-anchor" href="#tabs-3"
    role="presentation" tabindex="-1">Aenean lacinia</a>
</li>
</ul>
```

The following code shows how to extend Selenium to build customized functions for simulating user actions on this tab widget.

1. First, a JQueryTab class is created with its getter and setter properties.

```
import java.util.List;

import org.openqa.selenium.By;
import org.openqa.selenium.WebElement;
public class JQueryTab {
private WebElement jQueryTab;
public JQueryTab(WebElement jQueryTab) {
        this.setjQueryTab(jQueryTab);
}
/*
 * @desc: get jQuery tab widget element
 * @return: returns jQuery tab widget tab element
 */
public WebElement getjQueryTab(){
        return jQueryTab;
}

/*
 * @desc: set jQuery tab widget element
 */
```

```
public void setjQueryTab(WebElement jQueryTab){
        this.jQueryTab = jQueryTab;
}
```

2. Add a method to retrieve all the tab elements

```
/*
 * @desc: get all tabs
 * @return List<WebElement> of all tabs
 */
public List<WebElement> getAllTabs(){
        List<WebElement> tabs = jQueryTab.findElements(
          By.cssSelector("ul.ui-tabs-nav>li"));
        return tabs;
}
```

3. Add a method to retrieve all the tab counts.

```
/*
 * @desc: get tab count
 * @return int number of tabs
 */
public int getTabCount(){
        return this.getAllTabs().size();
}
```

4. Add a method to get the selected tab elements.

```
/*
 * @desc: get selected tab element
 * @return WebElement selected tab element
 */
public WebElement getSelectedTab(){
        WebElement selectedTab = jQueryTab.findElement(
          By.cssSelector("ul.ui-tabs-nav>li[aria-
            selected='true']"));
        return selectedTab;
}
```

5. Add a method to get the name of the selected tab element.

```
/*
 * @desc: get name of the selected tab
 * @return String name of the selected tab
 */
public String getSelecetdTabName(){
        return this.getSelectedTab().getText();
}
```

6. Add a method to get the index of the selected tab element.

```
/*
 * @desc: get position or index of the selected tab
 * @return int index of the selected tab
 */
public int getSelecetdTabIndex(){
        int tabIndex=0;
        List<WebElement> tabs = this.getAllTabs();
        for (tabIndex=0;tabIndex<tabs.size();tabIndex++){
                if (isTabSelected(tabs.get(tabIndex))) break;
        }
        return tabIndex;
}
```

7. Add a method to select the tab element with the specified name.

```
/*
 * @desc: select tab by tab name
 * @return WebElement selected tab
 */
public WebElement selectTabByName(String tabName) throws Exception{
        Boolean isTabFound = false;
        WebElement selectedTab = null;
        List<WebElement> tabs = this.getAllTabs();
        for(int i=0;i<tabs.size();i++){
                if (tabs.get(i).getText().contentEquals(tabName)){
                        isTabFound=true;
                        tabs.get(i).click();
                        selectedTab = tabs.get(i);
                        break;
                }
        }
        if (!isTabFound) throw new Exception ("Could not find
          tab '" + tabName + "'");
        return selectedTab;
}
```

8. Add a method to select the tab element with the specified index.

```
/*
 * @desc: select tab by index
 * @return WebElement selected tab
 */
public WebElement selectTabByIndex(int tabIndex) throws Exception{
        Boolean isTabFound = false;
        WebElement selectedTab = null;
```

```
        List<WebElement> tabs = this.getAllTabs();
        for(int i=0;i<tabs.size();i++){
                if (i==tabIndex){
                        isTabFound=true;
                        tabs.get(i).click();
                        selectedTab = tabs.get(i);
                        break;
                }
        }
        if (!isTabFound) throw new Exception
          ("Could not find tab with index '" + tabIndex + "'");
        return selectedTab;
}
```

9. Add a method to find whether the specified tab is selected or not.

```
/*
  * @desc: Is the specified tab selected
  * @return Boolean true or false
  */
private Boolean isTabSelected(WebElement tab){
        Boolean isSelected = false;
        if (tab.getAttribute("aria-selected").
          contentEquals("true")){
                isSelected = true;
        }
        return isSelected;
    }
}
```

EXAMPLE 20.2 Website jqueryui.com/tabs/ has a tab widget as shown in Figure 20.2. This tab element is inside a frame. Write a code to get the tab count and to select the 3rd tab.

The following code shows how to use the above developed selenium extender to easily work with jQuery tabs.

```
        @Test
        public void testJQueryTab(){
                WebDriver driver = new FirefoxDriver();
                driver.get("http://jqueryui.com/tabs/");
                //switch to the frame that contains this
                  Datepicker widget
                driver = driver.switchTo().frame(
                  driver.findElement(By.XPath("//iframe")));

                //get jQuery tab element
                WebElement tab = driver.findElement(By.
                  id("tabs"));
```

```
        //get an instance of jQueryTab extension class
        JQueryTab jQueryTab = new JQueryTab(tab);

        //get tab count
        System.out.println(jQueryTab.getTabCount());
          //Output::3

        //get selected tab name
        System.out.println(jQueryTab.
          getSelecetdTabName());//Output::Nunc tincidunt

        //select 3rd tab
        try {
                jQueryTab.selectTabByIndex(2);
        } catch (Exception e) {
                e.printStackTrace();
        }

        //get selected tab index
        System.out.println(jQueryTab.
          getSelecetdTabIndex());//Output::2

        //get selected tab name
        System.out.println(jQueryTab.
          getSelecetdTabName());//Output::Aenean lacinia
}
```

20.4 | CREATING AN EXTENSION FOR WEB TABLE

Selenium Webdriver provides a generic `WebElement` class to work with various elements on a web page. It also provides helper classes such as `Select` to work with list box elements. However, there is no built-in class to support web tables. Section "Creating an Extension Class for Web Tables" of Chapter 11 discusses in detail on how to develop extension class for web table.

20.5 | CREATING AN EXTENSION TO SET WEBELEMENTS' ATTRIBUTE VALUE

In certain times, we are faced with situations where we need to directly set the attribute value of the element. One most common example is the text box where date is selected as shown in Figure 20.4. Assume that the text box is disabled and date can only be selected using the calendar tool. It may happen that the calendar element is not recognized by the tool. In this situation, we may want to set the value of the text box explicitly. Since the text box is disabled, method sendKeys will not work. So we will have to find a mechanism with which we can set the value of this text box. One approach could be to set the value attribute of the element at run-time using Javascript code.

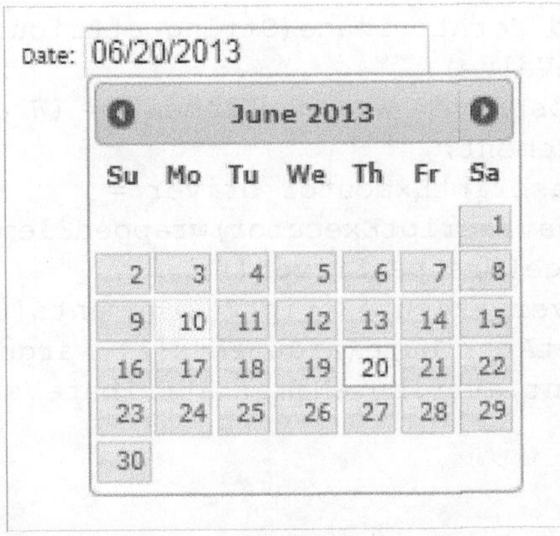

FIGURE 20.4 | Setting attribute value of a text box element

The following code shows how Selenium can be extended to set the attribute values of an element explicitly by executing Javascript code within the browser window.

```
import org.openqa.selenium.JavascriptExecutor;
import org.openqa.selenium.WebElement;
import org.openqa.selenium.internal.WrapsDriver;

public class SeleniumExtender{

        private WebElement element;

        public SeleniumExtender(WebElement element) {
                this.setElement(element);
        }
        /*
         * @desc: get element
         * @return: returns the element
         */
        public WebElement getElement(){
                return element;
        }
        /*
         * @desc: set element
         */
        public void setElement(WebElement element){
                this.element = element;
        }

        /*
         * @desc: set the attribute value of the element
         */
```

```
        public void setAttribute(String attributeName, String
          attributeValue){
               WrapsDriver wrappedElement = (WrapsDriver)
                 element;
               JavascriptExecutor driver =
                 (JavascriptExecutor)wrappedElement.
                   getWrappedDriver();
               driver.executeScript("arguments[0].
                 setAttribute(arguments[1], arguments[2])",eleme
                   nt,attributeName, attributeValue);
        }
}
```

EXAMPLE 20.3 Write a code to set the attribute *value* of the text box element of Figure 20.4 to '06/13/2013'.

```
  @Test
  public void testSetAttributeValue(){
        WebDriver driver = new FirefoxDriver();
        driver.get("http://jqueryui.com/datepicker/");
        //switch to the frame that contains this Datepicker
          widget
        driver = driver.switchTo().frame(driver.findElement
          (By.XPath("//iframe")));
        //get text box element
        WebElement dateTextBox =
          driver.findElement(By.cssSelector("input#datepicker"));
        SeleniumExtender seleniumExtender = new
          SeleniumExtender (dateTextBox);
        seleniumExtender.setAttribute("value", "06/13/2013");
        //verify date value is set
        System.out.print(dateTextBox.getAttribute("value"));
        //Output::06/13/2013
}
```

EXAMPLE 20.4 Write a code to set the attribute *value* of the checkbox element as 'true' to select the checkbox shown in Figure 20.5.

FIGURE 20.5 | Setting value attribute of checkbox as 'true'

The attribute of the checkbox element that determines whether checkbox is selected or not is '*checked*' attribute. A checkbox element can be selected by setting this value to 'true' and can be deselected by setting it to 'false'.

The following code shows how Selenium code can be extended to set the *value* attribute of the checkbox element explicitly by executing Javascript code within the browser window.

```
@Test
      public void testSetCheckboxAttributeValue(){
            WebDriver driver = new FirefoxDriver();
            driver.get("........");
            //Assume id attribute of the Checkbox element
            'US' is 'id0'
            WebElement checkbox = driver.findElement(By.
            id("id0"));
            SeleniumExtender seleniumExtender =
            new SeleniumExtender(checkbox);
            seleniumExtender.setAttribute("checked",
            "true");
            //verify that checkbox is selected
            System.out.println(checkbox.isSelected());
            //Output::true
      }
```

20.6 | CREATING AN EXTENSION CLASS TO HIGHLIGHT ELEMENTS

Since Selenium tests execute very fast, there is no way to find out to which element its interacting with when the selenium test execution is in process. Certain times it may happen that a dynamic element which is recognized in *Firepath* test while execution may fail to recognize the same element during run-time. It generally happens if there are more than one element with same attribute. For example, two elements – text box and checkbox both exist with same name say 'add'. In this case, the 'XPath' value "//input[@name='add']" will highlight both the elements in Firefox browser. Suppose textbox appears in application code before the checkbox element. Now assume we use code `driver.findElement(By.XPath("//input[@name='add']")).click()` to select the checkbox. In this case, though the code will get executed successfully but checkbox will never get selected. This happens because the above code will be taking a click action on the text box element. It becomes difficult to debug such piece of code. To making debugging easier in such scenarios we can use the trick of highlighting the element before taking any user action on it. This will help us know with which element the code is interacting.

Now let us see how an element can be highlighted. Highlighting an element will essentially mean creating a coloured border around the element as shown in Figures 20.6 and 20.7. We can also add the feature for this border to blink twice or thrice to differentiate this element from other elements and to attract users attention.

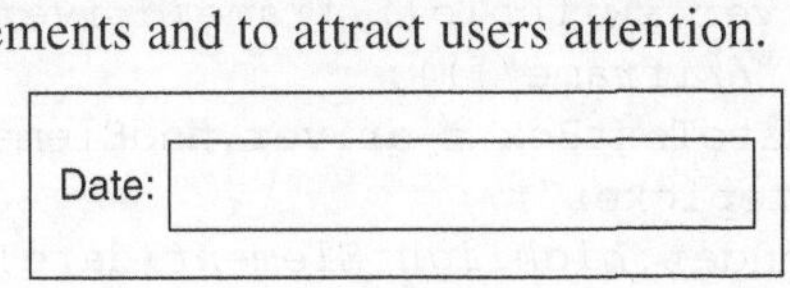

FIGURE 20.6 | Original element

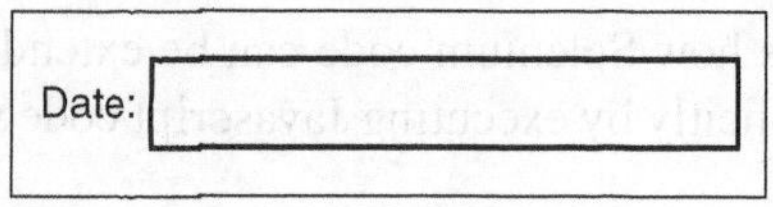

FIGURE 20.7 | Highlighted element

Border around the element can be created by setting the *style* attribute of the element using Javascript code. Blinking effect can be created by setting the style attribute of the element to display border and then resetting it to original attributes in loop. Following code shows how Selenium can be extended to highlight an element during run-time.

```
public class SeleniumExtender {
        /*
         * @desc: highlight element
         */
        public static void highlightElement(WebElement element){
                WrapsDriver wrappedElement;
                for (int i=0;i<10;i++){
                        wrappedElement = (WrapsDriver) element;
                        JavascriptExecutor driver =
                          (JavascriptExecutor)wrappedElement.
                            getWrappedDriver();
                        //create border and set its color to red
                        driver.executeScript("arguments[0].
                          setAttribute('style',arguments[1]);",
                            element,"red;border:2px solid red;");
                        //reset the element style attribute to
                          original
                        driver.executeScript("arguments[0].
                          setAttribute('style',arguments[1]);",
                            element,"");
                }
        }
}
```

EXAMPLE 20.5 Write a code to highlight the text box of Figure 20.6 as shown in Figure 20.7.

```
@Test
public void testHighlightElement(){
        WebDriver driver = new FirefoxDriver();
        driver.get("http://jqueryui.com/datepicker/");
        driver = driver.switchTo().frame(driver.findElement
           (By.XPath("//iframe")));
        WebElement dateTextBox = driver.findElement(By.cssSelector
           ("input#datepicker"));
        SeleniumExtender.highlightElement(dateTextBox);
}
```

Note: Highlighting elements slows down the code execution. It is advisable to use this feature while code debugging only.

20.7 | CREATING AN EXTENSION FOR CAPTURING SCREENSHOT OF ELEMENTS

In test automation, screenshots are an effective way of analysing what caused the tests to fail during run-time. Automation framework is to be designed in a way that it captures screenshot of the active screen at the very point of test failure. Selenium WebDriver provides *TakesScreenshot* interface to capture screenshots of the active screen while tests are executing. This interface allows capturing screenshots of the entire page, current active window, visible part of the page or the complete desktop depending on the type of browser. However, certain times, the requirement could be to capture screenshots of only certain parts of the page or certain elements. One example of such requirement could be to implement bitmap checkpoint.

The following code discusses how we can develop an extension class for capturing screenshots of specific elements. In the following code, `wrapsDriver` class gets the underlying `driver` instance of the element. This `driver` instance is then used to capture screenshot of the page. Then this screenshot is cropped as per the x,y ordinates of the element. This gives us an image of the element.

```
public class SeleniumExtender {
        /**
         * @desc: capture screenshot of the specified element
         * @param: WebElement element whose image needs to be captured
         * @param: String format of the image (png, bmp, etc.)
         * @return: File image file object
         */     public static File captureElementScreenshot(
                    WebElement element, String imageFormat){
                //get x,y ordinates of the upper left corner of
                  the element
                Point elementXY = element.getLocation();

                //get element height
                int elementHeight = element.getSize().getHeight();
                //get element width
                int elementWidth = element.getSize().getWidth();

                //get rectangular area of the element
                Rectangle elementRectArea =
                  new Rectangle(elementWidth, elementHeight);

                WrapsDriver wrapsDriver = (WrapsDriver)element;
                //Take screenshot of the page
                File pageImage = ((TakesScreenshot) wrapsDriver.
                  getWrappedDriver()).getScreenshotAs(OutputType.
                    FILE);
```

```
                    //describe image as accessible buffer of image data
                    BufferedImage bufferedImg = null;
                    try {
                              bufferedImg = ImageIO.read(pageImage);
                    } catch (IOException e1) {
                              e1.printStackTrace();
                    }
                    //get subimage as defined by the specified
                    //rectangular region from the buffer image
                    BufferedImage elementImage = bufferedImg.
                      getSubimage( elementXY.getX(), elementXY.getY(),
                        elementRectArea.width, elementRectArea.height);
                    //write the subimage to the file pageImage
                    try {
                              ImageIO.write(elementImage, imageFormat,
                                pageImage);
                    } catch (IOException e) {
                              e.printStackTrace();
                    }
                    //return the subimage file
                    return pageImage;

          }
   }
```

EXAMPLE 20.6 Write a WebDriver code to capture screenshot of the logo *jQuery user interface* of website jqueryui.com as shown in Figure 20.8.

FIGURE 20.8 | Capturing screenshot of logo jQuery user interface

Assume HTML code of the *jQueryUI* logo to be:

```
<h2 class="logo">
<a title="jQuery UI" href="/">jQuery UI</a>
```

```
</h2>
```

Following code shows how to capture the screenshot of this element.

```
@Test
public void testCaptureElementScreenshot(){
      WebDriver driver = new FirefoxDriver();
      driver.get("http://jqueryui.com");
      //get the element whose screenshot needs to be captured
      WebElement logoImage = driver.findElement(By.XPath(
        "//div[@id='logo-events']//a[@title='jQuery UI']"));
      //capture the screenshot of the specified element
      File elementImage = SeleniumExtender.
        captureElementScreenshot(logoImage, "png");
      //save the image to a location in hard drive
      try {
             FileUtils.copyFile(elementImage,
              new File("c:\\temp\\jQueryUILogo.png"));
      } catch (IOException e) {
             e.printStackTrace();
      }
}
```

Output of the above code is the image file shown in Figure 20.9.

FIGURE 20.9 | Output of the code testCaptureElementScreenshot()

20.8 | CREATING EXTENSION FOR COMPARING IMAGES

In test automation, many times the requirement is to compare two images by their pixels (bitmap checkpoint). For example, tests may require validating that various icons, images or links are rendering correctly.

Selenium provides the feature to capture screenshots but does not provide any method to compare two images. Following code shows how we can build extension classes for comparing two images by their pixels. The following code uses `Toolkit.getDefaultToolkit().getImage()` method to get Image object. Next it uses `PixelGrabber` class to grab the pixels of these images. `java.awt.Image` namespace has been used to work with images.

```
public class SeleniumExtender {
      /**
        * @desc: Compare two images
```

```
   * @param: File base image
   * @param: File actual image
   * @return: Result
   */
  public static Boolean compareImage(
    String baseImageLocation, String actualImageLocation){
  Boolean isImageMatch=true;

  Image baseImage = Toolkit.getDefaultToolkit().
    getImage(baseImageLocation);
  Image actualImage = Toolkit.getDefaultToolkit().
    getImage(actualImageLocation);
  PixelGrabber baseImagePixels =
    new PixelGrabber(baseImage,0,0,-1,-1,false);
  PixelGrabber actualImagePixels =
    new PixelGrabber(actualImage,0,0,-1,-1,false);

  int[] baseImagePixelData = (int[]) baseImagePixels.
    getPixels();
  int[] actualImagePixelData = (int[]) actualImagePixels.
    getPixels();

  //compare image size
  if ((baseImagePixels.getHeight()!=actualImagePixels.
    getHeight()) ||(baseImagePixels.
    getWidth()!=actualImagePixels.
      getWidth())){
          isImageMatch=false;
          logger.info("Mismatch in image size:" +
            baseImagePixels.getHeight());

          logger.info("base image height:" +
            baseImagePixels.getHeight());
          logger.info("base image width:" +
            baseImagePixels.getWidth());

          logger.info("actual image height:" +
            actualImagePixels.getHeight());

          logger.info("actual image width:" +
            actualImagePixels.getWidth());
  } else if (!java.util.Arrays.equals(baseImagePixelData,
    actualImagePixelData)){
          isImageMatch=false;
  }
  return isImageMatch;
  }

}
```

Example 20.7 Write a WebDriver code to compare the jQueryUI image of example above with its baseline image.

Assume the base image file is kept at path "C:\temp\jQueryUILogo.png". The following code captures the screenshot of the element, saves it to a location and then uses the `compareImage` method of `SeleniumExtender` class to compare base and actual image.

```
@Test
public void testCompareImage(){
        String baseImage = "c:\\temp\\jQueryUILogo.png";
        String actualImage = "c:\\temp\\jQueryUILogo_Actual.png";

        //get actual image
        WebDriver driver = new FirefoxDriver();
        driver.get("http://jqueryui.com");
        WebElement logoImage = driver.findElement(By.XPath(
          "//div[@id='logo-events']//a[@title='jQuery UI']"));
        File elementImage = SeleniumExtender.captureElementScree
          nshot(logoImage, "png");
        //save the image to a location in hard drive
        try {
                FileUtils.copyFile(elementImage, new
                  File(actualImage));
        } catch (IOException e) {
                e.printStackTrace();
        }

        //compare images
        Boolean isImageMatches = SeleniumExtender.
          compareImages(baseImage, actualImage);
        assertTrue("Image does nott match", isImageMatches);
}
```

INTERVIEW QUESTIONS

1. Write Selenium extension code to automate the *datepicker* element shown in Figure 20.2.
2. Write Selenium helper class to take screenshot of an element.
3. Write code to compare two images.
4. Write code to enter text on a disabled text field.

21 CHAPTER

Testing HTML 5 Web Applications

HTML 5 is a markup language for structuring and presenting web contents. It is the fifth revision of HTML (created in 1990) and is a W3C candidate recommendation. HTML 5 is gaining lot of popularity because of its latest support to multimedia and graphic contents. Previously, users had to resort to proprietary plugins to implement these. HTML 5 adds many syntactic features. These include <video>, <audio> and <canvas> elements. It also integrates scalable vector graphics content and MATHML for mathematical formulas. New elements such as <section>, <article>, <header> and <nav> enrich the semantic content of documents. With its new features, HTML 5 is a potential candidate for cross-platform mobile applications. Many features of HTML 5 have been developed with the consideration of being able to run on low-powered devices such as smart phones and tablets. In today's world, almost all major browsers support HTML 5.

Selenium WebDriver supports testing of HTML 5 web applications on certain browsers. For rest of the browsers, JavaScript can be used for testing.

Note: JavaScript can also be used to test HTML 5 features on all browsers.

In this chapter, we will discuss the most important features of HTML 5 and how to test them.

21.1 | AUTOMATING HTML 5 VIDEO PLAYER

Before HTML 5, there was no standard for displaying videos on web pages. Most of the browsers were dependent upon plugins such as flash to playback videos. Different browsers had different plugins.

HTML 5 defines a new element `<video>` to play videos on web browsers. This standard is uniform across all browsers.

The browsers that support `<video>` element are: Internet Explorer 9+, Firefox, Opera, Chrome and Safari.

Consider the video shown in Figure 21.1. The section below explains how to write WebDriver code to simulate user actions on this video.

FIGURE 21.1 | Video player on a web page

Assume HTML code of the video to be:

```
<video id="vplayer" width="320" height="240" autoplay="autoplay"
  controls="controls">
<source src="movie.mp4" type="video/mp4">
<source src="movie.ogg" type="video/ogg">
Your browser does not support this video.
</video>
```

Following code shows how to verify the source of the video.

```
@Test
public void testVideoSource(){
      WebDriver driver = new FirefoxDriver();
      driver.get("http://www.808.dk/?code-html-5-video");
      WebElement videoPlayer = driver.findElement(By.
        tagName("video"));
      JavascriptExecutor je = (JavascriptExecutor) driver;
      String source = (String)je.executeScript
        ("return arguments[0].currentSrc;", videoPlayer);
      assertEquals(http://www.HTML5video.com/pics/video/
        technews.mp4, source);
}
```

HTML5 tags for video can contain one or more attributes. These attributes decide how videos should appear or behave. Table 21.1 describes some of the video attributes.

TABLE 21.1 HTML 5 Video Attributes

Attribute	Description
src	Specifies the location(URI) of the video file.
crossOrigin	Attributes crossOrigin allows to configure CORS (Cross Origin Resource Sharing). If this attribute is not specified, CORS is not used at all. Possible values are: **Values : Description** anonymous : Cross-origin CORS requests for the element will not have the credentials flag set. It implies, there will be no exchange of user credentials via cookies, client-side SSL certificates or HTTP authentication. user-credentials : Cross-origin CORS requests for the element will have the credentials flag set.
poster	Specifies the image (URI) to use while the video is unavailable (or hasn't loaded yet)

networkState	Specifies the state of the network. Possible values:
	`0: "NETWORK_EMPTY"`
	`1: "NETWORK_IDLE"`
	`2: "NETWORK_LOADING"`
	`3: "NETWORK_NO_SOURCE"`

preload	Specifies whether the video should be preloaded or not and if so, how it should be preloaded. Possible values:
	`none`
	`metadata`
	`auto`

mediaGroup	This attribute allows specifying media elements to link together. It is defined as a String. For example: `mediagroup=movie`. Videos/media elements with the same value are automatically linked by the user agent/browser.
canPlayType	Specifies whether the given video type can be played or not (supported or not).

loop	Specifies whether to keep re-playing the video once it has finished. Possible values:
	`[Empty string]`
	`loop`

controls	Specifies whether or not to display video controls (such as a play/pause button, etc).
duration	Specifies the length (total time duration) of the video.

(continued)

TABLE 21.1 | *(continued)*

Attribute	Description
readyState	Specifies whether video is ready for playback. Possible values: 0: "HAVE_NOTHING" 1: "HAVE_METADATA" 2: "HAVE_CURRENT_DATA" 3: "HAVE_FUTURE_DATA" 4: "HAVE_ENOUGH_DATA"
autoPlay	Specifies whether the video will play automatically or not
play	Plays the video
pause	Pauses the video
currentTime	Specifies the current playback time of the video.
volume	Specifies the volume of the video.
muted	Specifies whether video is muted or not.
height	Specifies the width, in pixels, to display the video.
width	Specifies the height, in pixels, to display the video.
errorState	Specifies the error if video playback fails. Possible values: 1: "MEDIA_ERR_ABORTED" 2: "MEDIA_ERR_NETWORK" 3: "MEDIA_ERR_DECODE" 4: "MEDIA_ERR_SRC_NOT_SUPPORTED"

EXAMPLE 21.1 Write code to find the various attributes of a HTML5 video.

Following code shows the methods to be used to find the various attributes of a HTML5 video.

```
@Test
public void testHTML5Video(){
        WebDriver driver = new FirefoxDriver();
        driver.get("http://www.longtailvideo.com/html5/
          autoloop/");
        WebElement videoPlayer = driver.findElement(By.
          tagName("video"));
        //Alernatively,
        //WebElement videoPlayer = driver.findElement(By.
          id("video"));

        JavascriptExecutor je = (JavascriptExecutor) driver;

        waitFor(2000);

        //find the location (URI) of the video file
        String source = (String)je.executeScript(
          "return arguments[0].src", videoPlayer);
```

```
//find the current source of the video
String currentSrc = (String)je.executeScript(
  "return arguments[0].currentSrc", videoPlayer);
System.out.println("Video current source:" +
  currentSrc);
//Output::Video current source:
  // http://content.bitsontherun.com/videos/bkaovAYt-
  52qL9xLP.mp4

//Find the crossOrigin settings
String crossOrigin = (String)je.executeScript(
  "return arguments[0].crossOrigin;", videoPlayer);

//Find the image (URI) to use while the video is
  unavailable (or hasn't //loaded yet)
String poster = (String)je.executeScript(
  "return arguments[0].poster", videoPlayer);
System.out.println("Poster:" + poster);
//Output::Poster: http://content.bitsontherun.com/
  thumbs/bkaovAYt-320.jpg

//Find the video network state
Long networkState = (Long)je.executeScript(
  "return arguments[0].networkState", videoPlayer);
System.out.println("Network state:" + networkState);
//Output::Network state:1

//Find the preload attribute of teh video
String preload = (String)je.executeScript(
  "return arguments[0].preload", videoPlayer);

//Find the media elements of the video
String mediaGroup = (String)je.executeScript(
  "return arguments[0].mediaGroup", videoPlayer);

//seeking
Boolean seeking = (Boolean)je.executeScript(
  "return arguments[0].seeking", videoPlayer);

//Find if video will keep re-playing
Boolean loop = (Boolean)je.executeScript(
  "return arguments[0].loop", videoPlayer);
System.out.println("Loop:" + loop);
//Output::Loop:true

//Find if video controls will be enabled or not
Boolean controls = (Boolean)je.executeScript(
   "return arguments[0].controls", videoPlayer);
System.out.println("Controls:" + controls);
//Output::Controls:true
```

```
//Find if video is set to play automatically or not
Boolean autoplay = (Boolean)je.executeScript(
  "return arguments[0].autoplay", videoPlayer);
System.out.println("Autoplay:" + autoplay);
//Output::Autoplay:true

//Find the video length
Double duration = (Double)je.executeScript(
  "return arguments[0].duration", videoPlayer);
System.out.println("Duration:" + duration);
//Output::Duration:33.005

//Find if video is ready to be played
Long readyState = (Long)je.executeScript(
  "return arguments[0].readyState;", videoPlayer);
System.out.println("Ready state:" + readyState);
//Output::Ready state:4

//Find if video type "video/mp4" can be played or not
String mediaType = "video/mp4";
String canPlayType = (String)je.executeScript("return
  arguments[0].canPlayType(arguments[1])",
    videoPlayer,mediaType);
System.out.println("Can play type video/mp4:" +
  canPlayType);
//Output::Can play type video/mp4:maybe

//Find the default playback rate of the video
Long defaultPlaybackRate = (Long)je.executeScript(
  "return arguments[0].defaultPlaybackRate",
    videoPlayer);
System.out.println("Default playback rate:" +
  defaultPlaybackRate);
//Output::Default playback rate: 1

//Find the playback rate of the video
//(playback rate can be changed using controls)
Long playbackRate = (Long)je.executeScript(
  "return arguments[0].playbackRate", videoPlayer);
System.out.println("Current Playback rate:" +
  playbackRate);
//Output::Current Playback rate:1

//Find if video will be default muted when it starts to play
Boolean defaultMuted = (Boolean)je.executeScript(
  "return arguments[0].defaultMuted", videoPlayer);
System.out.println("Default muted:" + defaultMuted);
//Output::Default muted:true

//Find video is playing or not
```

```
Boolean isPaused = (Boolean)je.executeScript(
  "return arguments[0].paused", videoPlayer);
System.out.println("Is video paused:" + isPaused);
//Output::Is video paused:false

//Play the video if its paused
if (isPaused){
       je.executeScript("arguments[0].play();",
         videoPlayer);
}

waitFor(2000);

//Find the error if video playback fails
String errState = (String)je.executeScript(
  "return arguments[0].error", videoPlayer);
System.out.println("Error State:" + errState);
//Output::Error state:null

//Find if video is currently muted or not
Boolean muteState = (Boolean)je.executeScript(
  "return arguments[0].muted", videoPlayer);
System.out.println("Mute state:" + muteState);
//Output::Mute state:true

//Find the current playback time of the video
Double currentTime = (Double)je.executeScript(
  "return arguments[0].currentTime", videoPlayer);
System.out.println("Current playback time:" +
  currentTime);
//Output::Current playback time: 4.325782

//Find the played state of the video
ArrayList played = (ArrayList)je.executeScript(
  "return arguments[0].played", videoPlayer);

//Pause the video playback
je.executeScript("arguments[0].pause();", videoPlayer);

//Take screenshot for later verification
File imageSrcFile = ((TakesScreenshot)driver).
  getScreenshotAs(OutputType.FILE);
try {
FileUtils.copyFile(imageSrcFile, new
  File("C:\\temp\\pause.png"));
} catch (IOException e1) {
       e1.printStackTrace();
}
waitFor(2000);

//Find video is playing or not
```

```
isPaused = (Boolean)je.executeScript(
  "return arguments[0].paused", videoPlayer);
System.out.println("Is video paused:" + isPaused);
//Output::Is video paused:true

//Play the video
je.executeScript("arguments[0].play();", videoPlayer);

//Find the volume level of the video
Long volume = (Long)je.executeScript(
  "return arguments[0].volume", videoPlayer);
System.out.println("Volume:" + volume);
//Output::Volume:1

//Find video playback has ended or not
Boolean ended = (Boolean)je.executeScript(
  "return arguments[0].ended", videoPlayer);
System.out.println("Is playback ended:" + ended);
//Output::Is playback ended:false

//Find the current playback time of the video
currentTime = (Double)je.executeScript(
  "return arguments[0].currentTime", videoPlayer);
System.out.println("Current playback time:" +
  currentTime);
//Output::Current playback time:8.647641

//Find the initial time of the video
Long initialTime = (Long)je.executeScript(
  "return arguments[0].initialTime", videoPlayer);
System.out.println("Initial time:" + initialTime);
//Output::Initial time:0

//Find the start offset time of the video
Long startOffsetTime = (Long)je.executeScript(
  "return arguments[0].startOffsetTime", videoPlayer);

//Find height
Long height = (Long)je.executeScript(
  "return arguments[0].height", videoPlayer);
System.out.println("Height:" + height);
//Output::Height:270

//Find video height
Long videoHeight = (Long)je.executeScript(
  "return arguments[0].videoHeight;", videoPlayer);
System.out.println("Video height:" + videoHeight);
//Output::Video height:270

//Find width
Long width = (Long)je.executeScript(
  "return arguments[0].width;", videoPlayer);
```

```
        System.out.println("Width:" + width);
        //Output::Width:480
        //Find video width
        Long videoWidth = (Long)je.executeScript(
          "return arguments[0].videoWidth;", videoPlayer);
        System.out.println("Video width:" + videoWidth);
        //Output::Video width:480
}
public void waitFor(long milliSeconds){
        try {
                Thread.sleep(milliSeconds);
        } catch (InterruptedException e) {
                e.printStackTrace();
        }
}
```

EXAMPLE 21.2 Write a code for the following tests:

(a) Wait till video is ready for playback
(b) Play/pause video
(c) Mute/unmute video
(d) Increase/decrease volume
(e) Play video from specified time

Following WebDriver code shows how to simulate the above scenarios.

```
@Test
public void testHTML5Video1() {
        WebDriver driver = new FirefoxDriver();
        driver.get("http://www.longtailvideo.com/html5/
          autoloop/");
        WebElement videoPlayer = driver.findElement(By.id("v"));
        JavascriptExecutor je = (JavascriptExecutor) driver;

        //wait till video is ready for playback
        waitForVideoReadyState4(je, videoPlayer);

        //find video duration
        Double videoDuration = getVideoDuration(je,
          videoPlayer);
        //verify video duration
        System.out.println("Video duration:" + videoDuration);
        //Output::Video duration:33.995

        //find video is playing or not
        Boolean isVideoPaused = isVideoPaused(je, videoPlayer);
        //play video if video is not playing
        if (!isVideoPaused) playVideo(je,videoPlayer);
```

```
//verify video is playing
System.out.println("Video paused state:" +
  isVideoPaused(je, videoPlayer));
//Output::Video paused state:false
//For assertion use,
//assertEquals("Video is paused.",
  isVideoPaused(je, videoPlayer), false);

//find sound is muted or not
Boolean isVideoSoundOnMute = isVideoSoundMuted(je,videoP
  layer);
//unmute sound if sound is muted
if (isVideoSoundOnMute) muteVideoSound(je,videoPlayer,
  false);
//verify sound is not on mute
System.out.println("Video mute state:" +
  isVideoSoundMuted(je,videoPlayer));
//Output::Video mute state:false
//assertEquals("Video is muted.",
//      isVideoSoundMuted(je,videoPlayer),false);

//set volume level to 0.8
setVolumeLevel(je,videoPlayer,0.8);
//find the current volume level
Double volumeLevel = getVolumeLevel(je,videoPlayer);
//verify volume level is set to 0.8
System.out.println("Current volume is:" +
  getVolumeLevel(je,videoPlayer));
//Output::Current volume is:0.8

//find current video playback time
Double currentPlaybackTime = getVideoPlaybackTime(je,
  videoPlayer);
System.out.println("Current playback time:" +
  currentPlaybackTime);
//Output::Current playback time:4.640158

//play video from time 10.6 seconds
setVideoPlaybackTime(je, videoPlayer, 15.76);
//verify video playback time is now >=15.76 seconds
currentPlaybackTime = getVideoPlaybackTime
  (je, videoPlayer);
System.out.println("Current playback time=15.76s:" +
  currentPlaybackTime);
//Output::Current playback time=15.76s:15.76

//play video from time 9.7 seconds
setVideoPlaybackTime(je, videoPlayer, 9.7);
//verify video playback time is now >=9.7 seconds
currentPlaybackTime = getVideoPlaybackTime
  (je, videoPlayer);
```

```
        System.out.println("Current playback time=9.7:" +
          currentPlaybackTime);
        //Output::Current playback time=9.7s:9.7
  }
  //wait till video is ready for playback
  public void waitForVideoReadyState4(JavascriptExecutor je,
    WebElement videoElement){
        Long readyState;
        int cntr=0;
        do{
                readyState = (Long)je.executeScript( "return
                  arguments[0].readyState;", videoElement);
                cntr = cntr + 1;
                waitFor(500);
        }while ((readyState!=4)||(cntr<10));
  }
  //plays the video
  public void playVideo(JavascriptExecutor je, WebElement
    videoElement){
        je.executeScript("return arguments[0].readyState;",
          videoElement);
  }
  //pauses video playback
  public void pauseVideo(JavascriptExecutor je, WebElement
    videoElement){
        je.executeScript("arguments[0].pause();", videoElement);
  }
  //find if video is in paused state
  public Boolean isVideoPaused(JavascriptExecutor je, WebElement
    videoElement){
        Boolean isPaused = (Boolean)je.executeScript(
          "return arguments[0].paused", videoElement);
        return isPaused;
  }
  //mutes or unmutes video sound
  //mutes video sound if muteVideo is true else unmutes the
    video
  public void muteVideoSound(JavascriptExecutor je,
    WebElement videoElement, Boolean muteVideo){
        je.executeScript("arguments[0].muted=" + muteVideo,
         videoElement);
  }
  //find if video sound is muted
  public Boolean isVideoSoundMuted(JavascriptExecutor je,
    WebElement videoElement){
```

```
        Boolean muteState = (Boolean)je.executeScript(
          "return arguments[0].muted", videoElement);
        return muteState;
    }
    //set video volume level
    //volumeLevel can be any value betweem 0 and 1
    public void setVolumeLevel(JavascriptExecutor je,
      WebElement videoElement,Double volumeLevel){
        je.executeScript("arguments[0].volume=" + volumeLevel,
          videoElement);
    }
    //get video volume level
    public Double getVolumeLevel(JavascriptExecutor je, WebElement
      videoElement){
        Double volumeLevel = (Double)je.executeScript(
          "return arguments[0].volume", videoElement);
        return volumeLevel;
    }
    //plays video from the specified time say 2.3seconds
    //fromTime can be any double value between 0 and video duration
    public void setVideoPlaybackTime(JavascriptExecutor je,
      WebElement videoElement,Double fromTime){
        je.executeScript("arguments[0].currentTime=" + fromTime,
          videoElement);
    }
    //get current video playback time
    public Double getVideoPlaybackTime(JavascriptExecutor je,
      WebElement videoElement){
        Double playbackTime = (Double)je.executeScript(
          "return arguments[0].currentTime", videoElement);
        return playbackTime;
    }
    //get video duration
    public Double getVideoDuration(JavascriptExecutor je,
      WebElement videoElement){
        Double duration = (Double)je.executeScript(
          "return arguments[0].duration", videoElement);
        return duration;
    }
```

21.2 | AUTOMATING HTML5 CANVAS ELEMENT

HTML5 introduces a new `<canvas>` element to help developers create drawing applications within web browser. This element helps to build drawing and charting applications by using JavaScript. Canvas has several methods for drawing lines, boxes, circles, characters and adding images.

The browsers that support <canvas> element are: Internet Explorer 9+, Firefox, Opera, Chrome and Safari.

Figure 21.2 shows ‘sketchpad’ application similar to ‘mspaint’ application of MS Windows. The difference is ‘sketchpad’ is a web application developed using HTML5 Canvas while ‘mspaint’ is a desktop-based application.

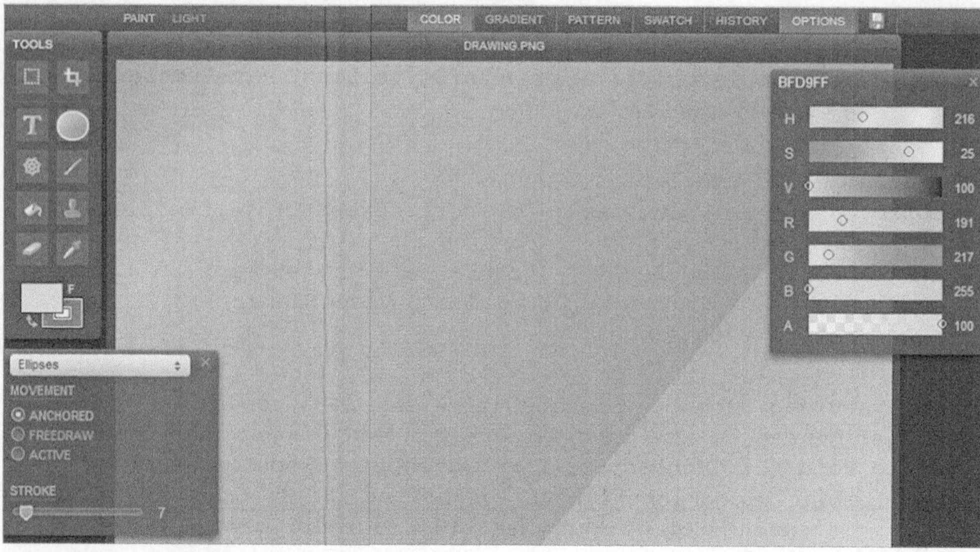

FIGURE 21.2 | Sketchpad app developed using HTML5

Suppose the test requirement is to test whether user can draw a circle, using paint brush and write text using this application or not. Following code shows how WebDriver can be used to test this application.

Assume HTML code of the element canvas 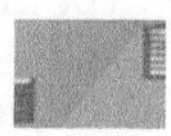 (where drawing can be done) to be:

```
<canvas id=″ctx_marquee″ style=″z-index: 6; left: 0px; top:
0px;″ width=″700″ height=″575″/>
```

Assume HTML code of element ‘Shape’  to be:

```
<div onclick=″gui_tools.imageCurrent(‘Shape_’+vars.shape)″
  style=″background-position: 5px -437px;″ title=″Shape″>
<img class=″plus″ alt=″Shape″ src=″media/gui/sw_add.png″
style=″display: none;″/>
<img class=″Shape_ellipses Shape_polygon Shape_star Shape_burst
Shape_gear″ alt=″Shape″ src=″media/gui/tools/Shape_ellipses_2.
png″ style=″width: 40px; height: 40px; top: -12.5px; left:
-12.5px; display: block;″/>
</div>
```

Assume HTML code of element 'Brush'  to be:

```
<div onclick="gui_tools.imageCurrent(vars.draw)"
  style="background-position: 5px 5px;" title="Brush">
<img class="plus" alt="Draw" src="media/gui/sw_add.png"
  style="display: none;"/>
<img class="Brush Calligraphy Pencil" alt="Draw" src="media/
  gui/tools/Brush_2.png" style="width: 40px; height: 40px; top:
    -12.5px; left: -12.5px; display: block;"/>
</div>
```

Assume HTML code of element 'Text'  to be:

```
<div onclick="gui_tools.imageCurrent('Text')"
  style="background-image: url("media/gui/tools/Tools.png");
    background-position: 5px -593px;" title="Text">
<img class="Text" alt="Text" src=""/>
</div>
```

Assume HTML code of the element for selecting brush colour (hue)  to be:

```
<canvas id="Hue" width="120" height="18" onmousedown="gui_
  color.core('HueCur',event,function(a,b,m) { gui_color.
    cur(b.X,'HSV','Hue',m); })"/>
```

After clicking on the 'Text' element a new text box element appears (refer to Figure 21.3) on the screen to specify what text to write on the screen. As Figure 21.3 shows, the text box has some pre-defined text written on it. Thus the automation steps would be to clear the text first and then write the specified text to the text box.

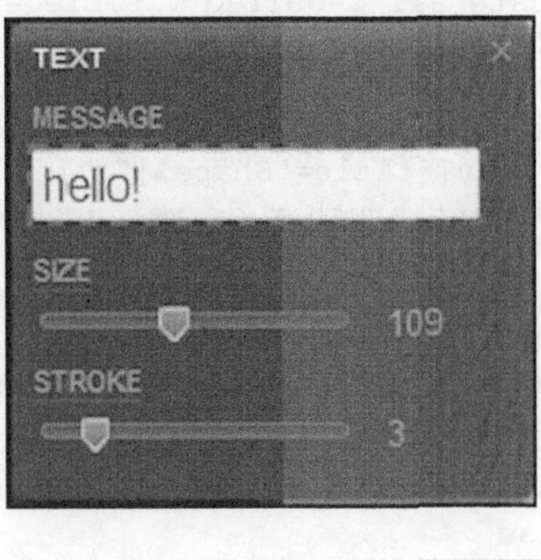

FIGURE 21.3 | Text box

Assume HTML code of the text box to be:

```
<div id="text" style="padding-bottom: 13px">
<span style="font-size: 11px; -moz-user-select: none; -khtml-
  user-select: none; user-select: none; ">MESSAGE</span>
<br/>
<input type="text" value="hello!" style="width: 90%; font-size:
  16px" onkeyup="vars.textMessage=this.value;" onkeydown="vars.
  textMessage=this.value;" onmousedown="preventDefault = false;"/>
</div>
```

As we know all user drawing actions on this application either involves keyboard or mouse operation. Thus, we will use *Action* class of WebDriver to simulate these events. Following code shows how to test this application.

In the following code, first we launch the 'sketchpad' application (which is built on HTML5 Canvas). Then we create an instance of WebDriver's *Action* class. We use this action class to simulate various user actions involving mouse and keyboard events. First we draw a circle. Then put some paint on it using brush. Next we write some text on the canvas window. Then we draw a spirograph. Finally, we do image comparison of the current drawing with an existing image to verify our test.

```
@Test
public void testHTML5Canvas() {
        WebDriver driver = new FirefoxDriver();
        driver.get("http://mudcu.be/sketchpad/");
        //Pause code execution till canvas element to be
          clickable on the page
        WebDriverWait wait =new WebDriverWait(driver,2);
        wait.until(ExpectedConditions.
          elementToBeClickable( By.id("ctx_marquee")));

        //Locate all required visible elements
        WebElement canvas = driver.findElement(By.id("ctx_
          marquee"));
        WebElement shape = driver.findElement(By.xpath
          ("//div[@title='Shape']"));
        WebElement brush = driver.findElement(By.xpath
          ("//img[@alt='Draw']"));
        WebElement text = driver.findElement(By.xpath
          ("//div[@title='Text']"));
        WebElement pickColor = driver.findElement
          (By.id("Hue"));

        //Simulate user action of drawing using Action
          class
```

```
Actions builder = new Actions(driver);
//draw a circle
builder.click(shape)
        .clickAndHold(canvas)
        .moveByOffset(100, 100)
        .release()
        .build()
        .perform();

//use brush to paint circle
builder.click(brush)
        .click(pickColor)
        .moveToElement(canvas, 360, 330)
        .clickAndHold()
        .moveByOffset(60,0)
        .release()
        .build()
        .perform();

//Click on the Text element.
//New text box element is displayed after click.
builder.click(text).build().perform();
//Note: findElement code for any element needs to
  be executed once
// it is visible on the screen.
WebElement textBox = driver.findElement
  (By.xpath("//div[@id='text']//input"));
//delete the existing text from text box
builder.sendKeys(textBox, Keys.BACK_SPACE)
        .sendKeys(textBox, Keys.BACK_SPACE)
        .sendKeys(textBox, Keys.BACK_SPACE)
        .sendKeys(textBox, Keys.BACK_SPACE)
        .sendKeys(textBox, Keys.BACK_SPACE)
        .sendKeys(textBox, Keys.BACK_SPACE)
        .sendKeys(textBox, Keys.BACK_SPACE)
        .sendKeys(textBox, Keys.BACK_SPACE)
        .build()
        .perform();
//Specify text to be written on text box and
  then draw this text on the //screen
//Note: FindElement method can also be called as
  shown below
builder.sendKeys(driver.findElement(By.xpath(
  "//div[@id='text']//input")), "HTML5 Canvas Test")
        .moveToElement(canvas,20,100)
        .click()
```

```
                .build()
                .perform();

        //Take screenshot of the Canvas element after
          drawing and
        //compare it with the base image
        //to verify if the image drawn is correct
        File elementImage;
        try {
                elementImage = this.
                  takeElementScreenshot(canvas, "png");
                FileUtils.copyFile(elementImage, new
                  File("c:\\temp\\actualDrawing.png"));
        } catch (IOException e) {
                e.printStackTrace();
        }
        //Compare the current drawing with basline
          drawing image.
        //refer chapter extending Selenium for method
          Compare Image
        assertEquals("Drawing not correct",this.
          CompareImage("c:\\temp\\baseDrawing.png","c:\\
            temp\\actualDrawing.png"));
}

//capture image of the specified element in the specified
  format

public File takeElementScreenshot(WebElement element,
  String imageFormat) throws IOException{

//get x,y ordinates of the upper left corner of the
  element
Point elementXY = element.getLocation();

//get element height
int elementHeight = element.getSize().getHeight();
//get element width
int elementWidth = element.getSize().getWidth();

//get rectangular area of the element
Rectangle elementRectArea = new Rectangle(elementWidth,
  elementHeight);

WrapsDriver wrapsDriver = (WrapsDriver)element;
//Take screenshot of the page
File pageImage = ((TakesScreenshot) wrapsDriver.
  getWrappedDriver()).getScreenshotAs(OutputType.FILE);
```

```
        //describe image as accessible buffer of image data
        BufferedImage bufferedImg = ImageIO.read(pageImage);

        //get subimage as defined by the specified rectangular
        //region from the buffer image
        BufferedImage elementImage = bufferedImg.
          getSubimage(elementXY.getX(), elementXY.getY(),
            elementRectArea.width, elementRectArea.height);
        //write the subimage to the file pageImage
        ImageIO.write(elementImage, imageFormat, pageImage);
        //return the subimage file
        return pageImage;
    }
```

Figure 21.4 shows the diagram drawn using the selenium code.

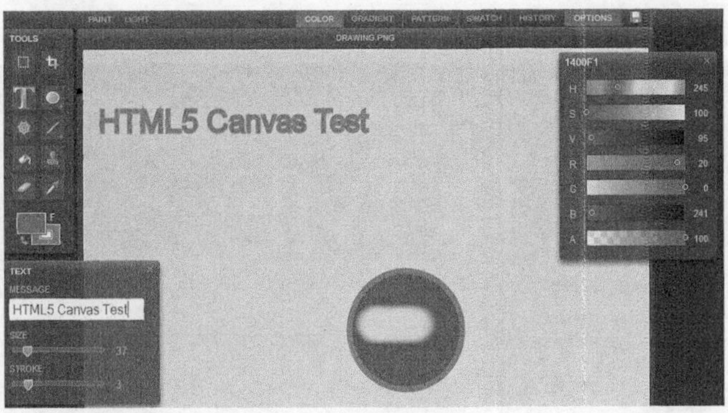

FIGURE 21.4 | Diagram drawn by code

21.3 | WEB STORAGE

Web Storage is a new HTML5 API offering important benefits over traditional cookies. Web Storage is a more secure and faster way of storing data locally within user's browser. Previously, this was done using cookies. In Web Storage, data is not included with every server request and used only when asked for. It can also store large amount of data without degrading the website's performance. The data is stored as *key/value* pairs and a web application can only access data stored by itself.

HTML5 Web Storage provides two new objects for storing data on the client (user's machine):

- **Local storage:** Stores data with no expiration date
- **Session storage:** Stores data for one session

21.3.1 | How to View Web Storage Data in Firefox and Chrome

In day-to-day testing, it is required to view/edit the web storage data for various tests. Web Storage data can be viewed in Firefox by installing *FireStorage Plus!* add-in. While in Chrome, it can be viewed in resources tab.

To view web storage data in Firefox, open *Firebug* and then click on the tab *FireStorage Plus!* as shown in Figure 21.5.

FIGURE 21.5 | Viewing localStorage and sessionStorage data in Firefox

To view web storage data in Chrome, open *InspectElement* and then click on the tab *Resources* as shown in Figure 21.6.

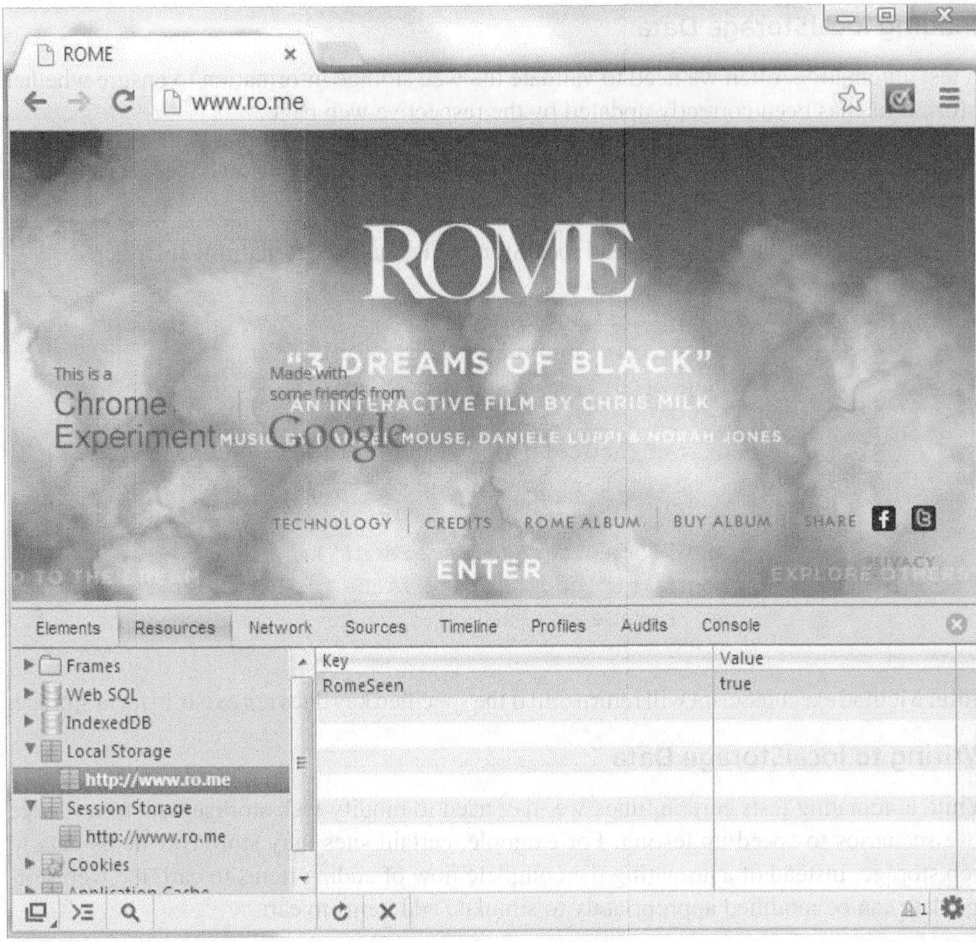

FIGURE 21.6 | Viewing localStorage and sessionStorage data in Chrome

Note: Web Storage data is created by HTML5 sites only. To view these data, a HTML5 site which creates this data be opened first. Not every HTML5 site necessarily uses web storage.

21.3.2 | Local Storage

Local storage stores the data with no expiration date. This means data is available even when the browser is closed.

Selenium WebDriver JavascriptExecutor class can be used to read, write or delete localStorage data.

Reading localStorage Data

In test automation, often we need to validate the web storage information to ensure whether information has been correctly updated by the respective web page.

EXAMPLE 21.3 Write a code to read value of localStorage key 'RomeSeen' as shown in Figure 21.6.

Following code shows how to read localStorage data using Selenium WebDriver.

```
@Test
    public void readLocalStorage(){
        WebDriver driver = new FirefoxDriver();
        driver.get("http://www.ro.me");

        JavascriptExecutor je = (JavascriptExecutor)driver;
        //get local storage data whose key is 'RomeSeen'
        String romeSeenValue = (String) je.executeScript(
          "return localStorage.RomeSeen;");
        assertEquals("localStorage value for RomeSeen is wrong.",
          "true",romeSeenValue);
    }
```

Note: Method executeScript will return null if the specified key does not exists in localStorage.

Writing to localStorage Data

While automating tests certain times we may need to modify web storage data to test edge case scenarios to speed up testing. For example, certain sites may store cart items data to web storage. Instead of automating the complete flow of adding items to cart, the web storage data can be modified appropriately to simulate add items to cart.

EXAMPLE 21.4 Write a code to update value of localStorage key 'RomeSeen' of Figure 21.6.

Following code shows how to write to localStorage data.

```
@Test
public void writeToLocalStorage(){
    WebDriver driver = new FirefoxDriver();
    driver.get("http://www.ro.me");

    JavascriptExecutor je = (JavascriptExecutor)driver;
    //Set localStorage key 'RomeSeen' value as 'false'
    je.executeScript("localStorage.RomeSeen=false;");
    //Verify localStorage key 'RomeSeen' value is updated
    String romeSeenValue = (String) je.executeScript(
    "return localStorage.RomeSeen;");
    assertEquals("localStorage value for RomeSeen is not
      updated.", "false",romeSeenValue);
}
```

Deleting localStorage Data

In test automation, when tests are executed in batch mode almost every time we need to delete the web storage data before executing a new test. This is done because web storage data of previous test execution may result in false results in current test execution.

EXAMPLE 21.5 Write a code to delete a specific key 'RomeSeen' from localStorage data of Figure 21.6.

Following code shows how to read specific localStorage key.

```
@Test
public void deleteLocalStorageData(){
      WebDriver driver = new FirefoxDriver();
      driver.get("http://www.ro.me");

      JavascriptExecutor je = (JavascriptExecutor)driver;
      //Delete localStorage key 'RomeSeen'
      je.executeScript("localStorage.
        removeItem('RomeSeen');");
      //Get localStorage key value of key 'RomeSeen'
      //Returns null if key does not exist
      String romeSeenValue = (String) je.executeScript
        ( "return localStorage.RomeSeen;");
      assertEquals("localStorage key RomeSeen still exists.",
        null,romeSeenValue);
}
```

EXAMPLE 21.6 Write a code to delete all localStorage data of Figure 21.6.

Following code shows how to delete all localStorage data.

```
@Test
public void deleteAllLocalStorageData(){
      WebDriver driver = new FirefoxDriver();
      driver.get("http://www.ro.me");

      JavascriptExecutor je = (JavascriptExecutor)driver;
      //Delete all localStorage data
      je.executeScript("localStorage.clear();");
      //Get localStorage key value of key 'RomeSeen'
      //Returns null if key does not exist
      String romeSeenValue = (String) je.executeScript(
        "return localStorage.RomeSeen;");
      assertEquals("localStorage key RomeSeen still exists.",
        null,romeSeenValue);
}
```

Session Storage

Session storage stores the data for one browser session only. This means data is deleted as soon as the browser is closed.

Selenium WebDriver JavascriptExecutor class can be used to read, write or delete sessionStorage data.

Reading sessionStorage Data

Following code shows how to read specific sessionStorage key.

```
@Test
public void readSessionStorage(){
        WebDriver driver = new FirefoxDriver();
        driver.get("http://www....");

        JavascriptExecutor je = (JavascriptExecutor)driver;
        //get sessionStorage data whose key is 'KeyName'
        String keyValue = (String) je.executeScript(
          "return sessionStorage.KeyName;");
        assertEquals("sessionStorage value for KeyName is
          wrong.", "KeyValue",keyValue);
        }
```

Writing to sessionStorage Data

Following code shows how to write to sessionStorage data.

```
@Test
public void writeToSessionStorage(){
        WebDriver driver = new FirefoxDriver();
        driver.get("http://www....");

        JavascriptExecutor je = (JavascriptExecutor)driver;
        //Set sessionStorage key 'KeyName' value as 'KeyValue'
        je.executeScript("sessionStorage.KeyName=KeyValue;");
        //Verify sessionStorage key 'KeyName' value is updated
        String keyValue = (String) je.executeScript(
          "return sessionStorage.KeyName;");
        assertEquals("sessionStorage value for KeyName is not
          updated.",
         "KeyValue",keyValue);
}
```

Deleting sessionStorage Data

Following code shows how to delete specific sessionStorage key.

```
@Test
public void deleteSessionStorageData(){
```

```
        WebDriver driver = new FirefoxDriver();
        driver.get("http://www....");

        JavascriptExecutor je = (JavascriptExecutor)driver;
        //Delete sessionStorage key 'KeyName'
        je.executeScript("sessionStorage.
          removeItem('KeyName');");
        //Get sessionStorage key value of key 'KeyName'
        //Returns null if key does not exist
        String keyValue = (String) je.executeScript(
          "return sessionStorage.KeyName;");
        assertEquals("sessionStorage key KeyName still exists.",
          null,keyValue);
}
```

Following code shows how to delete all localStorage data.

```
@Test
public void deleteAllSessionStorageData(){
        WebDriver driver = new FirefoxDriver();
        driver.get("http://www...");

        JavascriptExecutor je = (JavascriptExecutor)driver;
        //Delete all sessionStorage data
        je.executeScript("sessionStorage.clear();");
        //Get sessionStorage key value of key 'KeyName'
        //Returns null if key does not exist
        String keyValue = (String) je.executeScript(
          "return sessionStorage.KeyName;");
        assertEquals("sessionStorage key KeyName still exists.",
          null,keyValue);

}
```

INTERVIEW QUESTIONS

1. Explain how to test a HTML5 video player.
2. Write code to test play, pause and volume functionality of HTML5 video player.
3. What is the difference between session storage and local storage?
4. How to add a new cookie information to session storage?
5. Write a code to delete a specific local storage cookie.

22 CHAPTER

Working with Flat Files

A flat file is a file storing data which can be stored and accessed sequentially. Often information is stored in flat files in non-structured way. Notepad file and CSV files are common examples of flat files.

Flat files are generally used in Selenium automation to store test data. However, other uses of flat files in test automation include defining framework settings, execution status flags, error logs, etc.

22.1 | WORKING WITH NOTEPAD WITH JAVA LIBRARY

Notepad is a basic text editor used to create simple documents. In test automation, Notepad files can be used to store automation framework settings, test execution status, error logs or other information.

The basic operations that need to be performed on a Notepad file from test automation perspective are as follows:

- Creating a notepad file
- Writing to a notepad file
- Reading a notepad file
- Editing a notepad file
- Appending a notepad file

22.1.1 | Creating a Notepad File

Java library java.io.File can be used to create a new file. Following code creates an instance of *File* class. Method createNewFile creates a new file if the file does not exist. This method returns *true* if file is created, else it returns *false*.

```
@Test
public void testCreateNotepadFile() {
       try {
         //create a notepad file
          String absoluteFilepath = "C:/temp/test.txt";
          File textFile = new File(absoluteFilepath);
          Boolean isCreated = textFile.createNewFile();
```

```
            if(isCreated) {
                System.out.println("File created");
            } else {
                System.out.println("File already exists");
            }
        } catch (IOException e) {
            e.printStackTrace();
        }
    }
```

The above code uses the absolute path to create a notepad file. Files can also be created at a specific location in the project by referring the projects logical path. Assume a file *test.txt* needs to be created at path '*com/webdriver/testdata/test.txt*' as shown in Figure 22.1.

FIGURE 22.1 | Creating a text file

Java code to create a file by specifying project logical path is as follows.

```
String folderPath = "/com/webdriver/testdata";
String absoluteFolderPath = getClass().getResource(folderPath).
  getFile();
String absoluteFilepath = absoluteFolderPath + "/test.txt";
System.out.print(absoluteFilepath);
//Output::/F:/workspaces/Selenium/bin/com/webdriver/testdata/test.txt
```

The absolute file path so obtained can be used in the code above to create a notepad file at the given location.

Note: File is created in the *bin* directory and not in *src* directory. All files under source directory are copied to the working directory which happens to be *bin* directory. All operations are performed on files which are in the working directory. This is the reason why the text file in above case is created inside *bin* directory and not inside *src* directory.

22.1.2 | Writing to a Notepad File

Java class 'Writer' can be used to write to notepad files. Following code shows how to write text 'Hello World!!!' to text file.

```
@Test
public void testWriteToNotepadFile() {
        try {
                String folderPath = "/com/webdriver/testdata";
                String absoluteFolderPath = getClass().
                  getResource(folderPath).getFile();
                String absoluteFilepath = absoluteFolderPath +
                  "/test.txt";
                 File textFile = new File(absoluteFilepath);
                 FileOutputStream fos = new FileOutputStream
                   (textFile);
                 OutputStreamWriter osw = new OutputStreamWriter(fos);
                 Writer w = new BufferedWriter(osw);
                 w.write("Hello World!!!");
                 w.close();
            } catch (IOException e) {
                 e.printStackTrace();
        }
}
```

Note: `FileOutputStream` overwrites the existing file, if file already exists.

22.1.3 | Reading a Notepad File

BufferedReader class can be used to read a character-input stream. This class buffers characters so as to provide for efficient reading of characters, arrays and lines. The buffer size may be specified, or the default size may be used.

Following code shows how to read a notepad file using BufferedReader and FileReader class.

```
@Test
public void testReadNotepadFile() {
        try {
                String folderPath = "/com/webdriver/testdata";
                String absoluteFolderPath = getClass().
                  getResource(folderPath).getFile();
                String absoluteFilepath = absoluteFolderPath +
                  "/test.txt";
          FileReader textFile = new FileReader(absoluteFilepath);
          BufferedReader reader = new BufferedReader(textFile);
          //read the file till end of line
        String line;
        while((line=reader.readLine())!=null){
                System.out.println(line);
        }
```

```
            } catch (IOException e) {
                e.printStackTrace();
        }
    }
```

Note: `FileReader` is meant for reading streams of characters. For reading streams of raw bytes, consider using `FileInputStream`.

22.1.4 | Editing a Notepad File

Many times we may have to edit the contents of a notepad file, for example, changing the status flags in notepad, changing the settings value, etc. Replace method can be used to edit the contents of a notepad file.

Section 22.2.7 shows how to edit the contents of notepad file.

22.1.5 | Appending a Notepad File

Constructor FileWriter(String fileName, Boolean append) can be used to append a text file. The Boolean value of *append* is to be set as *true*. Following code shows how to append the file of the example above.

```
@Test
public void testAppendNotepadFile() {
        try {
                String folderPath = "/com/webdriver/testdata";
                String absoluteFolderPath = getClass().
                  getResource(folderPath).getFile();
                String absoluteFilepath = absoluteFolderPath +
                  "/test.txt";
                 File textFile = new File(absoluteFilepath);
                 FileOutputStream fos = new FileOutputStream
                   (textFile,true);
                 OutputStreamWriter osw = new OutputStreamWriter
                   (fos,"UTF-8");
                 Writer w = new BufferedWriter(osw);
                 w.append("Appended text: Hello World Again!!!");
                 w.close();
        } catch (IOException e) {
                 e.printStackTrace();
        }
}
```

22.2 | WORKING WITH NOTEPAD WITH APACHE COMMONS IO LIBRARY

Apache Common IO is a library of utilities to help in developing IO functionality. It contains utility classes, stream implementations, file filters, file comparators, endian transformation classes and much more. There are six main areas included in the Commons IO library:

1. **Utility classes:** Contains static methods to perform common tasks.
2. **Input:** Contains useful Input Stream and Reader implementations.
3. **Output:** Contains useful Output Stream and Writer implementations.
4. **Filters:** Contains various implementations of file filters.
5. **Comparators:** Contains various implementations of java.util.Comparator for files.
6. **File monitor:** Contains a component for monitoring file system events.

Apache Commons IO library can be downloaded from site: http://commons.apache.org/proper/commons-io/download_io.cgi.

In the following section, we will discuss how to use Apache Commons IO library for performing various operations on notepad files.

22.2.1 | Creating a Notepad File

Apache Commons IO library provides *FileUtils* class to perform various operations on files and folders. Method *touch* of this class can be used to create any new flat file say .txt, .vbs, .ini, etc. This method creates a new file with size 0. If the file exists already, it is opened and closed without modifying it, but updating the file date and time.

Following code shows how to create a new text file 'textFile.txt' inside framework path *com/webdriver/testData.*

```
@Test
public void testCreateNotepadFile(){
        String folderPath = "/com/webdriver/testdata";
        String absoluteFolderPath = getClass().
          getResource(folderPath).getFile();
        String absoluteFilepath = absoluteFolderPath +
          "/textFile.txt";
        System.out.println(absoluteFilepath);
        //Output::/F:/workspaces/Selenium/bin/com/
        //webdriver/testdata/textFile.txt
        File file = new File(absoluteFilepath);
        FileUtils.touch(file);
        System.out.println("Size:" + FileUtils.sizeOf(file));
        //Output::Size:0
}
```

22.2.2 | Verifying File Existence

File class provides a method called *isFile* to check if the specified file exists or not. Following code verifies whether a file has been created or not.

```
@Test
public void testIsExistsNotepadFile(){
        String folderPath = "/com/webdriver/testdata";
        String absoluteFolderPath = getClass().
          getResource(folderPath).getFile();
        String absoluteFilepath = absoluteFolderPath +
          "/textFileNew.txt";
        System.out.println(absoluteFilepath);
        File file = new File(absoluteFilepath);
        System.out.println("File exists:" + file.isFile());
        //Output::File exists:false
        FileUtils.touch(file);
        System.out.println("File exists:" + file.isFile());
        //Output::File exists:true
}
```

22.2.3 | Deleting a Notepad File

FileUtils class provides three methods to delete a file. They are as follows:

1. **deleteQuietly:** This method deletes a file, never throwing an exception. That is, no exception is thrown if the file cannot be deleted.
2. **forceDelete:** This method deletes a file and throws an exception if the file cannot be deleted.
3. **forceDeleteOnExit:** This method schedules deletion of the file when JVM exits. An exception is thrown if file cannot be deleted.

Following code shows how to quietly delete the file 'textFileNew.txt' created in the example above.

```
@Test
public void testDeleteNotepadFile(){
        String filePath = "/com/webdriver/testdata/textFileNew.txt";
        String absoluteFilepath = getClass().
          getResource(filePath).getFile();
        File file = new File(absoluteFilepath);
        FileUtils.deleteQuietly(file);
        System.out.println("File exists:" + file.isFile());
        //Output::File exists:false
}
```

22.2.4 | Writing to a Notepad File

FileUtils class provides various methods to write to a file. All these methods also creates the file if it does not exist, else it overwrites the existing file. These methods also provide the option to define the encoding type. A *null* value for the encoding means default coding of the system will be used. These methods are as follows:

- **write:** This method writes CharSequence to a file.
- **writeByteArrayToFile:** This method writes a byte array to a file.
- **writeStringToFile:** This method writes any text stream to a file.
- **writeLines:** This method writes multiple lines of text stream to a file.

Figure 22.2 shows the list of methods that can be used to write to a file.

```
write(File file, CharSequence data) : void - FileUtils
write(File file, CharSequence data, boolean append) : void - FileUtils
write(File file, CharSequence data, Charset encoding) : void - FileUtils
write(File file, CharSequence data, String encoding) : void - FileUtils
write(File file, CharSequence data, Charset encoding, boolean append) : void - FileUtils
write(File file, CharSequence data, String encoding, boolean append) : void - FileUtils
writeByteArrayToFile(File file, byte[] data) : void - FileUtils
writeByteArrayToFile(File file, byte[] data, boolean append) : void - FileUtils
writeLines(File file, Collection<?> lines) : void - FileUtils
writeLines(File file, Collection<?> lines, boolean append) : void - FileUtils
writeLines(File file, Collection<?> lines, String lineEnding) : void - FileUtils
writeLines(File file, String encoding, Collection<?> lines) : void - FileUtils
writeLines(File file, Collection<?> lines, String lineEnding, boolean append) : void - FileUtils
writeLines(File file, String encoding, Collection<?> lines, boolean append) : void - FileUtils
writeLines(File file, String encoding, Collection<?> lines, String lineEnding) : void - FileUtils
writeLines(File file, String encoding, Collection<?> lines, String lineEnding, boolean append) : void - FileUtils
writeStringToFile(File file, String data) : void - FileUtils
writeStringToFile(File file, String data, boolean append) : void - FileUtils
writeStringToFile(File file, String data, Charset encoding) : void - FileUtils
writeStringToFile(File file, String data, String encoding) : void - FileUtils
writeStringToFile(File file, String data, Charset encoding, boolean append) : void - FileUtils
writeStringToFile(File file, String data, String encoding, boolean append) : void - FileUtils
```

FIGURE 22.2 | FileUtils class methods to write to a flat file

Note: Above methods overwrite the existing data of the file.

Following code shows how to write text 'Hello World!!!' to an already existing notepad file 'textFile.txt'. Assume file is blank (0 kb).

```
@Test
public void testWriteToNotepadFile(){
        String filePath = "/com/webdriver/testdata/textFile.txt";
```

```
        String absoluteFilePath = getClass().getResource(filePath).
          getFile();
        File file = new File(absoluteFilePath);
        System.out.println("File size:" + FileUtils.sizeOf(file));
        //Output::File size:0
        FileUtils.writeStringToFile(file, "Hello World First!!!");
        System.out.println("File size:" + FileUtils.sizeOf(file));
        //Output::File size:20
        FileUtils.writeStringToFile(file, "Hello World!!!");
        System.out.println("File size:" + FileUtils.sizeOf(file));
        //Output::File size:14
}
```

Generally, the requirement could be write single or multiple lines of text to a file. Following code shows how to write multiple lines of a text to a notepad file using UTF-8 encoding.

```
@Test
public void testWriteMultipleLinesToNotepadFile(){
        String filePath = "/com/webdriver/testdata/textFile.txt";
        String absoluteFilePath = getClass().
          getResource(filePath).getFile();
        File file = new File(absoluteFilePath);
        List<String> lines = Arrays.asList("line 1", "line 2", "line 3");
        FileUtils.writeLines(file, lines);
}
```

Alternatively,

```
        ArrayList<String> lines = new ArrayList<String>();
        lines.add("line 1");
        lines.add("line 2");
        lines.add("line 3");
        FileUtils.writeLines(file, lines);
```

Figure 22.3 shows output of the above code.

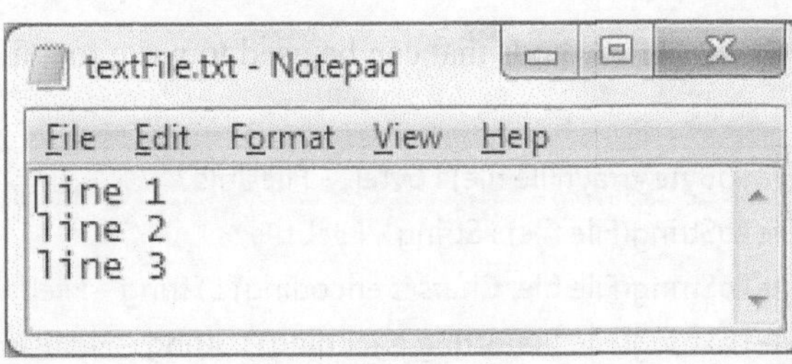

FIGURE 22.3 | Output of test *testWriteMultipleLinesToNotepadFile*

FileUtils class also provides the flexibility to define the line separator to distinguish between two lines. A null value for the *lineSeparator* implies system default line separator will be used. Following code uses dot ('.') as a line separator.

```
@Test
public void testWriteMultipleLinesUsingLineSeparatorToNotepadFile() {
       String filePath = "/com/webdriver/testdata/textFile.txt";
       String absoluteFilePath = getClass().getResource(filePath).
         getFile();
       File file = new File(absoluteFilePath);
       ArrayList<String> lines = new ArrayList<String>();
       lines.add("line 1");
       lines.add("line 2");
       lines.add("line 3");
       FileUtils.writeLines(file, "UTF-8", lines, ".");
}
```

Figure 22.4 shows output of the above code.

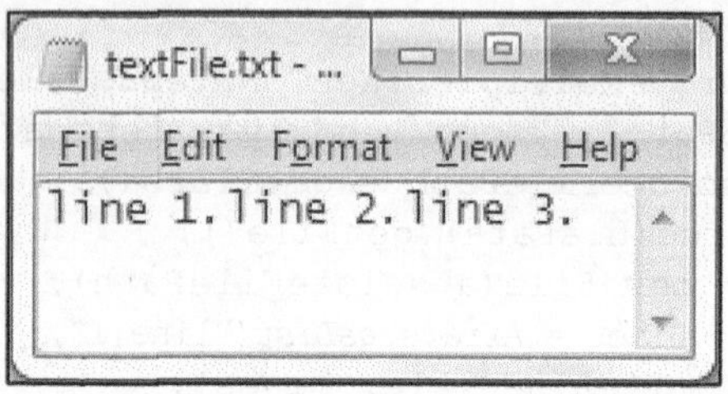

FIGURE 22.4 | Output of test testWriteMultipleLinesUsingLineSeparatorToNotepadFile

22.2.5 | Reading a Notepad File

FileUtils class provides various methods to read contents of a flat file. The methods close the file once it is read. These methods include the following:

- **readFileToByteArray:** This method reads the contents of a file into a byte array.
- **readFileToString:** This method reads the contents of a file into a String.
- **readLines:** This method reads the contents of a file line by line into a List of Strings.

Figure 22.5 shows the list of methods that can be used to write to a file.

FIGURE 22.5 | *FileUtils* class methods to read a flat file

Following code shows how to read the contents of a notepad file of the example code above where the line separator is system default.

```
@Test
public void testReadNotepadFile(){
        String filePath = "/com/webdriver/testdata/textFile.txt";
        String absoluteFilePath = getClass().getResource(filePath).
          getFile();
        File file = new File(absoluteFilePath);

        //read file as string
        String fileContent = FileUtils.readFileToString(file);
        System.out.println("File contents:" + fileContent);

        //read file line by line
        List<String> fileConentsByLines = FileUtils.readLines(file);
        for (String line:fileConentsByLines){
                System.out.println(line);
        }
}
```

Output of above code is shown in Figure 22.6.

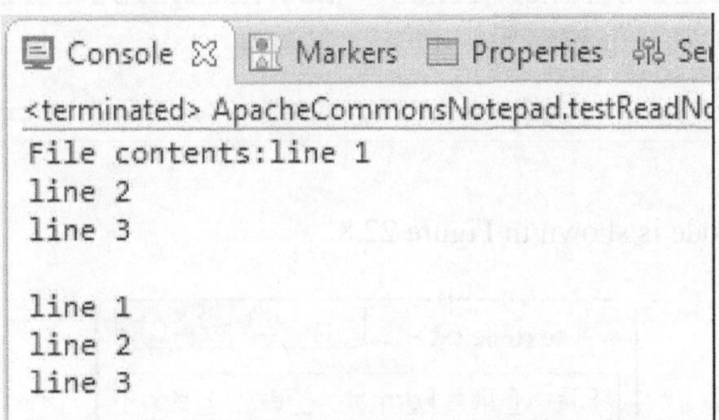

FIGURE 22.6 | Output of test code `testReadNotepadFile()`

22.2.6 | Appending a Notepad File

FileUtils class provides overloaded write methods to append or edit a flat file. Figure 22.7 shows the list of those methods.

The Boolean *append* value to be set to *true* to append a text string or text line. The text stream is added at the end of the file. If this value is set to *false* then the file is overwritten.

```
write(File file, CharSequence data, boolean append) : void - FileUtils
write(File file, CharSequence data, Charset encoding, boolean append) : void - FileUtils
writeByteArrayToFile(File file, byte[] data, boolean append) : void - FileUtils
writeLines(File file, Collection<?> lines, boolean append) : void - FileUtils
writeLines(File file, Collection<?> lines, String lineEnding, boolean append) : void - FileUtils
writeLines(File file, String encoding, Collection<?> lines, boolean append) : void - FileUtils
writeLines(File file, String encoding, Collection<?> lines, String lineEnding, boolean append) : void - FileUtils
writeStringToFile(File file, String data, boolean append) : void - FileUtils
writeStringToFile(File file, String data, Charset encoding, boolean append) : void - FileUtils
writeStringToFile(File file, String data, String encoding, boolean append) : void - FileUtils
```

FIGURE 22.7 | FileUtils class methods to append or edit a flat file

Following code shows how to append the *textFile.txt* with two lines of text 'line 4' and 'line 5'.

```
@Test
public void testAppendNotepadFile(){
        String filePath = "/com/webdriver/testdata/textFile.txt";
        String absoluteFilePath = getClass().getResource(filePath).
          getFile();
        File file = new File(absoluteFilePath);
        ArrayList<String> lines = new ArrayList<String>();
        lines.add("line 4");
        lines.add("line 5");
        FileUtils.writeLines(file, "UTF-8", lines, true);
}
```

Result of above code is shown in Figure 22.8.

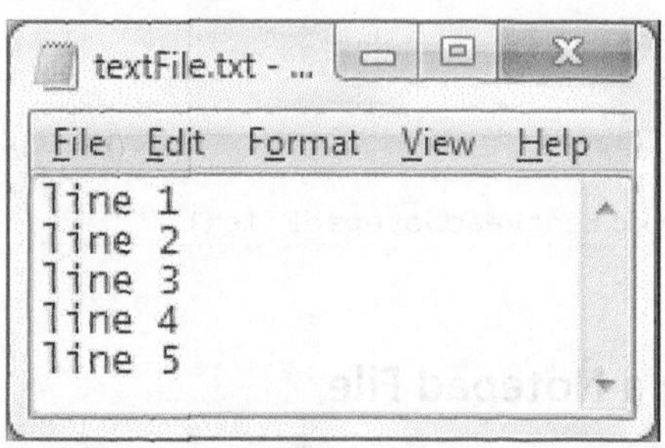

FIGURE 22.8 | Result of test code testAppendNotepadFile

Method `writeLines(file, encoding, lines, lineEnding, append)` can be used to append a file with text stream separator by specific line separator.

22.2.7 | Editing a Notepad File

Editing a file in Java can be done by reading the notepad contents to memory, making changes to the contents to memory and then overwriting the file with the changed content from memory.

Figure 22.9 shows a notepad file with some information. Suppose requirement is to add text 'overwritten' to line 4. Figure 22.10 shows the file contents after file editing. Following code shows how to replace text 'line 4' with text 'line 4 overwritten' in the notepad file shown in Figure 22.9.

```
@Test
public void testEditNotepadFile() throws IOException{
        String filePath = "/com/webdriver/testdata/textFile.txt";
        String absoluteFilePath = getClass().getResource(filePath).
          getFile();
        File file = new File(absoluteFilePath);
        List<String> fileConentsByLines = FileUtils.readLines(file);
        for (int i=0;i<fileConentsByLines.size();i++){
                if (fileConentsByLines.get(i). equalsIgnoreCase
                  ("line 4")){
                          fileConentsByLines.set(i, "line 4 overwritten");
                }
        }
        FileUtils.writeLines(file, fileConentsByLines);
}
```

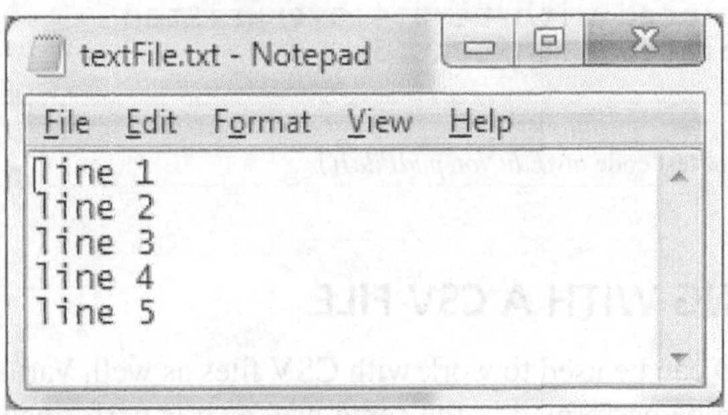

FIGURE 22.9 | Notepad contents before editing the file

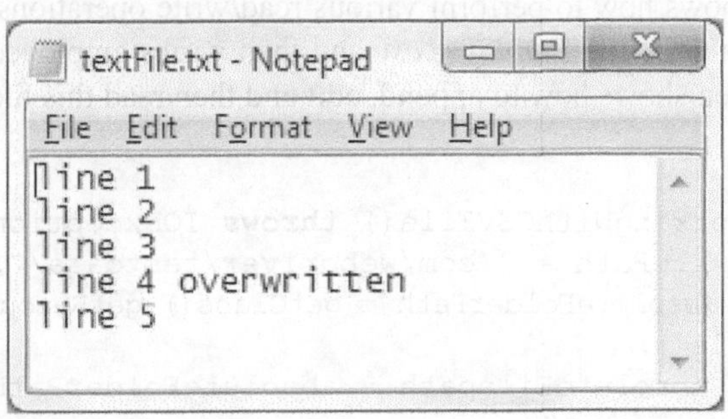

FIGURE 22.10 | Notepad contents after editing the file

Many times we may have to replace all instances of a specific text in a file with a different text stream. Following code shows how to replace all instances of text 'line' in the above notepad file to text stream 'replaced with text'.

```
@Test
public void testEditNotepadFile1(){
        String filePath = "/com/webdriver/testdata/textFile.txt";
        String absoluteFilePath = getClass().getResource(filePath).
          getFile();
        File file = new File(absoluteFilePath);
        String contents = FileUtils.readFileToString(file);
        contents = contents.replaceAll("line", "replaced with text");
        FileUtils.write(file, contents);
}
```

Figure 22.11 shows the result of above code.

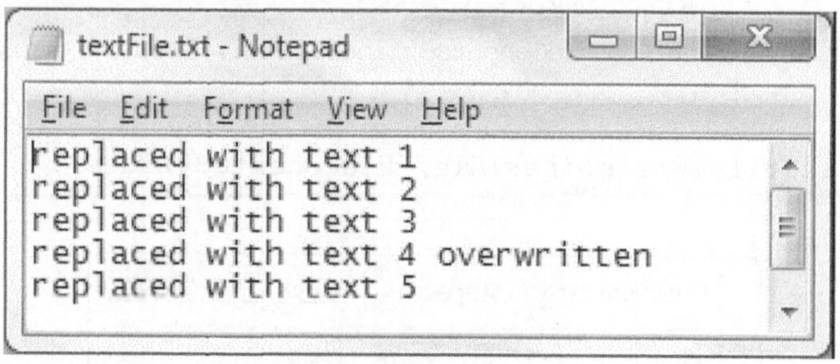

FIGURE 22.11 | Result of test code *testEditNotepadFile1()*

22.3 | WORKING WITH A CSV FILE

Apache Commons IO can be used to work with CSV files as well. Various read/write operations on CSV file can be performed in the same way as it is performed on any flat file (say notepad file).

Following code shows how to perform various read/write operations on a CSV file. The code below creates a CSV file *Employee.csv* and then writes employee test details data to this file. The code then shows how to append, edit and then read this file.

```
@Test
public void workingWithCSVFile() throws IOException{
        String filePath = "/com/webdriver/testdata/";
        String absoluteFolderPath = getClass().getResource(filePath).
          getFile();
        String absoluteFilepath = absoluteFolderPath + "/" +
          "Employee.csv";
```

```
        File csvFile = new File(absoluteFilepath);
        //create CSV file
        FileUtils.touch(csvFile);

        //write to csv file
        ArrayList<String> lines = new ArrayList<String>();
        lines.add("Employee ID,Employee Name,Age");
        lines.add("10656,Anne Schwarz,22");
        lines.add("10636,Stewart Larsen,24");
        FileUtils.writeLines(csvFile, lines);

        //append csv file
        ArrayList<String> appendLine = new ArrayList<String>();
        appendLine.add("13423,Lee Charles,25");
        FileUtils.writeLines(csvFile, appendLine, true);
        //replace employee name 'Stewart Larsen' with name
          'John Larsen'
        String contents = FileUtils.readFileToString(csvFile);
        contents = contents.replaceAll("Stewart Larsen",
          "John Larsen");
        FileUtils.write(csvFile, contents);

        //read contents of csv file
        String fileContents = FileUtils.readFileToString(csvFile);
        System.out.println(fileContents);
}
```

Figure 22.12 shows the output of above code as seen on Eclipse's *Console* tab.

```
Employee ID, Employee Name, Age
10656, Anne Schwarz, 22
10636, John Larsen, 24
13423, Lee Charles, 25
```

FIGURE 22.12 | Output of test code `workingWithCSVFile()`

22.3.1 | Extending *FileUtils* to Read Test Data Stored in a CSV File

In selenium automation, the most common use of CSV file is used for storing test data. In this section, we will discuss how to write extended class for reading test data from a CSV file.

Figure 22.13 shows *CurrencyConverter.csv* file which contains currency conversion test data. The first row of the file denotes field names and the row thereafter contains field values. Field *'Key'* assigns a unique number to each row of test data. This unique key can be used to easily identify and read any specific row of data from the CSV file. However, this method has one drawback. Numeric key values makes the code less readable. In the test code, from the value of this unique key, it would be difficult to know which type of test data is being used in the test. A better approach would to use *key names* for each row of

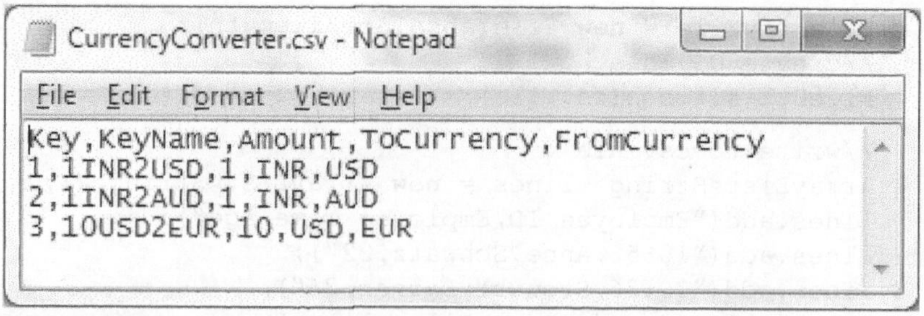

FIGURE 22.13 | CurrencyConverter.csv file

data. The *keyName* to be defined in a way that makes it unique for a given data set and also conveys the type of test data it is referring to. Figure 22.13 shows currency conversion test data CSV file with *keyName* defined for each row.

Now let us see how we can write an extension class for selenium for reading test data from the CSV file. Following code provides method *getData(key_or_keyName)* to read specific row of data from the CSV file. Either of row *key* value or *keyName* value can be used as input parameter to read the specific row data. The test data is returned as key/value pairs as an instance of Map object.

```
import java.io.File;
import java.io.IOException;
import java.util.HashMap;
import java.util.List;
import java.util.Map;

import org.apache.commons.io.FileUtils;
import static org.junit.Assert.*;

public class CSVFile {
        public static File csvFile;
        public static List<String> fileContents;

        public CSVFile(String filename) {
        String frameworkPath= "/com/webdriver/testdata/";
        String logicalFilepath = frameworkPath + filename;
        String absoluteFilepath = getClass().
         getResource(logicalFilepath). getFile();
        csvFile = new File(absoluteFilepath);
        fileContents = CSVFile.getFileContents();
        }

        /**
         * @desc: Read the line contents as key/value pairs with key as
         *         field name and value as value of that line
         *         corresponding to the specific field
         * @param: int index - line number to read
```

```
 * @return: Map - Key/Value pairs
 */
public static Map<String, String> getData(int key){
        int index = key;
        return readLine(index);
}
/**
 * * @desc: Read the line contents as key/value pairs with key as
 *          field name and value as value of that line
 *          corresponding to the specific field
 * @param: String ketyName - KeyName of the line to read
 * @return: Map - Key/Value pairs
 */
public static Map<String, String> getData(String keyName){
        int index = getIndex(keyName);
        return readLine(index);
}

//read specified line from file
private static Map<String,String> readLine(int index){
        Map<String, String> map = new HashMap<String,String>();
        String[] keys = getKeys();
        String[] values = getLine(index);
        for(int i=0;i<keys.length;i++){
                map.put(keys[i], values[i]);
        }
        return map;
}

//get keyName index
private static int getIndex(String keyName){
        int keyNameIndex=-1;
        for (int i=1;i<fileContents.size();i++){
                if (fileContents.get(i).contains(keyName)){
                        keyNameIndex=i;
                }
        }
        assertNotEquals("Key name '" + keyName + "' not found
          for file:" + csvFile.getName(),-1, keyNameIndex);
        return keyNameIndex;
}

//get contents of line with the specified line number
private static String[] getLine(int index){
        return fileContents.get(index).split(",");
}

//get contents of first line
private static String[] getKeys(){
```

```
                return fileContents.get(0).split(",");
        }
        //get file contents
        private static List<String> getFileContents(){
                try {
                                fileContents = FileUtils.readLines(csvFile);
                } catch (IOException e) {
                                e.printStackTrace();
                }
                return fileContents;
        }
}
```

EXAMPLE 22.1 Write code to retrieve fields *Amount* and *ToCurrency* for second row of test data.

The second row of test data has *Key* value as '2' and *KeyName* value as '1INR2AUD'. Following code shows how to read the fields *Amount* and *ToCurrency* for second row of test data.

```
@Test
public void testSeleniumExtensionApacheIOCommonsCSV() {
        new CSVFile("CurrencyConverter.csv");
        Map<String,String> map = CSVFile.getData(2);
        System.out.println("Amount:" + map.get("Amount"));
        //Output::Amount:1
        System.out.println("ToCurrency:" + map.get("ToCurrency"));
        //Output::ToCurrency:INR

        map = CSVFile.getData("1INR2AUD");
        System.out.println("Amount:" + map.get("Amount"));
        //Output::Amount:1
        System.out.println("ToCurrency:" + map.get("ToCurrency"));
        //Output::ToCurrency:INR
}
```

Note: It is advisable to use *KeyName* value to retrieve tests data in tests. This helps make test code more readable.

INTERVIEW QUESTIONS

1. Which Java API will you use to work with flat files?
2. How will you edit a notepad file?
3. Write code to edit and append data to a CSV file.
4. Write extension class to retrieve test data from a CSV file.

23

CHAPTER

Working with MS Excel

Microsoft Excel is a spreadsheet application developed by Microsoft Corporation for storing, organizing and manipulating data. It features calculation, graphic tools, pivot tables and a macro programming language called Visual Basic for Applications (VBA). Generally, in test automation, MS Excel is used as test data sheets for storing the test input data. There are two ways in which we can access MS Excel file in test automation:

- MS Excel as workbook
- MS Excel as database

MS Excel object model is used to access MS Excel as workbook. In case of using it as database, MS Excel is treated as any other database such as MS Access and SQL queries are executed on it. In test automation, using MS Excel as database has specific advantages over using MS Excel as workbook.

23.1 | MS EXCEL OBJECT MODEL

The MS Excel object model contains thousands of objects, properties, methods and predefined enumerated values. This chapter describes some of the most important items of MS Excel object model required for test automation. Figure 23.1 shows a part of the MS Excel object model. The application object is the root object of the MS Excel object model. All the other objects in the MS Excel object model can only be accessed through the application object.

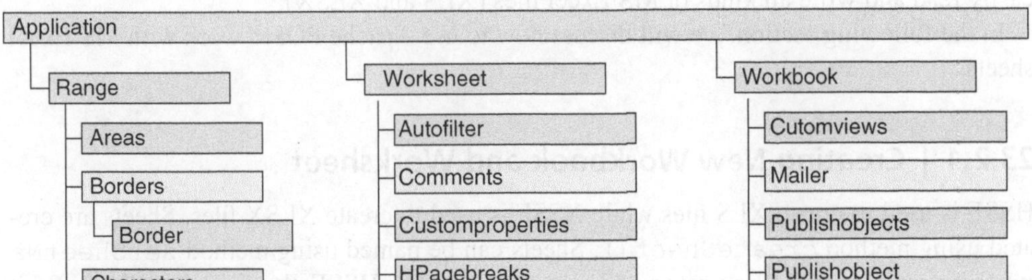

FIGURE 23.1 | MS Excel object model

The Workbooks collection represents a collection of currently opened workbooks. The Workbook object represents a single open MS Excel workbook file containing one or more worksheets. The methods of Workbook allow finding and manipulating the worksheets. The Worksheets collection represents a collection of worksheets in the referenced open workbook. The Worksheet object represents a single worksheet in the referenced open workbook. The properties and methods of the object allow manipulating the contents of the worksheet's cells. The Worksheet object's Range property returns a Range object that represents a rectangular block of cells on the worksheet. Range object is used to manipulate groups of data in the Excel sheet.

23.2 | APACHE POI: JAVA API FOR MICROSOFT DOCUMENTS

Apache Foundation provides Apache POI API to work with MS Office documents using Java. Apache POI library provides API to interact with MS documents such as Excel, Word, PowerPoint, Visio, etc. The API supports manipulating various file formats based upon the Office Open XML standards (OOXML) and Microsoft's OLE 2 Compound Document format (OLE2).

OLE2 files include MS Office files such as XLS, DOC and PPT.

Office Open XML format is the new standards based XML file format found in MS Office 2007, 2008 and 2010. This includes XLSX, DOCX and PPTX.

Listed as follows are APIs components of Apache POI:

- Excel (SS=HSSF+XSSF)
- Word (HWPF+XWPF)
- PowerPoint (HSLF+XSLF)
- OpenXML4J (OOXML)
- OLE2Filesystem (POIFS)
- OLE2Document Props (HPSF)
- Outlook (HSMF)
- Visio (HPBF)

Note: HSSF library to be used to read/write a XLS format Excel file while XSSF library to be used to read/write a XLSX format excel file. The combines SS interface can be used to easily read and write all kinds of MS Excel files (XLS and XLSX).

In the following section, we will discuss how to use Apache POI to work with MS Excel sheets.

23.2.1 | Creating New Workbook and Worksheet

HSSF is used to create XLS files while XSSF is used to create XLSX files. Sheets are created using method `createSheet()`. Sheets can be named using method `setSheetName(sheetindex,"SheetName",encoding)`. For HSSF, the name may be in 8-bit encoding format (`HSSFWorkbook.ENCODING_COMPRESSED_UNICODE`) or Unicode (`HSSFWorkbook.ENCODING_UTF_16`). Default encoding for HSSF is 8-bit per char. For XSSF, the name is automatically handled as unicode.

Following code shows how to create a new XLS format workbook and worksheet at default working directory.

```
import java.io.FileOutputStream;
import java.io.IOException;
import org.apache.poi.hssf.usermodel.*;
import org.apache.poi.ss.usermodel.*;
import org.apache.poi.xssf.usermodel.*;
import org.junit.Test;
public class ApachePOIExcel {
      @Test
      public void testCreateXLS() throws IOException {
        //Create HSSF instance
        Workbook wb = new HSSFWorkbook();
        //Create workbook names workbook.xls as default
         working directory
        FileOutputStream fileOut = new FileOutputStream("workbook.
         xls");
        //Create workbooksheet with name 'new sheet 1'
        Sheet sheet1 = wb.createSheet("new sheet 1");
        Sheet sheet2 = wb.createSheet("new sheet 2");
        wb.write(fileOut);
        fileOut.close();
      }
}
```

Note: While actual code development test should not throw any exception. Instead exceptions need to be handled using try…catch block within the test code. For easy code illustration, 'throws' has been used throughout this chapter.

Code below shows how to create a XLSX file at location '/com/webdriver/testdata/'. Assume workbook file name is workbook.xlsx.

```
public void testCreateXLSX() throws IOException {
            //get absolute path of logical path
            String filePath = "/com/webdriver/testdata/";
            String absoluteFolderPath = getClass().
              getResource(filePath).getFile();
            String absoluteFilepath = absoluteFolderPath +
             "/" + "workbook.xlsx";

            //create new xlsx workbook and add worksheets to it
      Workbook wb = new XSSFWorkbook();
      FileOutputStream fileOut = new FileOutputStream(absoluteF
       ilepath);
      Sheet sheet1 = wb.createSheet("new sheet 1");
      Sheet sheet2 = wb.createSheet("new sheet 2");
```

```
        wb.write(fileOut);
        fileOut.close();
    }
```

The file is created at location 'F:\workspaces\Selenium\bin\com\webdriver\testdata\workbook.xlsx'. Figure 23.2 shows the MS Excel file created from the above code.

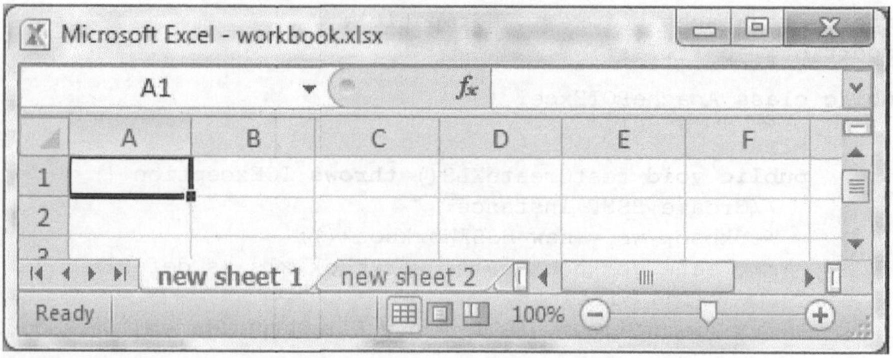

FIGURE 23.2 | Creating a new workbook

Note: Sheet name must not contain any special characters such as colon (:), backslash(/), asterisk(*), question mark(?), forward slash(\), opening or closing square brackets([ ]). Also, the sheetname must not exceed 31 characters. In order to safely create an MS Excel sheet without bothering about these restrictions, Apache POI provides method createSafeSheetName(<sheet name>). This method automatically filters out the special characters. For example,

```
        //Replace invalid characters with white space
        String validSheetName =
        WorkbookUtil.createSafeSheetName("Not/a\\valid:name?");
        System.out.println("validSheetName:" + validSheetName);
        //Output::validSheetName:Not a valid name
        wb.createSheet(validSheetName);
```

23.3 | WRITING TO A WORKBOOK

Writing to a new workbook involves creating the desired row and cell first and then writing to the cell. Following code shows how we can write to a newly created MS Excel file.

```
    @Test
    public void testWriteToXLSX() throws IOException,
      InvalidFormatException {
        // Create new xlsx workbook and add worksheets to it
        Workbook wb = new XSSFWorkbook();
        FileOutputStream fileOut = new
          FileOutputStream("workbook.xlsx");
```

```
        Sheet sheet1 = wb.createSheet();

        // Create a row and put some cells in it. Rows are 0 based.
        Row row = sheet1.createRow((short)0);
        // Create a cell and write integer value to it
        Cell cell = row.createCell(0);
        cell.setCellValue(1);
        // Create a cell and write float value to it
        row.createCell(1).setCellValue(1.2);
        //Create a cell and write string value to it
        row.createCell(2).setCellValue("This is a string");

        // Create a new row
        Row row2 = sheet1.createRow((short)1);
        //Create a cell and write boolean value to it
        row2.createCell(1).setCellValue(true);

        System.out.println(new Date());
        //Output::Thu Jul 11 21:30:11 PDT 2013
        //Create a cell and write date value to it
        row2.createCell(2).setCellValue(new Date());

        // Write the output to a file
        wb.write(fileOut);
        fileOut.close();
    }
```

Figure 23.3 shows the MS Excel file created from the code above.

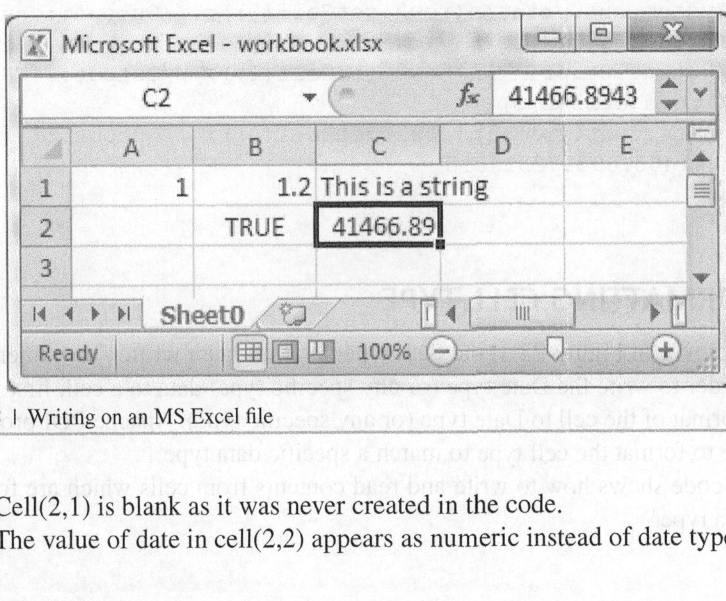

FIGURE 23.3 | Writing on an MS Excel file

Notes: 1. Cell(2,1) is blank as it was never created in the code.
2. The value of date in cell(2,2) appears as numeric instead of date type.

23.4 | READING A WORKBOOK

Apache POI provides methods `getRow()` to get instance of a specific row and method `row.getCell()` to retrieve contents of a specific cell.

Following code shows how to read contents of the workbook 'workbook.xlsx' of Figure 23.3.

```
@Test
public void testReadXLSX() throws InvalidFormatException,
  IOException{
        InputStream is = new FileInputStream("workbook.xlsx");
        Workbook wb = WorkbookFactory.create(is);
        Sheet sheet = wb.getSheet("Sheet0");
        //Alternatively,WorkSheet can also be located using index.
        //index value of sheet starts from 0.
        //Sheet sheet = wb.getSheetAt(0);
        //get first row
        Row row1 = sheet.getRow(0);
        //read cell(1,1)
        System.out.println(row1.getCell(0)); //Output:: 1.0
        //read cell(1,2)
        System.out.println(row1.getCell(1)); //Output:: 1.2
        //read cell(1,3)
        System.out.println(row1.getCell(2)); //Output:: This is
          a string
        //get row 1
        Row row2 = sheet.getRow(1);
        //read cell(2,1)
        System.out.println(row2.getCell(0)); //Output:: null
        //read cell(2,2)
        System.out.println(row2.getCell(1)); //Output:: TRUE
        //read cell(2,3)
        System.out.println(row2.getCell(2)); //Output::
          41466.895972314815
}
```

23.5 | FORMATTING CELL TYPE

As we can observe in Figure 23.3, the date type data has been written as numeric value in the cell. In order to write the Date type (or any specific type) data to a cell, first we need to change the format of the cell to Date type (or any specific type). Apache POI provides class `CellStyle` to format the cell type to match a specific data type.

Following code shows how to write and read contents from cells which are formatted to a specific data type.

```
@Test
public void testFormatCellsAndWrite() throws
  InvalidFormatException, IOException{
            //create new xlsx workbook and add worksheet to it
      Workbook wb = new XSSFWorkbook();
      FileOutputStream fileOut = new FileOutputStream("workbook.
        xlsx");
      Sheet sheet1 = wb.createSheet("new sheet");

      Row row1 = sheet1.createRow((short)0);

      // Create a cell and write integer value to it
      Cell cell11 = row1.createCell(0);
      cell11.setCellValue(1);

      // Create a cell and write numeric value as string to it
      Cell cell12 = row1.createCell(1);
      cell12.setCellValue(1);
      cell12.setCellType(Cell.CELL_TYPE_STRING);

      // Create a cell and write float data to it
      Cell cell13 = row1.createCell(2);
      cell13.setCellValue(1.2);
      cell13.setCellType(Cell.CELL_TYPE_NUMERIC);

      // Create a cell and write boolean data to it
      Cell cell14 = row1.createCell(3);
      cell14.setCellValue(true);
      cell14.setCellType(Cell.CELL_TYPE_BOOLEAN);

      // Create a cell and write Date data to it
      CreationHelper createHelper = wb.getCreationHelper();
      CellStyle cellStyle = wb.createCellStyle();
      cellStyle.setDataFormat(
        createHelper.createDataFormat().getFormat("mm-ddd-yy
           h:mm"));
       Cell cell15 = row1.createCell(4);
       cell15.setCellValue(new Date());
       cell15.setCellStyle(cellStyle);

      // Create a cell and write a formula to it
      Cell cell16 = row1.createCell(5);
      cell16.setCellType(Cell.CELL_TYPE_FORMULA);
      cell16.setCellFormula("SUM(A1,C1)");

      // Write the output to a file
      wb.write(fileOut);
      fileOut.close();
}
```

Figure 23.4 shows the MS Excel file created by the above code.

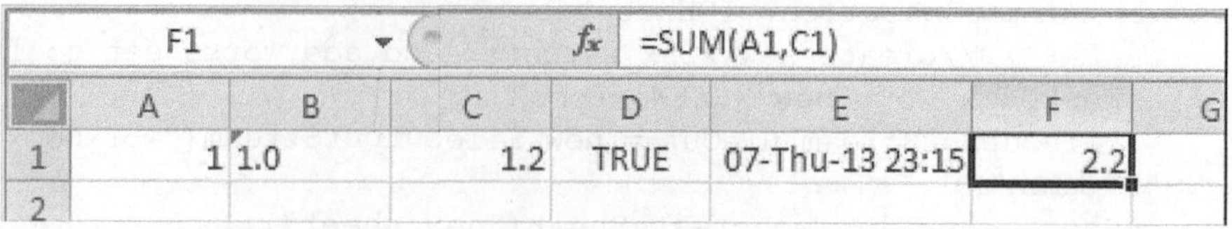

FIGURE 23.4 | Formatting cell type to store a specific data type

In order to retrieve cell contents, first we need to know the cell format type. Trying to retrieve a numeric value from a cell type formatted as string will throw NumberFormatException.

Following code shows how to read contents of MS Excel cells which are formatted to store a specific data type. The following code reads MS Excel file of Figure 23.4.

```
@Test
public void testReadFormattedCell() throws
  InvalidFormatException, IOException{
            InputStream is = new FileInputStream("workbook.
              xlsx");
            Workbook wb = WorkbookFactory.create(is);
            Sheet sheet1 = wb.getSheet("new sheet");
            //iterate over the used range of the sheet
            for (Row row : sheet1) {
              for (Cell cell : row) {
                    //get the name of the current cell. example
                      A1, A2...
                    CellReference cellRef =
                       new CellReference(row.getRowNum(),
                       cell.getColumnIndex());
                    System.out.print(cellRef.
                      formatAsString());
                    System.out.print(" - ");
                    //find the cell type and then get the
                      cell contents
                    switch (cell.getCellType()) {
                          case Cell.CELL_TYPE_STRING:
                            System.out.println(cell.
                               getRichStringCellValue().
                               getString());
                            break;
                          case Cell.CELL_TYPE_NUMERIC:
                            if (DateUtil.
                              isCellDateFormatted(cell)) {
                                  System.out.println(cell.
                                    getDateCellValue());
                            } else {
```

```
                System.out.println(cell.
                  getNumericCellValue());
            }
            break;
          case Cell.CELL_TYPE_BOOLEAN:
            System.out.println(cell.
              getBooleanCellValue());
            break;
          case Cell.CELL_TYPE_FORMULA:
            System.out.println(cell.
              getCellFormula());
            //evaluate cell value
            FormulaEvaluator evaluator =
              wb.getCreationHelper().
              createFormulaEvaluator();
            evaluator.evaluate
              FormulaCell(cell);
            System.out.println("Cell Value:" +
              cell.getNumericCellValue());
            break;
          default:
            System.out.println();
        }
      }
    }
  }
```

Figure 23.5 shows the output of the above code as visible on Eclipse *Console* tab.

```
A1 – 1.0
B1 – 1.0
C1 – 1.2
D1 – true
E1 – Thu Jul 11 23:15:15 PDT 2013
F1 – SUM(A1,C1)
Cell Value:2.2
```

FIGURE 23.5 | Reading contents of a formatted MS Excel of Figure 23.4

23.6 | EDITING A WORKBOOK

While automating a MS Excel, many times we may require to read and edit the contents of the file. Following code shows how to read an existing MS Excel file and then edit the cell contents.

Following code changes value of Cell A1 to 5 and adds new text value 'New Text' to Cell G1 to the MS Excel file of Figure 23.4.

```
@Test
public void testEditXLSX() throws IOException,
  InvalidFormatException{
        InputStream is = new FileInputStream("workbook.xlsx");
        Workbook wb = WorkbookFactory.create(is);
        Sheet sheet1 = wb.getSheetAt(0);
        Row row1 = sheet1.getRow(0);

        //read value of cell A1
        Cell cell1 = row1.getCell(0);
        System.out.println("Cell A1=" + cell1.
          getNumericCellValue());
        //Output::Cell A1=1.0

        //change value of cell A1 from 1 to 5
        Cell cell11 = row1.createCell(0);
        cell11.setCellType(Cell.CELL_TYPE_NUMERIC);
        cell11.setCellValue(5);

        //write text to blank cell G1
        Cell cell17 = row1.createCell(6);
        cell17.setCellType(Cell.CELL_TYPE_STRING);
        cell17.setCellValue("New Text");

        // Write the output to a file
        FileOutputStream fileOut = new
          FileOutputStream("workbook.xlsx");
        wb.write(fileOut);
        fileOut.close();
}
```

	A	B	C	D	E	F	G	H
1	5	1.0	1.2	TRUE	07-Thu-13 23:52	6.2	New Text	
2								

FIGURE 23.6 | Editing an existing MS Excel file

23.6.1 | Setting and Evaluating Cell Formula

In MS Excel automation, many times we may require using formulas in the cell of the file. While reading this MS Excel file, we would like to read the value of the cell calculated by the formula. Apache POI provides method `setCellFormula()` to write any formula to a cell. The value of this formula can be calculated by using the method `evaluate-FormulaCell()` of `FormulaEvaluator` class. Section *'Formatting Cell Type'* above explains how to set and evaluate a cell formula in a MS Excel file.

23.6.2 | Formatting Cell Attributes

Apache POI provides methods to modify the cell properties such as font, colour, text-alignment, background colour, etc., programmatically.

Following code shows how to modify cell attributes.

Setting Colour of Cell Text

Code below sets colour of cell text to red colour.

```
@Test
public void formattingCellAttributes() throws IOException,
  InvalidFormatException{
        Workbook wb = new XSSFWorkbook();
        FileOutputStream fileOut = new FileOutputStream
          ("workbook1.xlsx");
        Sheet sheet1 = wb.createSheet();
        Row row1 = sheet1.createRow((short)0);

        //***** Set cell(1,1) text color to RED ******
        Font font1 = wb.createFont();
        CellStyle style1 = wb.createCellStyle();
        Cell cell11 = row1.createCell(0);
        cell11.setCellValue("Text Color Test");
        font1.setColor((short)2);
        style1= wb.createCellStyle();
        style1.setFont(font1);
        cell11.setCellStyle(style1);
```

Setting Foreground Colour of a Cell

Code below sets foreground colour of cell to yellow colour.

```
//***** Set foreground color cell(1,2) to yellow ******
        Font font2 = wb.createFont();
        CellStyle style2 = wb.createCellStyle();
        Cell cell12 = row1.createCell(1);
        cell12.setCellValue("Cell Foreground Color Test");
        style2.setFillForegroundColor(IndexedColors.LIGHT_
          YELLOW.getIndex());
        style2.setFillPattern(CellStyle.SOLID_FOREGROUND);
        cell12.setCellStyle(style2);Setting border color of cell
```

Setting Font of a Cell Text

Code below sets font of cell text to 'Courier New' and font colour to red.

```
//***** Set font of cell(1,3) text to Courier New 24 ******
        Font font3 = wb.createFont();
```

```
        CellStyle style3 = wb.createCellStyle();
        font3.setFontHeightInPoints((short)12);
        font3.setFontName("Courier New");
        font3.setItalic(true);
        font3.setStrikeout(true);
        font3.setColor(font3.COLOR_RED);
        // Fonts are set into a style so create a new one to use.
        style3.setFont(font3);
        // Create a cell and put a value in it.
        Cell cell13 = row1.createCell(2);
        cell13.setCellValue("Fonts Test");
        cell13.setCellStyle(style3);
```

Setting Border Attributes of a Cell

Code below sets border attributes of a cell.

```
  //***** Set border attributes of cell(1,4) ******
        Font font4 = wb.createFont();
        CellStyle style4 = wb.createCellStyle();
        Cell cell14 = row1.createCell(3);
        style4.setBorderBottom(CellStyle.BORDER_DASHED);
        style4.setBottomBorderColor(IndexedColors.BLACK.
          getIndex());
        style4.setBorderLeft(CellStyle.BORDER_DASHED);
        style4.setLeftBorderColor(IndexedColors.GREEN.
          getIndex());
        style4.setBorderRight(CellStyle.BORDER_DASHED);
        style4.setRightBorderColor(IndexedColors.BLUE.
          getIndex());
        style4.setBorderTop(CellStyle.BORDER_MEDIUM_DASHED);
        style4.setTopBorderColor(IndexedColors.BLACK.
          getIndex());
        cell14.setCellValue("Cell Border Format Test");
        cell14.setCellStyle(style4);
```

Merging Cells

Code below shows how to merge two or more cells.

```
  //***** Merge cells cell(1,5) and cell(1,6) *****
        Cell cell15 = row1.createCell(4);
        cell15.setCellValue("Merged Cell");
        sheet1.addMergedRegion(new CellRangeAddress(
                0, //first row (0-based)
                0, //last row (0-based)
                4, //fifth column (0-based)
                5 //sixth column (0-based)
        ));
```

23.6.3 | Conditional Cell Formatting

Code below shows how to set conditional formatting for a cell.

```
//***** Conditional Formatting: Format font color to RED
//if cell value is >=10 for cell(1,7) and cell(1,8) *****
    Cell cell17 = row1.createCell(6);
    cell17.setCellValue(5);
    Cell cell18 = row1.createCell(7);
    cell18.setCellValue(15);
    SheetConditionalFormatting sheetCF =
      sheet1.getSheetConditionalFormatting();
    ConditionalFormattingRule rule1 =
      sheetCF.createConditionalFormattingRule(ComparisonOper
        ator.GE, "10");
    FontFormatting fontFmtg = rule1.createFontFormatting();
    fontFmtg.setFontStyle(true, false);
    fontFmtg.setFontColorIndex(IndexedColors.DARK_RED.index);

    //Format font color to GREEN if cell value is <10
    ConditionalFormattingRule rule2 =
      sheetCF.createConditionalFormattingRule(ComparisonOper
        ator.LT, "10");
    fontFmtg = rule2.createFontFormatting();
    fontFmtg.setFontStyle(true, false);
    fontFmtg.setFontColorIndex(IndexedColors.BRIGHT_GREEN.
      index);
    ConditionalFormattingRule [] cfRules = {rule1, rule2};
            CellRangeAddress[] regions = {
                    CellRangeAddress.valueOf("G1:H1")
            };
    sheetCF.addConditionalFormatting(regions, cfRules);

    // Write the output to a file
    wb.write(fileOut);
    fileOut.close();
}
```

Figure 23.7 shows the MS Excel file created using the code above.

	A	B	C	D	E	F	G	H
1	Text Color Test	Cell Foreground Color Test	~~Fonts Test~~	Cell Border Format Test	Merged Cell		5	***15***
2								

FIGURE 23.7 | Formatting cell attributes

23.7 | MS EXCEL AS DATABASE

Access is a good database application but as far as test automation is considered it is less readable. For test automation, the database should offer the same ease of reading/updating data manually or programmatically. Test automation requires that test input data be defined manually. The features of MS Excel such as list, sort, filter, etc., come handy and help in easy and fast manual update of the MS Excel file. In the absence of these features, it becomes a nightmare to update the MS Access database manually. During script execution, the MS Excel file can easily be updated by executing SQL queries. Moreover, use of MS Excel as database provides the flexibility to add any number of rows and columns to MS Excel within the existing columns without impacting the test scripts. Inserting of rows or columns within the existing rows or columns is required to keep the test data file readable and structured. For MS Access, this is not possible and such updates make the MS Access database complicated and less readable. In case of use of MS Excel as workbook, insertion of rows or columns within the existing columns requires script maintenance as ordinates of the cells change.

In order to use MS Excel as database, the data inside MS Excel needs to be structured in the list format. Figure 23.8 shows various database attributes as mapped to MS Excel sheets.

- Name of the excel workbook is the Excel database name.
- Sheet name is the table name of the Excel database. Each worksheet represents one table.
- First column of worksheet represents column names. Restriction of database and table apply to MS Excel to when accessing Excel as database. For example, no special character is to be used in the table attribute names.

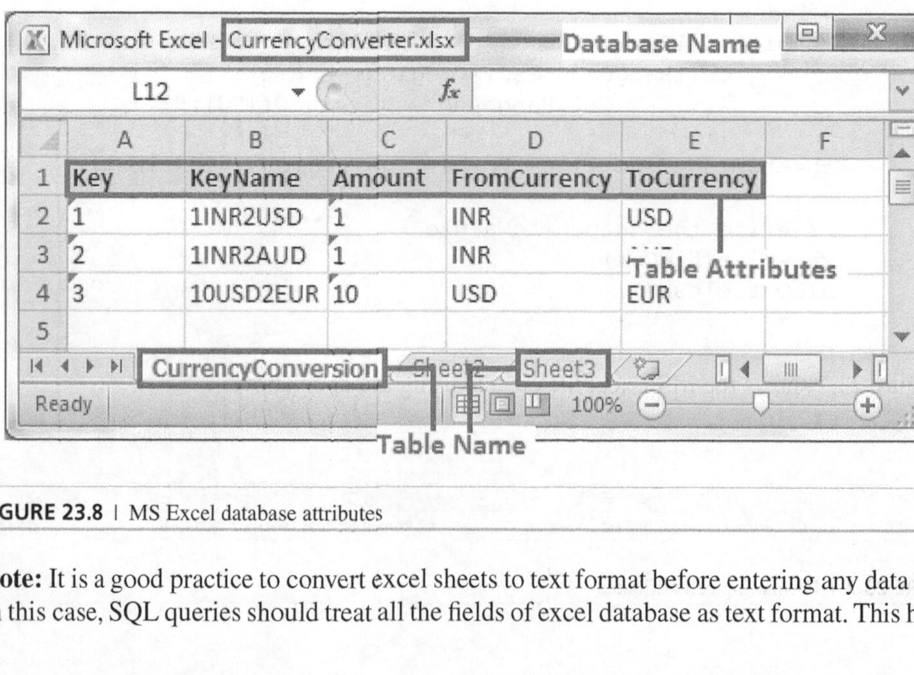

FIGURE 23.8 | MS Excel database attributes

Note: It is a good practice to convert excel sheets to text format before entering any data to it. In this case, SQL queries should treat all the fields of excel database as text format. This helps in avoiding confusion while reading or updating data to MS Excel database. For defining the table attributes, the restrictions of SQL apply such as the attribute name should not contain white spaces, should not start with numeric or special character, etc.

A database connection needs to be established with the MS Excel file before data can be read or updated to it. There are two ways to connect to a MS Excel database:

- ODBC (Open Data Base Connectivity) or DSN (Data Source Name) Connection
- DSN-less connection

In DSN connection, a separate DSN is created for each excel book. Thus with increase in excel database, the number of DSN that needs to be created goes on increasing. Moreover, the DSN needs to be created on all the machines from where the test script is to be executed. This makes maintenance difficult. To overcome this, a DSN-less connection is used to dynamically connect to any excel database. It does not require any machine-specific setup like ODBC creation. DSN-less connection requires excel file path and driver name to connect to excel database. The details once stored in the environment files can easily be accessed by all the test scripts to connect to the MS Excel database without any prior ODBC setup on the test execution machine. Since ODBC connection is not recommended for test automation, we will be discussing only the DSN-less database connection technique.

23.8 | DSN-LESS CONNECTION

In DSN-less connection, ADODB connection can be used to connect to excel database. Once connection is established, SQL queries can be executed on the MS Excel database. Results of queries are saved in RecordSet object.

23.8.1 | Connecting to a MS Excel File

Following code shows how to open a DB connection with a MS Excel file.

Method *getConnection* takes excel file absolute path as input parameter and returns the *Connection* object. The driver used for connecting to Excel database is *Microsoft Excel Driver*.

```
//get connection object
      private Connection getConnection(String excelFilepath){
             String username="";
             String password="";
             try {
                    Class.forName("sun.jdbc.odbc.
                      JdbcOdbcDriver");
                    String connString="jdbc:odbc:DRIVER={Micr
                      osoft Excel Driver (*.xls, *.xlsx, *.xlsm,
                        *.xlsb)};DBQ="+excelFilepath+"";
                    conn = DriverManager.getConnection
                      (connString, username,password);
```

```
        } catch (ClassNotFoundException e) {
                e.printStackTrace();
        } catch (SQLException e) {
                e.printStackTrace();
        }
        return conn;
}
```

Note: The above code may fail if both MS Excel and JRE are not of the same bit version. For example, trying to connect to MS Excel 32-bit with JRE 64-bit will throw an exception. If MS Excel is 32-bit, then JRE should also be 32-bit and if MS Excel is 64-bit, then JRE should also be 64-bit. A simple way of finding whether a program is 32-bit or 64-bit is to look for the installation directory of the file. A program is 64-bit if it is installed at location '*C:\Program Files*' while it is 32-bit if it is installed at location '*C:\Program Files (x86)*' for Win 7 OS.

Note: For above code to work MS Excel driver needs to be installed on the machine from where this code is to be executed. For MS Excel 2010, '*Microsoft Access Database Engine 2010*' can be downloaded from site http://www.microsoft.com/en-in/download/details.aspx?id=13255.

23.8.2 | Reading Data from a MS Excel File

SQL '*Select*' query is to be used to read data from MS Excel database.

EXAMPLE 23.1 Write a code to read second row of data from 'CurrencyConverter.xlsx' shown in Figure 23.8.

Folowing code reads all data from table *CurrencyConversion* whose *KeyName* (Primary Key) value equals '1INR2AUD'.

```
String sql = "Select * from [CurrencyConversion$] where
  KeyName='1INR2AUD'";
Statement stmt = conn.createStatement();
stmt.execute(sql);
//get ResultSet object
ResultSet resultSet = stmt.getResultSet();
ResultSetMetaData rsmd = resultSet.getMetaData();
int columns = rsmd.getColumnCount();
//read resultset data
while (resultSet.next()){
        for(int i=0 i<=columns; i++){
                System.out.println(resultSet.getString(i));
}
    }
```

23.8.3 | Updating Data to a MS Excel File

SQL '*Update*' query is to be used to update data to MS Excel database.

EXAMPLE 23.2 Write a code to update *Amount* value to 100 for row 1 data of 'CurrencyConverter.xlsx'.

```
String sql = "Update [CurrencyConversion$] Set Amount='100'
  Where KeyName='1INR2USD');
Statement stmt = conn.createStatement();
stmt.execute(sql);
```

23.8.4 | Deleting Data from a MS Excel File

SQL '*Delete*' query is to be used to delete data from MS Excel database.

EXAMPLE 23.3 Write a code to delete first row of data from 'CurrencyConverter.xlsx'.\

```
String sql = "Delete from [CurrencyConversion$] Where
  KeyName='1INR2USD');
Statement stmt = conn.createStatement();
stmt.execute(sql);
```

23.8.5 | Inserting Data to a MS Excel File

SQL '*Insert*' query is to be used to insert new row of data to Excel database.

EXAMPLE 23.4 Write code to insert a row of data to 'CurrencyConverter.xlsx'.

```
String sql = "Insert into [CurrencyConversion$]  (Key,KeyName,
  Amount,FromCurrency,ToCurrency)  Values ('4', '10INR2USD',
    '10', 'INR', 'USD') ";
Statement stmt = conn.createStatement();
stmt.execute(sql);
```

23.8.6 | Creating Extension Class for MS Excel DB

Selenium WebDriver does not provide any out-of-box support for connecting to MS Excel database. In this section, we will discuss how to create an extension class for reading and updating data to excel database.

Following code shows *ExcelDB* class. This class has two public methods: read() and update(). `read()` method executes a '*Select*' query and returns the result as list of hash map objects. `update()` method can execute either '*Update*' or '*Insert*' query. The method does not return anything.

```
import java.sql.Connection;
import java.sql.DriverManager;
import java.sql.ResultSet;
import java.sql.ResultSetMetaData;
import java.sql.SQLException;
import java.sql.Statement;
import java.util.ArrayList;
import java.util.HashMap;
import java.util.List;

import org.testng.Assert;

public class ExcelDB {
        private String excelFilepath;
        private int rowCount;
        private int columnCount;
        private Connection conn;
        private Statement stmt;

        private ResultSet resultSet;
        public ExcelDB(String filepath){
                excelFilepath = filepath;
        }

        /**
         * @desc: execute a 'Select' sql query against excel database
         * @param sql sql query
         * @return sql query results as List<HashMap<String, Object>>
         */
        public List<HashMap<String, Object>> read(String sql){
                ResultSet resultSet = this.executeSql(sql, true);
                List<HashMap<String, Object>> recordSet =
                  convertResultSetToList(resultSet);
                closeConnection();
                return recordSet;
        }

        /**
        * @desc: execute a 'Update/Insert/Delete' sql query
        * against excel database
        * @param sql sql query
        */
        public void update(String sql){
                this.executeSql(sql, false);
                closeConnection();
        }

        //execute the sql query and return ResultSet object
```

```
    private ResultSet executeSql(String sql, boolean read){
        String absolutePath = getAbsoluteFilepath(excelF
          ilepath);
        conn = getConnection(absolutePath, read);
        ResultSet resultSet = executeQueryOnExcel(conn,
          sql);
        return resultSet;
    }

    //get the absolute path of the excel file
    private String getAbsoluteFilepath(String excelFilepath){
        String filepath = getClass().getResource
          (excelFilepath).getFile();
        filepath = filepath.replaceFirst("/", "");
        return filepath;
    }

    //get connection object
    private Connection getConnection(String excelFilepath,
      boolean read){
        String username="";
        String password="";
        String connString;
        try {
                Class.forName("sun.jdbc.odbc.
                  JdbcOdbcDriver");
                if (read){
                        connString = this.getReadConnectio
                          nString(excelFilepath);
                } else{
                        connString = this.getWriteConnecti
                          onString(excelFilepath);
                }
                conn = DriverManager.getConnection(
                  connString,username,password);
        } catch (ClassNotFoundException e) {
                Assert.assertTrue(false, "Incorrect
                  driver class");
        } catch (SQLException e) {
                Assert.assertTrue(false, "Connection
                  with excel db failed");
        }
        return conn;
    }

    //get connection string for reading data from Excel
```

```
private String getReadConnectionString(String
  excelFilepath){
        String connString="jdbc:odbc:DRIVER={Microsoft
         Excel Driver (*.xls, *.xlsx, *.xlsm, *.xlsb)
          };DBQ="+excelFilepath+"";
        return connString;
}

//get connection string for writing data to Excel
private String getWriteConnectionString(String
  excelFilepath){
        String connString="jdbc:odbc:DRIVER={Microsoft
         Excel Driver (*.xls, *.xlsx, *.xlsm, *.xlsb)};
          DBQ="+excelFilepath+";ReadOnly=0;";
        return connString;
}

//execute the sql query and return ResultSet object
private ResultSet executeQueryOnExcel(Connection
  conn,String sql){
        try {
                        stmt = conn.createStatement();
                  stmt.execute(sql);
                        resultSet = stmt.getResultSet();
                  } catch (SQLException e) {
                  Assert.assertTrue(false, "Failed to
                   execute sql query.");
        }
return resultSet;
}

//store ResultSet object data to an ArrayList
private List<HashMap<String,Object>>
  convertResultSetToList(
ResultSet resultSet) {
        int rowCntr=0;
ResultSetMetaData rsmd = getResultSetMetaData(resultSet);
this.setColumnCount(resultSet);
List<HashMap<String,Object>> list =
  new ArrayList<HashMap<String,Object>>();
 try {
        while (resultSet.next()) {
                  HashMap<String,Object> row = new HashMap
                   <String, Object>(columnCount);
                  for(int i=1; i<=columnCount; ++i) {
                  row.put(rsmd.getColumnName(i),
                   resultSet.getObject(i));
```

```
                }
                rowCntr = rowCntr + 1;
                list.add(row);
                }
        } catch (SQLException e) {
                Assert.assertTrue(false, "Failed to convert
                  ResultSet to List.");
        }
    rowCount = rowCntr;
    return list;
}

//get total number of rows of data returned by the sql query
public int getRowCount(){
        return rowCount;
}

//get total columns of data returned by the sql query
public int getColumnCount(){
        return columnCount;
}

//get ResultSetMetadata Object
private ResultSetMetaData getResultSetMetaData
  (ResultSet rs){
        ResultSetMetaData rsmd = null;
        try {
                rsmd = rs.getMetaData();
        } catch (SQLException e) {
                e.printStackTrace();
        }
        return rsmd;
}

//set total number of columns of data returned by the
  sql query
private void setColumnCount(ResultSet resultSet){
        ResultSetMetaData rsmd = getResultSetMetaData
          (resultSet);
        try {
                columnCount = rsmd.getColumnCount();
        } catch (SQLException e) {
                Assert.assertTrue(false, "Failed to retrieve
                  column count.");
        }
}
```

```
        //close the DB connection
        private void closeConnection(){
                try {
                                stmt.close();
                                conn.close();
                        } catch (SQLException e) {
                                Assert.assertTrue(false, "Failed
                                  to close Excel db connection.");
                }
        }
}
```

EXAMPLE 23.5 Write a code to retrieve all test data from file *CurrencyConverter.xlsx* as shown in Figure 23.8.

The extension class `ExcelDB` can be used to execute select queries against MS Excel database. Following code creates an instance of `ExcelDB` with input argument of excel file path. Thereafter `read()` method of `ExcelDB` is called with the SQL query. This method returns the data returned by the query.

```
@Test
public void testExcelDBRead() {
        ExcelDB excelDB = new ExcelDB("/com/webdriver/
          testdata/CurrencyConverter.xlsx");
        String sql = "Select * from [CurrencyConversion$]";
        List<HashMap<String, Object>> resultSet = excelDB.
          read(sql);
        System.out.println("Row Count:" + excelDB.
          getRowCount());
        System.out.println("Column Count:" + excelDB.
          getColumnCount());
        for (int i=0;i<resultSet.size();i++){
                System.out.print(resultSet.get(i).get("Key") +
                  "\t");
                System.out.print(resultSet.get(i).get("KeyName")
                  + "\t");
                System.out.print(resultSet.get(i).get("Amount")
                  + "\t");
                System.out.print(resultSet.get(i).get
                  ("FromCurrency") + "\t");
                System.out.print(resultSet.get(i).get
                  ("ToCurrency") + "\t");
                System.out.println();
        }
}
```

The output of above code as visible on Eclipse *console* tab is shown in Figure 23.9.

```
Row Count:3
Column Count:5
1       1INR2USD     1     INR    USD
2       1INR2AUD     1     INR    AUD
3       10USD2EUR    10    USD    EUR
```

FIGURE 23.9 | Reading all data from MS Excel DB

EXAMPLE 23.6 Write a code to retrieve the field names of MS Excel table as returned by the query of Example 23.5.

The field names of the excel table can be found by executing method '*keySet*' on any of the Hasp Map object of the List Object. For example, any of the code below will return the field names of the MS Excel table.

```
Set<String> fieldNames = resultSet.get(0).keySet();
        Or,
//Set<String> fieldNames = resultSet.get(1).keySet(); and
  so on...
for (String fieldName:fieldNames){
        System.out.print(fieldName + "\t");
}
```

Figure 23.10 shows the output of the above code.

```
Amount   ToCurrency        Key        FromCurrency        KeyName
```

FIGURE 23.10 | Reading MS Excel DB table field names

EXAMPLE 23.7 Write a code to read the excel data returned by the query as array.

Method `toArray()` can be used to convert the `List<HashMap<String, Object>>` data to array.

```
Object[] arrResultSet = resultSet.toArray();
```

EXAMPLE 23.8 Write a code to read fields *Amount*, *ToCurrency* and *FromCurrency* for the row whose *KeyName–1INR2AUD*.

```
@Test
public void testExcelDBReadSpecificData() {
```

```
        ExcelDB excelDB = new
          ExcelDB("/com/webdriver/testdata/
            CurrencyConverter.xlsx");
                String sql = "Select Amount,ToCurrency,FromCurrency
                  from [CurrencyConversion$] Where
                    KeyName='1INR2AUD'";
                List<HashMap<String, Object>> resultSet =
                  excelDB.read(sql);
                  System.out.print(resultSet.get(0).get("Amount") +
                  "\t");
                System.out.print(resultSet.get(0).get
                  ("FromCurrency") + \t");
                System.out.print(resultSet.get(0).get
                  ("ToCurrency") + "\t");
                }
    }
```

EXAMPLE 23.9 Write a code to update *Amount* to 100 for row with *KeyName=1INR2AUD*

```
  @Test
  public void testExcelDBUpdate(){
                ExcelDB excelDB = new ExcelDB("/com/webdriver/
                  testdata/CurrencyConverter.xlsx");
                String sql = "Update [CurrencyConversion$] Set
                  Amount='100' Where KeyName='1INR2AUD'";
                excelDB.update(sql);
        }
```

EXAMPLE 23.10 Write a code to insert a new row of test data to the MS Excel file CurrencyConverter.xlsx

```
  @Test
  public void testExcelDBInsert(){
        ExcelDB excelDB = new ExcelDB("/com/webdriver/testdata/
          CurrencyConverter.xlsx");

        String sql = "Insert into [CurrencyConversion$] (Key,Key
          Name,Amount,FromCurrency,ToCurrency) Values ('4',
            '10INR2USD', '10', 'INR', 'USD') ";

        excelDB.update(sql);
    }
```

23.9 | ADVANTAGES OF USING MS EXCEL VERSUS MS ACCESS AS TEST CASES AND TEST DATA SET

MS Excel's advantage is its universal usage, comparative ease of use and quick solutions for simple databases. MS Access needs to be used in case of complex requirements. Test automation requires simple database with good text editing features. Editing features are required in case of manual addition/deletion/updation of test cases and test data in test data set. MS Excel provides excellent features to make list, sort and filter data, search specific data, etc. These features lower the cost and effort required to maintain test data set. We can create lists in MS Excel and restrict the data that a user can enter into it. This reduces the chances of manual error and increases efficiency as well. Multiple data can be easily created using drag features of excel. In case of Access, each data needs to be entered manually.

23.10 | ADVANTAGES OF USING MS EXCEL AS DATABASE OVER MS EXCEL AS WORKSHEET/DATA TABLE

TABLE 23.1 Benefits of using MS Excel as database

	Excel as Worksheet	Excel as Database
Co-ordinate dependency	Data is retrieved by specifying cell ordinates. Any insertion of row/column in between used rows/columns will change the cell ordinates. Since, cell ordinates are hardcoded in test scripts, all the scripts need to be changed to extract the required data.	Data is retrieved using SQL query. Any insertion of row/column in between used rows/columns will not impact data retrieved from SQL query. Because of this, no change in test scripts is required in case of addition/deletion of row/columns of worksheet.
Memory	Complete worksheet needs to be loaded in memory while reading/writing data from MS Excel file. If worksheet size is large, test scripts may hang while execution.	A connection is established and data is retrieved using the same connection. Since complete file is not loaded in memory, memory usage is less.
Speed	Data needs to be extracted cell by cell. This slows down the speed of execution. Only one cell can be read/updated at a time.	It generally takes less time to retrieve data using SQL query. Queries can be designed to read/update more than one cell values in one go as per requirement.

(*continued*)

TABLE 23.1 | *(continued)*

	Excel as Worksheet	Excel as Database
Code length	Programming logic needs to be coded to extract specific data from worksheets. For example, to extract specific row data from excel sheet as shown in example 4, extra code logic needs to be written. Most of the times it requires complex and lengthy codes to dynamically filter and sort excel data as per requirement.	Powerful SQL queries can be designed to retrieve filtered and sorted data from worksheets. Most of the times single line query will be sufficient.
Maintenance	Generally, in test automation data in test data sheets can vary from one regression run to another. For example, in one run test, cases need to be executed with 10 data sets while in another 23. Dynamic handling of these variations is difficult in use of excel as worksheet, as data retrieval is cell ordinate dependent. The cell ordinate changes with increase or decrease in data sets.	A query to extract all required data from worksheets. In the MS Excel sheet shown in Figure 23.8, we can add one more column that specifies whether to use the specific row data for testing or not. We can name this column UseAsTestData. A value 'Y' for this column implies this test data can be used for testing. Now suppose, if for one run, only 10 data sets are marked 'Y' in excel sheet for the mentioned condition then all 10 datasets will be retrieved. While for another regression run if 20 data sets are marked 'Y' in excel, then 20 data sets will be retrieved automatically.

Quick Tips

1. It is advisable to use MS Excel as database as compared to MS Access or any other database.
2. MS Excel object model is used to access MS Excel as a workbook.
3. Accessing MS Excel as database has lot more advantages for test automation than accessing it as workbook.
4. Use DSN-less connection to connect to the MS Excel database.

INTERVIEW QUESTIONS

1. Why it is better to use excel as test data file than as compared to any other database?
2. Why it is advisable to access excel as database than as worksheet in test automation?
3. What is an excel Application object?
4. Write code to create a new excel file, write data to it and save it.
5. Write code to add worksheet to an existing workbook.
6. Write code to access data from an already opened MS Excel file.
7. Write code to retrieve data from an excel database.

24
CHAPTER
Working with Database

In test automation, we may often require to connect to the application database to verify if the database has been updated correctly and to validate the front-end contents against back-end data. Suppose we are automating a retail banking web site and we need to validate the transaction amount is equal to the amount debited from the debtor account. In this case, we can directly connect to the AUT database and can compare the amount deducted from the debtor account to the transaction amount. Also, an important use of connecting to application database is to retrieve the right test data that can be used to execute a test. For example, in order to execute a 'Funds transfer' test, we would need a debtor account that has a positive balance to transfer. Suppose we specify this debtor account number in test data file. Then every time we run the test, the amount gets exhausted rendering the account unusable for next test run. An alternative solution to this is to run a query in database for an account that has balance and use the same account as debtor account in test.

Selenium WebDriver does not provide any out-of-box support to connect to a database. In this chapter, we will learn how to connect to various databases using Java code.

24.1 | CONNECTING TO ORACLE DATABASE

The Oracle Database (commonly referred to as Oracle RDBMS or simply as Oracle) is an object-relational database management system produced and marketed by Oracle Corporation.

Oracle provides a variety of Java ODBC drivers to connect to various Oracle databases in different OS environments. These exist as jar files and can be downloaded from the site: http://www.oracle.com/technetwork/database/enterprise-edition/overview/index.html

These jar files needs to be associated to the Eclipse project build path before it can be used to connect to a database.

Following code shows how to connect to oracle database. Method executeOracleDB-Query takes four input parameters: host name, port number, service name and the SQL query to execute. Host name, port number and service name of a database can be found in tnsnames.ora file. This file can be found both on oracle server and client. A typical connection string for a DB in tnsnames.ora file looks like as shown below:

SERVER=(DESCRIPTION=(ADDRESS=(PROTOCOL=TCP)(HOST=MyHost)(PORT=1521))(CONNECT_DATA=(SERVICE_NAME=MyOracleSID)));

```
import java.sql.Connection;
import java.sql.DriverManager;
import java.sql.ResultSet;
import java.sql.ResultSetMetaData;
import java.sql.SQLException;
import java.sql.Statement;
import org.junit.Test;
public class DB {

    @Test
    public void testOracleDBConnect(){
        String host="HostName";
        int port = 1521;
        String service_name = "ServiceName";
        String sql="Select * from dual";
        this.executeOracleDBQuery(host, port, service_
          name, sql);
    }
    private void executeOracleDBQuery(String host, int port,
      String service_name, String sql){
        Connection connection = null;
        Statement stmt = null;
        try{
            Class.forName("oracle.jdbc.driver.
            OracleDriver");
            String connUrl = "jdbc:oracle:
              thin:dbread/looksee@//" + host + ":" +
                port + "/" + service_name ;
            connection = DriverManager.
              getConnection(connUrl);
            stmt = connection.createStatement ();
            ResultSet rs = stmt.executeQuery (sql);
            ResultSetMetaData rsmd = rs.getMetaData ();
            int columnCount = rsmd.getColumnCount ();
            while(rs.next()){
              for (int colCntr=0;colCntr<columnCount
                ;colCntr++){
                  System.out.println(rsmd.
                    getColumnName(colCntr+1) + ":" +
                      rs.getString(colCntr+1));
              }

            }
        }catch (Exception e){
            e.printStackTrace();
        }finally{
            if (connection != null){
```

```
                        try {
                         if (stmt!=null) stmt.close();
                         connection.close ();
                        } catch (SQLException e) {
                         e.printStackTrace();
                        }
                    }
                }
            }
    }
```

24.2 | CONNECTING TO IBM DB2 DATABASE

IBM DB2 is a relational model database server developed by IBM. There are three main products in the DB2 family: DB2 for LUW (Linux, Unix and Windows), DB2 for z/OS (mainframe) and DB2 for iSeries (formerly OS/400).

Selenium being a web-based automation tool cannot be used to automate desktop-based applications like AS400. This poses a challenge in situations where we need to test integration between web-based and desktop-based applications. Very often, we may require to validate if data has moved correctly to/from web-based apps to AS400 app. This problem can be solved by directly connecting to AS400 DB and retrieving the data that needs to be validated. In this section, we will learn how to connect to a DB2 for mainframes (AS400) application.

IBM provides a library of Java classes to access IBM i (i5/OS) data and resources from Java code. JTOpen is the open source version of Toolbox for Java. JTOpenLite is delivered since JTOpen 7.7.1. JTOpenLite is a set of lightweight Java classes suitable for use on mobile devices. It provides Java application access to IBM i: DDM access, basic JDBC access, command call, program call access, etc. JTOpen can be downloaded from site: http://sourceforge.net/projects/jt400/. Once downloaded, the jar files needs to be associated to the Eclipse project's build path before it can used to connect to the DB2 database.

Following code shows how to connect to DB2 database using JTOpen jar files. Method executeDB2DBQuery takes four input parameters: AS400 application name, username used to login to AS400, password and the SQL query.

```
@Test
public void testAS400DBConnect(){
       String as400Box="AS400QA";
       String username = "username";
       String password = "password";
       //Select all the rows from DSN81010.EMP by ascending
         hire date
       String sql="SELECT * FROM DSN81010.EMP ORDER BY
         HIREDATE";
       this.executeDB2DBQuery(as400Box, username, password, sql);
}
```

```
private void executeAS400DBQuery(String as400Box, String
  username, String password, String sql){
        Connection connection = null;
        Statement stmt = null;
        try{
                DriverManager.registerDriver(new com.ibm.as400.
                  access.AS400JDBCDriver());
                connection = DriverManager.getConnection
                  ("jdbc:as400://" + as400Box ,username,password);
                DatabaseMetaData dmd = connection.getMetaData ();
                stmt = connection.createStatement ();
                ResultSet rs = stmt.executeQuery (sql);
                ResultSetMetaData rsmd = rs.getMetaData ();
                int columnCount = rsmd.getColumnCount ();
                while(rs.next()){
                        for (int colCntr=0;colCntr<columnCount;c
                          olCntr++){
                             System.out.println(rsmd.
                               getColumnName(colCntr+1) + ":" +
                                 rs.getString(colCntr+1));
                        }
                }
        }catch (Exception e){
                e.printStackTrace();
        }finally{
                if (connection != null){
                        try {
                             if (stmt!=null) stmt.close();
                               connection.close ();
                        } catch (SQLException e) {
                               e.printStackTrace();
                        }
                }
        }
}
```

Note: For details on DB2 SQL queries refer link http://pic.dhe.ibm.com/infocenter/dzichelp/v2r2/index.jsp?topic=%2Fcom.ibm.db2z10.doc.sqlref%2Fsrc%2Ftpc%2Fdb2z_sql_select-statementexamples.htm

24.3 | CONNECTING TO MS ACCESS DATABASE

Microsoft Access is a database management system from Microsoft that combines the relational Microsoft Jet Database Engine with a graphical user interface and software development tools. It is a member of the Microsoft Office suite of applications.

Assume MS Access database named Database11.accdb is stored at location c:\temp. Following code shows how to connect to MS Access 2010 database and retrieve the contents of a table named 'Table1'.

```
@Test
public void testMSAccess2010DBConnect(){
        String dbPath="C:\\temp\\Database11.accdb";
        String username = "";
        String password = "";

        String sql="SELECT * from Table1";
        this.executeMSAccessDBQuery(dbPath, username, password, sql);
}

private void executeMSAccessDBQuery(String dbPath, String username,
  String password, String sql){
        Connection connection = null;
        Statement stmt = null;
        try{
                Class.forName("sun.jdbc.odbc.JdbcOdbcDriver").
                  newInstance();
                String connString = "jdbc:odbc:Driver={
                  Microsoft Access Driver (*.mdb, *.accdb)};DBQ="
                    + dbPath;
                connection = DriverManager.getConnection
                  ( connString,username,password);
                DatabaseMetaData dmd = connection.getMetaData ();
                stmt = connection.createStatement ();
                ResultSet rs = stmt.executeQuery (sql);
                ResultSetMetaData rsmd = rs.getMetaData ();
                int columnCount = rsmd.getColumnCount ();
                while(rs.next()){
                        for (int colCntr=0;colCntr<columnCount;c
                          olCntr++){
                                System.out.println(rsmd.
                                  getColumnName(colCntr+1) +  ":" +
                                    rs.getString(colCntr+1));
                        }
                }
        }catch (Exception e){
                e.printStackTrace();
        }finally{
                if (connection != null){
                        try {
                                if (stmt!=null) stmt.close();
                                connection.close ();
                        } catch (SQLException e) {
```

```
                        e.printStackTrace();
                    }
                }
            }
    }
```

Note: The above code may fail if both MS Access and JRE are not of the same bit version. For example, trying to connect to MS Access 32-bit with JRE 64-bit will throw an exception. If Access is 32-bit, then JRE should also be 32-bit and if Access is 64-bit, then JRE should also be 64-bit. A simple way of finding whether a program is 32-bit or 64-bit is to look for the installation directory of the file. A program is 64-bit if it is installed at location '*C:\Program Files*', while it is 32-bit if it is installed at location '*C:\Program Files (x86)*' for Win 7 OS.

24.4 | CONNECTING TO MS EXCEL DATABASE

Microsoft Excel is a spreadsheet application developed by Microsoft for Microsoft Windows and Mac OS X. It features calculation, graphing tools, pivot tables and a macro programming language called Visual Basic for Applications. MS Excel can also be used as database for updating and retrieving data. For details refer Chapter 20.

Assume MS Excel database named Emp.xlsx is stored at location c:\temp. following code shows how to connect to MS Excel 2010 database and retrieve the contents of a table named 'Sheet1'.

```
@Test
public void testMSExcel2010DBConnect(){
        String dbPath="C:\\temp\\Emp.xlsx";
        String username = "";
        String password = "";
        String sql="SELECT * from [Sheet1$]";
        this.executeMSAccessDBQuery(dbPath, username, password, sql);
}

private void executeMSExcelDBQuery(String excelFilepath,
   String username, String password, String sql){
        Connection connection = null;
        Statement stmt = null;
        try{
                Class.forName("sun.jdbc.odbc.JdbcOdbcDriver");
                String connString="jdbc:odbc:DRIVER={Microsoft
                  Excel Driver (*.xls, *.xlsx, *.xlsm, *.xlsb)};D
                    BQ="+excelFilepath+"";
                connection = DriverManager.getConnection
                  ( connString,username,password);
```

```
                DatabaseMetaData dmd = connection.getMetaData ();
                stmt = connection.createStatement ();
                ResultSet rs = stmt.executeQuery (sql);
                ResultSetMetaData rsmd = rs.getMetaData ();
                int columnCount = rsmd.getColumnCount ();
                while(rs.next()){
                        for (int colCntr=0;colCntr<columnCount;
                          colCntr++){
                              System.out.println(rsmd.
                                getColumnName(colCntr+1) + ":" +
                                  rs.getString(colCntr+1));
                        }
                }
        }catch (Exception e){
                e.printStackTrace();
        }finally{
                if (connection != null){
                        try {
                              if (stmt!=null) stmt.close();
                              connection.close ();
                        } catch (SQLException e) {
                              e.printStackTrace();
                        }
                }
        }
}
```

Note: The above code may fail if both MS Excel and JRE are not of the same bit version. For example, trying to connect to MS Excel 32-bit with JRE 64-bit will throw an exception. If Excel is 32-bit, then JRE should also be 32-bit and if Excel is 64-bit, then JRE should also be 64-bit. A simple way of finding whether a program is 32-bit or 64-bit is to look for the installation directory of the file. A program is 64-bit if it is installed at location '*C:\Program Files*', while it is 32-bit if it is installed at location '*C:\Program Files (x86)*' for Win 7 OS.

INTERVIEW QUESTIONS

1. Write code to connect to Oracle DB.
2. Write code to read data from MS Access DB.

25 CHAPTER

Working with XML

XML stands for extensible markup language. XML is a universal file format for storing and exchanging structured information. Some common uses of XML on the web are web development, documentation and database development. A number of new Internet languages have been created with XML. Some of them are as follows:

- XHTML
- WSDL for describing available web services
- WAP and WML as markup languages for handheld devices
- RSS languages for news feeds
- RDF and OWL for describing resources and ontology
- SMIL for describing multimedia for the web

Java provides methods to allow parsing and manipulating XML files. This chapter discusses about how to access, manipulate and create an XML file.

25.1 | XML STRUCTURE

The elements in an XML document form a document tree. The tree starts at the root and branches to the lowest level of the tree. The first node in an XML file is called the *root* node. In the following example, node *<Bookstore>* is the root node. Node <Book> has four *child* nodes: <title>, <author>, <year> and <price>. Child nodes are the children of an enclosing parent node. Node *<Book>* is called the *parent* node of these child nodes. Value assigned to any particular node is called *node value*. Node <title> has node value Harry Potter. A node can have *attributes*. For example, third node of book has two attributes: *category* and *cover* with attribute values *technical* and *paperback,* respectively.

```
<?xml version="1.0" encoding="UTF-8"?>
<Bookstore>
        <Book category="children">
                <title lang="en">Harry Potter</title>
                <author>J. K. Rowling</author>
                <year>2005</year>
                <price>29.99</price>
        </Book>
        <Book category="children">
```

```
            <title lang="en">Alice in Wonderland </title>
            <author>Lewis Carroll</author>
            <year>1865</year>
            <price>39.95</price>
        </Book>
        <Book category="technical" cover="paperback">
            <title lang="en">Learning XML</title>
            <author>Eric Thomson </author>
            <author>James Lyod </author>
            <year>2010</year>
            <price>49.95</price>
        </Book>
</Bookstore>
```

There are two programming models for working with XML infosets: Streaming and the Document Object Model (DOM).

The DOM model creates in-memory objects representing an entire document tree and the complete infoset state of an XML document. Once in memory, DOM trees can be navigated freely and parsed arbitrarily. This provides maximum flexibility to developers while working with XML files. However, if file size is large then memory can be an issue.

Streaming refers to a programming model where in XML infosets are transmitted and parsed serially at runtime. Data transmission and parsing often happens real-time and often from dynamic sources whose contents are not precisely known beforehand. Also, stream-based parsers can start generating output immediately and the used infoset elements can be immediately discarded and garbage collected. While streaming provides lesser memory footprint, the trade-off is infoset state can be read at one location at one time in the document.

Streaming model of XML is essentially useful in application which has strict memory restrictions such as cell phone running on Java platform.

25.2 | JAVA API FOR XML PROCESSING (JAXP)

The Java API for XML Processing (JAXP) is for processing XML data using applications written in the Java programming language. JAXP supports both DOM as well as Streaming programming model for working with XML. In the following section, we will discuss how to work with XML using DOM.

The XML Document Object Model (DOM) defines a standard way for accessing and manipulating XML documents. The DOM models XML as a set of node objects. JAXP provide *DocumentBuilderFactory* to load XML files. Following code shows how to access XML file using *DocumentBuilderFactory*.

Assume the XML code mentioned above is saved at path *'/com/webdriver/testData/Books.xml'*. Code below shows how to access a XML file.

```
String xmlFilepath = getClass().getResource("/com/webdriver/
  testdata/Books.xml").getFile();
File xmlFile = new File(xmlFilepath);
```

```
DocumentBuilderFactory dbFactory=DocumentBuilderFactory.newInstance();
DocumentBuilder dBuilder = dbFactory.newDocumentBuilder();
Document doc = dBuilder.parse(xmlFile);
```

25.3 | READING XML FILES

XML DOM provides an application programming interface for working with XML data. As an XML representation, it conforms to the W3C DOM specification. As a set of API, XML DOM objects are COM objects that implement interfaces and can be used in XML applications written in programming languages such as Java, C/C++, Visual Basic, VBScript and JScript.

25.3.1 | Methods to Read XML Files

Described as follows are some of the methods of the JAXP to read XML files.

getElementById Returns the `Element` that has an ID attribute with the given value

Note: Attributes with the name "ID" or "id" are not of type ID unless so defined.

getElementsByTagName Returns a `NodeList` of all the `Elements` in document order with the specified tag name.

Following code shows how to find the count of nodes whose tag name equals *Book*.

```
@Test
public void testXML(){
        String xmlFilepath =
                getClass().getResource("/com/webdriver/testdata/
                  Books.xml").getFile();
        File xmlFile = new File(xmlFilepath);
        DocumentBuilderFactory dbFactory =
                    DocumentBuilderFactory.newInstance();
        DocumentBuilder dBuilder = dbFactory.newDocumentBuilder();
        Document doc = dBuilder.parse(xmlFile);

        NodeList nodelist = doc.getElementsByTagName("Book");
        System.out.println(nodelist.getLength()); //Output::3
}
```

Following code shows how to retrieve all <author> nodes from the XML file.

```
NodeList nodelist = doc.getElementsByTagName("author");
for (int i=0;i<nodelist.getLength();i++){
System.out.println(nodelist.item(i).getNodeName() + ":" +
                        nodelist.item(i).getTextContent());
}
```

```
//Output::
author:J K. Rowling
author:Lewis Carroll
author:Eric Thomson
author:James Lyod
```

getNodeType Returns the type of the node. Following code shows how to check if a node is an element node or not.

```
NodeList nodelist = doc.getElementsByTagName("Book");
if (nodelist.item(0).getNodeType()==doc.ELEMENT_NODE){
       System.out.println("This is element node");
}else if (nodelist.item(0).getNodeType()==doc.TEXT_NODE){
       System.out.println("This is text node");
}
//Output:: This is element node
```

getNodeName Returns the name of the node
Following code shows how to read the name of the node.

```
System.out.println(nodelist.item(0).getNodeName());//Output::Book
```

getNodeValue Returns the value of the specific node.

Note: Calling *getNodeValue* on a node always returns null as value of an element node is always null. To get the value of the node, *getNodeValue* method needs to be called on the text node. An another option is to call method *getTextContent()* of the element node. Code below shows how to read the tag value of *title* node.

```
NodeList nodelist = doc.getElementsByTagName("title");
System.out.println(nodelist.getLength()); //Output::3
System.out.println(nodelist.item(0).getNodeValue());//
Output::null
System.out.println(nodelist.item(0).getTextContent());
//Output:: Harry Potter
```

getTextContent Returns the text content of this node and its descendants. Code below shows how to retrieve the value of the first `<author>` node

```
NodeList nodelist = doc.getElementsByTagName("author");
System.out.println(nodelist.item(0).getTextContent());
//Output:: J K. Rowling
```

getUserData Returns the DOMUserData associated to the given key on this node, or null if there was none.

getAttribute: Returns the value of the specified attribute of the current node. Following code shows how to retrieve the values of attribute 'category' of first <Book> node.

XML Node:

```
<Book category="children">
....
<Book category="children">
....
<Book category="technical" cover="paperback">
```

Code below shows how to read the value of attribute *category* of *Book* node.

```
NodeList nodelist = doc.getElementsByTagName("Book");
for (int i=0;i<nodelist.getLength();i++){
        //verify if the current node is an element node
        if (nodelist.item(i).getNodeType()==doc.ELEMENT_NODE){
                Element element = (Element) nodelist.item(i);
                System.out.println(element.getTagName());
                //Output::Book
                //get value of attribute category
                System.out.println(element.getAttribute
                  ("category"));
                //Output::children
                break;
        }
}
```

getAttributes Returns all the attributes of the specific node. Following code shows how to read the attributes of third 'Book' node of XML mentioned above.

```
NodeList nodelist = doc.getElementsByTagName("Book");
NamedNodeMap attr = nodelist.item(2).getAttributes();
System.out.println(attr.getNamedItem("category"));
//Output:: category="technical"
System.out.println(attr.getNamedItem("cover"));
//Output:: cover="paperback"
System.out.println(attr.getLength());
                                        //Output::2
System.out.println(attr.item(0).getNodeName());
                                        //Output::category
System.out.println(attr.item(0).getTextContent());
                                        //Output::technical
System.out.println(attr.item(1).getNodeName());
                                        //Output::cover
System.out.println(attr.item(1).getNodeValue());
                                        //Output::paperback
System.out.println(attr.item(1).getTextContent());
                                        //Output::paperback
```

getParentNode Returns the parent of the current node. Following code shows how to retrieve the parent node of the `<author>` node.

```
NodeList nodelist = doc.getElementsByTagName("author");
String nodeName = nodelist.item(0).getParentNode().
getNodeName();
System.out.println("Parent node of <author> node:" + nodeName);
//Output:: Parent node of <author> node:Book
```

Note: All nodes, except `Attr`, `Document`, `DocumentFragment`, `Entity` and `Notation` may have a parent.

getChildNodes Returns all the child nodes of the current node. Following code retrieves the child nodes of the nodes `<Bookstore>` and `<Book>`.

```
//retrieve the first Book node/element
NodeList bookNodes = doc.getElementsByTagName("Book");
Element firstBookElement = null;
for (int i=0;i<bookNodes.getLength();i++){
        if (bookNodes.item(i).getNodeType()==doc.ELEMENT_NODE){
                firstBookElement = (Element) bookNodes.item(i);
                break;
        }
}
System.out.println(firstBookElement.getTagName());//Output::Book

//does firstfirstBookstoreElement has child nodes
System.out.println(firstBookElement.hasChildNodes());//Output::true

//get all the child nodes of first Book element
NodeList bookChildNodes = firstBookElement.getChildNodes();
//get the node name and node values of the <Book> child nodes
for (int i=0;i<bookChildNodes.getLength();i++){
        if (bookChildNodes.item(i).getNodeType()==doc.ELEMENT_NODE){
                System.out.println(bookChildNodes.item(i).get
                  NodeName() +
                        ":" + bookChildNodes.item(i).getText
                          Content());
        }
}
//Output::
title:Harry Potter
author:J K. Rowling
year:2005
price:29.99
```

Note: If there are any white spaces between two <object> nodes, then white spaces are considered as childnodes and are returned as #text. In such cases, it is advisable to verify whether the specific node is an element node or not before performing any operations on it.

getFirstChild Returns the first child of the current node. The first child node of the node <Book> is node <title>. Following code shows how to retrieve the first child node of the <Book> node.

```
Node node = doc.getElementsByTagName("Book").item(0);
System.out.println(node.getFirstChild().getNodeName());//Output::title
```

getLastChild Returns the last child of the current node. The last child node of the node <Book> is node <price>. Following code shows how to retrieve the last child node of the <Book> node.

```
Node node = doc.getElementsByTagName("Book").item(0);
System.out.println(node.getLastChild().getNodeName());//Output::price
```

getNextSibling Returns the next sibling node of the current node. The next sibling node of node <title> is node <author>. Following code shows how to retrieve the next sibling node of the <title> node.

```
Node node = doc.getElementsByTagName("title").item(0);
System.out.println(node.getNextSibling().getNodeName());//Output::author
```

getPreviousSibling Returns the previous sibling node of the current node. The previous sibling node of node <author> is node <title>. Following code shows how to retrieve the previous sibling node of the <author> node.

```
Node node = doc.getElementsByTagName("author").item(0);
System.out.println(node.getPreviousSibling().getNodeName());
//Output::title
```

25.4 | READING XML FILE FROM URL

In WebService automation, many a times a web service URL returns a XML file. Suppose the requirement is to verify if the XML response is correct or not. Following code shows how to read the XML response from Jenkins servers.

Assume the URL for test resports for Jenkins job 'regression' to be 'http://jenkins.com/job/ regression/lastBuild/testReport/api/xml'. Figure 25.1 shows the XML response from the server for the specified URL.

```
public void readXMLResponseFromURL() {
    String url="http://jenkins.com/job/regression/lastBuild/
        testReport/api/xml"
    DocumentBuilderFactory dbf = DocumentBuilderFactory.new
      Instance();
```

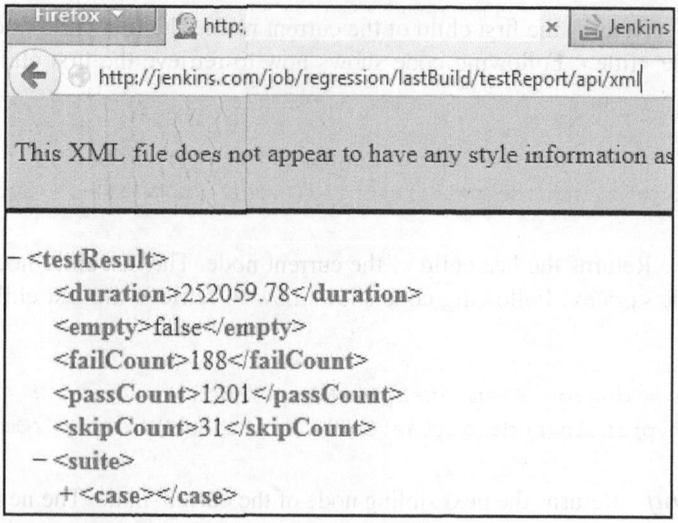

FIGURE 25.1 | Reading XML file dynamically opened in a browser

```
        DocumentBuilder db = dbf.newDocumentBuilder();
        //get XML response
        Document doc = db.parse(new URL(url).openStream());
        //read 'failCount' tag value from XML response
        NodeList nodelist = doc.getElementsByTagName("failCount");
        System.out.println(nodelist.getLength()); //Output::1
        for (int i=0;i<nodelist.getLength();i++){
                System.out.println(nodelist.item(i).getNodeName()
                  + ":" + nodelist.item(i).getTextContent());
        }
        //Output:: failCount:188
}
```

25.5 | EDITING XML FILES

Generally in Web service automation, often we need to change the values of certain node elements of those related to date, amount, etc., before posting the XML. Described as follows are some of the methods to edit an XML value.

setTextContent Sets the value of the current node to the specified value. Following code shows how to change the value of the node `<title lang="en">Harry Potter</title>` to *Harry Potter II*.

```
@Test
public void testEditXMLFile(){
        try{
```

```
String xmlFilepath = getClass().getResource(
  "/com/webdriver/testdata/Books.xml").getFile();
File xmlFile = new File(xmlFilepath);
DocumentBuilderFactory dbFactory = DocumentBuilder
  Factory.newInstance();
DocumentBuilder dBuilder = dbFactory.newDocument
  Builder();
Document doc = dBuilder.parse(xmlFile);
doc.getDocumentElement().normalize();

//edit xml file
Node node = doc.getElementsByTagName("title").item(0);
node.setTextContent("Harry Potter II");
//write the content into xml file (bin directory)
TransformerFactory transformerFactory =
                  TransformerFactory.newInstance();
Transformer transformer = transformerFactory.new
  Transformer();
DOMSource source = new DOMSource(doc);
StreamResult result = new StreamResult(xmlFile);
transformer.transform(source, result);
}catch (Exception e){
          e.printStackTrace();
}
}
```

Note: The code above uses one generalized try…catch statement for the complete part of the code. This has been done so that it is easy to understand the above code. While developing the actual automation code, it needs to be ensured that the try…catch statement is always next to the statement expected to throw an error. This helps easy and quick identification of the line statement that is throwing error and the root cause of it.

setAttribute Sets the value of the given attribute to the specified value. In case the given attribute does not exist, then new attribute is created with the specified value. Following code shows how to change the value of the `'lang'` attribute of the node `<title lang="en">Harry Potter</title>` to *fr*.

```
//change value of attribute lang to fr
Node node = doc.getElementsByTagName("title").item(0);
Element element = (Element) node;
element.setAttribute("lang", "fr");
```

replaceChild Replaces the given child node with `the specified new child node` in the list of children and returns the `old child` node.

removeChild Removes the specified child node from the list of children and returns the removed child node.

25.6 | CREATING XML FILE

WebService automation many times require creating XML file dynamically before posting the XML file to aURL. In this section, we will discuss how a new XML file can be created during run-time.

- **createElement:** Creates an element with the specified tag name.
- **createAttribute:** Creates the specified attribute for the given node.
- **appendChild:** Adds the specified child element to a node.
- **cloneNode:** Returns a duplicate of the given node.
- **createComment:** Creates a Comment node with the specified string value.
- **createCDATASection:** Creates a CDATASection node with the specified string value.

EXAMPLE 25.1 Write a code to create a new xml file with contents as shown below.

```
<?xml version="1.0" encoding="UTF-8" ?>
<Bookstore>
        <Book category="children">
                <title lang="en">Harry Potter</title>
                <author>J K. Rowling</author>
                <year>2005</year>
                <price>29.99</price>
        </Book>
</Bookstore>
```

Following code shows how to create the above XML file. The following code uses one try…catch statement for the complete code. This is just done for ease in understanding code. While developing the actual automation code, try...catch statement needs to be always next to the code statement which is expected to throw exception. Also, instead of throwing generic Exception error, attempt is made to throw more explicit error object such as `ParserConfigurationException, SAXException, IOException,` etc., as applicable.

```
@Test
public void testCreateXMLFile(){
        try{
                DocumentBuilderFactory docFactory =
                            DocumentBuilderFactory.newInstance();
```

```
DocumentBuilder docBuilder = docFactory.newDocument
  Builder();

// root elements
Document doc = docBuilder.newDocument();
Element rootElement = doc.createElement("Bookstore");
doc.appendChild(rootElement);

// book elements
Element book = doc.createElement("Book");
rootElement.appendChild(book);

// set attribute to book element
Attr attr = doc.createAttribute("category");
attr.setValue("children");
book.setAttributeNode(attr);
//Alternatively,
//book.setAttribute("category", "children");

//add title element
Element title = doc.createElement("title");
//set attribute
title.setAttribute("lang", "en");
//add title node
title.appendChild(doc.createTextNode("Harry Potter"));
book.appendChild(title);

//add author element
Element author = doc.createElement("author");
author.appendChild(doc.createTextNode("J. K. Rowling"));
book.appendChild(author);

//add year element
Element year = doc.createElement("year");
year.appendChild(doc.createTextNode("2005"));
book.appendChild(year);

//add price element
Element price = doc.createElement("price");
price.appendChild(doc.createTextNode("29.99"));
book.appendChild(price);

// write the content into xml file
TransformerFactory transformerFactory =
                TransformerFactory.newInstance();
```

```
            Transformer transformer = transformerFactory.new
              Transformer();
            DOMSource source = new DOMSource(doc);
            StreamResult result = new StreamResult(new
                    File("C:\\temp\\xmlfile.xml"));

            //Output to console for testing
            //StreamResult result = new StreamResult(System.out);

            transformer.transform(source, result);
            }catch(Exception e){
                 e.printStackTrace();
            }
    }
```

25.7 | LOCATING XML ELEMENTS USING XPATH QUERY

XPath is XML path language based on a tree representation of the XML document. It is a query language for selecting nodes from XML document. It provides the ability to navigate around the tree by selecting nodes by using a variety of criteria. XPath is very useful in locating dynamic elements of an XML file. A dynamic XML element can be one whose tag name is not fixed and keeps on changing from one run session to another. In such situations, the explicit path (position in xml tree) can be used to locate the element using XPath.

25.7.1 | Developing XPath Expression for XML

XPath for an element in XML file can be developed by developing the node navigation path of the XML DOM. Two nodes in XPath expression are separated by symbol slash '\'. All the axis of the XPath such as child, parent, ancestor, following-sibling, etc., can be used to develop an XPath expression.

Firefox *Firebug* add-on `FirePath` can be used to verify whether the developed XPath expression locates the specified element in XML DOM tree or not. The identified element is highlighted in the `FirePath` window. In order to develop XPath for locating an XML element, following steps is to be followed.

1. Open the XML file in Firefox browser
2. Activate the Firebug *Firepath* tab
3. Write down the XPath expression in *Firepath* `XPath` text box.

Figure 25.2 shows how to locate all the `<title>` elements of the Bookstore XML file.

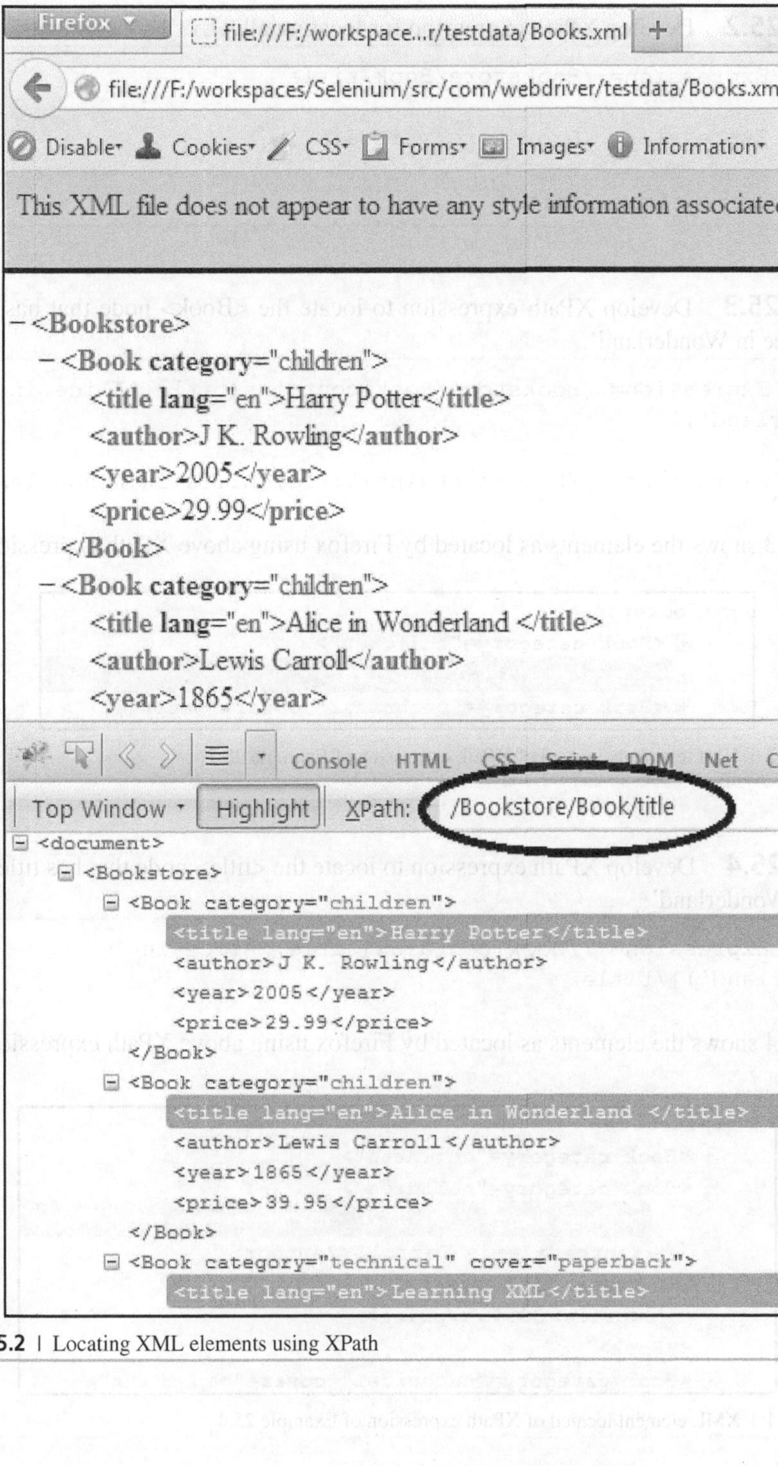

FIGURE 25.2 | Locating XML elements using XPath

EXAMPLE 25.2 Develop XPath expression for locating all `<title>` elements.

```
XPath Expression= /Bookstore/Book/title
Or,
XPath Expression= /Bookstore//title
Or,
XPath Expression= //title
```

EXAMPLE 25.3 Develop XPath expression to locate the <Book> node that has title element 'Alice in Wonderland'.

```
XPath Expression= /Bookstore/Book[contains(title,'Alice in
Wonderland')]
Or,
XPath Expression= //Book[contains(title,'Alice in Wonderland')]
```

Figure 25.3 shows the elements as located by Firefox using above XPath expression.

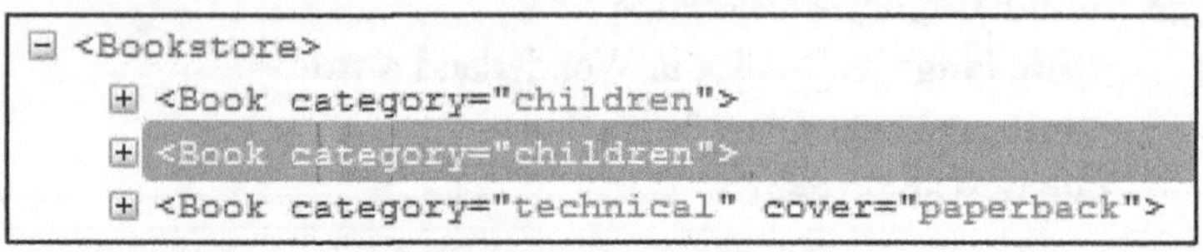

FIGURE 25.3 | XML elements located of XPath expression of Example 25.3

EXAMPLE 25.4 Develop XPath expression to locate the <title> node that has title element 'Alice in Wonderland'.

```
XPath Expression= //Book[contains(title,'Alice in
Wonderland')]/title
```

Figure 25.4 shows the elements as located by Firefox using above XPath expression.

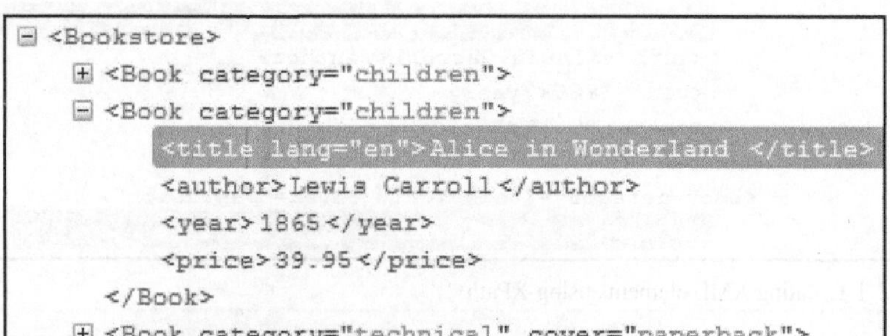

FIGURE 25.4 | XML element located of XPath expression of Example 25.4

EXAMPLE 25.5 Develop XPath expression to locate the <price> node that has title element 'Alice in Wonderland'.

```
XPath Expression= //Book[contains(title,'Alice in Wonderland')]/price
```

EXAMPLE 25.6 Develop XPath expression to locate all <Book> node whose <price> element value ends in .95.

```
XPath Expression= //Book[contains(price,'.95')]
```

Figure 25.5 shows the elements as located by Firefox using above XPath expression.

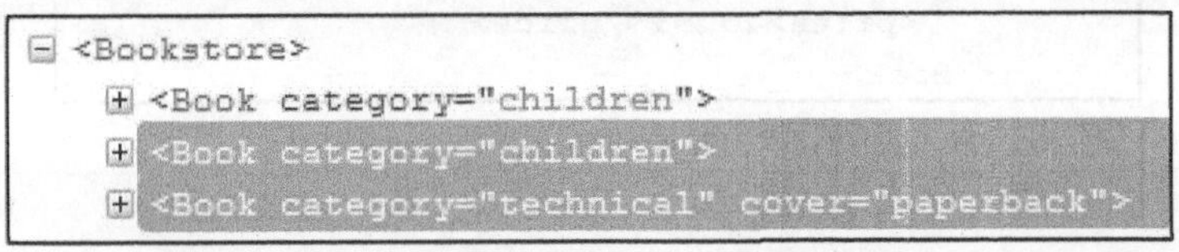

FIGURE 25.5 | XML Elements located of XPath expression of Example 25.6

EXAMPLE 25.7 Find all the books (title) which has been published in year 2005.

```
XPath Expression= //Book[contains(year,'2005')]/title
Or,
XPath Expression= //year[contains(.,'2005')]/parent::Book/title
```

EXAMPLE 25.8 Find all the nodes next to the node <author> for all books whose author is J.K. Rowling.

```
XPath Expression= //Book[contains(author,'Rowling')]/author/
following-sibling::*
```

Figure 25.6 shows the elements as located by Firefox using above XPath expression.

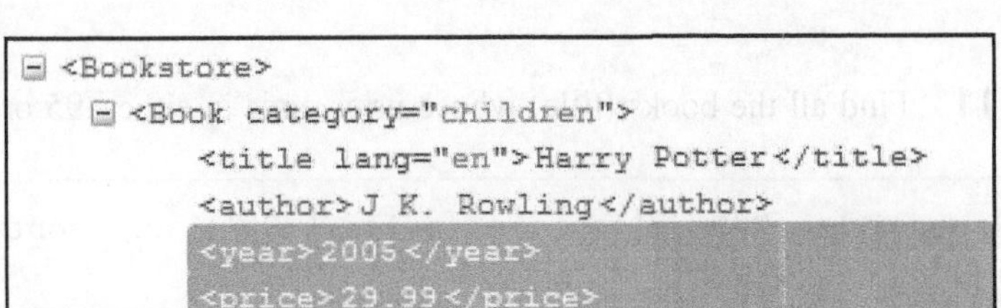

FIGURE 25.6 | XML elements located of XPath expression of Example 25.8

EXAMPLE 25.9 Find the node next to the node <author> for all books whose author is J. K. Rowling.

```
XPath Expression= //Book[contains(author,'Rowling')]/author/
following-sibling::*[1]
```

Figure 25.7 shows the elements as located by Firefox using above XPath expression.

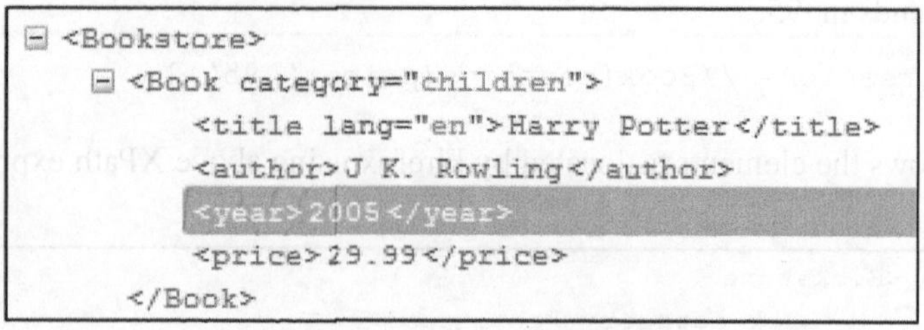

FIGURE 25.7 | XML elements located of XPath expression of Example 25.9

EXAMPLE 25.10 Find all the attributes (child nodes) of book whose author is J. K. Rowling.

```
XPath Expression= //Book[contains(author,'Rowling')]/child::*
```

Figure 25.8 shows the elements as located by Firefox using above XPath expression.

FIGURE 25.8 | XML elements located of XPath expression of Example 25.10

EXAMPLE 25.11 Find all the books (title) whose price ends in either .95 or is published in year 2010.

```
XPath Expression= //Book[contains(price,'.95') or contains(year,
'2010')]/title
```

EXAMPLE 25.12 Find all the books (title) whose price ends in .95 and is published in year 2010

```
XPath Expression= //Book[contains(.,'.95')][contains(.,'2010')]/title
```

EXAMPLE 25.13 Find all Books (<Book> nodes) whose category is 'children.

```
XPath Expression: //Book[@category=children]
```

Figure 25.9 shows the elements as located by Firefox using above XPath expression.

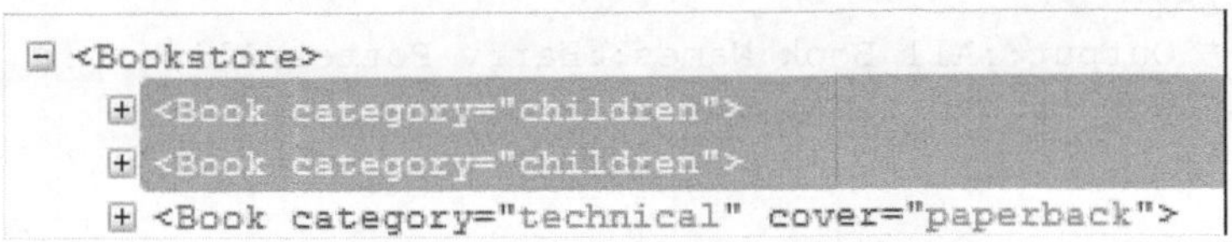

FIGURE 25.9 | XML elements located of XPath expression of Example 25.13

EXAMPLE 25.14 Find all Books (<Book> nodes) whose category is 'technical' and cover is 'paperback'.

```
XPathExpression://Book[@category='technical'][@cover='paperback']
```

25.8 | READING XML FILE USING XPATH QUERY

Java provides methods *compile* and *evaluate* to retrieve XML elements as located by XPath query. Method *compile* compiles an XPath expression for later evaluation. Method *evaluate* evaluates the compiled XPath expression in the specified context and returns the result as the specified type.

Following code shows how to locate XML elements and read XML nodes using XPath Query.

```
@Test
public void readXMLByXPath(){

        String xmlFilepath = getClass().getResource(
                "/com/webdriver/testdata/Books.xml").getFile();
        File xmlFile = new File(xmlFilepath);
        DocumentBuilderFactory docFactory =
                        DocumentBuilderFactory.newInstance();
        docFactory.setNamespaceAware(true);
        DocumentBuilder dBuilder = docFactory.newDocumentBuilder();
        Document doc = dBuilder.parse(xmlFile);
        XPath xpath = XPathFactory.newInstance().newXPath();
```

```
//XPath Query for retrieving all elements with tagname = title
        //Compile XPath expression for later evaluation.
        XPathExpression expr = xpath.compile("//title");
        //Evaluate the compiled XPath expression
        Object result = expr.evaluate(doc, XPathConstants.NODESET);
        NodeList nodes = (NodeList) result;
        System.out.print("All Book Names:");
        for (int i = 0; i < nodes.getLength(); i++) {
              System.out.print(nodes.item(i).getTextContent() + ",");
        }
        System.out.println();
        /**
        * Output::All Book Names::Harry Potter,Alice in
        * Wonderland ,Learning XML,
        */

        //XPath Query to retrieve all <Book> nodes whose price
          ends with.95
        expr = xpath.compile("//Book[contains(price,'.95')]");
        result = expr.evaluate(doc, XPathConstants.NODESET);
        //get total number of books whose price ends in .95
        nodes = (NodeList) result;
        System.out.println("Total# books whose price ends
          with .95=" + nodes.getLength());
        //get the book names
        System.out.print("All books whose price ends with .95:");
        for (int i=0;i<nodes.getLength();i++){
              NodeList bookChildNodes = nodes.item(i).getChildNodes();
              for (int j=0;i<bookChildNodes.getLength();j++){
                      if (bookChildNodes.item(j).getNodeName().
                                              contains("title")){
                            System.out.print(bookChildNodes.
                                        item(j).getTextContent() + ",");
                            break;
                      }
              }
        }
        System.out.println();
        /**Output::
        * Total# books whose price ends with .95=2
        * All books whose price ends with .95:Alice in Wonderland,
        * Learning XML,
        */

        //XPath Query to retrieve all the books (title) whose
        //price ends in .95 and is published in year 2010
        expr = xpath.compile("//Book[contains(.,'.95')]
          [contains(.,'2010')]/title");
```

```
result = expr.evaluate(doc, XPathConstants.NODESET);
//get total number of books whose price ends in .95
nodes = (NodeList) result;
//get the book names
System.out.print("All books whose published year=2010
  and price ends with .95:");
for (int i=0;i<nodes.getLength();i++){
        System.out.println(nodes.item(i).getTextContent()
          + ",");

}
/**
* Output::
* All books whose published year=2010 and price ends
*   with .95:Learning XML,
*/
//XPath Query to retrieve all Books (<Book> nodes) whose
//category is 'technical' and cover is 'paperback'
expr = xpath.compile("/Book[@category='technical'][
  @cover='paperback']/title");
result = expr.evaluate(doc, XPathConstants.NODESET);
//get total number of books whose price ends in .95
nodes = (NodeList) result;
//get the book names
System.out.print("All books whose category=technical
  and cover=paperback:");
for (int i=0;i<nodes.getLength();i++){
        System.out.println(nodes.item(i).getTextContent() + ",");

}
/**
* Output::
* All books whose category=technical and
* cover=paperback:Learning XML,
*/
}
```

INTERVIEW QUESTIONS

1. Which Java API will you use to read an XML file?
2. What is the difference between XML streaming and XML DOM methods of reading XML file?
3. Write code to create a new XML file.
4. Write code to update an existing XML file.
5. Write code to read an XML file from a web URL.
6. Write code to read an XML file using XPath query.

26

CHAPTER

Selenium Server

Selenium Grid is part of the Selenium Suite that allows running of multiple tests across different browsers, operating systems and machines in parallel. That is, executing multiple tests at the same time against different machines running different browsers and operating systems. In short, Selenium Grid allows running tests in distributed test execution environment.

Selenium grid has two versions: Grid 1 and Grid 2. Grid 2 is the latest version. In this chapter, we will focus only on Grid 2 as Grid 1 is being gradually deprecated by Selenium team.

26.1 | WHEN TO USE IT

Selenium Grid reduces Selenium suite execution time by distributing the execution load to different machines. It further speeds up execution by allowing running more than one test parallel in a machine. That is, at a time, more than one test can be executed on a machine. It also supports executing Selenium tests against different browsers and operating systems. That is, it provides central point control for managing test runs against various environments. Following are the reasons why Selenium grid should be used in a Selenium Automation Project:

- To reduce execution time by scheduling test suite to run against multiple machines
- To execute tests against various browsers and browser versions
- To execute test against browsers running on different operating systems

Selenium Grid speeds up test execution by distributing the execution load among various machines. For example, we have a test suite of around 1000 tests which takes around 500 minutes to execute against a single machine. Now assume Selenium Grid is setup to execute the tests against 4 machines (virtual machines or physical machines). Since, now tests are running in parallel against 4 machines the execution time will be reduced by 4 (125 minutes).

Total time taken to execute tests = 500/4 = 125 minutes

Again, Selenium Grid provides the option to run more than one test parallel on a machine. Assuming Selenium Grid is setup to execute 5 tests parallel on a machine, the total time taken to execute the Selenium suite now is

Total time taken to execute tests = (500/5)/4 = 25 minutes

Thus, Selenium Grid reduces execution time from 500 minutes to 25 minutes. This is significant saving in execution time.

Selenium Grid supports running tests against variety of browsers and operating systems. For example, a 'grid' of virtual machines (VMs) can be setup with each supporting a different browser. Assume machine 1 has Internet Explorer, machine 2 has Firefox 10, machine 3 has Chrome and machine 4 has Firefox 12. When Selenium test suite is executed, Selenium Grid executes the test against its required browser by scheduling it for run against specific machine. Also, a grid of same browser versions can also be created like creating a grid of four machines with Firefox 12 installed on each machine.

26.2 | HOW SELENIUM GRID WORKS

Selenium Grid consists of single hub and one or more nodes. Hub is the central point where all tests are loaded into. There should be one hub in a grid. Nodes are the Selenium instances that execute the tests that are loaded on the hub. Nodes can be launched on multiple machines with each machine on a different OS platform and browser.

Hub knows the configuration of each node that has registered to the hub. The hub receives a test to be executed along with information on which browser and platform the test is to be executed. The hub then selects the node that has the specific browser–platform combination. Once the node is selected, the Selenium commands of the test are passed on to the hub which in turn passes it on to the selected node. The node then executes the Selenium commands against the specific browser.

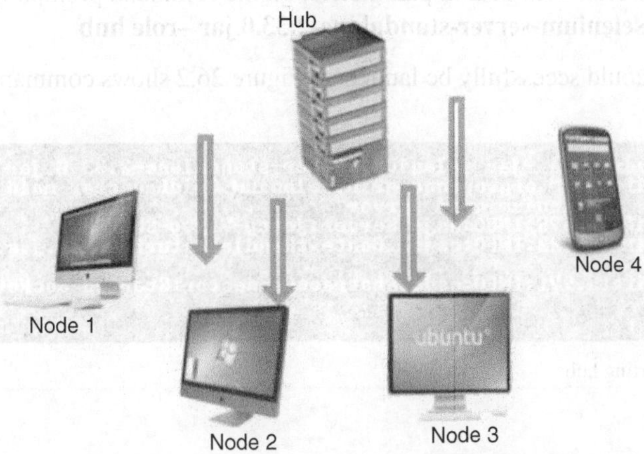

FIGURE 26.1 | Selenium grid

26.2.1 | Installation

Selenium Grid 2 is available as part of Selenium Server suite. Selenium Server can be downloaded from site http://code.google.com/p/selenium/downloads/list. There are two Selenium Server suites at the time of writing this book:

- Selenium-server-2.xx.x.zip
- Selenium-server-standalone-2.xx.x.jar

The former includes all variants of the Selenium Server: Selenium-server-standalone-2.xx.x.jar, jar with dependencies and sources. Selenium server standalone is to be used when the requirement is to use Selenium RC or Remote WebDriver or Grid 2 without needing any additional dependencies.

Let us assume we have two machines Machine A and Machine B. Machine A is used as Hub and Machine B as node. Let us call Machine A as Hub Machine and Machine B as Node Machine. Assume Selenium server standalone jar file is kept at local C:\SeleniumServer on Hub machine and C:\SeleniumNode on Node machine.

Note: For readers who are using this book for self-learning on local machine, it would be difficult for them to create two different hub and node machines. To avoid this problem, readers can use the same machine as both hub and node server. All the setup and configuration steps remain the same.

26.2.2 | Start the Hub

- Open command prompt on Hub machine.
- Navigate to the directory C:\SeleniumServer on command prompt.
- To start the Hub with default parameters, on the command prompt, type **java –jar selenium-server-standalone-2.33.0.jar –role hub**

  The hub should sccessfully be launched. Figure 26.2 shows command prompt output.

```
c:\SeleniumServer>java -jar selenium-server-standalone-2.33.0.jar -role hub
Aug 3, 2013 1:41:12 PM org.openqa.grid.selenium.GridLauncher main
INFO: Launching a selenium grid server
2013-08-03 13:41:15.675:INFO:osjs.Server:jetty-7.x.y-SNAPSHOT
2013-08-03 13:41:15.722:INFO:osjsh.ContextHandler:started o.s.j.s.ServletContext
Handler{/,null}
2013-08-03 13:41:15.971:INFO:osjs.AbstractConnector:Started SocketConnector@0.0.
0.0:4444
```

FIGURE 26.2 | Starting hub

Notes:

1. This will work on all the supported platforms, Windows Linux or Mac.
2. The above command starts Hub on default port 4444. In order to start Hub on a specific port, define an additional parameter –port while running the command.

- In order to verify Hub has successfully started open browser and navigate to: http://localhost:4444/grid/console. Figure 26.3 shows the browser window output.
- Also, we can check if Node machine can access Hub machine's web interface. This can be checked by opening a browser on Node machine and navi-

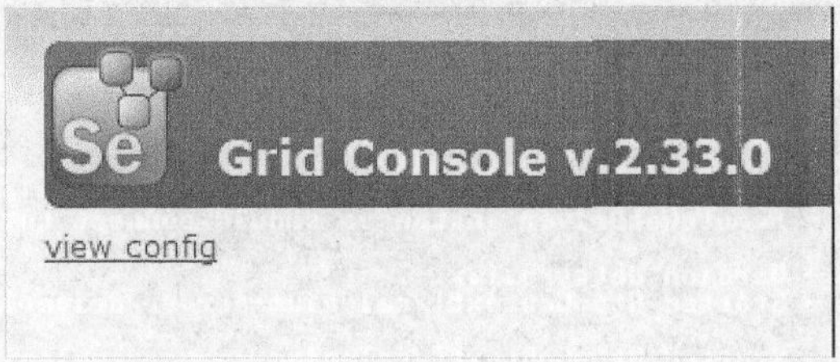

FIGURE 26.3 | Verifying hub has started

gating to URL: http://IPorHostNameOfHubMachine:4444/grid/console where "IPorHostNameOfHubMachine" should be the IP address or Host name of the Hub machine. For example: http://192.168.0.110:4444/grid/console. The output would be same as Figure 26.3.

26.2.3 | Start the Node

- Open command prompt on Node machine and navigate to C:\SeleniumNode drive.
- To start the node type on Command Prompt:

```
java -jar selenium-server-standalone-2.33.0.jar -role
node -hub http://192.168.0.110:4444/grid/register
```

Or, use below command specifically for WebDriver hub

```
java -jar selenium-server-standalone-2.33.0.jar -role
node -webdriver http://192.168.0.110:4444/grid/register
```

Note: The port defaults to 5555 if not specified whenever the "-role" option is not hub. In order to start node on specific port say 5566, type:

```
java -jar selenium-server-standalone-2.33.0.jar -role
node -hub http://192.168.0.110:4444/grid/register -port
5566
```

Note: Settings such as browser type for test execution and number of browser instances for parallel test execution can also be defined for a node as shown below:

```
java -jar selenium-server-standalone-2.33.0.jar -role
node -hub
http://192.168.0.110:4444/grid/register
-browser browserName=firefox,maxInstances=3
```

Figure 26.4 shows the Command Prompt output of the above command with default port 5555.

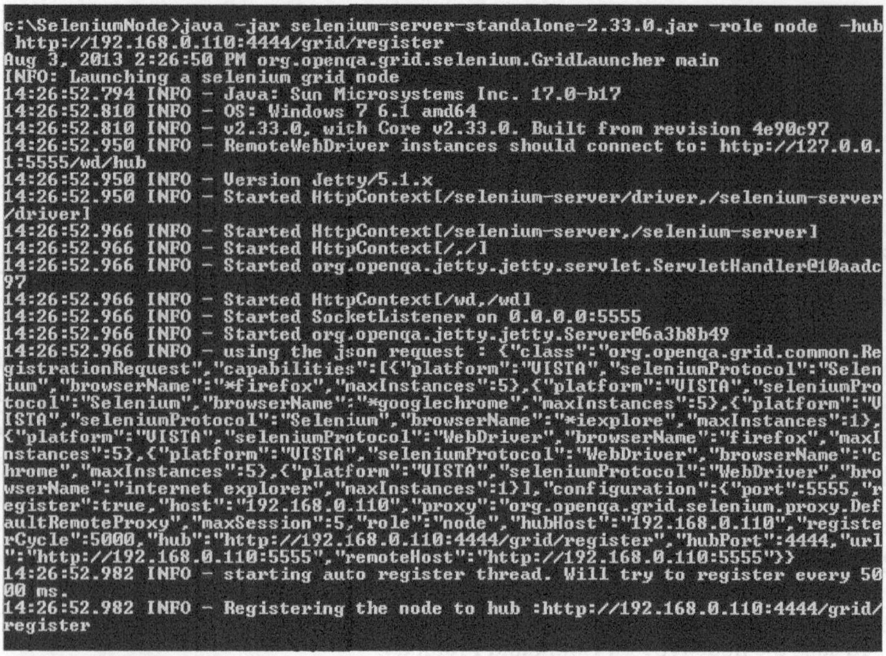

```
c:\SeleniumNode>java -jar selenium-server-standalone-2.33.0.jar -role node  -hub
 http://192.168.0.110:4444/grid/register
Aug 3, 2013 2:26:50 PM org.openqa.grid.selenium.GridLauncher main
INFO: Launching a selenium grid node
14:26:52.794 INFO - Java: Sun Microsystems Inc. 17.0-b17
14:26:52.810 INFO - OS: Windows 7 6.1 amd64
14:26:52.810 INFO - v2.33.0, with Core v2.33.0. Built from revision 4e90c97
14:26:52.950 INFO - RemoteWebDriver instances should connect to: http://127.0.0.
1:5555/wd/hub
14:26:52.950 INFO - Version Jetty/5.1.x
14:26:52.950 INFO - Started HttpContext[/selenium-server/driver,/selenium-server
/driver]
14:26:52.966 INFO - Started HttpContext[/selenium-server,/selenium-server]
14:26:52.966 INFO - Started HttpContext[/,/]
14:26:52.966 INFO - Started org.openqa.jetty.jetty.servlet.ServletHandler@10aadc
97
14:26:52.966 INFO - Started HttpContext[/wd,/wd]
14:26:52.966 INFO - Started SocketListener on 0.0.0.0:5555
14:26:52.966 INFO - Started org.openqa.jetty.jetty.Server@6a3b8b49
14:26:52.966 INFO - using the json request : {"class":"org.openqa.grid.common.Re
gistrationRequest","capabilities":[{"platform":"VISTA","seleniumProtocol":"Selen
ium","browserName":"*firefox","maxInstances":5},{"platform":"VISTA","seleniumPro
tocol":"Selenium","browserName":"*googlechrome","maxInstances":5},{"platform":"V
ISTA","seleniumProtocol":"Selenium","browserName":"*iexplore","maxInstances":1},
{"platform":"VISTA","seleniumProtocol":"WebDriver","browserName":"firefox","maxI
nstances":5},{"platform":"VISTA","seleniumProtocol":"WebDriver","browserName":"c
hrome","maxInstances":5},{"platform":"VISTA","seleniumProtocol":"WebDriver","bro
wserName":"internet explorer","maxInstances":1}],"configuration":{"port":5555,"r
egister":true,"host":"192.168.0.110","proxy":"org.openqa.grid.selenium.proxy.Def
aultRemoteProxy","maxSession":5,"role":"node","hubHost":"192.168.0.110","registe
rCycle":5000,"hub":"http://192.168.0.110:4444/grid/register","hubPort":4444,"url
":"http://192.168.0.110:5555","remoteHost":"http://192.168.0.110:5555"}}
14:26:52.982 INFO - starting auto register thread. Will try to register every 50
00 ms.
14:26:52.982 INFO - Registering the node to hub :http://192.168.0.110:4444/grid/
register
```

FIGURE 26.4 | Starting node

- In order to verify Node has been successfully started, refresh the browser already opened in previous steps on node machine (http://192.168.0.110:4444/grid/console). The browser window should look like as shown in Figure 26.5.

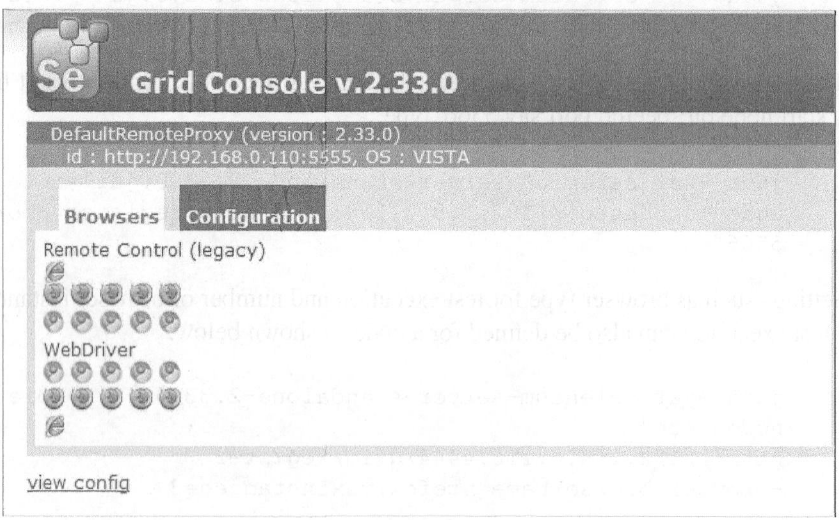

FIGURE 26.5 | Verifying if node has started

Note: Command "netstat –a" can be used to see the ports used by all running programs on the machine.

26.2.4 | Designing Tests That Can Run on Grid

In order to design tests that can run on the Grid, we need to use DesiredCapabilities and RemoteWebDriver objects. DesiredCapabilities defines browser version and OS against which test is to be executed. **RemoteWebDriver** defines the node (machine) where test is to be executed.

Following code defines the test execution browser as Firefox and OS as Windows.

```
DesiredCapabilities capability = DesiredCapabilities.
  firefox();
capability.setBrowserName("firefox");
capability.setPlatform(Platform.WINDOWS);
```

Following code defines the node machine where test execution should happen.

```
WebDriver driver = new RemoteWebDriver(new
  URL("http://192.168.0.110:5555/wd/hub"),capability);
```

Following is a simple WebDriver JUnit code that can be created in Eclipse on any Eclipse machine. Once this test is run from Hub machine, execution is performed on Node machine.

```
import java.net.MalformedURLException;
import java.net.URL;

import org.junit.After;
import org.junit.Before;
import org.junit.Test;
import org.openqa.selenium.By;
import org.openqa.selenium.Platform;
import org.openqa.selenium.WebDriver;
import org.openqa.selenium.remote.DesiredCapabilities;
import org.openqa.selenium.remote.RemoteWebDriver;

public class SeleniumGrid {
        WebDriver driver=null;
        @Before
        public void setUp(){
                String nodeMachineURL =
                  "http://192.168.0.110:5555/wd/hub";
```

```
                DesiredCapabilities capability = DesiredCapabilities.
                  firefox();
                capability.setBrowserName("firefox");
                capability.setPlatform(Platform.WINDOWS);
                try {
                        driver = new RemoteWebDriver(new
                          URL(nodeMachineURL),capability);
                } catch (MalformedURLException e) {
                        e.printStackTrace();
                }
        }
        @Test
        public void testGrid() {
                //Open google search site and search for
                  'Selenium Grid'
                driver.get("https://www.google.com");
                driver.findElement(By.name("q")).
                 sendKeys("Selenium Grid");
                driver.findElement(By.id("gbqfb")).click();
        }
        @After
        public void tearDown(){
                driver.quit();
        }
}
```

Note: In order to schedule the run against server and let server decide the node to use for execution, the RemoteWebDriver object instance is to be initiated for Server URL as shown below.

```
driver = new RemoteWebDriver(new URL(serverMachineURL),capability);
```

26.3 | HOW TO FIND THE BROWSER AND OS VERSIONS SUPPORTED BY VARIOUS NODES

Selenium Grid provides the option to schedule test executions against specific browser and OS versions. If there are no nodes with the specific configuration and the specific tests will not get executed. Thus, before scheduling the run, we would like to check if the node machines are upgraded to support these executions. One way of verifying is to log-in to all machines and check the same. An easy option to check the same is by looking into Selenium Grid's web interface. Launch URL: http://192.168.0.110:4444/grid/console on the node machine. A web interface similar to Figure 26.6will show up.

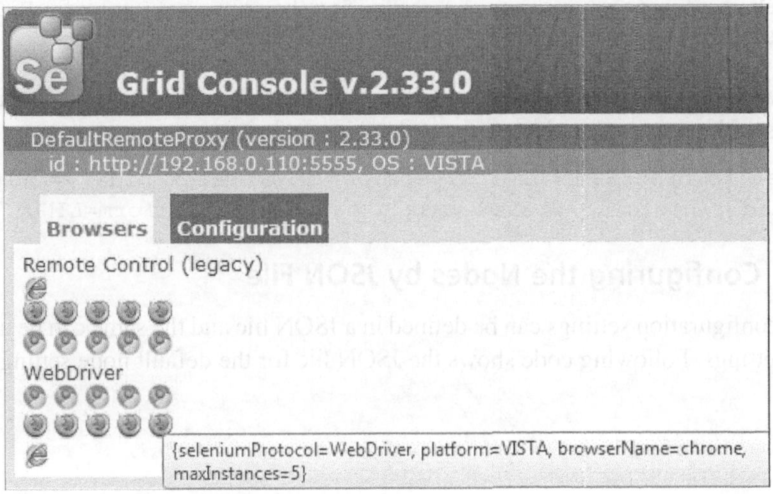

FIGURE 26.6 | Selenium Grid Console

As Figure 26.6 suggests the Node machine supports execution against three browser types: Firefox, Chrome and IE. Also, it supports executing 5 instances of Chrome or Firefox at one time while 1 instance of IE. The OS platform is VISTA.

26.3.1 | Configuring the Nodes

Nodes can be configured in two ways. One by specifying parameters in command line parameters and the other by specifying a JSON file.

26.3.2 | Configuring the Nodes by Command Line

As shown in Figure 26.2, the default configuration of node starts 11 browsers: 5 Firefox, 5 Chrome and 1 Internet Explorer. The maximum number of concurrent tests is set to 5. To change these settings and other settings as well, we can pass in parameters to each browser switch. Each switch represents a node based on the parameters passed. If –browser parameter is used then the default browser will be ignored and only the command line specified browser would be used. For example, the following command sets browser to be Firefox 19 and platform as Windows.

```
-browser browserName=firefox,version=19.0,maxInstances=5,
 platform=WINDOWS
```

If the node machine has multiple versions of Firefox installed, then we can map the location of each binary to a particular version on the same machine:

```
-browser browserName=firefox,version=18.0,firefox_binary=c:\Program
Files\firefox18\firefox,maxInstances=3,platform=WINDOWS -browser
```

```
browserName=firefox,version=19.0,firefox_binary c:\Program Files\
firefox19\firefox,maxInstances=4,platform=WINDOWS
```

Note: If we need to provide a space somewhere in browser parameters, then surround the parameters with quotation marks:

```
-browser "browserName=firefox,version=19.0,firefox_binary=/home/
  myhomedir/firefox18/firefox ,maxInstances=3, platform=LINUX"
```

26.3.3 | Configuring the Nodes by JSON File

The node configuration settings can be defined in a JSON file and the same can be used to set the node settings. Following code shows the JSON file for the default node settings.

```
{
    "capabilities":
        [
            {
                "browserName": "*firefox",
                "maxInstances": 5,
                "seleniumPrococol": "Selenium"
            },
            {
                "browserName": "*googlechrome",
                "maxInstances": 5,
                "seleniumProtocol": "Selenium"
            },
            {
                "browserName": "*iexplore",
                "maxInstances": 1,
                "seleniumProtocol": "Selenium"
            },
            {
                "browserName": "firefox",
                "maxInstances": 5,
                "seleniumProtocol": "WebDriver"
            },
            {
                "browserName": "chrome",
                "maxInstances": 5,
                "seleniumProtocol": "WebDriver"
            },
            {
                "broserName": "internet explorer",
                "maxInstances": 1,
                "seleniumProtocol": "WebDriver"
            }
        ],
```

```
    "configuration":
    {
       "proxy": "org.openqa.grid.selenium.proxy.DefaultRemoteProxy",
       "maxSession": 5,
       "port": 5555,
       "host": ip,
       "register": true,
       "registerCycle": 5000,
       "hubPort": 4444,
       "hubHost": ip
    }
 }
```

Assume file name is nodeConfig.json. Then command line command to set Node settings using JSON file is:

```
java -jar selenium-server-standalone.jar -role node -nodeConfig
nodeConfig.json
```

26.3.4 | Configuring the Hub by JSON File

The hub configuration settings can be defined in a JSON file and the same can be used to set the node settings. Following code shows the JSON file for the default hub settings.

```
{
  "host": null,
  "port": 4444,
  "newSessionWaitTimeout": -1,
  "servlets": [],
  "prioritizer": null,
  "capabilityMatcher": "org.openqa.grid.internal.utils.
     DefaultCapabilityMatcher",
  "throwonCapabilityNotPresent": true,
  "nodePolling": 5000,

  "cleanUpCycle": 5000,
  "timeout": 300000,
  "browserTimeout": 0,
  "maxSession": 5
}
```

Assume file name is hubConfig.json. Then command line command to set Node settings using JSON file is:

```
java -jar selenium-server-standalone.jar -role hub -hubConfig
hubConfig.json
```

26.3.5 | Configuring Optional Parameters for Node

-port

This parameter specifies port of the Node. Default port for node is 4444.

-timeout

This parameter specifies the time in seconds before the hub automatically releases a node that has not received any requests for time greater than timeout time. Default timeout time is 30 sec. After this time, the node is released for another test in the queue. This helps to clear client crashes without manual intervention. To remove the timeout, specify timeout 0 and the hub will never release the node.

Note: This is not the WebDriver timeout for "wait for WebElement" type of commands.

-maxSession

This parameter specifies the maximum number of browsers that can run in parallel on the node. Default is 5. This is different from the maxInstance of supported browsers.

For example, for a machine with Firefox 18.0, Firefox 19.0 and IE8 browsers and maxSession=1 will only run one browser session at a time, either IE or Firefox. If maxSession=2, then two Firefox sessions (tests) can be run at the same time or one Firefox and one IE session (tests) can be run at the same time.

-browser <params>

This parameter specifies the browser run settings. Default is a node will start with 5 Firefox, 5 Chrome and 1 IE instance on windows OS. This parameter is to be set multiple times to define multiple types of browsers.
Allowed parameters for -browser are:

```
-browser: browserName={android, chrome, firefox, htmlunit,
internet explorer, iphone, opera} version={browser version}
firefox_binary={path to executable binary} chrome_binary={path to
executable binary} maxInstances={maximum number of browsers of
this type} platform={WINDOWS, LINUX, MAC}
```

-registerCycle

This parameter specifies how often (in milliseconds) the node will try to register itself again each hub. This parameter gives the flexibility to restart the hub without requiring to restart the node.

26.3.6 | Parallel Test Execution for Maven Project

Both TestNG and JUnit provide the feature to execute tests in parallel. In this section, we will discuss how to execute tests in parallel for a Maven project. The first step would be to configure the maven project. Maven project configuration involves configuring pom.xml file.

Configuring POM.xml File

The first step in configuring pom.xml file is to the maven surefire plugin. Below mentioned code shows a sample configuration of pom.xml file.

```
<build>
..................
    <plugins>
    ..................
        <plugin>
                <groupId>org.apache.maven.plugins</groupId>
        <artifactId>maven-compiler-plugin</artifactId>
                <version>3.1</version>
        <configuration>
                <source>1.7</source>
                <target>1.7</target>
        </configuration>
        </plugin>
        <plugin>
                <groupId>org.apache.maven.plugins</groupId>
                <artifactId>maven-surefire-plugin</artifactId>
                <version>2.5</version>
                <configuration>
                        <parallel>methods</parallel>
                        <threadCount>4</threadCount>
                        <perCoreThreadCount>true</perCoreThreadCount>
                        <suiteXmlFiles>
                        <suiteXmlFile>src/test/resources/testng.
                            xml</suiteXmlFile>
                </suiteXmlFiles>
                </configuration>
        </plugin>
    </plugins>
</build>
```

Notes: 1. The latest version of the plugins can be found out from maven site.

2. For complete pom.xml file for TestNG and JUnit, refer to Chapter 3.

The significance of various `<configuration>` parameters for maven-surefire-plugin is discussed below.

`<parallel>` attribute defines parallel test execution attributes. For TestNG, it can take any of the three values: *methods*, *classes* or *both*. If value is *methods*, then it implies that all tests (methods) of various classes will be executed in parallel. If value is *classes*, then it implies that all test classes will be executed in parallel. In this case, two methods of the same classes cannot be executed in parallel. For JUnit, the acceptable values are—*suites*, *suitesAndClasses*, *suitesAndMethods*, *classesAndMethods* or *all*.

`<threadCount>` attribute defines number of threads (methods) to be allocated for test execution. For the above configuration, four tests (methods) will be executed in parallel on a machine at a time.

`<perCoreThreadCount>` attribute defines thread count per CPU core. (Only for JUnit 4.7 onwards)

`<suiteXmlFile>` attribute defines the location of test suite. (Only for TestNG)

Notes: 1. The complete list of maven-surefire-plugin parameters along with its description can be found at site: http://maven.apache.org/surefire/maven-surefire-plugin/test-mojo.html.

2. For parallel test execution using *parallel* attribute, the concurrency happens within the same JVM process. Though this efficiently utilizes memory and execution time, it is more vulnerable towards race conditions or other unexpected and hard to reproduce behaviours. Another option of parallel test execution is to set the parameter `<forkCount>` to a value higher than 1. Following section describes the same.

Forked Test Execution

`<forkCount>` parameter defines the maximum number of JVM processes that Surefire will spawn concurrently to execute the tests. If the value is terminated with 'C', then that value will be multiplied with the number of CPU cores available in the system. For example, forkCount=2.5C on a Quad-Core system will result in forking up to 10 concurrent JVM processes that execute tests.

Parameter `<reuseForks>` can be used along with parameter `<forkCount>` to define whether to terminate the spawned process after one test class and to create a new process for the next test in line or not.

Default setting is `forkCount=1/reuseForks=true`, which implies Surefire creates one new JVM process to execute all tests in one maven module.

Setting `forkCount=1/reuseForks=true` implies east test class is executed in its own JVM process, one after another. Though this option offers highest level of separation, it greatly increases the execution time. Therefore, this option should only be used as a last resort.

Combining Parameters: ForkCount and Parallel

Fork count modes `forkCount=0` and `forkCount=1/reuseForks=true` can be combined freely with the available settings for parameter `parallel`. As `reuseForks=false` creates a new JVM process for each test class, using parameter `parallel=classes` would have no effect.

For parameter option, `reuseForks=true` and `forkCount,` value greater than one test classes are handed over to the forked process one-by-one. In this case, option `parallel=classes` would have no effect. However, option `parallel=methods` would execute classes in `forkcount` concurrent processes. In this case, each of the processes can then use `threadCount` threads to execute the methods of one class in parallel.

26.3.7 | TestNG Test Suite Creation and Execution

`TestNG` provides the feature to create TestNG test suites and execute them in serially or in parallel. There are two ways of executing TestNG test suites—one by configuring TestNG dependency in pom.xml file and other by defining test suite XML. In this section, we will discuss the configuration settings required for the automation project to support parallel execution of TestNG test suite as well as the framework setup that supports parallel execution of TestNG tests.

Configuring TestNG Dependency in `POM.xml`

In order to configure project to support TestNG, include the following dependency in the pom.xml file.

```
<dependency>
<groupId>org.testng</groupId>
<artifactId>testng</artifactId>
<version>6.8.5</version>
<scope>test</scope>
</dependency>
```

Notes: 1. The complete pom.xml file is discussed in detail in Chapter 3.

2. Users are required to create tests in test source directory (eg, `src/test/java`). The tests are to be named using defaults such as *Test.java so that tests can be run by Surefire as TestNG tests. '*' here can be any valid test name (without spaces and special characters). In order to use a different naming scheme, parameter *includes* needs to be defined.

Suite XML Files

TestNG provides an alternative way of executing TestNG test suite by creating a test suite XML files. In this method, two XML files are created—one defines the test suite attributes while the other XML file defines the tests that makes up the test suite. However, pom.xml needs to be configured first to support XML test suites.

Configuring pom.xml File

The first step would be to configure the pom.xml file to support TestNG test suites. The following XML code shows a sample configuration of Surefire plugin.

```
<plugins>
    [...]
      <plugin>
        <groupId>org.apache.maven.plugins</groupId>
        <artifactId>maven-surefire-plugin</artifactId>
        <version>2.5</version>
```

```
        <configuration>
           <suiteXmlFiles>
              <suiteXmlFile> src/test/resources/testng.xml</
                 suiteXmlFile>
           </suiteXmlFiles>
        </configuration>
     </plugin>
   [...]
 </plugins>
```

Note: This configuration overrides the includes and excludes patterns and runs all tests in the suite files.

Specifying Test Parameters

TestNG allows developing tests that accept parameters with the @Parameter annotation. Maven allows passing these parameters to TestNG tests from pom file itself. These parameters are specified as system properties in pom.xml file as follows.

```
 <plugins>
   [...]
     <plugin>
        <groupId>org.apache.maven.plugins</groupId>
        <artifactId>maven-surefire-plugin</artifactId>
        <version>2.5</version>
        <configuration>
           <systemPropertyVariables>
              <propertyName>firefox</propertyName>
           </systemPropertyVariables>
        </configuration>
     </plugin>
   [...]
 </plugins>
```

The aforementioned xml file browser type is one of the system properties. TestNG tests can use this parameter to decide against which browser type respective test is to be executed.

Specifying Test Groups

TestNG allows to group the tests in various categories say functional tests, regression tests, security tests, performance tests, etc. Users are to use *group* parameter of maven-surefire-plugin to achieve this with Surefire. For example,

```
 <plugins>
   [...]
     <plugin>
```

```
        <groupId>org.apache.maven.plugins</groupId>
        <artifactId>maven-surefire-plugin</artifactId>
        <version>2.5</version>
        <configuration>
          <groups>functest,regtest,sectest,perftest</groups>
        </configuration>
      </plugin>
    [...]
</plugins>
```

Likewise parameter `<excludedGroups>` to be used to run all but a certain set of groups.

Running Tests in Parallel

TestNG allows to run both TestNG as well as JUnit tests in parallel. To achieve this, maven-surefire-plugin parameters *parallel* and *threadCount* needs to be set as follows:

```
</plugins>
    [...]
      <plugin>
        <groupId>org.apache.maven.plugins</groupId>
        <artifactId>maven-surefire-plugin</artifactId>
        <version>2.5</version>
        <configuration>
          <parallel>methods</parallel>
          <threadCount>10</threadCount>
        </configuration>
      </plugin>
    [...]
</plugins>
```

Note: Refer to section 'Parallel Test Execution for Maven Project' for detailed description of these parameters.

Step by Step Guide for Creating and Executing TestNG Test Suite

In this section, we will discuss how to create a TestNG so that test suite and execute it in parallel. The first step would be to create TestNG tests as per the framework that supports parallel test execution. Next step would to create test suite XML files. Here two XML files are created. One is testng.xml file which defines test suite attributes. Next is the test suite XML file which defines which tests make up the test suite.

Notes: 1. Hub and node server needs to be started before TestNG so that test suite can be executed in parallel on node machine.

2. For readers who are using this book for self-learning on local machine, it would be difficult for them to create two different hub and node machines. To avoid this problem, readers can use the same machine as both hub and node server. All the setup and configuration steps would remain the same.

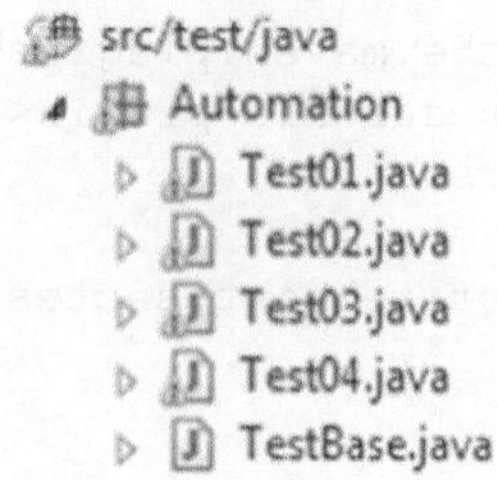

FIGURE 26.7 | TestNG Test Suite Code

26.3.8 | Developing TestNG Test Suite

Let us assume a Java project or Maven project is already created (refer Chapter 3). First step towards test development would be to create a base class for tests. This class is to be used for defining basic components for all tests such as browser profile, driver initialization, etc. Assume name of this class is *TestBase* and it is inside package *Automation* as shown in the following figure.

Developing Base Class

Following code shows a sample *TestBase* class. This class creates:

- a new RemoteWebDriver.
- defines `setup()` method and annotates it as @BeforeMethod. This method will always be executed before initiating any test execution.
- defines `teardown()` method and annotates it as @AfterMethod. This method will always be executed before exiting any test execution.
- `getDriver()` method. This driver instance will be used for test execution.

```
package Automation;

import java.net.MalformedURLException;
import java.net.URL;

import org.openqa.selenium.WebDriver;
import org.openqa.selenium.firefox.FirefoxDriver;
import org.openqa.selenium.firefox.FirefoxProfile;
import org.openqa.selenium.remote.DesiredCapabilities;
import org.openqa.selenium.remote.RemoteWebDriver;
import org.testng.annotations.AfterMethod;
import org.testng.annotations.BeforeMethod;

public class TestBase {

protected ThreadLocal<RemoteWebDriver> threadDriver = null;
```

```
@BeforeMethod
public void setUp(){
        String nodeMachine = "http://192.168.1.110:5555/wd/hub";
        //else, to execute on server machine
        //serverMachine = "http://localhost:4444/wd/hub";
threadDriver = new ThreadLocal<RemoteWebDriver>();
DesiredCapabilities dc = new DesiredCapabilities();
FirefoxProfile fp = new FirefoxProfile();
dc.setCapability(FirefoxDriver.PROFILE, fp);
dc.setBrowserName(DesiredCapabilities.firefox().getBrowserName());
try {
               threadDriver.set(new RemoteWebDriver(new
                 URL(nodeMachine), dc));
               //threadDriver.set(new RemoteWebDriver(new
                 URL(serverMachine), dc));
               } catch (MalformedURLException e) {
               e.printStackTrace();
        }
    }

public WebDriver getDriver() {
return threadDriver.get();
    }

@AfterMethod
public void closeBrowser() {
getDriver().quit();

    }
}
```

Developing Test Class

Now, let us create test classes. Following code shows test code for four test classes. *Thread.* `sleep()` has been used in all classes to help readers visualize parallel test execution while executing the suite.

```
package Automation;
import org.testng.annotations.Test;

public class Test01 extends TestBase{
    @Test
    //if test groups are defined in pom.xml, then
    //test groups can be annotated to a test method as:
  // @Test(groups = { "functest", "perftest" })
public void testFacebookLink()throws Exception{
        getDriver().get("http://facebook.com");
```

```
        Thread.sleep(20000);
    }
}
package Automation;

import org.testng.annotations.Test;

public class Test02 extends TestBase{
    @Test
    public void testTwitterLink()throws Exception{
        getDriver().get("http://twitter.com");
        Thread.sleep(20000);
    }
}

package Automation;

import org.testng.annotations.Test;

public class Test02 extends TestBase{
    @Test
    public void testGoogleLink()throws Exception{
        getDriver().get("http://www.google.com");
        Thread.sleep(20000);
    }
}

package Automation;

import org.testng.annotations.Test;

public class Test02 extends TestBase{
    @Test
    public void testAmazonLink()throws Exception{
        getDriver().get("http://www.amazon.com");
        Thread.sleep(20000);
    }
}
```

26.3.9 | Creating Suite XML Files

Now next step is to create XML files that define test suite attributes (testing.xml) and tests that make up the test suite. Let us assume this file is created at path *src/test/resources/testng.xml*.

Following is the XML code for testng.xml.

```
<suite name="Test Suite 1">
      <suite-files>
              <suite-file path="src/test/resources/
                  testsuite1tests.xml" />
      </suite-files>
</suite>
```

Notes: 1. Logical path can also be used for suite-file path as:

```
<suite-file path="./resources/testsuite1tests.xml" />
Or,
<suite-file path="//resources/testsuite1tests.xml" />
```

2. For maven project, *<suite-file path>* path is to be the same as *<suiteXml-File>* mentioned in the pom.xml file.

Next step is to create the XML file that defines the tests that makes up the test suite as well as defines the test execution attributes. Let us assume the file name to be 'testSuite1tests.xml' and its path is *src/test/resources/TestSuite1Tests.xml*

```
<!DOCTYPE suite SYSTEM "http://testng.org/testng-1.0.dtd">
<suite name="Test Suite 1 Tests" parallel="tests" thread-
count="3">

<test name="T_01">
    <classes>
        <class name="Automation.Test01" ></class>
    </classes>
</test>
<test name="T_02">
    <classes>
        <class name="Automation.Test02" ></class>
    </classes>
</test>
<test name="T_03">
    <classes>
        <class name="Automation.Test03" ></class>
    </classes>
</test>
<test name="T_04">
    <classes>
        <class name="Automation.Test04" ></class>
    </classes>
</test>
</suite>
```

Where *Automation* is the name of the package, tests reside as shown in Figure 26.1. *threadCount* defines the number of tests that would be executed in parallel. Since, here we have defined three, out of the four available tests in the test suite; only three tests will be executed at a time. The fourth test will be triggered when execution of one of the test is complete.

Note: In case of multiple test suites, multiple *testng* files can be created as testng1.xml, testng2.xml and so on. Multiple test suite xml can also be created in the same way as testsuite1tests.xml, testsuite2tests.xml and so on.

Triggering Parallel Execution of Tests of Test Suite XML from Eclipse

In order to trigger parallel execution of the test suite tests from Eclipse, right click on the file *testing.xml* → Select *Run As* → Select *TestNG Suite.*

Note: Hub and node server needs to be started before TestNG test suite can be executed in parallel on node machine.

Triggering Parallel Execution of Tests of Test Suite XML from Command Prompt

TestNG offers the flexibility to execute the test suite from command line. Assuming that the class path of TestNG is set, the simplest way to invoke TestNG tests execution is as follows:

```
java org.testng.TestNG testng1.xml [testng2.xml
  testng3.xml ...]
```

```
The complete list of parameters that can be passed from
command prompt for executing TestNG tests can be found
at site - http://testng.org/doc/documentation-main.
html#parameters-testng-xml
```

Note: For a maven project, it is advisable to use maven commands to execute TestNG tests. Maven offers wide range of options to execute tests such as executing a single test, a single class, specific groups (as defined in test annotation), all tests, all tests with specific name pattern, etc.

Triggering Parallel Execution of Tests of Maven Project from Command Prompt

POM.xml file needs to be configured first to enable parallel test execution of maven projects TestNG or JUnit tests. Section 'Configuring POM.xml File' explains in detail the configuration settings to execute tests in parallel.

The configuration settings of pom.xml file may or may not define a TestNG test suite xml. Steps below shows how to execute the xml test suite using maven command:

a. Open command prompt and go to the maven project directory that has pom.xml file

```
cd E:\WebDriverProject\amazonretail
```

b. Type

```
mvn  test  -U  -Pselenium-tests
```

Aforesaid command executed the xml file mentioned for parameter <suiteXmlFiles>:

```
<suiteXmlFiles>
     <suiteXmlFile>src/test/resources/testng.xml</
       suiteXmlFile>
</suiteXmlFiles>
```

In the absence of test suite xml file parameter in pom.xml file, maven command line features to be used to execute specific group of tests. This is a preferred method of test execution as it prevents the need to create test suite xml files. In situations, where tests are huge in number say >1000 and tests are getting added/removed from the test suite continuously, it becomes very difficult and time consuming to keep the test suite xml file updated. To resolve this problem, it is advisable to use maven command line features which automatically and dynamically creates a test suite and executes it.

EXAMPLE 26.1 Write maven command to execute test testFacebookLink of class Test01.

Maven command to execute a specific test method is as follows:

```
mvn -Dtest=Test01#testFacebookLink test
```

EXAMPLE 26.2 Write maven command to execute all tests of class Test01.

```
mvn -Dtest=Test01 test
```

EXAMPLE 26.3 Write maven command to execute all tests of classes Test01, Test02 and Test03.

```
mvn -Dtest=Test01,Test02,Test03 test
```

EXAMPLE 26.4 Write maven command to execute all classes whose name starts with text 'Test'.

```
mvn -Dtest=Test* test
```

EXAMPLE 26.5 Write maven command to execute all tests whose name begins with text 'test' for class Test01.

```
mvn -Dtest=Test01#test* test
```

EXAMPLE 26.6 Write maven command to execute tests that below to group 'functest'

```
mvn -Dgroups=functest test
```

Notes: 1. Use command *mvn clean* to prepare for a clean build.
2. Use command *mvn install* to compile, build and run tests.
3. Use command *mvn test-compile* to compile a build.
4. Use command *mvn—version* to find installed maven version.
5. Refer to the site http://maven.apache.org/maven-1.x/reference/command-line.html for the complete list of command line options.

26.3.10 | JUnit Test Suite Creation and Execution

JUnit tests can be executed from command prompt using maven-surefire-plugin. Maven commands can be used to dynamically and automatically create test suites and execute them. Maven commands as shown earlier can be used to execute JUnit tests.

Parallel Execution of JUnit Tests

JUnit 4.7 and above supports parallel execution of tests. Maven-surefire-plugin can be used to execute JUnit tests in parallel. POM file is to be configured the same way as it has been discussed in previous 'Configuring pom.xml File' sections. However, while defining the dependency instead of TestNG, JUnit dependency needs to be defined in the pom.xml file as shown as follows:

```
<dependency>
    <groupId>junit</groupId>
    <artifactId>junit</artifactId>
    <version>4.8.1</version>
    <scope>test</scope>
</dependency>
```

Section *Configuring pom.xml file* for topic 'Parallel Test Execution for Maven Project' explains a generic pom.xml file for a maven project which has both TestNG and JUnit framework installed. If the maven project has only JUnit framework installed then following *<plugin>* configuration for pom.xml file is to be used.

```
<build>
.................
        <plugins>
        ......................
          <plugin>
                <groupId>org.apache.maven.plugins</groupId>
          <artifactId>maven-compiler-plugin</artifactId>
                <version>3.1</version>
          <configuration>
                <source>1.7</source>
```

```
            <target>1.7</target>
      </configuration>
      </plugin>
      <plugin>
            <groupId>org.apache.maven.plugins</groupId>
            <artifactId>maven-surefire-plugin</artifactId>
            <version>2.5</version>
            <configuration>
                  <parallel>methods</parallel>
                  <threadCount>4</threadCount>
                  <perCoreThreadCount>true</
                      perCoreThreadCount>
            </configuration>
        </plugin>
     </plugins>
</build>
```

Step by Step Guide for Creating and Executing JUnit Test Suite

Described as follows are the steps to execute JUnit test suite tests in parallel.

1. Configure pom.xml file as discussed earlier and rebuild project using 'mvn clean install'.
2. Start Selenium Hub and Selenium Node as discussed earlier.
3. Develop Selenium WebDriver JUnit test.
4. Execute WebDriver tests from eclipse or from command prompt using maven Surefire commands.

Quick Tips

1. Selenium grid is used to run multiple tests simultaneously in different browsers and platforms.
2. Grid uses hub-node concept. Hub is the central point where tests are loaded. Nodes are the instances where test execution of the tests loaded in hub takes place.
3. There are two ways to verify whether hub is running or not. One is through command prompt and another through grid's web interface.
4. To run tests on the Grid, DesiredCapabilities and RemoteWebDriver objects are to be used.
5. DesiredCapabilities sets the type of browser and platform on which the tests should be executed execute.
6. RemoteWebDriver sets the node machine on which test execution should take place.
7. Configuration timeout time defines the time hub would wait before releasing a node in case hub receives no response from node within that time.
8. Configuration timeout time should be greater than socket lock timeout (45 secs) and WebDriver.manage.timeouts().

27
CHAPTER

Agile Methodology

Agile methodology is a software development method based on iterative and incremental development, where requirements and solutions evolve through collaboration between self-organizing, cross-functional teams and customer feedback. It promotes adaptive planning and evolution development and delivery. Delivery is based on time-boxed iterative approach. It encourages rapid and flexible response to change with minimum change impact. It requires very frequent and tight interactions with all the stakeholders throughout the development cycle.

In agile methodology, complete software is developed in small iterative and incremental development. It lays emphasis on compacting the software development life cycle rather than changing it as shown in Figure 27.1.

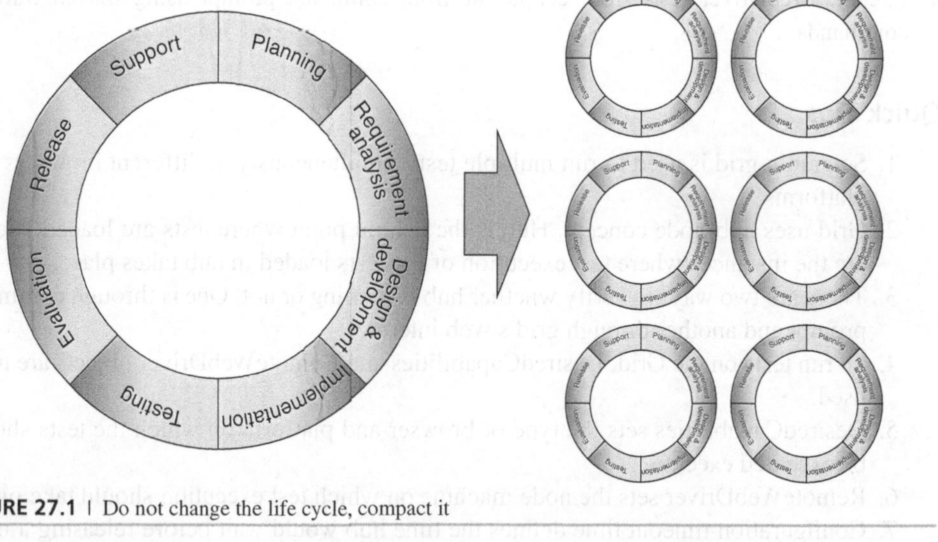

FIGURE 27.1 | Do not change the life cycle, compact it

27.1 | AGILE VALUES

Agile development term was derived from the Agile Manifesto, which was written in 2001 by a group that included the creators of Scrum, Extreme Programming (XP), etc. The agile values as listed in the manifesto are as follows:

- **Individuals and interactions over processes and tools:** Agile software development methodology lays emphasis on self-organization, motivation and interactions such as co-location and pair programming as compared to any process or tool.
- **Working software over comprehensive document:** Working software is valued more useful than presentation documents in client meetings. Self-explanatory code is valued more than hundreds of pages of documents.
- **Customer collaboration over contract negotiation:** Agile methodology accepts the fact that with the ever-changing world change to software development requirements is a continuous process and all requirements cannot be fully collected at the beginning of the project. Therefore, continuous customer and stakeholder interaction is must at short periodic intervals.
- **Responding to change over following a plan:** Agile development focusses on quick response to change to minimize delivery to customer time.

27.2 | AGILE PRINCIPLES

Agile manifesto is based on the following 12 principles:

1. Customer satisfaction by rapid delivery of useful software.
2. Welcome changing requirements, even late in development.
3. Working software is delivered frequently (weeks rather than months).
4. Working software is the principal measure of progress.
5. Sustainable development, able to maintain a constant pace.
6. Close, daily cooperation between business people and developers.
7. Face-to-face conversation is the best form of communication (co-location).
8. Projects are built around motivated individuals, who should be trusted.
9. Continuous attention to technical excellence and good design.
10. Simplicity—the art of maximizing the amount of work not done—is essential.
11. Self-organizing teams.
12. Regular adaptation to changing circumstances.

27.3 | WHY AGILE?

Agile methodology of software development has lots of advantages over traditional methods of software development. The most important being reduced product delivery time and fast feedback loops. Table 27.1 explains some of the benefits of agile methodology of software development.

TABLE 27.1 | Benefits of agile methodology

Benefits	Description
 Revenue	Agile methodology delivers the features incrementally, thereby, helping some of the revenues to be gained early while the product is still under development.
 Risk Management	Continuous small deliveries help to identify the blocking issues early and quick adaptability to a change.
 Speed to Market	Continuous incremental deployments helps to release some of the product features early to the market.
 Quick Resolution	Agile methodology lays emphasis on quick small discussions based on practical ground realities to solve issues rather than holding meetings based on big specs. Developing specs, helping stakeholders understand them and holding discussion on it consumes time and money.
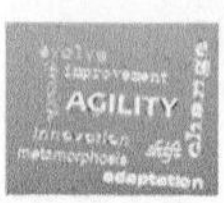 Agility	Agile methodology accepts change as an integral part of software development process. In agile development, timescale is fixed while requirements emerge and evolve as product is developed. Acceptance of change among active stakeholders helps to make necessary trade-off decisions faster.
 Faster Customer Feedback	Early release of some product features helps to receive customer inputs while the product is still getting developed. This helps to tweak the product feature as per customer expectations as per budget overruns.
 Quality	Agile methodology integrates testing to the SDLC to the very beginning stage of software development. This helps to catch software issues early in SDLC. Since, feature gets developed in small chunks it is easier to fix the bugs. This helps product stability quickly.
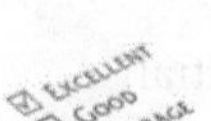 Customer Satisfaction	Continuous change to the product features as per customer feedbacks helps to achieve customer satisfaction.
 Visibility	Agile methodology lays stress on involving business owners and stakeholders throughout the development cycle. This helps to effectively manage stakeholders' expectations.
 More Enjoyable	Agile methodology replaces big specs and large group meetings with smaller workshop discussions based on practical facts. This results in active involvement and co-operation within agile team which makes it a fun place to work.

27.4 | AGILE METHODOLOGIES AND PRACTICES

Agile development is not a methodology in itself. It is set of methodologies and practices that aid in rapid software development. These methodologies include: Scrum, XP (Extreme Programming), Crystal, Test Driven Development (TDD), FDD (Feature Driven Development), DSDM (Dynamic System Development Method), Lean Practices, etc. In this section, we will discuss some of the agile methodologies and practices as mentioned in Table 27.2.

TABLE 27.2 | Some of the agile methodologies/practices

Agile methodology/Practice		Objectives
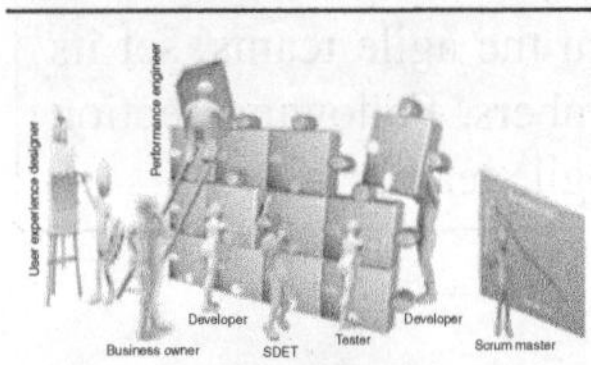	Agile team dynamics	Explains team formation
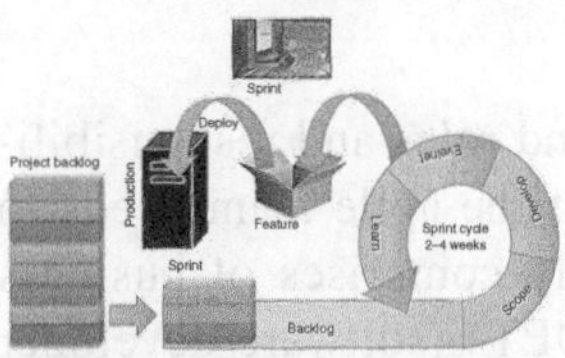	Scrum	Describes development methodology details
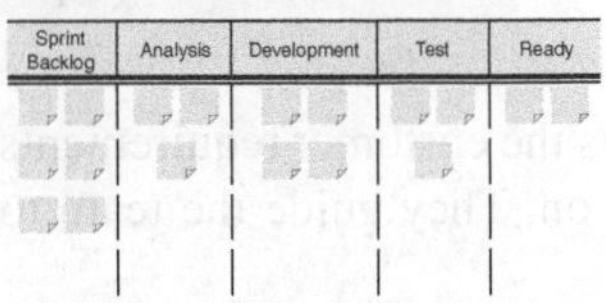	Kanban	Describes how to manage the development work
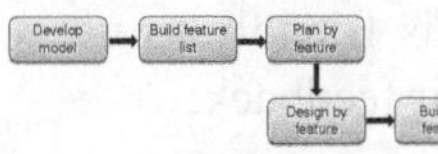	Feature Driven Development (FDD)	Development framework based on featured based development
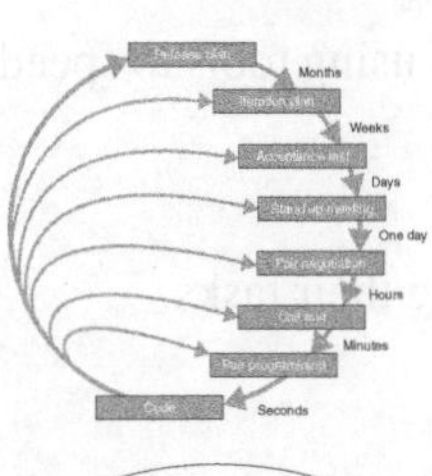	eXtreme Programming (XP)	Development framework describing programming practice to follow
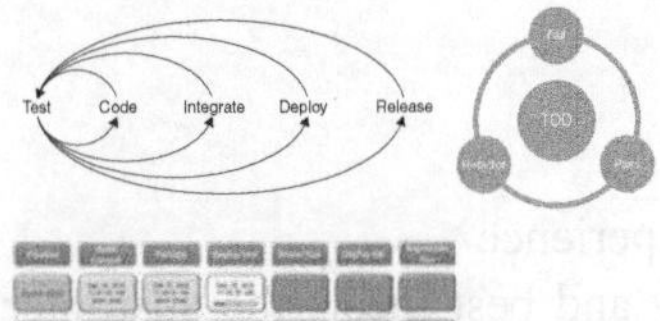	Test Driven Development (TDD)	Development framework that integrates testing practice within development practice
	Continuous Integration (CI)	Practice that describes how to automate build deployment process

In this section, we will discuss how various agile methodologies and practices can be utilized to develop a true agile software development process for a project. We will *first* discuss how to form an agile team and define the role and responsibilities of the team members. Second, we will discuss the development methodology (Scrum) to be implemented for development. *Third,* we will discuss how the requirements to be chosen for development (FDD). Fourth, we will discuss the programming practices (XP) to be followed for development. *Fifth,* we will discuss how to integrate the testing practices within development to ensure a high quality defect-free deployment build (TDD). *Finally*, we will discuss how we can automate the complete build deployment process to ensure the complete agile process works smoothly (CI).

The first step before implementing any agile project is to form the agile teams, set its goals and define the role and responsibilities of the team members. Following section 'Agile Team Dynamics' explains in detail the formation of an agile team.

27.5 | AGILE TEAM DYNAMICS

Agile team dynamics defines the structure of the agile team and roles and responsibilities of the various team members. Generally, the team size of the agile team needs to be small, around seven team members. Agile teams generally comprises of business owners, scrum masters, developers, functional testers and SDETs (software developer engineers in test).

- **Business owner** carries out customer surveys and converts the customer requirements into meaningful themes on which agile teams can work on. They guide the team to develop the theme that meets the customer expectations.
- **User experience designers** design the user experience which is friendly to users. They sometimes, also, take this design back to customers for their feedback.
- **Developers** write the code to develop the feature.
- **Functional testers** test the functionality of the code while SDETs using tools to speed up testing.
- **Performance engineers** test the performance of the code.

Figure 27.2 shows an agile team with their team members performing their tasks.

27.5.1 | User Experience Designer

The role of user experience designer in agile team is to:

- Carry out customer surveys to identify the best user experience
- Design graphical user experience that is user-friendly and best meets the customer expectations

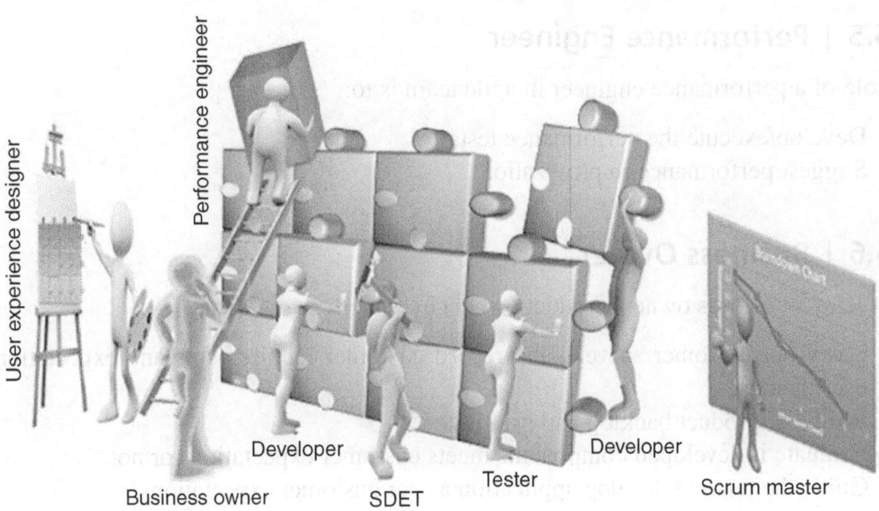

FIGURE 27.2 | Agile team dynamics

27.5.2 | Developer

The role of a developer in agile team is to:

- Develop the application code.
- Deploy the code to testing environments (build manager).
- Fix bugs.
- Develop/execute unit/integration tests.

27.5.3 | Functional Tester

The role of a functional tester in agile team is to:

- Design traceability matrix.
- Develop manual tests.
- Test the feature under development.
- Targeted testing for the developed feature.
- Suggest user design experience improvizations.

27.5.4 | Software Developer Engineer in Test (SDET)

The role of SDET (software developer engineer in test) in agile team is to:

- Develop/automate unit/integration/functional/regression/security/cross-platform/… tests.
- Execute automated tests.
- Test the application under development.
- Suggest technical (code) improvizations.

27.5.5 | Performance Engineer

The role of a performance engineer in agile team is to:

- Develop/execute the performance tests.
- Suggest performance improvizations.

27.5.6 | Business Owner

The role of a business owner (product owner) in an agile team is to:

- Carry out customer surveys and record customer requirements and expectations as user themes.
- Build the product backlog and prioritize it.
- Evaluate if developed components meets customer expectations or not.
- Guide the team to develop application as per customer expectations.

27.5.7 | Scrum Master

The role of a scrum master in an agile team is to:

- Build and prioritize the sprint backlog.
- Co-ordinate to resolve blocking issues.
- Motivate the team, evaluate progress and publish Burndown charts.
- Synchronize business owner/management expectations and teams capabilities.

Once agile teams have been formed and their goals set; next step is to define the development framework for the agile team. In agile methodology, each agile team is free to decide the development framework it will follow. Among all the development frameworks Scrum is very popular. It best describes the process right from selecting requirements to work on to production ready requirements. Following section describes in detail Scrum development framework and how to implement it.

27.6 | SCRUM

Scrum is an iterative and incremental agile software development framework for managing software projects. It promotes a flexible product development strategy where the agile team works as a unit to achieve a common goal. It enables teams to self-organize by encouraging physical co-location of all team members and daily face to face communication among all team members and disciplines in the project.

Scrum framework accepts the fact that in this dynamic and ever-changing world continuous change to requirements is obvious and hence, requirements can never be frozen. It also accepts that all requirements cannot be gathered in the initial phase of the project. Hence, scrum framework lays emphasis on working on smallest possible deliverable units first.

Customers and stakeholders are encouraged to suggest their feedbacks and changes. The suggestions are then implemented during the future sprint cycles. Scrum emphasizes on production ready work being delivered by the end of the sprint.

27.6.1 | Sprint

A sprint (or iteration) is the basic unit of scrum development framework. The sprint is 'time-boxed', i.e., it is restricted to specific time duration. This duration is fixed in advance by the agile team and may vary from 2 to 4 weeks. Each sprint starts with sprint planning meeting where the team identifies the themes for implementation and creates tasks (or sub-stories) for the same. Sprint ends with sprint review-and-retrospective meeting where the progress is reviewed and lessons for the next sprint is identified. Figure 27.3 shows sprint cycles (iteration cycles) followed by different agile teams for a typical project. Agile team I has 2 week sprint cycle; agile team II has 4 week sprint cycle and agile team III has 1 week sprint cycle.

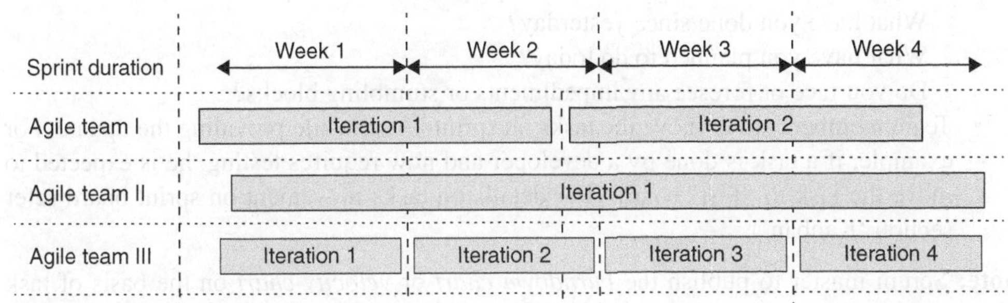

FIGURE 27.3 | Sprint cycles

27.6.2 | Sprint Meetings

Scrum advices few meetings to ensure smooth functioning of the team.

Backlog Grooming Meeting

Backlog Grooming Meeting is organized by the p*roduct owner* (*business owner*) of the team. Product owners walkthrough the team on the various themes available in backlog for development. The team can ask questions and clarify their doubts regarding the 'ask' from the theme or functionality to be implemented as per the theme. Backlog grooming meeting generally lasts for 2–4 hrs.

The team then uses this information to estimate the implementation feasibility of stories and effort required for the same.

Sprint Planning Meeting

Sprint planning meeting is organized by the *scrum master* of the team. The objective of this meeting is to identify the set of prioritized stories that the team is comfortable delivering for the current sprint. This set of stories form the spring backlog. Also, tasks are created for each story and each task is assigned an owner. Sprint planning meeting generally lasts for 4–6 hrs.

For example, for a specific story, the generalized tasks would be analysis, UI design, development and testing.

Daily Scrum Meeting (Daily Stand-up Meeting)

Daily scrum meeting is organized by the scrum master. This meeting is scheduled to occur first thing in the morning every day during the sprint. This meeting has some specific guidelines:

- The meeting duration is time-boxed to 15 minutes.
- All members of the team to come prepared to the meeting.
- The meeting starts precisely on the same time and same location every day, even if some team members fail to make it on time.
- All team members are to give a summary update on below points:
  - What have you done since yesterday?
  - What have you planned to do today?
  - Do you face or foresee any impediments or stumbling blocks?
- Team members are to move the tasks on sprint board while providing the update. For example, if a task is done by a developer and now requires testing, he is expected to move the task to 'Test' board. (For details on tasks movement on sprint board refer section 'Kanban').

Note: Scrum master to publish the *burndown chart* or *velocity chart* on the basis of task completed. The objective of burndown chart or velocity chart is to help the team understand that with current development pace will the team be able to accomplish all the goals of the sprint. If not, then how much they can cover. Based on this, team can hold separate discussions to resolve the bottlenecks. If team foresees, it has more bandwidth left, then they can decide to add more themes to sprint backlog from product backlog.

- Scrum master to document the identified impediments and work outside this meeting to resolve them.
- No detailed discussion is to happen in this meeting.

Sprint Retrospective Meeting

Sprint review-and-retrospective meeting is organized by the scrum master at the end of the sprint. During this meeting, the team discusses to identify:

- What went well?
- What did not go well?
- What are the lessons learnt?
- What are the areas of improvement?

Sprint Demo Meeting

Sprint demo meeting is organized by the customer at the end of the sprint or as per a pre-defined schedule. All agile teams, stakeholders and customers are to be part of this meeting. In this meeting, agile team gives a demo of the working feature developed or in progress. The work done is reviewed by the stakeholders and customers. For precisely this reason, this meeting is also called *review meeting*.

Note: Some agile teams may also choose to hold the retrospective and demo meeting together. This is called sprint review-and-retrospective meeting. This meeting is attended by the respective agile team, concerned business owners of other teams, concerned stakeholders and customer. Whatever, be the strategy for a given project, all agile teams are to follow the same process. That is, all agile teams of a project are to hold a sprint review-retrospective meeting or spring retrospective and sprint review meeting.

27.7 | HOW SCRUM WORKS?

In this ever-changing dynamic world where the technology and requirements change very fast, application design and development is getting more and more complex with every second day. Scrum provides a framework that allows agile teams to successfully work on complex projects. Section 'Agile Team Dynamics' explains in detail how the various members of the agile team work to deliver a successful product.

27.8 | SCRUM WORKFLOW

Figure 27.4 describes the work flow of scrum framework.

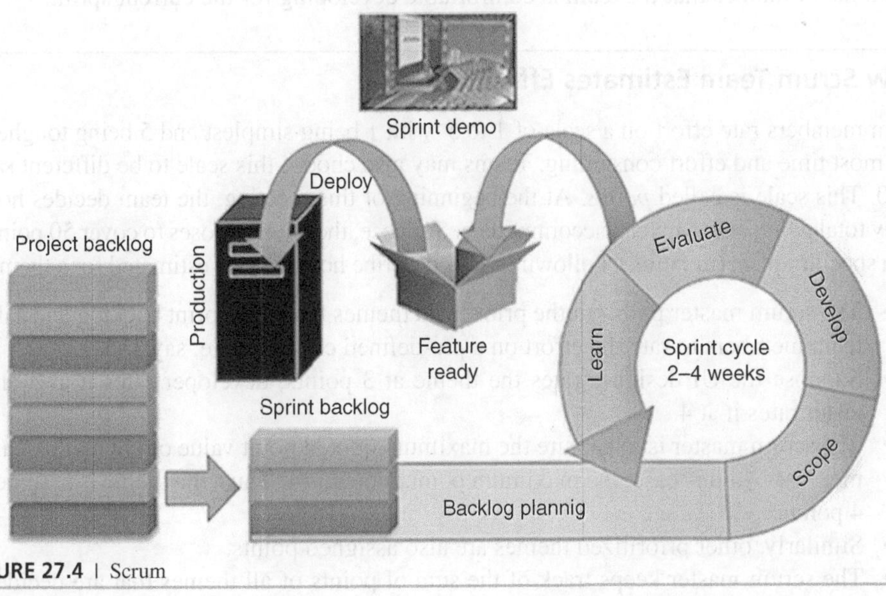

FIGURE 27.4 | Scrum

27.8.1 | Product Backlog

The product backlog is a prioritized features list, containing short descriptions of all functionality or features desired in the product.

- Product backlog exists in the form of user themes
- Each user theme is a short and simple description of the desired functionality from the perspective of the user

27.8.2 | Backlog Planning

Beginning of every sprint cycle, business owner organizes a *Backlog Grooming Meeting*.

- Objective of this meeting is to groom the team on the prioritized list of user themes that can be taken up for development in the current sprint.
- On the basis of team feedback, the business owner creates a list of user themes which is to be developed for the current sprint. This list is called *Sprint Backlog*.

27.8.3 | Scope

After the backlog grooming meeting, the scrum master organizes a *Sprint Planning Meeting*.

- Objective of this meeting is identify the effort required to develop the sprint backlog themes
- Each team member submits his effort estimation for each and every theme
- On the basis of the teams' feedback, the scrum master refines the sprint backlog list to a list of themes that the team is comfortable developing for the current sprint.

How Scrum Team Estimates Effort?

Team members rate effort on a scale of 1 to 5, with 1 being simplest and 5 being toughest and most time and effort consuming. Teams may also choose this scale to be different say 1–10. This scale is called *points.* At the beginning of this meeting, the team decides how many total points the team can accommodate. Suppose, the team chooses to cover 50 points for a specific sprint (iteration). Following steps describe how effort is estimated for a theme:

- The scrum master pulls out the prioritized themes from the sprint backlog and asks team members to rate the effort on a pre-defined chosen scale, say 1–5.
- Suppose the UI designer rates the theme at 3 points; developer rates it at 3 and tester rates it at 4.
- The scrum master is to capture the maximum quoted point value out of all the team members. In this case, the maximum point quoted is 4. Thus, the theme is assigned 4 points.
- Similarly, other prioritized themes are also assigned points.
- The scrum master keeps track of the sum of points of all themes that are decided to be worked upon.

- The scrum master stops pulling themes from sprint backlog as soon as total points equal 50.
- If the themes in sprint backlog are over and still total points does not equals 50, then team can ask the product owner to move some more prioritized themes to the sprint backlog. However, as a general practice, business owners are encouraged to pull sufficient themes to sprint backlog during backlog planning phase itself.
- If the total number of points has reached 50 and still there are some themes in the sprint backlog then the scrum master updates the business owner of the themes that cannot be accommodated. The business owner then pulls these themes back to the project backlog.
- Once the sprint planning meeting is over, all team members are expected to identify (create) their tasks for each theme and update the scrum master.
- The scrum master then updates the scrum task board with list of all stories in spring backlog and all identified tasks for each theme. This is discussed in detail in the following section 'Scrum Task Board'
- The scrum master also publishes the Burndown chart and Velocity chart on a daily basis to update the team on its current progress and current pace of achieving sprint goals. This is discussed in detail in the following section 'BurnDown chart' and 'Velocity chart'.

The team members are expected to quote points to a theme on the basis of the knowledge they gathered during backlog grooming meeting and their experience. The team members quote the points more on their gut-feeling. This is accepted in scrum as at this phase no team member has a clear perception of what actually needs to be developed and tested. However, if during later stages it turns out that the effort required is more, then themes or sub-themes are to be created and assigned points accordingly. Once created, these can again be prioritized by the business owner with feedback from the team. These stories can then be pulled in Sprint backlog or can be pushed to Project backlog as team deems fit.

Scrum is a continuous evolving process. Hence, no hard bound rules are drafted for Scrum. Scrum methodology provides the full flexibility to the team to choose how they can add maximum value to the business.

Develop

After sprint planning meeting, the team starts to develop the user themes. Table 27.3 shows the list of tasks performed by different team members of the agile team.

Test

Once the components have been developed, the components are merged with the regression environment. In the regression environment, further testing takes place such as regression testing, multi-browser testing, performance testing, security testing, etc.

TABLE 27.3 | List of tasks performed by different team members of the agile team

	User design	Developer	QA	Scrum Master	Business owner
Agile tasks	Designs the user experience design as small recursive components	Develops the business logic code Develps the GUI components for which user experience design is ready Fixes bugs	Builds test and automation strategy Tests the developed components of code Deveops the automated tests Identifies areas/scope of improvement	Co-ordinates inter and intra team meetings Publishes burn-down chart Analyses impact of blocking issues and co-ordinates to mitigate them	Evaluates developed components on the grounds of customer expecations Provides feedback and improvements

Evaluate

Once a user theme is fully developed, the business owner analyses the developed theme to check whether it meets the customer expectations.

- If yes, then the user story is marked 'Ready' for deployment to production.
- If no, then the team is required to work on the suggested improvements.

Learn

At the end of the sprint, the scrum master organizes a *retrospective meeting*. In this meeting, the team discusses on

- What the team did well?
- What went wrong?
- Areas of improvement

Feature Ready

A list of features ready for go-live is collected by the *build deployment manager*. The build deployment manager syncs up with various agile teams to collect dependencies for various features going live. Next, go-live steps for various features are drafted. This is to ensure minimum impact to go-live and no undesirable impact to production environment.

The go-live schedule could be daily, weekly or sprint end. Agile teams are free to choose the go-live schedule. However, all agile teams are encouraged to for a daily go-live so that features can be delivered early to the customers. In scenarios wherein feature is partially developed or feature developed has dependency on code being developed by other teams, a toggle switch is developed for the feature. Code as developed is pushed to production with toggle switch switched off, so that essentially the features do not go-live though code is already live in production.

Note: Only that code is marked ready which has been successfully tested and marked ready for go-live.

Sprint Demo

At the end of the sprint (or as per the demo schedule), all agile teams give a demo to all the stakeholders on:

- The features that have been deployed to production or are ready for production deployment
- The features which are under development
  - Development progress of the features under development
  - Expected production-ready date of the features under development

Note: For sprint demo, agile teams are encouraged to walk through the stakeholders through the working or the developed feature of the actual application. Presentations or any sort of documented presentation is discouraged for sprint demo meetings.

27.8.4 | Scrum Task Board

Scrum task board provides an effective way to track the various tasks of the sprint as well as the impediments. Scrum task board is designed in a way that it is visible in both plan mode and work mode. That is, the scrum board helps the team plan out the various tasks for the sprint as well as to track progress. Figure 27.5 shows a typical scrum task board.

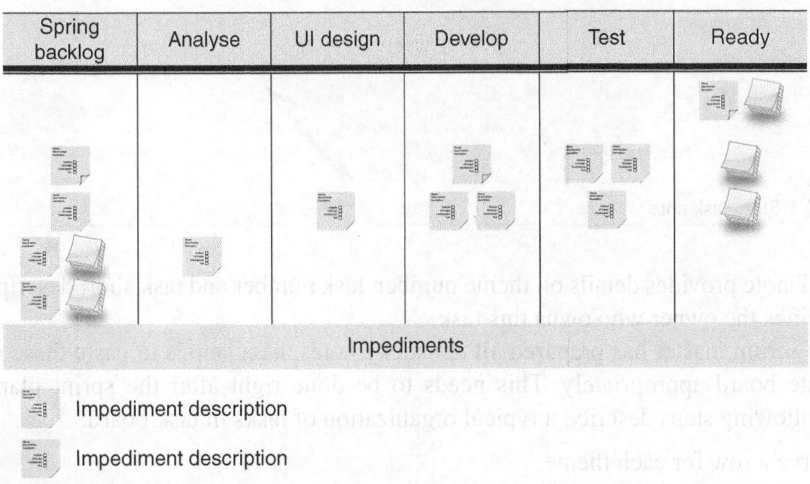

FIGURE 27.5 | Scrum task board

Once all the themes and its tasks have been identified, the scrum master prepares sticky notes. For every story, there exists one sticky note as shown in Figure 27.6 and multiple task notes as shown in Figure 27.7.

Story note provides details on: Theme number, theme points and theme short description. It also contains status checkboxes for different phases of story development. The respective owner of that phase is required to check the checkbox when they have completed their respective phases.

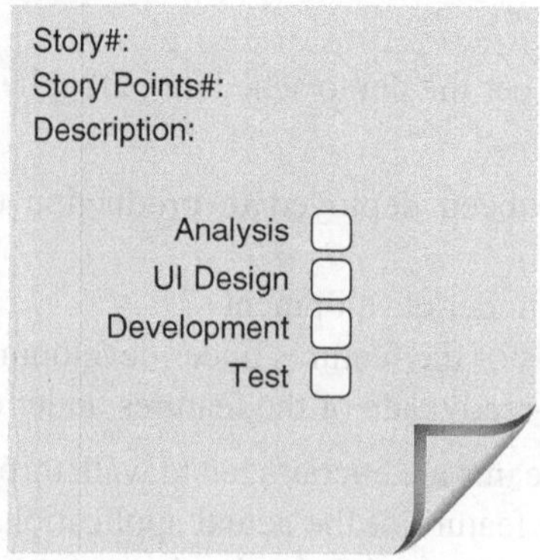

FIGURE 27.6 | Story note

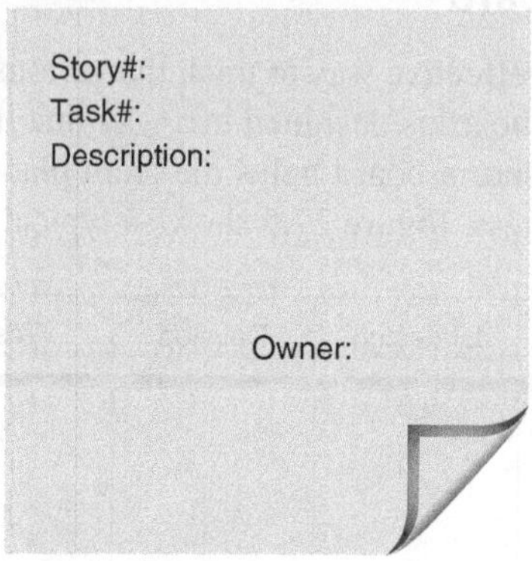

FIGURE 27.7 | Story task note

Story task note provides details on theme number, task number and task short description. It also specifies the owner who owns this task.

Once the scrum master has prepared all the sticky notes, next step is to paste these notes on the white board appropriately. This needs to be done right after the sprint planning meeting. Following steps describe a typical organization of tasks in task board:

- Reserve a row for each theme.
- Paste the theme note and task notes against column 'Sprint Backlog'. Task notes are to be stacked upon one another and placed next to story note as shown in Figure 27.5.

During the daily scrum meetings, respective owners of task update the scrum task board by moving the tasks around the board. Team member need to:

- Move the theme task note around the board appropriately
  - For example, if a developer team member is ready to pick new task then he is to move that task from column 'Spring Backlog' to column 'Develop'.
  - Or, If a developer team member has completed a specific task, then he is to move the specific task from column 'Develop' to column 'Ready'.

- Update the story note
    - For example, if a developer team member has completed all the development tasks of a story, he is to check the 'Develop' task of the story note.

Also, when a scrum master observes that all the tasks for a specific theme is complete or the other words theme has been successfully been implemented, then he is to move the specific tasks from column 'Spring Backlog' to column 'Ready'.

If any impediments are found for a theme, then the respective theme and all its tasks are to be moved to the 'Impediment' section of the board. Also, a short description of the impediment is to be written.

27.8.5 | Burndown Chart

A *Burndown Chart* is a graphical representation of work left to do versus time.It measures whether with the current pace of development, team will be able to complete all spring tasks or not. The horizontal axis shows the time while the vertical axis shows the outstanding work (or backlog). Outstanding work can be in terms of themes or tasks or points.

Suppose, for a sprint cycle scrum team has chosen 10 themes for development. These themes have total of 45 tasks and the total points is 50.

Figure 27.8 shows a sample Burndown chart of a typical sprint cycle of 2 weeks. The vertical axis shows outstanding tasks while horizontal axis shows sprint days (time). Teams are to make an attempt to ensure that the current outstanding task line graph is close to ideal task remaining line graph. Ideal tasks remaining line graph is always a straight line with maximum outstanding tasks on day 1 and zero task on final sprint day which in this case is 10. This line is drawn as a reference line to show that the development pace is to match this line.

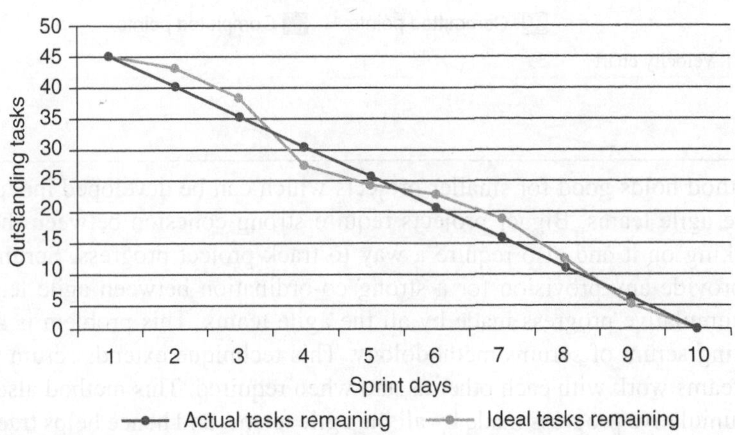

FIGURE 27.8 | Burndown chart

The scrum master is to publish this chart to team daily. This chart helps team to:

- Understand the current pace of development
- Understand whether team is on the track to achieve its sprint goals or not
- Warn if team may miss its sprint goals
- Show the impact of decisions

27.8.6 | Velocity Chart

The *velocity chart* measures the amount of value delivered by each sprint as compared to the committed value. This enables agile teams to estimate how much work the team can get done in future sprints. It is essentially useful during sprint planning meeting to help decide how much work the team is feasible to commit.

Velocity of a team is estimated by plotting a comparative bar graph between total points committed Vs total points completed (delivered) for various sprints. Figure 27.9 shows a sample velocity chart for the last 5 sprints.

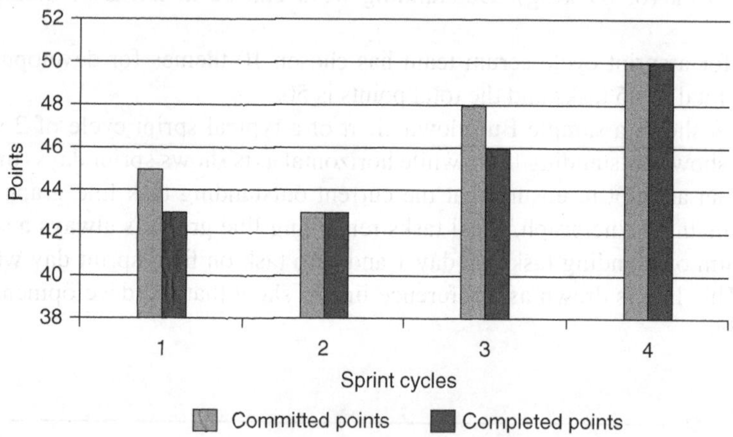

FIGURE 27.9 | Velocity chart

> Scrum method holds good for smaller projects which can be developed independently by separate agile teams. Bigger projects require strong cohesion between the various teams working on it and also require a way to track project progress. Scrum method does not provide any provision for a strong co-ordination between agile teams or to track the cumulative progress made by all the agile teams. This problem is solved by implementing scrum of scrums methodology. This technique extends scrum to ensure that agile teams work with each other as and when required. This method also helps to track the cumulative progress made by all the agile teams, and hence helps track project progress.

27.9 | SCRUM OF SCRUMS

Scrum of Scrums is a technique to scale scrum for bigger projects that involve large development groups. This methodology allows clusters of scrum teams to discuss their work, focusing especially on areas of overlap and integration.

27.9.1 | How Does Scrum of Scrum Works?

In scrum of scrums method, each scrum team works as normal but from each team one person is nominated as ambassador of the team (generally scrum masters or business owners). The responsibility of ambassador is to update higher management and enterprise architects on team progress, current impediments and issues faced. This update occurs in a meeting which is attended by all ambassadors and the stakeholders. This meeting is analogous to scrum meeting and is called *scrum of scrums meeting*. This meeting may occur daily or on alternate days. Figure 27.10 shows an illustration of scrum of scrums meeting.

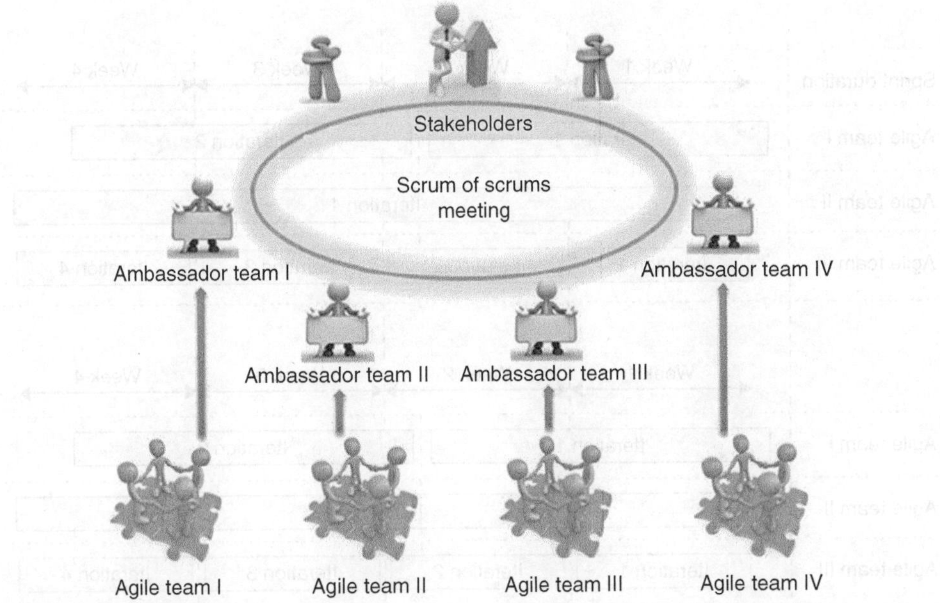

FIGURE 27.10 | Scrum of scrums meeting

The agenda of scrum of scrums meeting is analogous to daily scrum meeting and includes the following:

- What has your team done since we last met?
- What will your team do before we meet again?
- Is anything slowing your team down or getting in their way?
- Are you about to put something in another team's way?

Another technique that makes easier management of large projects using scrum of scrums is the alignment of iterations. Agile teams work on different project sizes, and also each agile team has a specific velocity, production capacity and learning curve. This results is different sprint duration (sizes) followed by different agile teams. As visible in Figure 27.3, agile team I follows 2 week sprint cycle; agile team II follows 4 week sprint cycle; and agile team III follows 1 week sprint cycle. As evident from this figure, start and end of sprint cycles of each team is different and is not in sync. This could be a major problem when multiple agile teams are working on a project which has huge dependency on each other. It may happen that agile team 3 may have to wait for a module developed by agile team I before they can work on their next iteration. Now in this case, since start and end of sprint cycles of agile teams I and III are different, agile team III may have to wait till agile team I completes their iteration cycle before it can begin its next iteration. To avoid this problem, start and end iteration cycles of all the agile teams is to be synchronized as shown in Figure 27.11. This helps align all the agile teams with project milestones. For example, plan the deployment of a new version of the product on a specific date.

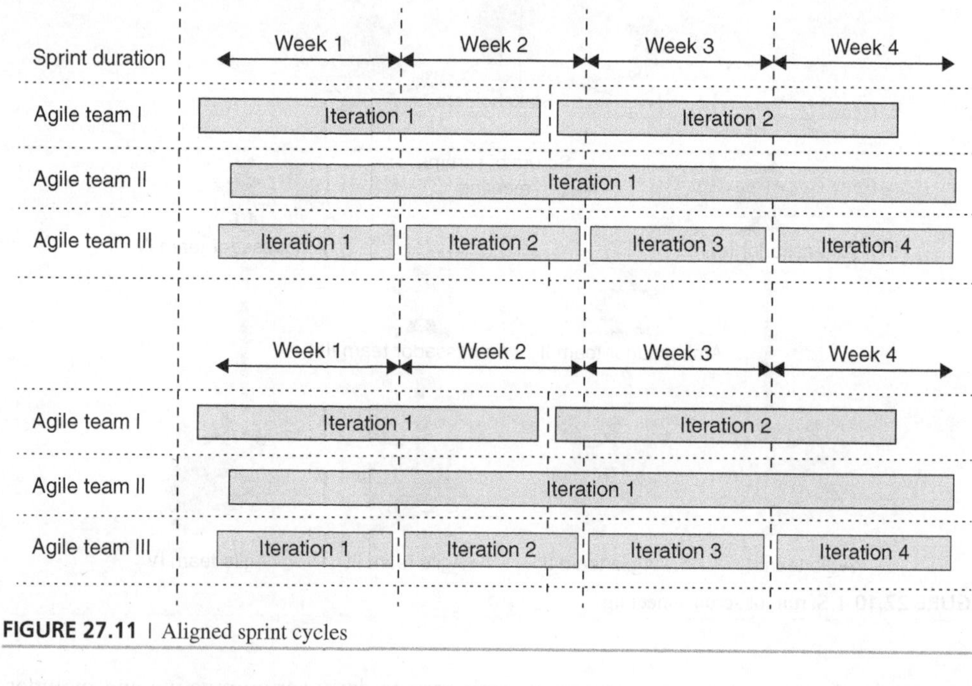

FIGURE 27.11 | Aligned sprint cycles

27.10 | KANBAN

Kanban is a visual process-based project management tool first developed in Japan by Toyota.

Kanban is a way to visualize the work of all team members, and to limit the amount of work in progress at any one time. Figure 27.12 shows a very simple Kanban big board. It consists of all the tasks and the status they are in. This board shows the development phases as column items. Each phase has the maximum limit counter. This maximum limit counter signifies these many tasks can be completed for the specific development phase in the given time period. If the task count exceeds the maximum limit counter for the specific phase, then a red flag is raised. Figure 27.12 shows maximum counter limit as 6 for Analysis phase 6 for development phase, and 4 for testing phase.

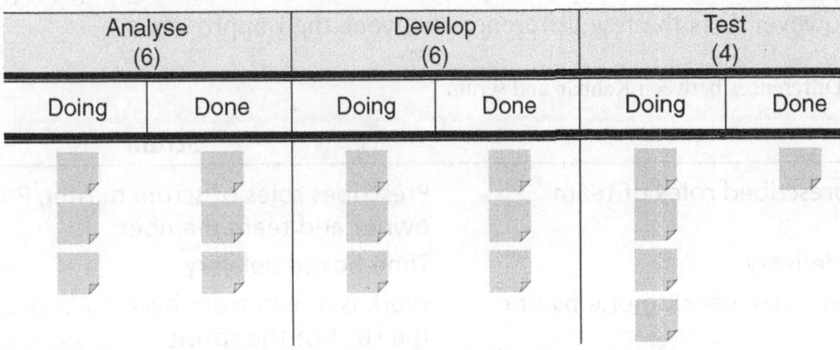

FIGURE 27.12 | Simple kanban board

27.10.1 | Kanban Principles

Kanban has three following core principles:

1. **Visualize what you have now:** Visualizing all the items in context of each other can be very informative
2. **Limit the amount of work in progress (WIP):**This helps to balance the flow-based approach so that teams do not overcommit.
3. **Enhance flow:** Continuously improving the way you work makes you more effective and happier.

Kanban promotes continuous collaboration and encourages active, ongoing learning and improving by letting the team define the best possible team workflow. Decisions in Kanban are made based on the scientific method instead of 'gut' feeling. Kanban discourages the idea of multi-tasking. This is because though multi-tasking gives an impression that lot is being done but in reality lot of time is lost when switching between works.

27.10.2 | Why Kanban?

Kanban board is very effective in finding bottlenecks in the agile software development process. As in the case of Figure 27.7, analysts can analyse maximum of 6 themes, developers can develop 5 themes and testers can test 4 theme. On any given day, it is observed that testers have 5 themes to test which 2 themes greater than what testers can handle. Though developers can deliver 6 themes but only 4 can be production ready as testers do not have bandwidth to test the remaining two. That is, here testers are bottleneck in the system.

If the team is not aware of this bottleneck, then with each development cycle backlog of work will begin to pile up in front of the testers. Work sitting in the pipeline ties down investment, creates distance from the market and drops in value as time goes by. To keep up, testers may start to cut corners. This will further result in bugs getting leaked to production.

On the other hand, if the team is made aware of the bottleneck in time, then they could have redeployed resources to help relive the test team. For example, analysts could have helped testing while developers could have helped develop automated tests.

How is Kanban different from Scrum? Kanban and scrum both focus on releasing software early and often. Both require highly-collaborative and self-managed agile teams. Table 27.4, however, lists the few differences between their approaches.

TABLE 27.4 | Differences between Kanban and scrum

Kanban	Scrum
No specific prescribed roles of team members	Prescribes roles of scrum master, Product owner and team member
Continuous delivery	Time-boxed delivery
Work is pulled from backlog one by one	Work is pulled from backlog in batches at the start of the sprint
Cycle time	Velocity
More appropriate in operational environments with a high degree of variability in priority	More appropriate in situations where work can be prioritized in batches that can be left alone

27.11 | FEATURE-DRIVEN DEVELOPMENT (FDD)

Feature-driven development (FDD) is a client-centric and architecture-centric agile software development methodology. Here client refers to stakeholders/customers. As the name suggests, features are an important aspect of FDD. In FDD, *feature* is defined as small client deliverable functionality. For example, 'Password rest', 'Authorize a transaction', 'Validate password strength', etc.

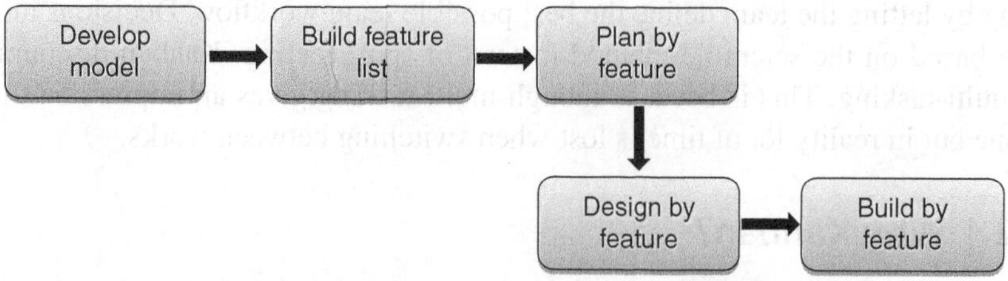

FIGURE 27.13 | Feature-driven development

FDD consists of five main activities as shown in Figure 27.13. These include:

1. **Develop Overall Model:** The project starts with a high-level walkthrough of the system and its scope. Next detailed walk throughs are held for each module area with the help of small groups. Each group prepares a model after appropriate peer reviews and discussions. Finally, the model is integrated to come up with a high-level model of the system.

2. Build Feature List: The overall model is used to decompose the complete functionality into small deliverable features.

3. Plan by Feature: Next, ownership for development of various features is assigned to chief programmers.

4. Design by Feature: Chief programmers select the list of features which can be developed in two week iteration. The team works out a detailed sequence diagram for each feature and refines the overall model. Next, the team writes class and method prologues and finally a design inspection is held.

5. Build by Feature: After a successful design inspection, team works to develop the complete client-valued function (feature).

There are six primary roles for an FDD project: project manager, chief architect, development manager, chief programmer, class owner and domain expert.

27.12 | EXTREME PROGRAMMING (XP)

Extreme programming (XP) is an agile software development methodology which advocates frequent releases to production and improved programmers responsiveness to changing customer requirements. Extreme programming lays emphasis on pair programming, simplicity and clarity in code and frequent interaction code developers with customers. Pair programming involves extensive code reviews and continuous unit and integration testing of all code. Figure 27.14 shows the panning and feedback loops of XP methodology.

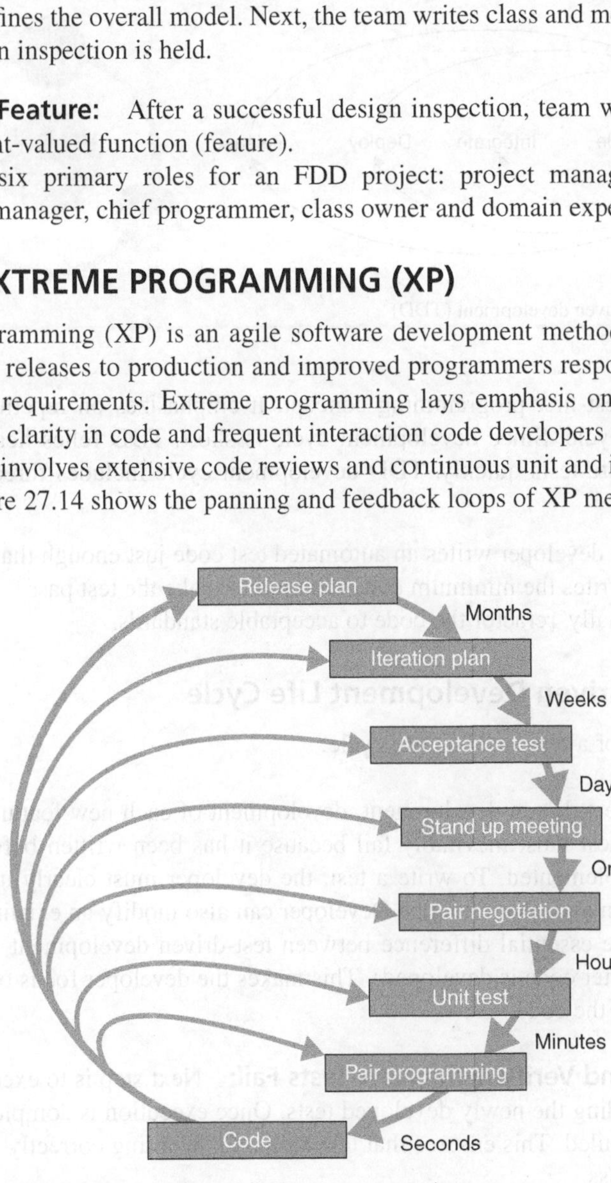

FIGURE 27.14 | Planning/Feedback loops of eXtreme programming

27.13 | TEST-DRIVEN DEVELOPMENT (TDD)

Test-driven development (TDD) is an agile practice that interweaves testing within the development practice. TDD promotes on very short development cycles with each cycle followed by a testing phase. As shown in Figure 27.15 tests are executed after each phase of development—coding, integrating, deploying and releasing. The developed code is rejected if either of development code or test code fails.

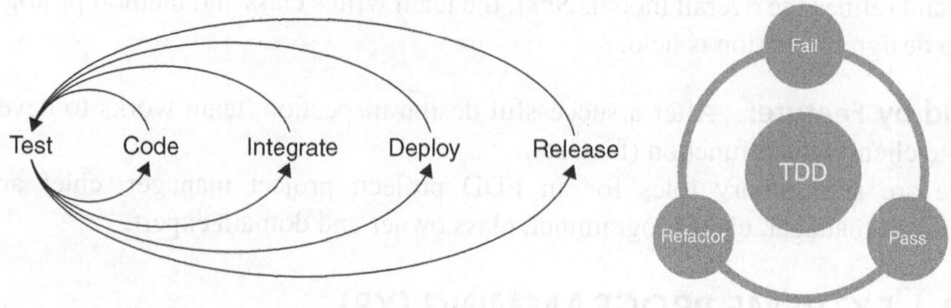

FIGURE 27.15 | Test-driven development (TDD)

TDD advocates test-first programming concept. It emphasizes on repetition of a very short development cycle. Since development cycle is short, TDD relies heavily on automated tests to execute tests quickly. TDD development cycle includes three phases: fail, pass and refactor.

1. **Fail:** First the developer writes an automated test code just enough that it fails.
2. **Pass:** Next, writes the minimum code required to make the test pass.
3. **Refactor:** Finally, refactor the code to acceptable standards.

27.13.1 | Test-driven Development Life Cycle

There are six steps for a typical TDD life cycle:

1. Add Test: In test-driven development, development of each new feature begins with writing a test. This test must inevitably fail because it has been written before the actual feature has been implemented. To write a test, the developer must clearly understand the feature's specification and requirements. Developer can also modify an existing test, if that deems fit. This is the essential difference between test-driven development and unit tests (which are written after code is developed). This makes the developer focus on the requirements *before* writing the code.

2. Run All Tests and Verify If the New Tests Fail: Next step is to execute the complete test suite including the newly developed tests. Once execution is complete, verify the new tests that have failed. This ensures that test harness is working correctly and new tests do not give a false pass.

3. Write Code: Next step is to write some code that causes the test to pass. At this stage, code is not expected to adhere to the project coding standards, so anything that just works fine (passes) is acceptable.

4. Run Tests: Run all the tests to ensure all tests pass and meets all the testing requirements.

5. Refactor Code: Next step is to clean up the code and move it to appropriate place in the test automation framework. Also, refactor code so that it adheres to the test automation framework standards. Any duplicate code needs to be removed at this stage.

6. Repeat: The size of changes made to code should always be restricted to small, say 1 to 10, edits between each test run. The code increments including external library file increments should always be small with each increment followed by the complete life cycle as discussed earlier.

27.14 | CONTINUOUS INTEGRATION (CI)

Continuous integration (CI) is a development practice that requires developers to merge their code into a centralized shared repository several times a day. Each check-in is verified by an automated build. This allows teams to detect problems early. Also, since build size is small, it makes it easier to track down the buggy code in case the code has defects. Moreover, since code commits are less it is easier to track the person whose code commit caused this bug. In short, bug detection, bug fix ownership assignment and buggy code detection becomes a lot faster and easier with continuous integration.

27.14.1 | CI Principles

CI emphasizes on the practice of frequent integration on one's code with the existing code repository. This should happen frequently enough that no intervening window remains between commit and build. Any error in code check-in or build creation should create an alarm and should be addressed with no loss of time. The reason being a failed build or commit may block the continuous integration pipeline defeating the main objective on continuous integration of frequent deployment and frequent testing. CI hugely relies on complete automation of build creation and deployment and builds certification process. Following are some of the principles and practices of CI.

- Maintain a code repository
- Automate the build
- Make the build self-testing
- Everyone commits to the baseline every day
- Every commitment should build on integration machine
- Keep the build fast
- Test in a clone of the production environment

- Make it easy to get the latest executables
- Everyone can see the complete build pipeline and what is happening in there including the results of the builds
- Automate deployment

27.14.2 | How CI Works?

In CI, multiple builds are committed in a day with each build on an eligible candidate of go-live build. If the build successfully passes the complete cycle then this build is deployed to production servers. Else if the build fails at any stage, then this build is rejected for go-live and next incoming build is considered. This loop continuously goes repeating.

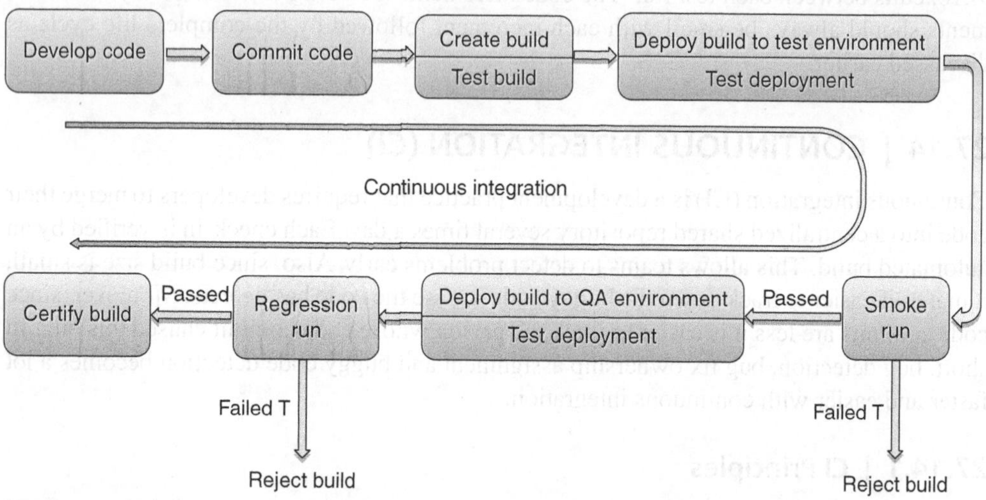

FIGURE 27.16 | Continuous integration cycle

Figure 27.16 shows a typical CI cycle. In CI cycle, developers commit code to the centralized repository multiple times in a day. As soon as the code is committed, the code is packaged as a build and a build test is run to ensure build is fine. Next, the build is deployed to test servers where smoke run is executed. The smoke run can comprise of API tests, unit tests, integration tests, GUI tests, security tests, performance tests, etc. If smoke run fails, then the build is rejected and further steps of life cycle are not executed. Else, if smoke run passes, the build is deployed to QA servers and tests are executed to test that deployment has happened successfully. After deployment regression run is executed. Regression run can comprise of API tests, integration tests, GUI tests, security tests, performance tests, cross-platform tests, etc. If regression run passes, then the build is considered certified for production deployment.

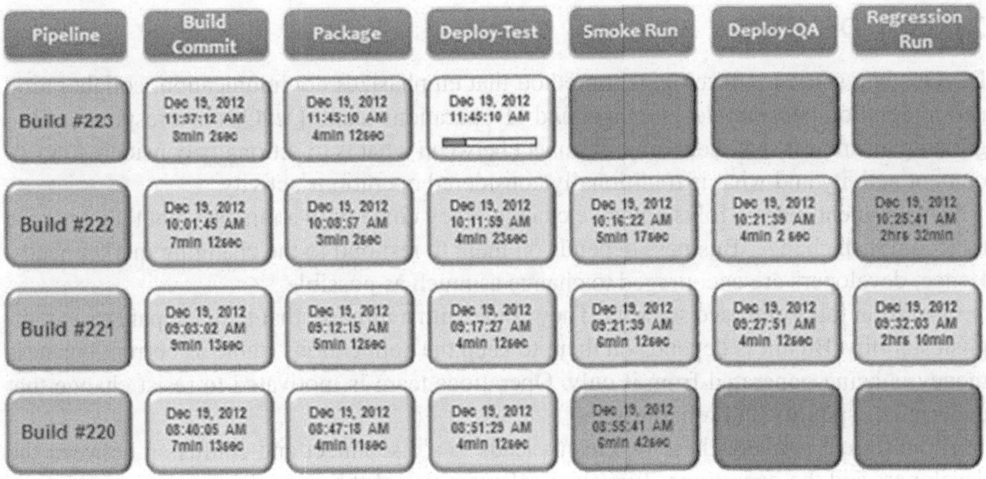

FIGURE 27.17 | Continuous integration pipeline

One of the tools to easily achieve complete automation of CI cycle is Jenkins. An important feature of CI is both the application code and the test code flows in the same pipeline. So say if some new application code has been developed then the test code to test this application should also be checked in with the same build. This ensures any new code or changed code is tested. This is very essential as in CI every build is an eligible candidate of go-live. Figure 27.17 shows a typical CI pipeline of Jenkins. As the figure shows there is continuous code commits (8:40 am, 9:03 am, 10:01 am and 11:37 am). Each code commit is built and assigned a build number (or pipeline number). If the build fails at any stage during the pipeline, then that build is rejected (as candidate of go-live build) and the pipeline waits for the next build. Any failure in this pipeline generates an alarm. Whenever there is an alarm, developers or SDETs need to quickly develop a fix and commit it. For example, Build #220 in the figure failed at 'Smoke Run' stage. Hence, this build was rejected (as candidate of go-live build) and further stages of the pipeline were never executed. Build #221 in the pipeline passes all the stages and hence the build is certified for go-live. Again, Build #222 failed at 'Regression Run' stage. In this case, the agile team needs to analyse the failures for the root cause. If the failure is because of a problem in the test then the test needs to be fixed quickly and committed. If the failure is because of a bug, then the severity and priority of the bug is to be discussed with the business owner. If the team feels that the bug is of low severity and a fix for the same can be deployed within next few builds, then this build can be certified for go-live. In case bug severity is high, this build is again rejected (as candidate of go-live build). Build #223 pipeline shows that this build has successfully been packaged, and deployment of the build to TEST servers is in progress.

27.15 | DEVOPS

DevOps is a software development method that emphasizes communication, collaboration and integration between development and IT operations team. DevOps is a response to the growing awareness that there is a disconnect between what is traditionally considered development activity and what is traditionally considered operations activity.

Development-centric folks embrace change. They come with a mindset that they are paid to accomplish change. Business depends on them to respond to the changing market needs. Hence, developers are encouraged to change as much as possible.

Operation folks embrace stability. They come with a mindset that they are paid to accomplish stability. Business depends on them to keep the applications stable as current business money is being generated from it only. Operations team is motivated to resist change that undermines stability and reliability.

The different goals of these two teams leads to a disconnect and confusion between the developers and the operations. Two classical examples of the same disconnect are:

1. Operations team saying that the release cannot be built as it is missing some components while developer team saying that it is getting built perfectly on their local machine.
2. Operations team saying that the release has bugs while the developer team saying that the bug is not reproducible on their local machine.

To bridge the gap between these two teams, a new practice of software development called DevOps was developed. DevOps overcomes the gaps by automating both development and IT operations. DevOps relies heavily on creating an automated pipeline right from build commits to production deployment. This pipeline is similar to 'Continuous Integration' pipeline discussed earlier with production deployment phase also included in this pipeline. Figure 27.18 describes a DevOps pipeline.

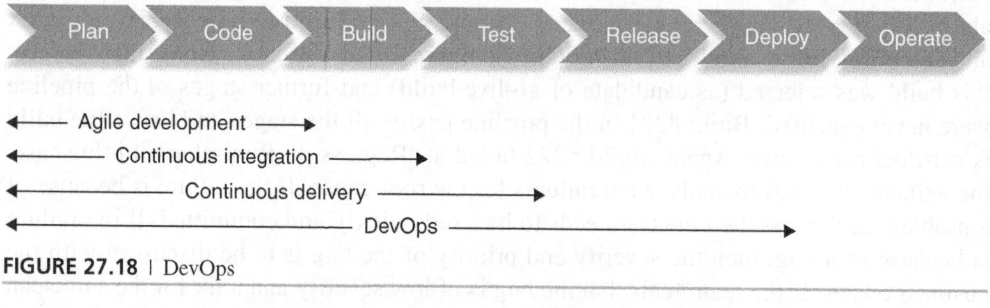

FIGURE 27.18 | DevOps

DevOps aids in easy release management of a software application by standardizing both development as well as operations environments. In recent times, DevOps has evolved an enterprise standard for continuous software delivery that enables organizations to respond to market opportunities and customer feedbacks rapidly, and balance speed, cost, quality and risk. It has evolved as a practice that fully automates processes of development, technology operations and QA to achieve an end-to-end automated release management cycle. Figure 27.19 shows DevOps as intersection of development, quality assurance and technology operations.

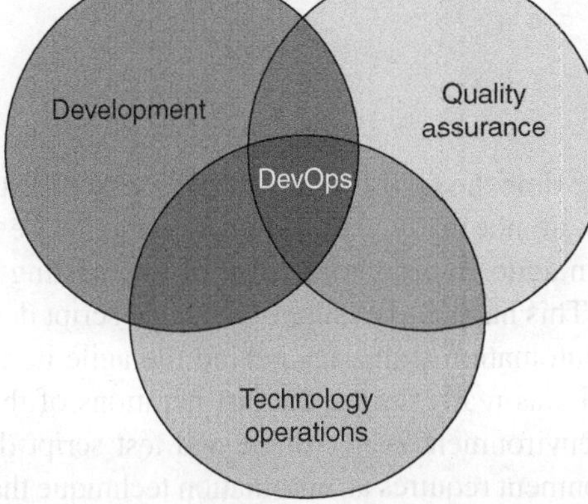

FIGURE 27.19 | DevOps as intersection of development, QA and technology operations

By implementing DevOps, enterprises can:

- Automate continuous delivery and DevOps processes.
- Facilitate real-time collaboration between teams.
- Establish common standards and protocols for all teams.
- Avoid problems arising because of communication gaps between different teams.
- Reduce lifecycle costs.

28

CHAPTER

Agile Automation Framework*

In agile environment by the time the GUI is ready there is very little time left for automation. Moreover, if the test cases are not ready, then automation cannot be started. This makes test automation very difficult in agile environment. Most of the existing frameworks fail to support agile test automation. This happens because of the huge script development effort associated with them. The test automation team lags behind the agile iteration cycle. Most of the time, reasons are that GUI was ready during the last iterations of the agile cycle, test cases were developed too late, environment is not stable and test script development takes time. Automation in agile environment requires an automation technique that supports fast and reliable script development method, minimum dependency of script development on GUI and no dependency on the manual test cases. In short, it requires an agile test automation framework.

Agile automation framework is a dynamic framework designed to achieve rapid automation. This framework minimizes the automation development and maintenance effort. The framework setup cost of agile automation framework is also very low. The complete framework can be setup within few hours and the test automation activity can be started. This framework enables the users to dynamically automate the test cases from component tables. This saves a lot of time and effort. The framework offers the flexibility to the users to dynamically design the regression suite. Users can dynamically design the automation suite to do any of the testing types—selective testing, comprehensive testing, life-cycle testing, positive testing, negative testing, smoke testing, etc. Agile automation framework can be implemented to achieve low-cost rapid scale automation. It is not necessary for the application development model to be agile to use this framework. This automation framework supports all types of application development models and has special features to easily support agile application development model.

The life cycle stages of the agile automation framework are so chosen that it best fits into the agile development environment. The automation developers can carry out the task of test automation in parallel with the application development. Automation developers engage themselves in knowledge gathering and component tables (test cases) design while the GUI is getting developed. Once the application is developed, automation developers quickly start developing test scripts by automating one page at a time. All the functionalities of the page are coded in the respective page component itself. Functionalities that are common to more than one page are automated in common page component package. This requires extensive programming skills. This framework is the first object-oriented framework.

*This framework has been designed and developed by the author, Rajeev Gupta.

Prior to data-driven framework, record/playback method of script design was used. With data-driven framework came the concept of scripting methods of script design. Keyword-driven method brought out the concept of complex scripting to make test automation easier with a compromise on the automation cost. Agile automation framework brings in the concept of 'programming' or 'coding' to develop test automation scripts. The concept of programming reduces the cost of test automation by an extensive margin. Agile automation framework greatly reduces the framework setup, test development and test maintenance costs. Agile automation framework achieves this by implementing the concepts of object-oriented programming—abstraction, inheritance, polymorphism and encapsulation.

Agile automation framework uses the business-scenario driven approach to increase the test coverage and also reduces the test development effort. In agile automation framework, automation developer is expected to have the business knowledge of the functionality under implementation. The automation developer is responsible for identifying the test scenarios and test cases for automation. In this framework, first of all a rough model of the business scenario is developed. This model helps in identifying the page components, common page components, business components and the decision logic 'keywords'. Decision logic keywords control the execution logic of both the page component and the business component. In this framework, for every page in application under test (AUT) there exists an automated script called *Page Component*. All the permutations and combinations of the page functionality is coded in the page components using various methods and logical statements. If a specific feature is common to more than one page, then the code for the same is written in separate *Common Page Component* package. *Business Components* make a call to various page components to automate the smallest reusable business functionality. The decision to execute the specific functionality is decided at run-time by the decision logic keywords. Each and every page component and business component have verification logic coded within them. It helps to check whether the respective script has executed successfully or not. It helps to identify the exact reason and point of error in case of script failure. This layout of agile automation framework helps in maximizing reusability of the test scripts. Since all the functionality of the page is coded in the page component, it can easily be reused for automating any other business scenario that uses this page. The decision logic to execute the specific functionality of the page components or the business components is controlled by the keywords defined in the component tables. These keywords form the decision logic inside the page components and the business components. The test script reads the data tables and executes the test case as specified by the 'keyword' combination. The combination of these keywords can be varied to dynamically automate more and more test cases of the same business scenario. The excel sheets are designed in a way that allow the users to dynamically decide which test cases to execute and which not. It even offers to perform negative testing easily by defining negative data in the data sheets. The driver script automatically captures the error reason along with the application page shot and writes them to the data sheet. In this framework, data sheets also act as test reports. All pass/fail status along with fail reason and error page shots are updated in the data sheet itself. It helps in quick analysis of test results.

28.1 | FRAMEWORK COMPONENTS

The agile automation framework segregates the automation activities into several independent packages called framework components. Each framework component refers to a specific test automation activity. These framework components are loosely coupled to each other and offer a one-point centralized maintenance control. All the framework components are designed to be independently managed. Figure 28.1 shows the framework components of the agile automation framework. It includes the following components:

- com.webdriver.envVariables
- com.webdriver.library
- com.webdriver.pageComponents
- com.webdriver.commonPageComponents
- com.webdriver.businessComponents
- com.webdriver.pageComponentTable
- com.webdriver.businessComponentTable
- com.webdriver.tests
- com.webdriver.settings
- com.webdriver.errScreenshots
- com.webdriver.resultLog

FIGURE 28.1 | Framework components

28.2 | FRAMEWORK ARCHITECTURE

Agile automation framework is designed to achieve rapid automation. This framework has been developed to reduce cost on test automation. The architecture of this framework is robust and agile enough to support both positive and negative testings and as well offer an easy test development and maintenance environment. This framework offers centralized development, maintenance and execution control. 'Settings' package contains Java files that define the WebDriver settings and AUT settings. These files contain code that prepares the Selenium WebDriver environment for test development and execution. It can include settings that define Selenium tool configuration settings, loads system dll and custom dll files, presets the test environment, and defines the application configuration settings. In short, the purpose of this file is to prepare the *Test Automation Bed*. Figure 28.2 shows the architecture of agile automation framework.

28.3 | PAGE COMPONENTS

These are reusable methods that exist inside *pageComponents* package. These methods implement the smallest reusable business functionality. Page components and common page components are the only components that are allowed to interact with GUI end in this framework. For each page in AUT, there exists one page component. All the functionalities of the page are implemented as various methods. A page of an application may implement

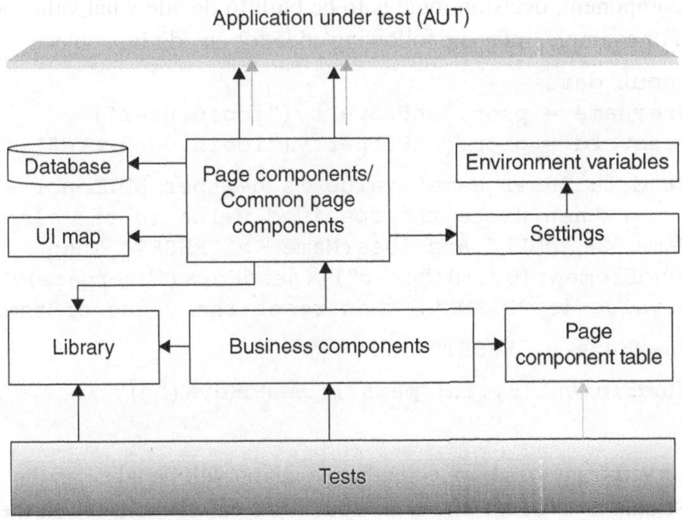

FIGURE 28.2 | Framework architecture

various application functionalities. Scripts are coded to implement all the functionalities of the page. Decision logic is used to decide which functionality to execute during run-time. A decision is made on the basis of 'keywords' present in the component table. For every page component there exits one page component table. All the keywords and data required to execute a page component is defined in these tables. The keywords and test data are passed to the page components using input parameters of an action. The test output data is sent back to the calling method. The page component methods are allowed to throw exceptions for any unexpected run-time errors. These exceptions are to be handled by tests developed in *test* package to determine test pass/fail status. Page components can either receive the test input data as value or as keyword. The various combinations that are allowed include:

- **AUTO:** Page component should itself select or extract the test input data that is required to execute the specific page component. Business components can execute SQL queries on AUT database to extract the valid test input data. It is always advisable to retrieve the valid test input data from the AUT database. This helps to:
  - Reduce the chances of error while defining test input data in the component tables.
  - Save time as user need not specify the test input data.
- **NULL or "":** Keyword 'NULL' or en empty value ("") in test input data implies the page component should not take any action on the element whose test input data is specified as 'NULL'.
- **RESET:** Keyword 'RESET' in test input data implies the page component should reset the value of the element whose test input data is specified as 'BLANK'.
- **<value>:** Any other values, other than the above mentioned values implies that the page component should set the value of the object as specified in the input parameter.

In the page component, decision logic is to be built to decide what value needs to be set for the object. For example, refer the following code for an edit box object.

```
// Test input data
String iUsername = prop.getProperty("login.user")
String iPassword = prop.getProperty("login.password")
// If test data 'User Name' value is neither NULL nor RESET,
//          then write the specified value to the element
If iUserName <> "NULL" And iUserName <> "RESET" Then
  driver.findElement(By.id("user")).sendKeys(iUsername);
// If the value is 'BLANK', then reset the value of the element
ElseIf iUserName = "RESET" Then
  driver.findElement(By.id("pass")).sendKeys("");
End If
```

It can be observed from the above code that no action will be taken on the element if the value of the test data is 'NULL'. The same code logic can be built for all the GUI objects including radio buttons, list box, check box, edit box, buttons, etc.

28.3.1 | Common Page Components

Common page components are methods developed for features that are common to multiple pages. For example, a free shipping banner is common to multiple pages. Automating the banner feature in multiple page components will result in code redundancy. So it is advisable to automate this feature inside *commonPageComponents* package. Common page components package is similar to *pageComponents* package with a difference: it only automates features that is common to multiple pages.

28.3.2 | Business Components

These are reusable methods which implement an end-to-end business functionality like booking a ticket, cancelling a ticket, etc., by calling the various page components. Business components never interact with GUI directly. It makes a call to page components which then perform desired user action on web pages.

Business components are coded to be flexible enough to implement most of the test scenarios of the business functionality. Business components are automated in a way to dynamically execute specific test case as per the input data passed. Business components can connect to the page component tables or database to identify the appropriate test input data. Ideally, the test input data should be provided by the tests (test method). The business component methods are allowed to throw exceptions for any unexpected run-time errors. These exceptions are to be handled by tests developed in *test* package to determine test pass/fail status. Business components can either receive the test input data as value or as keyword.

28.3.3 | Page Component Table

Page component table defines the test input data. For each and every web page with input fields, there exists a page component table. The test input data can exist in the form of 'keyword' or the exact data value. Page components table defines data for both positive and negative testing.

These keywords form the decision logic of the page components. The page components use these keywords to decide which test-sub scenario (code logic) to execute during run-time.

Note: There could be situations where two pages use the same test input data details. For example, billing and shipping address may be specified by the user in two different pages. In this case, creating two page component tables will result in creating multiple files with same information. This will make maintenance difficult. Thus it is advisable to create a common page component table 'customer address' for both billing and shipping address pages.

Figure 28.3 shows a design template layout of the page component table. The fields marked '*' are mandatory fields. The name of these fields should remain as it is across all the component tables. The various fields of the component table are:

- **SeqNo*:** Unique sequence identifier for the component table. It can take values 1, 2, 3 and so on.
- **DataDescription*:** Description of the test data.
- **iInputParam:** Indicates the test input data such as login username, password, etc. The name of this field should be named after the GUI object to which data is inputted. The name should be so chosen that it easily helps to identify the data type and data purpose. For example, if the input parameter is for inputting data to the 'UserName' edit box, then name of this field should be 'iUserName'. 'i' in 'iUserName' stands for test input data. Similarly, if the test input parameter is for inputting data to the 'Country' list box for specifying the country name, then this field should be written as 'iCountry'. All the input parameters can be specified one after another in sequence. The various acceptable values that can be specified for this field include:
    - ***<value>:*** Actual value that needs to be inputted to the page. For example, for 'UserName' edit box, the value can be 'Alex', Similarly, for list box 'Country', the value can be 'India'.
    - ***AUTO:*** Keyword 'AUTO' implies test scripts should itself extract or select the valid test data. For example, suppose the test case is to search and see if a transaction id can be searched in the GUI. In this case, test script can directly connect to the AUT database and retrieve a valid transaction id number. The same can be used as test input data for executing the test case. This relieves the user from manually searching the data in AUT and then specifying the same in the component table. This saves lot of time and effort.

SeqNo	DataDescription

iInputParam1	iInputParam2	iInputParam...n

iExpMsgOnPageLoad	iContinue	iSubmitPage	iExpMsgOnPageSubmit	iPageSubmitMsgLoc

FIGURE 28.3 | Design template layout of the page component table

- *NULL or "":* Keyword 'NULL' or an empty value ("") the page component should not take any action on the object for which this data is specified.
- *RESET:* Keyword 'RESET' implies the page component should reset the value of the object for which this data is specified.

All the test input data may not have all the options as mentioned earlier. Either a list of acceptable values is to be created or a comment is to be added for the excel cell defining the valid values that the column can accept as shown in Figure 28.4.

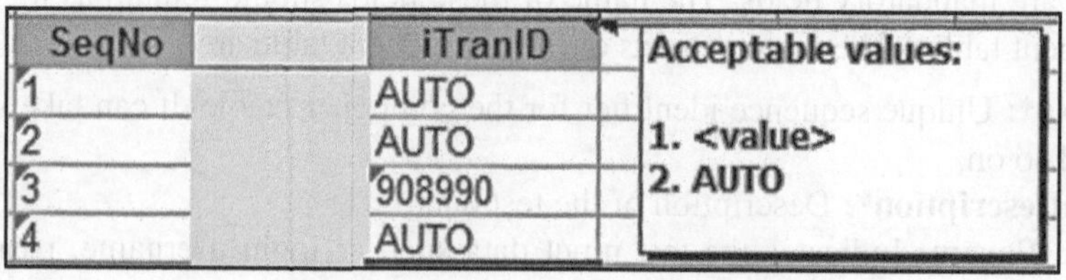

FIGURE 28.4 | Specifying valid acceptable values for a field as cell comment

Generally, after submitting a transaction on a page, a confirmation message appears on the page. This message can either appear on the same page, on a pop-up window or on the next page that loads. Assume an AUT, where after login, 'enter itinerary' page loads. Since page components automate one page at a time, it is not possible to verify the 'login successful' message in the login page component. As this message appears in the 'enter itinerary' page, it needs to be verified in the 'enter itinerary' page component only. Again, 'enter itinerary' page can also have messages on the page when this page is submitted. So, 'enter itinerary' page can contain two types of messages—one when the page loads and the other when the page is submitted. To implement the same, the component table contains two fields— *iExpMsgOnPageLoad* and *iExpMsgOnPageSubmit*. The first one specifies the messages of the page when the page loads and the other specify the messages of the page when the page is submitted. If this field is left 'blank' then it implies that the page component needs not verify the messages appearing on the page when the page loads. Again, if it is required to validate the messages on the page, there can be multiple conditions. Listed as follows are the various conditions that can occur at run-time.

- **Test Condition 1**
  - Verify page message when the page loads
  - Do not take action on page objects
  - Do not submit page
  - Do not verify page message on page submit
- **Test Condition 2**
  - Do not verify page message when the page loads
  - Take action on page objects
  - Do not submit page
  - Do not verify page message on page submit

- **Test Condition 3**
  - Do not verify page message when the page loads
  - Take action on page objects
  - Submit page
  - Verify page message on page submit
- **Test Condition 4**
  - Verify page message when the page loads
  - Take action on page objects
  - Submit page
  - Do not verify page message on page submit
- **Test Condition 5**
  - Verify page message when the page loads
  - Take action on page objects
  - Submit page
  - Verify page message on page submit

In order to implement these test conditions, two more fields are defined in the component table—*iContinue* and *iSubmitPage*.

- **iExpMsgOnPageLoad*:** Specifies the message to validate from the page when the page loads. If page message need not be verified on page load then this field is left blank.
- **iContinue*:** Indicates whether the page component will exit after validating the page message on page load or not. It can accept two values—'Yes' or 'No'. 'Yes' implies the page component should continue execution after validating the page message which appears on page load. 'No' implies the page component should exit after validating the page message.
- **iSubmitPage*:** This field specifies whether the page component should submit the page or not. It can take two values—'Yes' or 'No'. 'Yes' implies the page component should submit the page. 'No' implies the page component should not submit the page. It is not always required to submit the page after taking action on page objects. Also during automation maintenance phase, it may be required to add more functionality to the page component before submitting it. There are two ways of doing this—adding additional lines of code in the script component or writing another script component which can be called after the existing page component. But the second method requires that the page should not be submitted. In order to achieve the same, this field has been specified. If the value of this field is changed to 'No', then automatically the script component will not submit this page.
- **iExpMsgOnPageSubmit*:** Specifies the message to validate from the page when the page is submitted. If page message on page submit need not be validated then this field is left blank.
- **iPageSubmitMsgLoc*:** Specifies the location where the message can be expected after page submit. Generally, when the page is submitted the page message can either appear on the same page, next page or pop-up window. This field specifies where to look for the message on the page. It can take three values— CurrentPage, Pop-up or NextPage. *CurrentPage* implies the expected message will appear on the same submit page. *Pop-up* implies that the page message appears on the pop-up window. *NextPage*

implies that the page message appears on the next page that loads. 'NextPage' value has no significance for the page components script as page components can only automate one page at a time. It is just specified to make the component tables more user-friendly and readable. Any such verification need to be validated in the page component of the next page by specifying the 'iExpMsgOnPageLoad' field.

Note: It is advisable to create page component table as MS Excel file and access it as database. Accessing test input sheet as database has specific advantages over flat files. Flat files needs to be completely loaded in memory before it can be read. Also, flat files can only read sequentially. In case flat files are huge, time required to access data from flat files is also high. Reading test data sheets using SQL helps quick data access with minimum load on memory. Thus, it is advisable to read test data sheets as database.

28.4 | ENVIRONMENT VARIABLES

An environment variable in test automation is a variable whose scope is visible throughout the automation project. These variables are to be accessible through all the components of the automation framework. These variables are generally used to define application login details, application URL, database connection string, etc. Environment variables can also be used to store run-time data. For example, data returned by a SQL query or pass/fail status of the test script. Environment variables can be declared to be modifiable (static) or non-modifiable (static final). Environment objects can also be used to store values of multiple environment variables.

28.5 | SETTINGS

'Settings' package contains Java files that define AUT, Selenium WebDriver and agile automation framework settings. It can also define environment variables that control or switch various settings. Following variables are eligible to be defined in 'Settings' file:

- Variables that define the test automation bed such as application URL, application database details, etc.
- Variables that define the framework settings such as framework location, framework components path, etc.
- Variables that define the Selenium WebDriver settings such as WebDriver instance to create FirefoxDriver or InternetExplorerDriver or ChromeDriver, etc.
- Variables that help in executing the same test script across multiple browsers, various test environments, data bases, etc.

28.6 | LIBRARY

'Library' package contains Java files that define various methods to ease test development. These methods maximize code reusability. The scope of these methods is visible to page components, business components and tests.

Note: Library file should not contain any methods or should not make a call to any method that interacts with GUI.

28.7 | TESTS

'Tests' package contains automated tests. Test cases are automated in *Test* package by calling various methods of page components, business components and library file.

28.8 | UI MAP

UI Map contains definition of element attributes. These attributes are used to identify an element during test execution. UI Map can exist as a separate Java file or can be defined at the top of every page component. It is always advisable to avoid multiple definitions of the same element.

28.9 | FRAMEWORK STRUCTURE

Figure 28. 5 shows the framework structure of the agile automation framework.

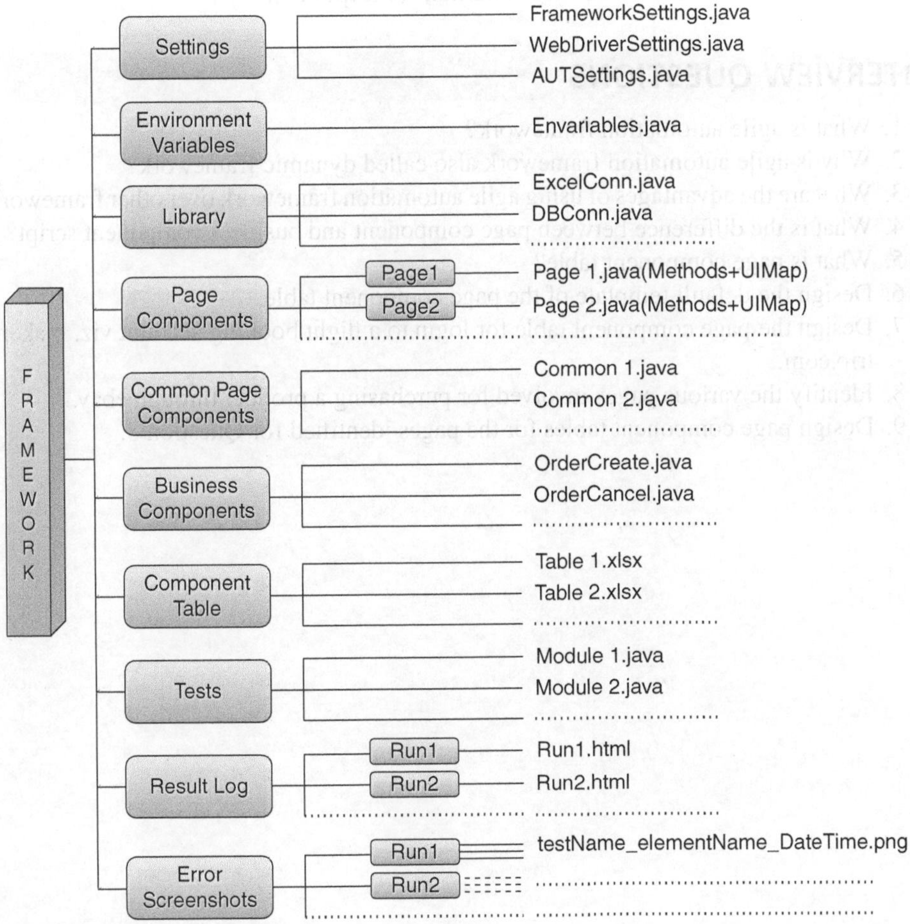

FIGURE 28.5 | Framework structure

Quick Tips

1. Use MS Excel as test data files.
2. SQL queries to be used to retrieve/update data to Excel files.
3. One page component should automate one page at a time.
4. Page and business components to be designed in a way that in case of script failure, test execution control is transferred back to the business components along with proper execution status flags and error messages.
5. Tests are to be designed in a way that current test execution should exit in case of test case failure with appropriate logging comments and AUT screenshots.
6. Test suite is to be designed in a way that complete test suite is executed even if an error occurs in a specific during test execution. In case of an error, the current test case execution is to be exited and the next test method should start executing the next test case.
7. Appropriate recovery scenarios are to be designed to ensure complete test suite is executed even in the worst case conditions (exceptions).

INTERVIEW QUESTIONS

1. What is agile automation framework?
2. Why is agile automation framework also called dynamic framework?
3. What are the advantages of using agile automation framework over other frameworks?
4. What is the difference between page component and business component script?
5. What is page component table?
6. Design the default template of the page component table.
7. Design the page component table for login to a flight booking account viz. makemytrip.com.
8. Identify the various pages involved for purchasing a product through ebay.
9. Design page component tables for the pages identified for Question 8.

Index